Lecture Notes in Artificial Intelligence　12387

Subseries of Lecture Notes in Computer Science

More information about this series at http://www.springer.com/series/1244

C. Maria Keet · Michel Dumontier (Eds.)

Knowledge Engineering and Knowledge Management

22nd International Conference, EKAW 2020
Bolzano, Italy, September 16–20, 2020
Proceedings

 Springer

Editors
C. Maria Keet 🆔
University of Cape Town
Cape Town, South Africa

Michel Dumontier 🆔
Institute of Data Science
Maastricht University
Maastricht, The Netherlands

ISSN 0302-9743   ISSN 1611-3349   (electronic)
Lecture Notes in Artificial Intelligence
ISBN 978-3-030-61243-6   ISBN 978-3-030-61244-3   (eBook)
https://doi.org/10.1007/978-3-030-61244-3

LNCS Sublibrary: SL7 – Artificial Intelligence

This Springer imprint is published by the registered company Springer Nature Switzerland AG
The registered company address is: Gewerbestrasse 11, 6330 Cham, Switzerland

Preface

This volume contains the proceedings of the 22nd International Conference on Knowledge Engineering and Knowledge Management (EKAW 2020), held as an online conference between September 16–20, 2020.

The special theme of EKAW 2020 was "Ethical and Trustworthy Knowledge Engineering". While recent reported breaches relate predominantly to machine learning systems, it is not impossible to envision ethical breaches in knowledge engineering more broadly and, conversely, devise methods and techniques to ensure no or minimal harm in knowledge acquisition, modeling, and knowledge-driven information systems. EKAW 2020 put a special emphasis on the importance of knowledge engineering and knowledge management to keep fostering trustworthy systems. It also included its usual topics, notably all aspects of eliciting, acquiring, discovering, modeling, and managing knowledge and construction of knowledge-intensive systems.

We invited three types of submissions for the main conference of EKAW 2020. First, original research papers that describe a novel method, technique, or analysis with appropriate empirical or other types of evaluations. The main assessment criteria for the research paper was novelty, technical soundness and depth, and clarity of writing. Second, in-use papers that describe applications of knowledge management and engineering in real environments. The main assessment criteria are the importance of the problem, technical soundness of the system, and quality of user evaluations. Third, position papers that offer original ideas, perspectives, and insights that contribute to a better understanding of these problems in the research community and may guide future research. The main assessment criteria was novelty, importance, and clarity of writing.

Overall, we received 88 abstract submissions, of which 72 were eventually accompanied by a full paper, which were reviewed by 78 reviewers and 15 subreviewers. Each paper received three to four reviews, and discussions were encouraged by both program chairs for papers that exhibited strongly divergent opinions. In total, 19 papers were accepted for publication in this volume, of which 8 are full length research papers, 7 are short research papers, 2 are in-use papers, and 2 are position papers.

Three distinguished keynote speakers were invited to present their work to the EKAW community to complement the technical program:

- Axel-Cyrille Ngonga Ngomo (Paderborn University, Germany), recognized for their expertise in knowledge graphs at scale, gave a talk entitled "Fact Checking and Knowledge Graphs."
- Diana Maynard (The University of Sheffield, UK), recognized for their expertise in NLP, gave a talk entitled "Integrating human expert knowledge and NLP tools for real-world applications."

- Toby Walsh (University of New South Wales, Australia), recognized for their expertise in social choice, constraint programming, and propositional satisfiability and interest in building trustworthy AI, gave a talk entitled "Preferences: Representing, Reasoning & Ethics."

This year's edition of EKAW 2020 was held as an online event, owing to the disruption in travel and large gatherings caused by the global spread of SARS-CoV-2, the novel infectious virus responsible for the COVID-19 disease.

EKAW 2020 included two workshops, held in collaboration with the FOIS 2020 workshops and ICBO 2020 conference. The first was the 5th International Workshop on Ontology Modularity, Contextuality, and Evolution (WOMoCoE 2020) organised by Stefano Borgo (LOA ISTC-CNR, Italy), Loris Bozzato (Fondazione Bruno Kessler, Italy), Till Mossakowski, (Otto von Guericke University Magdeburg, Germany), and Luciano Serafini (Fondazione Bruno Kessler, Italy). The second workshop was the Workshop on Scalable Knowledge Graph Engineering (SKALE), organized by Martin G. Skjæveland (University of Oslo, Norway), Daniel P. Lupp (University of Oslo, Norway), Ian Horrocks (University of Oxford, UK), Johan W. Klüwer (DNV GL, Norway), and Christian Kindermann (The University of Manchester, UK). EKAW 2020 also featured a P&D session.

The EKAW 2020 Organisation Committee involved the following individuals. The general chairs of EKAW 2020 were Oliver Kutz (Free University of Bozen-Bolzano, Italy) and Rafael Peñaloza (University of Milano-Bicocca, Italy). The program chairs of EKAW 2020 were Maria Keet (University of Cape Town, South Africa) and Michel Dumontier (Maastricht University, The Netherlands). The workshop and tutorial chairs were Anastasia Dimou (Ghent University, Belgium) and Karl Hammar (Jönköping University, Sweden). The poster and demo chairs were Daniel Garijo (University of Southern California, USA) and Agnieszka Ławrynowicz (Poznan University of Technology, Poland). The Local Committee chairs were Pietro Galliani (Free University of Bozen-Bolzano, Italy), Guendalina Righetti (Free University of Bozen-Bolzano, Italy), and Nicolas Troquard (Free University of Bozen-Bolzano, Italy). The publicity chair was Rafael Gonçalves (Stanford University, USA).

We wish to extend our gratitude to all members of the Organisation Committee, the Program Committee, the submitting authors, presenters, and attendees for their efforts and continued commitment in these trying times in making EKAW 2020 a successful event.

August 2020   Michel Dumontier
Maria Keet

Organization

General Chairs

Oliver Kutz   Free University of Bozen-Bolzano, Italy
Rafael Peñaloza   University of Milano-Bicocca, Italy

Program Committee Chairs

Michel Dumontier   Maastricht University, The Netherlands
Maria Keet   University of Cape Town, South Africa

Program Committee

Nathalie Aussenac-Gilles   IRIT CNRS, France
Olivier Bodenreider   US National Library of Medicine, USA
Alex Borgida   Rutgers University, USA
Stefano Borgo   ISTC-CNR, Italy
Christopher Brewster   Maastricht University, The Netherlands
Philipp Cimiano   Bielefeld University, Germany
Víctor Codocedo   Universidad Técnica Federico Santa María, Chile
Olivier Corby   Inria, France
Oscar Corcho   Universidad Politécnica de Madrid, Spain
Miguel Couceiro   Inria, France
Claudia d'Amato   University of Bari, Italy
Mathieu D'Aquin   National University of Ireland, Ireland
Daniele Dell'Aglio   University of Zurich, Switzerland
Anastasia Dimou   Ghent University, Belgium
Jérôme Euzenat   Inria and University Grenoble Alpes, France
Catherine Faron Zucker   Université Nice Sophia Antipolis, France
Dieter Fensel   University of Innsbruck, Austria
Jesualdo Tomás   Universidad de Murcia, Spain
   Fernández-Breis
Pablo Fillottrani   Universidad Nacional del Sur, Argentina
Aldo Gangemi   Università di Bologna and CNR-ISTC, Italy
Raúl García-Castro   Universidad Politécnica de Madrid, Spain
Daniel Garijo   University of Southern California, USA
Giancarlo Guizzardi   Free University of Bozen-Bolzano, Italy
Torsten Hahmann   University of Maine, USA
Harry Halpin   World Wide Web Consortium, USA
Karl Hammar   Jönköping University, Sweden
Martin Hepp   Universität der Bundeswehr München, Germany
Rinke Hoekstra   University of Amsterdam, The Netherlands

Antoine Isaac	Europeana and Vrije Universiteit Amsterdam, The Netherlands
Krzysztof Janowicz	University of California, Santa Barbara, USA
Clement Jonquet	University of Montpellier, LIRMM, France
Zubeida Khan	CSIR, South Africa
Manolis Koubarakis	National and Kapodistrian University of Athens, Greece
Francesco Kriegel	TU Dresden, Germany
Adila A. Krisnadhi	Universitas Indonesia, Indonesia
Markus Krötzsch	TU Dresden, Germany
Agnieszka Ławrynowicz	Poznan University of Technology, Poland
Danh Le Phuoc	TU Berlin, Germany
Maxime Lefrançois	MINES Saint-Etienne, France
Fabrizio Maria Maggi	Free University of Bozen-Bolzano, Italy
Suvodeep Mazumdar	The University of Sheffield, UK
Alessandro Mosca	Free University of Bozen-Bolzano, Italy
Till Mossakowski	University of Magdeburg, Germany
Enrico Motta	The Open University, UK
Axel-Cyrille Ngonga Ngomo	Paderborn University, Germany
Vit Novacek	National University of Ireland, Ireland
Francesco Osborne	The Open University, UK
Heiko Paulheim	University of Mannheim, Germany
Mohammad Taher Pilehvar	Iran University of Science and Technology, Iran
Antonella Poggi	Sapienza Università di Roma, Italy
María Poveda-Villalón	Universidad Politécnica de Madrid, Spain
Yannick Prié	LINA, University of Nantes, France
Ulrich Reimer	University of Applied Sciences, Switzerland
Mariano Rico	Universidad Politécnica de Madrid, Spain
Mariano Rodríguez Muro	Google NYC, USA
Oscar Rodríguez Rocha	Inria, France
Harald Sack	FIZ Karlsruhe and KIT Karlsruhe, Germany
Emilio Sanfilippo	University of Tours, France
Simon Scheider	University of Utrecht, The Netherlands
Stefan Schlobach	Vrije Universiteit Amsterdam, The Netherlands
Juan Sequeda	Data World, USA
Luciano Serafini	Fondazione Bruno Kessler, Italy
Barış Sertkaya	Frankfurt University of Applied Sciences, Germany
Cogan Shimizu	Kansas State University, USA
Derek Sleeman	University of Aberdeen, UK
Armando Stellato	University of Rome Tor Vergata, Italy
Mari Carmen Suárez-Figueroa	Universidad Politécnica de Madrid, Spain
Vojtêch Svátek	University of Economics, Prague, Czech Republic
Annette Ten Teije	Vrije Universiteit Amsterdam, The Netherlands
Andrea Tettamanzi	University Nice Sophia Antipolis, France

Ilaria Tiddi   Vrije Universiteit Amsterdam, The Netherlands
Konstantin Todorov   University of Montpellier, France
Frank Van Harmelen   Vrije Universiteit Amsterdam, The Netherlands
Iraklis Varlamis   Harokopio University of Athens, Greece
Guohui Xiao   Free University of Bozen-Bolzano, Italy
Fouad Zablith   American University of Beirut, Lebanon
Ondřej Zamazal   University of Economics, Prague, Czech Republic
Ziqi Zhang   The University of Sheffield, UK

Additional Reviewers

Kevin Angele   Jims Marchang
Germán Alejandro Braun   Amedeo Napoli
Genet Asefa Gesese   Rafael Peñaloza
Patrick Girard   Dimitrios Rafailidis
Larry González   Johann Schmidt
Fabian Hoppe   Umutcan Şimşek
Elias Kärle   Tabea Tietz
Antti Kuusisto   Roderick van der Weerdt

Contents

xii   Contents

In Use Papers

Position Papers

Research Papers

A Comparison of the Cognitive Difficulties Posed by SPARQL Query Constructs

Paul Warren(✉) ⓘ and Paul Mulholland ⓘ

Knowledge Media Institute, The Open University, Milton Keynes MK7 6AA, UK
{paul.warren,paul.mulholland}@open.ac.uk

Abstract. This study investigated difficulties in the comprehension of SPARQL. In particular, it compared the declarative and navigational styles present in the language, and various operators used in SPARQL property paths. The study involved participants selecting possible answers given a SPARQL query and knowledge-base. In general, no significant differences were found in terms of the response time and accuracy with which participants could answer questions expressed in either a declarative or navigational form. However, UNION did take significantly longer to comprehend than both braces and vertical line in property paths; with braces being faster than vertical line. Inversion and negated property paths both proved difficult, with their combination being very difficult indeed. Questions involving MINUS were answered more accurately than those involving negation in property paths, in particular where predicates were inverted. Both involve negation, but the semantics are different. With the MINUS questions, negation and inversion can be considered separately; with property paths, negation and inversion need to be considered together. Participants generally expressed a preference for data represented graphically, and this preference was significantly correlated with accuracy of comprehension. Implications for the design and use of query languages are discussed.

Keywords: SPARQL · User experience · Participant study

1 Introduction

The original specification of the SPARQL query language, SPARQL1.0 [1], employed a declarative syntax style, heavily influenced by SQL. Subsequently, SPARQL1.1 [2] introduced a number of new features, including a navigational syntax using *property paths*. This syntax was based on regular expressions and enabled the more compact expression of certain queries, besides the ability to define chains of unbounded length. The goal of the study reported here was to compare the ease of comprehension of the declarative and navigational styles, and to investigate the difficulties which people have with some of the property path features. The motivation for the work was to advise on the writing of easily intelligible queries; and to make recommendations for the future development of SPARQL and similar languages. The knowledge bases used in the study were expressed textually and graphically, and this also enabled a comparison of participants'

© Springer Nature Switzerland AG 2020
C. M. Keet and M. Dumontier (Eds.): EKAW 2020, LNAI 12387, pp. 3–19, 2020.
https://doi.org/10.1007/978-3-030-61244-3_1

reaction to the two formats. We used comprehension tasks because comprehension is fundamental to creating and sharing queries, and to interpreting the results of queries. A study such as this could usefully be complemented by a study involving query creation.

Section 2 reviews related work. Section 3 lists those features of the language which were used in the study, and describes the study's specific objectives. Section 4 describes how the study was organized. Sections 5 to 8 then describe each of the four study sections and present their results. Section 9 reports on what influence the prior knowledge of the participants had on their responses. Section 10 discusses the participant's usage of the textual and graphical forms of the knowledgebases. Finally, Sect. 11 summarizes the main findings and makes some recommendations.

2 Related Work

A number of researchers have analysed query logs from RDF data sources. Gallego et al. [3], and Rietveld and Hoekstra [4] looked at the frequency of use of various SPARQL features. Of relevance to this study, they found that UNION was among the more frequently used features. More recently, Bielefeldt et al. [5] have found appreciable usage of property path expressions. Bonifati et al. [6] looked at the relative usage of property path features. They found that negated property sets (!), disjunction (|), zero or more (*) and concatenation (/) were relatively frequently used. Complementing these studies, Warren and Mulholland [7] have surveyed the usage of SPARQL1.1 features. They report that 71% of their respondents used property paths. Similarly to Bonifati et al. [6], Warren and Mulholland [7] found that /, * and | were relatively frequently used operators. They also found that one or more (+) was relatively frequently used, and that ^ and ? were also used to a certain extent. However, ! was little used. By contrast, there has been little work reported on the user experience of query languages. There were a number of studies in the early days of database query languages, e.g. see Reisner [8]. More recently, there have been some studies of the usability of certain semantic web languages, e.g. Sarker et al. [9] have investigated rule-based OWL modelling and Warren et al. [10] have investigated Manchester OWL Syntax. However, to the authors' knowledge, there have been no studies investigating the usability of semantic web query languages.

3 SPARQL – Declarative and Navigational

The study made use of the following declarative features of the language: join, represented by a dot; UNION; and MINUS, i.e. set difference[1]. The property path features used were: concatenation (/); disjunction (|); inverse (^); negated property sets (!); and one or more occurrences of an element (+). We also used the braces notation, where, {m, n} after a path element implies that the element occurs at least m, and no more than n times. In fact, the braces notation was not included in the final W3C recommendation for SPARQL1.1. However, this notation was present in a working draft for SPARQL1.1

---

[1] Although part of the language's declarative style, MINUS was introduced in SPARQL1.1.

property paths [11], and is implemented in the Apache Jena Fuseki SPARQL server[2]. Moreover, the braces notation has been suggested for introduction in the next SPARQL standard[3]. Additionally, the SELECT and WHERE keywords were used. The use of these features is illustrated in Sects. 5 to 8. The specific objectives of the study were to:

- compare the original declarative syntax style used in SPARQL1.0 with the navigational style introduced in SPARQL1.1 (see Sect. 5);
- compare the use of braces, vertical line and plus in property paths; and compare these property path constructs with the use of UNION (see Sect. 6);
- investigate the understanding of inversion and negation in property paths (see Sects. 7 and 8).

Considering the last of these points, the study also considered the use of MINUS. This is another way of introducing negation into queries, albeit with a different semantics to that of negation in property paths. As described in Sect. 7, the study was able to compare how people reasoned about negation in the two cases.

4 Organization of the Study

The study was conducted on an individual basis, on the experimenter's laptop. The MediaLab application[4] was used to collect responses and record response times. There were 20 questions, divided over four sections. Each question displayed a small knowledgebase, shown on the left of the screen as a set of triples, and on the right diagrammatically. For each section, all the questions used the same knowledgebase, displayed in the same way. The screen also displayed a SPARQL query. This was in a simplified version of the language, in particular without any reference to namespaces. Finally, there were four possible solutions to the query. Participants were required to tick which of the four solutions were valid. It was made clear that the number of valid solutions could range between zero and four inclusive. Participants could then click on *Continue* at the bottom right to move on to the next question. MediaLab recorded the response or lack of response to each solution, and the time for the question overall. Figure 1 shows a sample screen, in this case for one of the questions in Sect. 5. For all screenshots see: https://doi.org/10.21954/ou.rd.11931645.v1.

Before the study the participants were presented with a six-page handout which described all the SPARQL features used in the study. Participants were asked to read the handout before beginning the study and encouraged to refer to the handout whenever necessary when completing the study. At the beginning of the study there were two

---

[2] https://jena.apache.org/documentation/fuseki2/.

[3] See https://github.com/w3c/sparql-12/issues/101. The likely reason for braces not being included in SPARQL1.1 property paths is the difficulty in deciding whether to opt for counting (bag) or non-counting (set) semantics. The former was the default in the original SPARQL standard. However, after the discovery of possible performance issues (see [12]), non-counting semantics were introduced in SPARQL1.1 specifically for property paths of unlimited length, i.e. using star (*) or plus (+); while leaving counting semantics as the default for all other SPARQL constructs.

[4] Provided by Empirisoft: http://www.empirisoft.com.

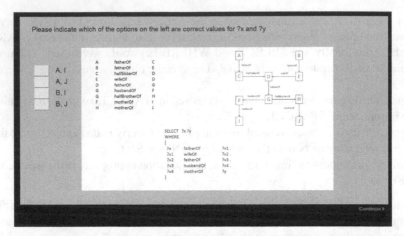

Fig. 1. Example question screen. This screen is for one of the questions discussed in Sect. 5.

screens providing more information about the study, and then a number of screens asking the participants for information on their knowledge of SPARQL, SQL, or any other query language, see Sect. 9. There was then a practice question, designed to introduce the participants to the format of the study; data from this question was not used in the analysis. For this question, and for this question only, the solution was subsequently presented to the participants. Participants then worked through the four sections. The order of presentation of the sections, and of the questions within the sections, were randomized. Randomization of the order of the sections mitigated the chance that performance might vary between the sections, e.g. the first because of unfamiliarity with the format of the question and the last because of fatigue. Randomization of the order of the questions similarly mitigated these effects, and also any learning effects between questions.

Participants were recruited from the authors' own institute and from a variety of other research and industrial environments. They were either computer scientists, with or without a knowledge of SPARQL, or else workers in other disciplines who made use of SPARQL. After a pilot with one participant, the study involved 19 participants, of whom 6 were female. The study was a within-participants study, so that between participant variability would equally affect all conditions. The research was approved by the Open University Human Research Ethics Committee (HREC/3175) and all participants signed a consent form prior to taking part. The study took place during March, April and May 2019.

The analysis was based on the accuracy and the response time. In each section below, accuracy is shown as the percentage of correct responses for each putative query solution. Comparisons of accuracy used logistic analysis of deviance, i.e. assumed a binomial distribution of correct/ not correct responses to each putative query solution. Response time data were collected per question. Analysis of the response time data indicated that they were positively skewed and hence did not follow a normal distribution. For this reason, non-parametric tests have been used in analyzing the response time data. Because this was a within-participants study, where appropriate these non-parametric tests are paired tests . All statistical analysis used the R statistical package [13]. Throughout,

$p < 0.05$ was taken as indicating statistical significance. Where pairwise analysis was undertaken, corrections were made for multiple testing.

5 Declarative Versus Property Path, Forward Versus Inverse

Questions. The four questions in this section were concerned with comparing participant performance on the declarative and property path syntactic styles, and on forward and inverse predicates. Figure 1 shows the question in the declarative style and using forward predicates. There is only one valid solution: (B, I). There was an analogous question, with the same solution, using a property path in the WHERE clause:

- { ?x fatherOf / wifeOf / fatherOf / husbandOf / motherOf ?y }

  The other two questions were in the declarative and property path styles, using inverse predicates, with the following WHERE clauses:

- { ?x ^motherOf ?v1 . ?v1 ^halfBrotherOf ?v2 . ?v2 ^fatherOf ?v3 . ?v3 ^halfSisterOf ?v4 . ?v4 ^fatherOf ?y }
- { ?x ^motherOf / ^halfBrotherOf / ^fatherOf / ^halfSisterOf / ^fatherOf ?y

  The proposed solutions for these two inverse predicate questions were (from top to bottom): (I, A), (I, B), (J, A), (J, B); (J, A) is the correct solution.

The four questions were designed so that, considering the diagram in Fig. 1, the correct solution for the two questions with forward predicates required a traversal from top right to bottom left; whereas for the other two questions with inverse predicates, a traversal from bottom right to top left was required. Thus, each of the four queries made similar traversals of the knowledgebase, to enable a meaningful comparison.

Results. Table 1 shows the percentage of correct responses, for each of the proposed solutions and overall for each question, besides the mean and standard deviation times for each question. In the table, and in subsequent similar tables, valid solutions are identified by showing their percentage of correct responses underlined and in bold. A two-factor analysis of deviance indicated a significant difference in accuracy between forward and inverse predicates ($p = 0.012$), but no significant difference between the declarative and property path styles ($p = 0.406$) and no interaction effect ($p = 0.947$). Paired Wilcoxon tests[5] showed a significant difference in response time between the forward and inverse predicates ($p = 0.0003$) but not between the two syntactic styles ($p = 0.405$). When the questions in the two styles were analyzed separately there was a significant difference in response time between the forward and inverse predicates for both the declarative questions ($p = 0.023$) and the property path questions ($p = 0.005$).

Discussion. Participants answered the questions with inverse predicates less accurately and they took longer to do so. Inversion can be seen as cognitively analogous to negation,

---

[5] The Wilcoxon test is a non-parametric test used in a within-participants study to compare two conditions. It can be considered as a non-parametric analogue of a paired t-test.

Table 1. Data for 'declarative versus property path, forward versus inverse' questions

Predicate direction	Syntax	Percentage Correct					Mean time (secs)	s.d. (secs)
- forward	Declarative	(A, I)	(A, J)	(B, I)	(B, J)	overall	75.7[a]	85.2
		100%	94.7%	**94.7%**	94.7%	96.1%		
	Property path	94.7%	94.7%	**94.7%**	94.7%	94.7%	48.1	29.2
- inverse	Declarative	(I, A)	(I, B)	(J, A)	(J, B)	overall	108.0	88.6
		100%	89.5%	**84.2%**	84.2%	89.5%		
	Property path	84.2%	84.2%	**73.7%**	100%	85.5%	114.3	103.3

[a]This time is increased by an outlier of 378 s. When this is removed, the time is 58.9 s.

which has been extensively studied, e.g. [14, 15]. They both require the construction of an initial mental model, which must then be inverted or negated, a process which both takes time and increases the probability of error.

6   Disjunction

Questions. This section of the study was concerned with comparing four ways of achieving disjunction in a query: using the UNION keyword in the declarative style; or using braces, vertical line or plus in the property path style. Figure 2 displays a portion of the screenshot for a question using the UNION keyword, showing the knowledgebase used for each question in the section.

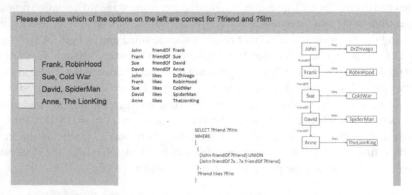

Fig. 2. Part of a question screen from the disjunction section.

There were also two analogous questions, using the vertical line and braces notations:

- {John friendOf| (friendOf/ friendOf) ?friend.?friend likes ?film}
- {John friendOf{1, 2} ?friend . ?friend likes ?film}

All three questions had the same proposed solutions, as shown in Fig. 2. Of these, (Frank, RobinHood) and (Sue, ColdWar) were valid. There were another three analogous questions using UNION, vertical line and braces, extending the 'reach' of the friendOf chain to four steps:

- {{{John friendOf ?friend} UNION

  {John friendOf ?x . ?x friendOf ?friend} UNION
  {John friendOf ?x . ?x friendOf ?y . ?y friendOf ?friend} UNION
  {John friendOf ?x . ?x friendOf ?y . ?y friendOf ?z . ?z friendOf ?friend}} . ?friend
  likes ?film}

- {John friendOf | (friendOf / friendOf)| (friendOf/ friendOf/ friendOf)

  | (friendOf/ friendOf/ friendOf/ friendOf)?friend . ?friend likes ?film}
- {John friendOf{1, 4} ?friend . ?friend likes ?film}

The same proposed solutions were used as in Fig. 2, and this time all were valid. Thus, there were six questions comparing UNION, vertical line and braces at what might be considered two levels of complexity, i.e. {1, 2} and {1, 4}. Thus, for each level of complexity, the three questions had the same solutions.

Finally, there was a seventh question, employing plus:

- {John friendOf + ?friend . ?friend likes ?film}
  For this question the topmost proposed solution, i.e. (Frank, RobinHood) was replaced with (John, DrZhivago); this was to test understanding of the plus operator. Thus, this topmost solution was not valid, whilst the remaining three were valid.

Results. Table 2 shows the data for each of the seven questions, with column headings identifying the proposed solutions by the value bound to *?friend*. Consider, first, the six questions excluding plus. A two-way analysis of deviance revealed that the accuracy of response for the three questions with reach 2 was significantly better than that for the three questions with reach 4 ($p = 0.009$), whilst there was no significant difference between the three operators ($p = 0.986$) and no interaction effect ($p = 0.297$). Turning to the response time data, a Wilcoxon test indicated no significant difference between the questions with reach 2 and reach 4 ($p = 0.769$). A Friedman test did indicate a significant difference between the three operators ($p = 0.0001$). In fact, a pairwise Wilcoxon test indicated a significant difference for each comparison (brace:union, $p = 0.0001$; brace:vertical, $p = 0.021$; vertical:union, $p = 0.030$). Friedman[6] tests also revealed a significant difference in response time between the operators at both levels of complexity (reach 2: $p = 0.016$; reach 4: $p = 0.004$).

A comparison was also made between the three questions with reach 4 and the question employing plus. For these questions, the analysis of accuracy excluded the

---

[6] The Wilcoxon test is a non-parametric test used in a within participants study to compare more than two conditions. It can be regarded as a non-parametric analogue of a repeated measures ANOVA.

Table 2. Data for the disjunctive questions. N.B. * indicates not significantly greater than chance (one-sided test)

Reach	Operator	Percentage correct					Mean time (secs)	s.d. (secs)
		Frank	Sue	David	Anne	Overall		
2	UNION	**84.2%**	**89.5%**	89.5%	94.7%	89.5%	95.3	86.3
	vert. line	**78.9%**	**68.4%***	84.2%	100%	82.9%	76.2	70.7
	braces	**78.9%**	**73.7%**	84.2%	100%	84.2%	53.0	68.1
4	UNION	**68.4%***	**63.2%***	**63.2%***	**94.7%**	72.4%	82.0	52.5
	vert. line	**84.2%**	**73.7%**	**73.7%**	**84.2%**	78.9%	66.7	51.3
	braces	**78.9%**	**68.4%***	**68.4%***	**89.5%**	76.3%	40.1	30.5
		John	Sue	David	Anne			
∞	plus	94.7%	**68.4%**	**68.4%**	**73.7%**	76.3%	73.8	39.2

topmost solution (i.e. leftmost in Table 2), which was different for the question with plus, i.e. it was based on the three solutions common to all four questions, which were all valid. On this basis, an analysis of variance indicated no difference in accuracy of response between the questions ($p = 0.851$). For the response time data, a Friedman test indicated a significant difference between the four operators ($p = 0.006$).

Discussion. The analysis of the six questions with UNION, vertical line and braces, indicated that the queries with longer reach were less accurately answered. On the other hand, the difference in reach made no significant difference to the response times. Conversely, the choice of operator made no significant difference to accuracy but did make a significant difference to response times, with the braces operator being significantly faster than the other operators. When the plus operator was included in the analysis, there was again a significant difference in response time but not in accuracy between the operators. The speed of interpretation of the braces operator may be due to the clarity of expression it permits, avoiding the combinatorial explosion which occurs with UNION and vertical line. The plus operator permits the same clarity of expression, but unlike the braces notation, its meaning is not explicit. The longer time for the plus operator, compared with the braces, may also be due to the difference in the sets of solutions.

7   MINUS and Negated Property Sets

Questions. This section contained six questions employing two forms of negation introduced into SPARQL1.1: MINUS and negated property sets. In each case there were three questions: with forward predicates, inverse predicates and a disjunction of forward and inverse predicates. The questions were designed to examine participants' reasoning with negation, with negation when combined with an inverse predicate; and also to compare participants' treatment of negation in negated property sets and in constructs with MINUS. Figure 3 displays the screenshot for the MINUS question with forward predicate. The other two MINUS questions have WHERE clauses:

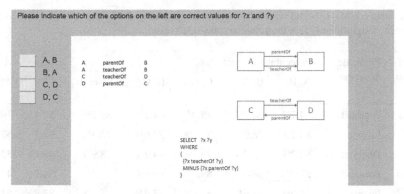

Fig. 3. Part of a question screen from the MINUS and negated property set section.

- {?x ^teacherOf ?y} MINUS {?x ^parentOf ?y}
- {?x teacherOf | ^teacherOf ?y} MINUS {?x parentOf | ^parentOf ?y}

The three questions with negated property sets have WHERE clauses:

- {?x !parentOf ?y}
- {?x !^parentOf ?y}
- {?x !(parentOf| ^parentOf)?y}

The first of these three is satisfied by using any predicate from *?x* to *?y*, other than *parentOf*. The second is satisfied by using any inverse predicate from *?x* to *?y*, other than the inverse of *parentOf*, i.e. it is equivalent to *?y !parentOf ?x*. The third is satisfied by using any forward or inverse predicate from *?x* to *?y* other than *parentOf* and its inverse, i.e. it is equivalent to *{?x !parentOf ?y} UNION {?y !parentOf ?x}*.

All six questions use the same knowledgebase and the same set of proposed solutions. It is important, however, to note that the semantics of MINUS and negated property sets are different. This can be seen in Table 3, which shows the data for this section and indicates the valid solutions, by showing the percentage of correct responses for these solutions underlined and in bold. For the question with MINUS and a disjunction of forward and inverse predicates, there are no valid solutions; whilst for the corresponding question with a negated property set, all the solutions are valid.

Results. A two-way analysis of deviance indicated a significant difference in accuracy between the MINUS and negated property path questions ($p = 10^{-11}$) and between the three uses of predicates ($p = 3 \times 10^{-8}$), with no interaction effect ($p = 0.311$). When the MINUS questions are considered separately, a one-way analysis of deviance indicated a significant difference in accuracy between the three uses of predicates ($p = 0.046$). A subsequent Tukey HSD analysis indicated a significant difference between the forward and inverse usages ($p = 0.045$), but not between forward and disjunction ($p = 0.283$) and inverse and disjunction ($p = 0.612$). A similar analysis for the negated property set questions again indicated a significant difference between the predicate usages ($p = 2 \times 10^{-7}$). A Tukey HSD also indicated a significant difference between forward and inverse usages ($p = 10^{-4}$) and in this case between forward and disjunction ($p = 10^{-4}$), but not

Table 3. Data for MINUS and negated property set questions. N.B. * not significantly greater than chance; † significantly less than chance (one-sided tests)

Form of negation	Predicate direction	Percentage correct					Mean time (secs)	s.d. (secs)
		A, B	B, A	C, D	D, C	Overall		
MINUS	Forward	94.7%	94.7%	**78.9%**	84.2%	88.2%	50.4	30.2
	Inverse	84.2%	78.9%	73.7%	**52.6%***	72.4%	93.2	52.4
	Disjunction	84.2%	73.7%	73.7%	84.2%	78.9%	146.1	133.4
Negated property sets	Forward	**57.9%***	68.4%*	**89.5%**	89.5%	76.3%	54.7	43.9
	Inverse	31.6%	**31.6%**	31.6%	**47.4%**	35.5%†	82.7	51.3
	Disjunction	**47.4%**	**36.8%**	**52.6%**	**26.3%**‡	40.8%	86.8	83.8

between inverse and disjunction (p = 0.782). The analysis indicates that the operator usage does have a significant effect on accuracy, and that effect is more extreme for the negated property set questions. It is particularly noteworthy that for the negated property set question employing only an inverse predicate, all the proposed solutions were responded to less accurately than chance; and for the negated property set question employing a disjunction of forward and inverse predicates, three of the four solutions were responded to less accurately than chance.

Turning to the response time, a Wilcoxon test showed no significant difference between the MINUS and the negated property set questions (p = 0.075), but a Fried-man test showed a significant effect of predicate usage (p = 0.006). However, this latter effect appears to originate from the MINUS questions. Considering the MINUS questions separately, there was a significant effect of predicate usage on response time (p = 0.006). Considering the property path questions separately, there was no significant effect of predicate usage (p = 0.331). For the MINUS questions, pairwise Wilcoxon tests indicated a significant difference between forward and inverse (p = 0.005), and between forward and disjunction (p = 0.0002), but not between inverse and disjunction (p = 0.087).

Discussion. The MINUS questions were answered significantly more accurately than the negated property set questions, but there was no significant difference in response times between the two sets of questions. The predicate usage had an effect on accuracy for both sets of questions, but on response time only for the MINUS questions. We can consider how the participants may be formulating answers to these questions. For the MINUS questions, participants are required to compute two sets and then find the set difference. For both sets they are required to think in terms of forward predicates, inverse predicates, and both forward and inverse predicates. Thinking in terms of inverse predicates is less accurate and slower than for forward predicates, because of the need to perform the inversion operations. Note that the mean time for the disjunction of forward and inverse predicates is close to the sum of the mean times in the other two cases. In part this effect is a chance effect occurring in aggregate. However, at the participant level, the response time for the question employing both forms of the predicate is generally relatively close to the sum of the times for the other two questions. This suggests that participants formed each of the two sets by considering the forward and inverse predicates separately.

For the MINUS questions, forming the set difference comes after the creation of the two sets, i.e. it is not required to consider negation and inverse at the same time. For the negated property set questions, the question using an inverse predicate and the question using the disjunction of forward and inverse predicates, require that negation and inverse be considered at the same time. This is likely to be the reason why, when using negated property sets, the inverse and disjunction questions were answered significantly less accurately than the forward question. For the negated property set questions, one might expect the disjunction of forward and inverse predicates to be answered less accurately than the question with solely an inverse predicate, since the former requires the manipulation of two mental models. However, for the question with a negated property set and the disjunction of predicate usages, all the solutions were valid. Two of the solutions, (A, B) and (C, D), required usage of the forward predicate, and these were the two where participants performed best; although not as well as for the question with forward predicate alone. The other two solutions required use of the inverse predicates, and here participants were less accurate. As a result, for the property path questions, the accuracy of the disjunctive question was between the other two.

8 Negated Property Sets and Braces

Questions. This section further examined the difficulties of negated property sets, in a situation where the braces notation was used. The questions were designed to examine participants' reasoning with negated property sets and inverse predicates in a more complex use than that for the questions in Sect. 7; in particular where a chain of predicates had to be considered. Figure 4 shows one of the questions, in this case using a forward predicate.

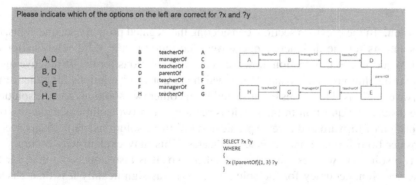

Fig. 4. Part of a question screen from the negated property set and braces section.

There were two other questions, using an inverse predicate and a disjunction of forward and inverse predicates:

- {?x (!^parentOf){1, 3} ?y}
- {?x (!(parentOf | ^parentOf)){1, 3} ?y}

All three questions used the same knowledgebase and the same proposed solutions.

Results. Table 4 shows the data for this section. A one-factor analysis of deviance indicated no significant difference in accuracy between the three questions (p = 0.293). A two-factor analysis, with both question and solution as factors indicated no significant difference for question (p = 0.292) or for solution (p = 0.851), but did indicate a significant interaction effect (p = 0.006). This is consistent with the data in Table 4, where it can be seen that the between-question variation is much greater for some solutions than it is overall. Turning to the response time data, a Friedman test indicates that there is no significant difference between the response times for the three cases (p = 0.368). The large mean time for the inverse predicate question is largely due to three response times of over 300 s each. The presence of these outliers is suggested by the large standard deviation. When they are removed, the mean time reduces to 90.4 s.

Table 4. Data for negated property set and braces questions. N.B. * not significantly greater than chance; † significantly less than chance (one-sided tests)

Predicate direction	Percentage correct					Mean time (secs)	s.d. (secs)
	A, D	B, D	G, E	H, E	Overall		
Forward	63.2%*	**84.2%**	57.9%*	57.9%*	65.8%	113.5	78.1
Inverse	68.4%*	26.3%†	**57.9%***	63.2%	53.9%*	144.8	144.6
Disjunction	**52.6%***	**78.9%**	**73.7%**	**47.4%**	63.2%	96.9	75.7
All questions	61.4%*	63.2%*	63.2%*	56.1%*	61.0%		

Discussion. In the previous section, considering the negated property set questions, the valid solutions for the disjunctive query were the union of the valid solutions for the other two queries. In this section, however, the valid solutions for the disjunctive query include two solutions, (A, D) and (H, E), which are not valid solutions for either of the other two questions. This arises because, unlike the other two solutions and the solutions for the disjunctive question in the previous section, these two solutions make use of a combination of forward and inverse predicates. For these solutions, participants needed to consider both forward and inverse predicates. This may explain why accuracy for these two solutions was less than for the other two. It is also noticeable that, for the inverse question, accuracy for the solution (B, D) was significantly less than chance. This is the solution which is valid for the forward predicate, so it seems likely that some participants were not inverting the predicate, and simply treating the question as they would the forward predicate question.

9   Effect of Prior Participant Knowledge

At the beginning of the study, participants were asked to rate their knowledge of SPARQL, SQL, and any other query language on a four-category scale. Table 5 shows the distribution of responses for each of the three questions.

Table 5. Expertise in query languages (percentage participants)

N = 19	No knowledge at all	A little knowledge	Some knowledge	Expert knowledge
SPARQL	36.8%	36.8%	21.1%	5.3%
SQL	21.1%	15.8%	42.1%	21.1%
Other query lang.	73.7%	5.3%	15.8%	5.3%

Tables 6 and 7 show the percentage of correct responses to solutions, over all the 80 proposed solutions, and the mean response time per question, for each of the categories of expertise in SPARQL and SQL. A one-sided Spearman's rank test indicated that accuracy did not significantly correlate with prior knowledge of SPARQL (rho = 0.12, p = 0.306)[7], or with knowledge of SQL (rho = 0.25, p = 0.148). However, the mean response time did significantly correlate with knowledge of SPARQL (rho = -0.44, p = 0.031), but not with knowledge of SQL (rho = 0.09, p = 0.358). Finally, it was thought that performance might depend on the overall knowledge of query languages, represented by highest level of expertise for each participant over the three questions. However, there was no significant correlation with accuracy (rho = 0.35, p = 0.071) or with response time (rho = -0.02, p = 0.462). In summary, the only significant effect of prior knowledge is that knowledge of SPARQL reduced response time, possibly because participants familiar with SPARQL spent less time referring to the handout.

Table 6. Accuracy and mean response time per SPARQL expertise category

	No knowledge at all	A little knowledge	Some knowledge	Expert knowledge
% age correct	75.4%	69.6%	80.6%	88.8%
Mean time; s.d. (secs)	104.1; 37.8	78.2; 32.3	75.5; 16.3	39.6; NA

---

[7] Spearman's rank correlation is a non-parametric measure of the correlation between the ranks of two variables. In this and subsequent Spearman's rank tests, the exact p-value could not be computed because of ties.

Table 7. Accuracy and mean response time per SQL expertise category

	No knowledge at all	A little knowledge	Some knowledge	Expert knowledge
% age correct	74.4%	66.3%	74.4%	83.8%
Mean time; s.d. (secs)	96.5; 41.8	54.3; 11.0	87.9; 30.7	91.3; 42.0

10   Textual and Graphical Representations

At the end of the study, participants were asked to describe their usage of the textual and graphical representations, according to the five categories shown in Table 8. These categories are arranged on an ordinal scale, going from an entirely textual approach at the top of the table, to an entirely graphical approach at the bottom. The table shows the percentage of participants in each of the categories, the percentage of correct responses to the proposed solutions, and the mean response time per question.

Table 8. Usage of textual and graphical information

	% age of respondents (N = 19)	% age correct responses	Mean response time (secs)	s.d. (secs)
I used only the textual information	5.3%	61.3%	97.3	NA
I used mostly the textual information, but also made some use of the graphical information	5.3%	67.5%	113.8	NA
I used the textual and graphical information about equally	10.5%	69.4%	74.4	49.3
I used mostly the graphical information, but also made some use of the textual information	57.9%	72.0%	87.0	40.9
I used only the graphical information	21.1%	91.6%	75.1	7.9

A two-sided Spearman's rank test showed that preference for the graphical representation correlated significantly with accuracy of response (rho = 0.50, p = 0.029). Thus, not only did the majority of participants prefer the graphical representation, but this preference correlated with increased accuracy. There was, however, no significant correlation with response time (rho = -0.11, p = 0.651). The questions in Sect. 5 permit a comparison of how this effect differs between the two styles. For the navigational style there was a significant correlation between preference for graphics and accuracy (rho = 0.56, p = 0.013); this was not the case for the declarative style (rho = 0.34, p = 0.161). For neither of the two styles was there a significant correlation with time (navigational: rho = -0.28, p = 0.241; declarative: rho = -0.38, p = 0.108).

11 Summary and Recommendations

Earlier in the paper we set out three goals. Firstly, we wanted to investigate whether there was any difference in the comprehension of questions in declarative and navigational form. Section 5 indicated that in general there was no significant difference in the styles. However, Sect. 6 does demonstrate a situation where the navigational style has a clear advantage; participants found the brace and vertical line notations significantly faster than the UNION keyword. The second goal was to determine any differences between various alternative property path constructs. Here the brace notation was significantly faster than the vertical line. The brace notation was also faster than the use of plus, although not significantly so on a pairwise comparison. The advantage of brace may well be that it is an obvious and easily understood notation which enables succinct expression of a query in a rapidly comprehensible form. The final goal was to investigate inversion and negation, and their interaction. Here, the indication is that thinking about either of them is hard. Thinking about both of them at the same time is very hard. This is particularly illustrated by the property path question combining inverse and negation in Sect. 7, where all the proposed solutions were answered less well than chance. Whilst the difficulties of inverse and negation are likely to be at root cognitive, they may be exacerbated by the non-intuitive symbolism used. Some property graph languages, e.g. Cypher [16], use forward and backward arrows to indicate the direction of a predicate, and this might be helpful for SPARQL. Adapting this notation to our context, *?x friendOf ?y* could be written *?x friendOf - > ?y*, whilst *?x ^friendOf ?y* could be written *?x < - friendOf ?y*. Johnson-Laird [17] describes the American philosopher C.S. Peirce's categorization of signs into: iconic, where representation depends on structural similarity; indexical, where representation depends on a physical connection; and symbolic, where representation depends on convention. The use of ^ is clearly symbolic, whilst the use of arrow is iconic. On the other hand, negation is generally represented symbolically. However, the exclamation mark may not for some people be associated with negation, and a more obvious usage, e.g. *not*, might be helpful. Finally, the analysis of Sect. 10 is evidence of the benefits offered by graphical representations. Previous work, e.g. [18], suggests that people have a preference either for textual or graphical reasoning. Our study indicates that, at least when thinking about graph databases, the graphical representation is a useful complement of the textual representation.

This leads us to four specific recommendations:

1. Query authors should use predicate paths with vertical line, or better the brace notation (if it is available) in preference to UNION. Where possible, they should minimise their use of negation and inverse, and in particular avoid using these two in combination.
2. Future developments of SPARQL should use more intuitive symbolism. In particular, an arrow notation could be used to represent directionality, in place of, or as an alternative to the use of ^; and *not* used as an alternative to !.
3. The next SPARQL standard should include the braces notation in property paths. In general, query languages should enable succinct and rapidly comprehensible queries, avoiding the need for verbosity.
4. SPARQL query engines should integrate with RDF visualization to support human reasoning about RDF knowledgebases, and in particular to support explanation of query engine results; this could be particularly useful with navigational queries.

Acknowledgements. The authors would like to thank all study participants; and also Enrico Daga for initial suggestions and assisting with participant contacts.

References

1. Prud'hommeaux, E., Seaborne, A.: SPARQL Query Language for RDF (2008) https://www.w3.org/TR/rdf-sparql-query/. Accessed 28 June 2019
2. Harris, S., Seaborne, A.: SPARQL 1.1 Query Language' (2013). https://www.w3.org/TR/sparql11-query/. Accessed 28 June 2019
3. Gallego, M.A., Fernández, J.D., Martínez-Prieto, M.A., de la Fuente, P.: An empirical study of real-world SPARQL queries (2011). Accessed 02 Nov 2015
4. Rietveld, L., Hoekstra, R.: Man vs. machine: Differences in SPARQL queries (2014)
5. Bielefeldt, A., Gonsior, J., Krötzsch, M.: Practical Linked Data Access via SPARQL: The Case of Wikidata (2018)
6. Bonifati, A., Martens, W., Timm, T.: An analytical study of large SPARQL query logs. VLDB J. **29**, 655–679 (2020). https://doi.org/10.1007/s00778-019-00558-9
7. Warren, P., Mulholland, P.: Using SPARQL – the practitioners' viewpoint. In: Faron Zucker, C., Ghidini, C., Napoli, A., Toussaint, Y. (eds.) EKAW 2018. LNCS (LNAI), vol. 11313, pp. 485–500. Springer, Cham (2018). https://doi.org/10.1007/978-3-030-03667-6_31
8. Reisner, P.: Human factors studies of database query languages: a survey and assessment. ACM Comput. Surv. CSUR **13**(1), 13–31 (1981)
9. Sarker, Md.K., Krisnadhi, A., Carral, D., Hitzler, P.: Rule-based OWL Modeling with ROWLTab protégé plugin. In: Blomqvist, E., Maynard, D., Gangemi, A., Hoekstra, R., Hitzler, P., Hartig, O. (eds.) ESWC 2017. LNCS, vol. 10249, pp. 419–433. Springer, Cham (2017). https://doi.org/10.1007/978-3-319-58068-5_26
10. Warren, P., Mulholland, P., Collins, T., Motta, E.: Improving comprehension of knowledge representation languages: a case study with description logics. Int. J. Hum.-Comput. Stud. **122**, 145–167 (2019)
11. Seaborne, A.: SPARQL 1.1 Property Paths (2010). https://www.w3.org/TR/sparql11-property-paths/. Accessed 28 June 2019

12. Arenas, M., Conca, S., Pérez, J.: Counting beyond a Yottabyte, or how SPARQL 1.1 property paths will prevent adoption of the standard. In: Proceedings of the 21st International Conference on World Wide Web, pp. 629–638 (2012)
13. R Core Team R: A language and environment for statistical computing. R Foundation for Statistical Computing, Vienna, Austria (2013). ISBN 3-900051-07-0, 2014
14. Khemlani, S., Orenes, I., Johnson-Laird, P.N.: Negation: a theory of its meaning, representation, and use. J. Cogn. Psychol. **24**(5), 541–559 (2012)
15. Orenes, I., Moxey, L., Scheepers, C., Santamaría, C.: Negation in context: evidence from the visual world paradigm. Q. J. Exp. Psychol. **69**(6), 1082–1092 (2016)
16. Robinson, I., Webber, J., Eifrem, E.: Graph Databases. O'Reilly Media Inc., Sebastopol (2013)
17. Johnson-Laird, P.N.: The history of mental models. In: Manktelow, K., Chung, M. (eds.) Psychology of reasoning: Theoretical and Historical Perspectives. p. 179. Psychology Press (2004)
18. Ford, M.: Two modes of mental representation and problem solution in syllogistic reasoning. Cognition **54**(1), 1–71 (1995)

What to Do When the Users of an Ontology Merging System Want the Impossible? Towards Determining Compatibility of Generic Merge Requirements

Samira Babalou$^{(\boxtimes)}$ ⓘ, Elena Grygorova ⓘ, and Birgitta König-Ries ⓘ

Heinz-Nixdorf Chair for Distributed Information Systems,
Institute for Computer Science, Friedrich Schiller University Jena, Jena, Germany
{samira.babalou,elena.grygorova,birgitta.koenig-ries}@uni-jena.de

Abstract. Ontology merging systems enable the reusability and interoperability of existing knowledge. Ideally, they allow their users to specify which characteristics the merged ontology should have. In prior work, we have identified Generic Merge Requirements (GMRs) reflecting such characteristics. However, not all of them can be met simultaneously. Thus, if a system allows users to select which GMRs should be met, it needs a way to deal with incompatible GMRs. In this paper, we analyze in detail which GMRs are (in-)compatible, and propose a graph based approach to determining and ranking maximum compatible supersets of user-specified GMRs. Our analysis shows that this is indeed feasible to detect the compatible supersets of the given GMRs that can be fulfilled simultaneously. This approach is implemented in the open source $\mathcal{C}o\mathcal{M}erger$ tool.

Keywords: Ontology merging · Merge requirements · Graph theory

1 Introduction

An ontology is a formal, explicit description of a given domain. It contains a set of entities, including classes, properties, and instances. Ontology merging [1] is the process of creating a merged ontology $\mathcal{O}_M$ from a set of source ontologies $\mathcal{O}_S$ with a set of corresponding pairs extracted from a given mapping. Various ontology merging systems [2–16] provide different sets of criteria and requirements that their merged ontologies should meet. In [17], we have analyzed the literature and determined which criteria, called Generic Merge Requirements (GMRs), are used by different approaches. Customizing the GMRs within an ontology merging system provides a flexible merging approach, where users can actively choose which requirements are important to them, instead of allowing only a very indirect choice by picking a merge system that uses their preferred set of

© Springer Nature Switzerland AG 2020
C. M. Keet and M. Dumontier (Eds.): EKAW 2020, LNAI 12387, pp. 20–36, 2020.
https://doi.org/10.1007/978-3-030-61244-3_2

criteria. Unfortunately, not all GMRs are compatible. For instance, one may want to preserve all properties contained in the original ontology in the merged ontology. On the other hand, one could wish to avoid cycles. Likely, these goals conflict.

The motivation behind this work is to enable merging systems to take user input into consideration, so ultimately, to have user-requirement driven ontology merging. Our proposal allows flexibility on the user side to select an arbitrary set of GMRs. Thus, once a user has chosen a set of important GMRs, a system is needed to check their compatibility and suggest a maximum set of requirements that can be met simultaneously. In this paper, we analyze in detail the (in)compatibility of GMRs and describe a graph based approach to determining maximal compatible sets for the given GMRs. Further, an automatic ranking method is proposed on the set of the system suggested compatible sets. The proposed framework is conservative and finds potential conflicts in GMRs. For a given ontology, not all of these potential conflicts may materialize. We discuss in Sect. 3, how the approach could be extended to leverage this. GMRs are implemented in $\mathcal{C}o\mathcal{M}erger$ [18] and are publicly available and distributed under an open-source license. We have empirically analyzed various merged ontologies for the given set of user-selected GMRs, and observed that there is a superset of compatible GMRs that can be fulfilled simultaneously.

The rest of the paper is organized as follows. Section 2 surveys GMRs. The proposed method of compatibility checker of GMRs is presented in Sect. 3. In Sect. 4, the compatible sets are ranked. An empirical analysis of GMRs is demonstrated in Sect. 5. The paper is concluded in Sect. 6.

2   Survey on Generic Merge Requirements

Generic Merge Requirements (GMRs) are a set of requirements that the merged ontology is expected to achieve. GMRs have been first introduced in the Vanilla system [1]. Later other merge approaches implicitly or explicitly took them into consideration [2–8,10–16,19,20]. To provide customizable GMRs in an ontology merging system, we surveyed the literature to compile a list of GMRs. This investigation lead to twenty GMRs [17], summarized in Table 1. They have been categorized in six aspects: completeness ($R1$–$R7$), minimality ($R8$–$R11$), deduction (R12), constraint ($R13$–$R15$), acyclicity ($R16$–$R18$), and connectivity ($R19$ and $R20$). This list has been acquired by studying three different research fields:

1. *Ontology and model merging methods*: The GMRs $R1$–$R6$, $R8$–$R16$, $R19$ have been extracted from existing ontology and model merging methods such as [2, 3,6]. These approaches aim to implicitly or explicitly meet at least one of the GMRs on their merged ontology.
2. *Ontology merging benchmarks*: The existing benchmarks [21,22] on the ontology merging domain introduced general desiderata and essential requirements that the merged ontology should meet. The criteria stated in

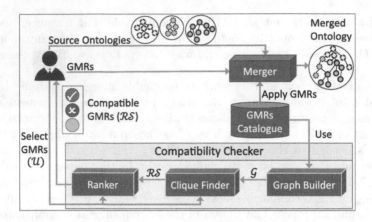

Fig. 1. The GMRs' compatibility checker within the ontology merge system.

these benchmarks are based on earlier research in [23], a study of the quality measurement of the merged ontology. In this respect, *R1*, *R4*, *R7–R9* have been extracted from these research studies.

3. *Ontology engineering*: Researchers of the ontology engineering domain [24–26] came up with a set of criteria to present the correctness of an ontology, which is developed in a single environment. It is worthwhile to consider these criteria also on the merged ontology because the newly created merged ontology may be viewed the same as the developed ontologies in this category. Not all of these criteria can be extended in the ontology merging scenario since some relate to the problem of the source ontologies modeling, in which the merge process can not affect them. In this regards, we recast *R15–R20* from this category.

To the best of our knowledge, there is no general compatibility checker between the GMRs in the literature. However, the approach in [27] proposed a resolution for conflicts that occurred by applying *R13* and *R14*.

3   Proposed Approach for Checking GMRs Compatibility

In this section, we describe our approach to finding maximum compatible supersets of user-specified GMR. Basically, what we do is first find subsets of the GMRs specified by the user that are compatible, and second, extend those by further GMRs, (out of those the user had not selected), while maintaining compatibility. Our intuition is that first, as much as possible of what the user wanted should be met and that second, adding further GMRs will, in general, improve the quality of the merged ontology.

Therefore, a framework is required to detect the compatibility of the user-selected GMRs. We propose such a framework within the ontology merge system, as shown in Fig. 1. The source ontologies are merged based on the user-selected GMRs. Users can request to check the compatibility of the selected

Table 1. Generic Merge Requirements (GMRs).

R1- **Class preservation**: All classes of source ontologies should be preserved in the merged ontology [1, 2, 4–11, 21–23]
R2- **Property preservation**: All properties of source ontologies should be preserved in the merged ontology [1, 2, 4, 5, 12]
R3- **Instance preservation**: All instances of source ontologies should be preserved in the merged ontology [1, 2, 4, 13]
R4- **Correspondence preservation**: The corresponding entities from source ontologies should be mapped to the same merged entity [1, 2, 8, 22]
R5- **Correspondences' property preservation**: The merged entity should have the same property of its corresponding entities [1, 8]
R6- **Property's value preservation**: Properties' values from the source ontologies should be preserved in the merged ontology [1, 8]
R7- **Structure preservation**: The hierarchical structure of source ontologies' entities should be preserved in the merged ontology [23]
R8- **Class redundancy prohibition**: No redundant classes should exist in the merged ontology [1, 2, 5, 10, 14–16, 21, 23]
R9- **Property redundancy prohibition**: No redundant properties should exist in the merged ontology [4, 12, 21]
R10- **Instance redundancy prohibition**: No redundant instances should exist in the merged ontology [7, 13]
R11- **Extraneous entity prohibition**: No additional entities other than the source ontologies' entities should be added in the merged result [1]
R12- **Entailment deduction satisfaction**: All entailments of the source ontologies should be satisfied in the merged ontology [3, 5]
R13- **One type restriction**: Any merged entity should have one data type [1]
R14- **Property value's constraint**: Restriction on property's values from source ontologies should be applied without conflict in the merged ontology [1, 3]
R15- **Property's domain and range oneness**: The merge process should not result in multiple domains or ranges defined for a single property [25]
R16- **Acyclicity in the class hierarchy**: The merge process should not produce a cycle in the class hierarchy [1, 2, 4, 6, 11, 19, 23–25]
R17- **Acyclicity in the property hierarchy**: The merge process should not produce a cycle between properties w.r.t. the is-subproperty-of relationship [20, 25]
R18- **Prohibition of properties being inverses of themselves**: The merge process should not cause an inverse recursive definition on the properties [25]
R19- **Unconnected class prohibition**: Each connected class from source ontologies should not be unconnected in the merged ontology [1, 6, 25]
R20- **Unconnected property prohibition**: Each connected property from the source ontologies should not be unconnected in the merged ontology [8, 25]

Table 2. Scope of changes by applying GMRs in the merged ontology.

Scope	Sub-Scope	Explanation
Scope 1- Classes	Scope 1_1	Classes origin from source ontologies
	Scope 1_2	Redundant classes
	Scope 1_3	Extra classes that do not belong to any source ontologies
Scope 2 Properties	Scope 2_1	Properties origin from source ontologies
	Scope 2_2	Redundant properties
	Scope 2_3	Extra properties that do not belong to any source ontologies
Scope 3- Instances	Scope 3_1	Instances origin from source ontologies
	Scope 3_2	Redundant instances
	Scope 3_3	Extra instances that do not belong to any source ontologies
Scope4- Values of properties	-	Values of properties in the merged ontology

GMRs. To achieve this, we build a graph $\mathcal{G}$ of the interactions between the GMRs. We then recast the problem at hand by selecting the maximal superset of the user-selected GMRs as $\mathcal{RS} = \{rs_1, rs_2, ..., rs_z\}$. These results are ranked, sorted, and returned to the user. More precisely, the framework performs the following steps:

1. A graph $\mathcal{G}$ is built based on the interactions between GMRs.
2. The compatible subsets of the user-selected GMRs are extracted from the $\mathcal{G}$. Then, they will be extended to the maximal compatible superset.
3. The detected sets are ranked and ordered.
4. An ordered list of compatible sets is returned to the user.

In the next sub-section, building the GMRs interaction graph $\mathcal{G}$ and extracting the compatible supersets in the graph will be explained.

3.1 Building GMRs Interactions Graph $\mathcal{G}$

The *Graph Builder* component in Fig. 1 takes as input the GMRs catalogue and creates the graph $\mathcal{G}$. The GMRs' interaction graph $\mathcal{G} = (V, E)$ demonstrates the interaction between GMRs, where V is the set of vertices representing the GMRs (see Table 1), and E is the set of edges. In this graph, two GMRs are connected via an edge if they are compatible. To define the compatibility of GMRs (existence of an edge between two GMRs in $\mathcal{G}$), two conditions are defined:

Condition I. The scope of changes by a GMR on the merged ontology can reveal its (in-)compatibility with others. Thus, two GMRs are compatible if they do not modify the same scope of entities. The changes made by each GMR are applied to the classes (scope 1), properties (scope 2), instances (scope 3), and value of properties (scope 4), defined by the union of sub-scopes, as shown in Table 2. We distinguish between two scopes:

– **Direct scope**: It is the main scope that is affected by applying a GMR. E.g., applying *R1* adds missing classes, so the direct scope of *R1* is the classes.

– **Indirect scope:** It is the scope that might be affected by the changes made on the direct scope. E.g., applying $R8$ deletes the redundant classes (direct scope is redundant classes). However, as a side effect of this operation, this might cause the properties connected to those classes to become unconnected, or their instance to be orphaned. Thus, the indirect scopes of $R8$ are properties and instances.

Condition II. Let us illustrate our intuition to require the second condition with an example by considering $R2$ (property preservation) and $R5$ (correspondences' property preservation). $R2$ may make changes to the properties, and $R5$ possibly makes changes to the properties of the corresponding classes. So, both GMRs apply changes on the same set of entities (Scope 2_1). However, it cannot be concluded that both GMRs are incompatible because the operations that both carry on the merged ontology do not have any contradiction. $R2$ uses the add operation to preserve the missing properties. $R5$ also uses the add operation to add missing properties of the corresponding classes. So, both these actions can be performed simultaneously in the merged ontologies without conflict. As a whole, three types of operation are performed to meet the GMRs and ensure their fulfillment: (1) Add: e.g., $R1$ uses the add operation to preserve the missing classes in the merged ontology. (2) Delete: e.g., $R8$ uses the delete operation to get rid of redundant classes. (3) A combination of add and delete: e.g., $R4$ uses add and delete operations, in which for two corresponding classes c_1 and c_2 that are not mapped to the integrated class c', first, c_1 and c_2 will be deleted, then c' will be added. Table 3 shows the scopes and operations of each GMR. For some GMRs, there are different possible operations. We followed one solution in this paper and marked the alternative one by the symbol $\star$.

Although applying each GMR may change direct and indirect scopes, their operations carry on the direct scope. Therefore, to determine the compatibility of the GMRs, the type of operations performed by each GMR on the direct scope should be taken into account. In this regards, when two GMRs change the same set of entities, they can still be compatible if both use the same operation. Let $\mu(R_j)$ be a set of entities that get affected by applying $R_j \in$ GMRs on the merged ontology, i.e., the direct scope. Given the conditions mentioned above, we define the compatibility between R_j and $R_k \in$ GMRs as:

Definition 1. R_j *is compatible with* R_k $(R_j \parallel R_k)$ *if* R_j *and* R_k *modify different scopes of entities in the merged ontology, i.e.,* $\mu(R_j) \neq \mu(R_k)$. *If* $\mu(R_j) = \mu(R_k)$, *the type of operation of the applying* R_j *and* R_k *should be the same.*

Accordingly, there could be four variants between the scope of changes and the types of operation, as:

Case A- Same Scopes and Same Operations: In this case, the scope of entities affected by applying R_j and R_k, is the same. Moreover, R_j and R_k use the same type of operations. Since both GMRs use the same operation on the same set of entities, they are compatible with each other.

- *Example:* $R2 \parallel R7$. $R2$ and $R7$ both make changes in the properties origin from the source ontologies. Moreover, $R2$ uses the add operation to add the missing properties. $R7$ uses the add operation to add the missing is-a properties in order to preserve the hierarchy structure of the source ontologies in the merged ontology. Thus, both are compatible.

Case B- Same Scopes with Different Operations: In this case, the set of entities, getting affected by applying R_j and R_k, is the same. However, R_j and R_k use different types of operations. Since both use the different operations on the same set of entities, they are incompatible with each other.

Table 3. The scopes and operations of each GMR. The symbol * indicates an alternative solution.

GMR	Direct Scope	Indirect Scope	Operation	Description
$R1$	$S1_1$	-	add	It adds missing classes of the source ontologies
$R2$	$S2_1$	-	add	It adds missing properties of the source ontologies
$R3$	$S3_1$	-	add	It adds missing instances of the source ontologies
$R4$	$S1_1$	$S2$	add &	If two corresponding classes c_1 and c_2 are not mapped to the one
		$S3$	delete	integrated class c', first, c_1 and c_2 is deleted, then c' will be added
	$S2_1$	$S1$	add &	It follows the procedure the same as the $R4$-scope 1-1
		$S3$	delete	but one the properties
$R5$	$S2_1$	-	add	It adds missing properties of the corresponding classes
$R6$	$S4$	-	add	It adds missing values of the properties
$R7$	$S2_1$	-	add	It adds is-a properties to the respective class
$R8$	$S1_2$	$S2, S3$	delete	It deletes redundant classes
$R9$	$S2_2$	$S1, S3$	delete	It deletes redundant properties
$R10$	$S3_2$	$S1$	delete	It deletes redundant instances
$R11$	$S1_3$ $S2_3$ $S3_3$	$S1, S2, S3$	delete	It deletes extra entities
$R12$	$S1_1$ $S2_1$ $S3_1$	- - -	add	It adds some entities to achieve the entailment the same as the source ontologies
$R13$	$S4$	-	delete	It keeps only one of the data types and deletes the other one
$R14$	$S4$	-	delete	It keeps only one value of the property and deletes the other one
$R15$	$S1_1$	$S2, S3$	add & delete	It might add multiple domains or ranges as the unionOf to the property
			delete*	It might delete multiple domains or ranges and only keep one of them
$R16$	$S2$	$S1$	delete	It might delete some properties to be free of cycles
	$S1$	$S2, S3$	delete*	It might delete some classes to be free of cycles
$R17$	$S2$	$S1$	delete	It deletes properties to be free of the cycle on the properties' hierarchy
$R18$	$S2$	$S1$	delete	It deletes the inverse of properties
$R19$	$S2$	-	add	It might add is-a relations to connect the unconnected classes
	$S1$	$S2, S3$	delete*	It might delete unconnected classes
$R20$	$S2$	$S1$	delete*	It might delete the unconnected properties
		-	add	It might use the add operation to connect the unconnected properties to the classes

- *Example*: $R2 \nparallel R17$. Both $R2$ and $R17$ change properties. $R2$ adds missing properties, whereas $R17$ may delete some properties to achieve acyclicity. Thus, it may happen that applying $R17$ reverses the changes made by $R7$ and vice versa.

Case C- **Different Scopes with the Same Operations**: In this case, the set of entities, getting effect by applying R_j and R_k, is different. Moreover, both use the same type of operations. Since both GMRs using the same operation but on different sets of entities, they are compatible.

- *Example*: $R1 \parallel R2$. Preserving the classes in the merged ontology will make some changes in the classes in $R1$. However, preserving the properties will modify the properties in $R2$. These two GMRs do not change the same group of entities. Moreover, both use the add operation for applying these GMRs. Since both GMRs use the same operation but on different sets of entities, they are compatible.

Case D- **Different Scopes and Different Operations**: In this case, applying R_j and R_k is performed on different sets of entities. Moreover, both use different

Table 4. Compatibility interaction between GMRs. f_d shows the compatibility degree.

GMR	Compatible GMRs	f_d
R1	*R2, R3, R5–R14, R16–R20*	0.89
R2	*R1, R3, R5–R15, R19, R20*	0.79
R3	*R1, R2, R4–R20*	1
R4	*R3, R6, R8–R11, R13, R14*	0.74
R5	*R1–R3, R6–R15, R19, R20*	0.79
R6	*R1–R5, R7–R12, R15–R20*	0.89
R7	*R1–R3, R5, R6, R8–R15, R19, R20*	0.79
R8	*R1–R7, R9–R20*	1
R9	*R1–R8, R10–R18*	0.89
R10	*R1–R9, R11–R20*	1
R11	*R1–R10, R12–R18*	0.89
R12	*R1–R3, R5–R11, R13, R14, R19, R20*	0.74
R13	*R1–R5, R7–R12, R14–R20*	0.95
R14	*R1–R5, R7–R13, R15–R20*	0.95
R15	*R2, R3, R5–R11, R13, R14, R16–R20*	0.84
R16	*R1, R3, R6, R8–R11, R13–R15, R17, R18*	0.63
R17	*R1, R3, R6, R8–R11, R13–R16, R18*	0.63
R18	*R1, R3, R6, R8–R11, R13–R17*	0.63
R19	*R1–R3, R5–R8, R10, R12–R15, R20*	0.68
R20	*R1–R3, R5–R8, R10, R12–R15, R19*	0.68

types of operations. Since both use different operations on the different entity sets, they are completely separated and do not have any effect on each other. So, they are compatible.

- *Example*: *R1* ∥ *R11*. *R1* makes changes in the classes origin from source ontologies (scope 1_1). *R11*, in addition to changing properties, modifies the extra classes (scope 1_3). So, the scopes of changes by these two GMRs are on the different entity sets. *R1* uses the add operation, while *R11* uses delete operation. Since both use the different operations on different sets of entities, they are compatible.

Considering the scope and the operation of each GMR, the interaction between GMRs can be concluded in Table 4, in which R_j is considered compatible with R_k if the intersection of all its sub-scopes is compatible. Thus, the graph G has edges between the compatible GMRs, as stated in Table 4. The compatibility degree f_d for each GMR R_j is the number of compatible GMRs with R_j divided by the total number of GMRs, as shown in the last column. *R3*, *R8*, and *R10* are compatible with all other GMRs. *R13* and *R14* have high compatibility as the scope of their changes is different from the others. *R16*, *R17*, and *R18* are the least compatible.

3.2   Clique Finder

Given the GMRs interaction graph G and the set U containing the GMRs the user is interested in, we aim to find the maximal superset of V containing all vertices out of U and no incompatible nodes. This may not always be achievable since the user might have chosen incompatible GMRs already. In this case, we search for a maximal superset of V in G that preserves as many nodes out of U as possible and contains compatible nodes only. Thus, the *Clique Finder* component in Fig. 1 takes as input a set of user-selected GMRs U alongside with the GMRs' interaction graph G. It returns a set of all possible compatible sets, namely $RS = \{rs_1, rs_2, ..., rs_l\}$. Each suggested compatible set $rs \in RS$ contains (all/part) of the user-selected compatible GMRs, and compatible GMRs additionally all other. For the given user-selected GMRs, each suggested compatible set rs is formulated in Eq. 1.

$$rs = U^C \cup U^{EC} \tag{1}$$

where, U^C is a compatible subset of U, and U^{EC} is an extra compatible set of GMRs related to U. To obtain the compatible set rs, we recast the problem at hand as clique extraction on the GMRs' interaction graph G, where it needs to be the maximal best match based on the user-selected GMRs. A clique is a set of fully connected vertices. Thus a compatible clique K^C-*Clique* is extracted, where K indicates the number of vertices in the clique, and C denotes that the clique is compatible.

Definition 2. *The K^C-Clique is a compatible clique iff between all vertices only the compatible relations exist.*

Compatible relations between GMRs are encoded by edges in the GMRs interaction graph $\mathcal{G}$. Thus, $\mathcal{K}^C$-*Clique* includes compatible GMRs from $\mathcal{U}$ (called $\mathcal{U}^C$) and additional compatible GMRs related to $\mathcal{U}$'s elements (called $\mathcal{U}^{EC}$). $\mathcal{K}^C$-*max-Clique* is a clique containing at least $\mathcal{K}$ vertices that is not a subset of any other cliques. To compute the $\mathcal{K}^C$-*max-Clique*, we use the CLIQUES algorithm described in [28]. To avoid enumerating all possible subgraphs, two constraints on the clique extraction are placed:

1. If a clique does not contain at least $\mathcal{K}$ vertices, then neither the clique nor any other sub-cliques can contain a $\mathcal{K}^C$-*Clique*, because, if the clique does not have the required number of vertices, it cannot be a $\mathcal{K}^C$-*Clique*.
2. Only vertices in a $\mathcal{K}^C$-*max-Clique* of $\mathcal{G}$ can form a $\mathcal{K}^C$-*Clique*, because a vertex that is not in a $\mathcal{K}^C$-*max-Clique* cannot be in any $\mathcal{K}^C$-*Clique*.

The first constraint contributes to reducing the search space, and the second one narrows the result to the maximal desired compatible GMRs. Moreover, Definition 2 guarantees that the selected GMRs are compatible.

4   Ranking the Compatible Sets

For each set of user-selected GMRs, there are different possible compatible GMRs sets. Let $\mathcal{RS} = \{rs_1, rs_2, ..., rs_l\}$ be all possible compatible sets based on the user-selected GMRs. To figure out which $rs_z \in \mathcal{RS}$ is the best choice, the *Ranker* component in Fig. 1 rates the elements of $\mathcal{RS}$ based on different criteria. The ranked values assign a confidence degree to each suggested compatible set. Assume that the user selected $\mathcal{U} = \{R7, R9, R10, R16\}$. The approach described before finds three possible compatible sets, $\mathcal{RS} = \{rs_1, rs_2, rs_3\}$[1], where $rs_1 = \{R1, R3, R6, R8, R9, R10, R11, R16, R17, R18\}$, $rs_2 = \{R1, R3, R8, R9, R10, R11, R13, R14, R16, R17, R18\}$, and $rs_3 = \{R2, R3, R5, R6, R7, R8, R9, R10, R11, R15\}$. To determine which rs is the best choice, we rank all compatible sets with three different criteria:

1. **The number of user-selected GMRs in each compatible set:** The intersection of the compatible set rs_z and the user-selected GMRs $\mathcal{U}$, $rs_z \cap \mathcal{U}$, comprises all elements which are contained in both rs_z and $\mathcal{U}$. Therefore, we count the number of elements that are available in both rs_z and $\mathcal{U}$. Let us consider that $|rs_z|$ is the number of GMRs in the compatible set rs_z, $|\mathcal{U}|$ is the number of GMRs in the user-selected GMRs ($\mathcal{U}$), $|\mathcal{U} \cap rs_z|$ is the number of GMRs contained in both rs_z and $\mathcal{U}$, and $|GMRs|$ the total number of GMRs in our system. Given these notations, Eq. 2 ranks each suggested compatible set based on considering the user preference in the first part and the power (important) of rs_z itself in the second part.

$$Score_1(rs_z) = \frac{|\mathcal{U} \cap rs_z|}{|\mathcal{U}|} + \frac{|rs_z|}{|GMRs|} \tag{2}$$

---

[1] For the given $\mathcal{U}$, there are 18 different maximal compatible sets. To make the example concise, we consider 3 compatible sets, only.

In the given example, rs_1 has $|rs_1| = 10$, $|\mathcal{U}| = 4$, $|\mathcal{U} \cap rs_1| = 3$, and $|GMRs| = 20$. Therefore, this score is obtained as $Score_1(rs_1) = \frac{3}{4} + \frac{10}{20} = 1.25$. Similarly, this score for rs_2 and rs_3 is calculated as $Score_1(rs_2) = 1.3$ and $Score_1(rs_3) = 1.25$.

2. **The number of user-selected aspects in each compatible set:** GMRs have been categorized in different aspects, which users can select. So, not only the number of user-selected GMRs has an effect on the ranking of each compatible set rs, also the user-selected aspects should be taken into account. Therefore, we calculate to which extent each suggested compatible set rs_z covers the user's intended aspects. Let us $\Psi(\mathcal{U})$ be the number of GMRs' aspects in $\mathcal{U}$, $\Psi(rs_z)$ the number of GMRs' aspects in rs_z, $\Psi(\mathcal{U} \cap rs_z)$ the number of common aspects in both rs_z and $\mathcal{U}$, and $|GMRs_{Aspect}|$ the total number of aspects in the GMRs catalouge. Given these notations, Eq. 3 ranks each suggested compatible set based on considering the user preference aspects in the first part and the power (important) of rs_z's aspect itself in the second part of the equation.

$$Score_2(rs_z) = \frac{\Psi(\mathcal{U} \cap rs_z)}{\Psi(\mathcal{U})} + \frac{\Psi(rs_z)}{|GMRs_{Aspect}|} \tag{3}$$

In the current example, rs_1 has $\Psi(\mathcal{U}) = 3$, $\Psi(rs_1) = 3$, $\Psi(\mathcal{U} \cap rs_1) = 3$, and $|GMRs_{Aspect}| = 6$. Thus, this score is obtained as $Score_2(rs_1) = \frac{3}{3} + \frac{3}{6} = 1.5$. Similarly, this score for rs_2 and rs_3 is achieved as $Score_2(rs_2) = 1.67$ and $Score_2(rs_3) = 1.5$.

green: your compatible GMRs, red:your incompatible GMRs, orange: extra compatible GMRs

☑Maximum compatible set: {1,3,8,9,10,11,13,14,16,17,18}, Incompatible GMR: {7}, Rank:1.0
☐Maximum compatible set: {3,8,9,10,11,13,14,15,16,17,18}, Incompatible GMR: {7}, Rank:1.0
☐Maximum compatible set: {2,3,5,7,8,9,10,11,12,13,14}, Incompatible GMR: {16}, Rank:0.975
☐Maximum compatible set: {3,6,8,9,10,11,15,16,17,18}, Incompatible GMR: {7}, Rank:0.97
☐Maximum compatible set: {1,2,3,5,7,8,9,10,11,13,14}, Incompatible GMR: {16}, Rank:0.963
☐Maximum compatible set: {2,3,5,7,8,9,10,11,13,14,15}, Incompatible GMR: {16}, Rank:0.963
☐Maximum compatible set: {1,3,6,8,9,10,11,16,17,18}, Incompatible GMR: {7}, Rank:0.957
☐Maximum compatible set: {2,3,5,6,7,8,9,10,11,15}, Incompatible GMR: {16}, Rank:0.934
☐Maximum compatible set: {2,3,5,6,7,8,9,10,11,12}, Incompatible GMR: {16}, Rank:0.933
☐Maximum compatible set: {1,2,3,5,6,7,8,9,10,11}, Incompatible GMR: {16}, Rank:0.921

Fig. 2. Top-10 maximum compatible sets for $\mathcal{U} = \{R7, R9, R10, R16\}$.

3. **Compatibility degree of each GMR:** Up to now, the proposed metrics consider the quantity measure. This results in obtaining an equal value for those sets that contain the same number of GMRs and aspects. In the running example, there is the same number of GMRs and aspects in rs_1 and rs_3, i.e., $|s_1| = 10$, $|s_3| = 10$, $\Psi(s_1) = 3$, and $\Psi(s_3) = 3$. Also, the number of common GMRs and aspects in these sets with user-selected ones is the same. Therefore, they obtained the same values for $Score_1$ and $Score_2$. However, these two

sets are distinct. To reflect the difference of suggested sets, the distinctive characteristics of each GMR belonging to the sets should be considered. As an indicator to represent a difference between GMRs, we use the compatibility degree of each GMR (see Table 4). Thus, the average value of the compatibility degree of each GMR in the suggested compatible set is used as the third ranking criteria. For the given $rs_z = \{R_i, ..., R_m\}$, the average compatibility degree of Rs in rs_z is shown in Eq. 4.

$$Score_3(rs_z) = \Sigma_{j=i}^{m} f_d(R_j) \times \frac{1}{\Sigma(rs_z)} \tag{4}$$

In the example, $Score_3(rs_1) = 0.845$, $Score_3(rs_2) = 0.86$, and $Score_3(rs_3) = 0.89$.

Thus, the total rank for each rs_z is defined by Eq. 5.

$$Total\_Score(rs_z) = w_1 \times Score_1 + w_2 \times Score_2 + w_3 \times Score_3 \tag{5}$$

For our example, considering empirical values of 0.8, 0.1, and 0.1 for w_1, w_2, and w_3, respectively, the total score is achieved as $Total\_Score(rs_1) = 1.23$, $Total\_Score(rs_2) = 1.29$, and $Total\_Score(rs_3) = 1.24$. The values are normalized between 0 and 1 and presented in the descending order to the user. Figure 2 shows the top-10 compatible sets, where the values for each set has been normalized and ordered in the GUI.

5   Empirical Analysis

We have implemented the GMRs within the $\mathcal{C}o\mathcal{M}erger$ [18][2]. In the ranking process, w_1, w_2, and w_3 have been empirically adjusted to 0.8, 0.1, and 0.1, respectively. For two sample source ontologies (see Fig. 3), we have created manually two different versions of the merged ontologies $\mathcal{O}_{M_1}$ and $\mathcal{O}_{M_2}$ (see Fig. 4) to reflect different GMRs[3]. To this end, we analyze three user-selected GMRs and then discuss the extent to which they can be fulfilled simultaneously on $\mathcal{O}_{M_1}$ and $\mathcal{O}_{M_2}$.

First Use Case: $\mathcal{U} = \{R2, R3, R8, R16\}$. In $\mathcal{O}_{M_2}$, $R3$ and $R8$ are fulfilled. However, properties p_{15}, p_{24}, and p_{25} are missing, so $R2$ is not fulfilled. Moreover, there is a cycle in $c_5c_{13} \sqsubseteq c_{16} \sqsubseteq c_{17} \sqsubseteq c_{18} \sqsubseteq c_6c_{19} \sqsubseteq c_5c_{13}$, which indicates that $R16$ also is not fulfilled in $\mathcal{O}_{M_2}$. $R2$ and $R16$ are incompatible. Because $R2$ will add the missing properties and will want to keep all properties. On the other side, $R16$ will delete the is-a properties to be free of cycles. By applying $R2$ in $\mathcal{O}_{M_2}$, properties p_{15}, p_{24}, and p_{25} will be added. Thus, all properties can be preserved at the merged ontology. However, by applying $R16$, property p_{28} will

---

[2] Detail of GMR implementation: http://comerger.uni-jena.de/requirement.jsp.
[3] Ontologies available at: https://github.com/fusion-jena/CoMerger/GMR.

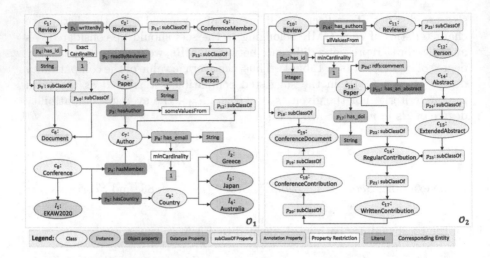

Fig. 3. Two sample source ontologies.

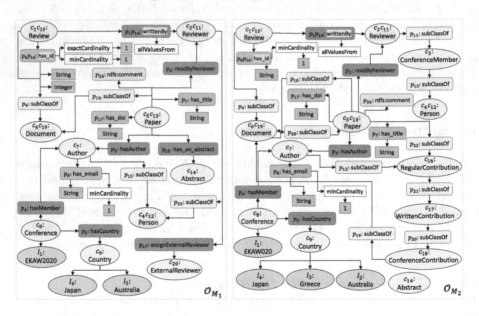

Fig. 4. Different versions of merged ontologies of Fig. 3.

be deleted in order to be free of cycles. This action causes that $R2$ failed. In this case, if $R2$ wants to add p_{28}, a cycle will be generated. So, $R2$ could not completely be fulfilled in the merged ontology. Three missing properties can be added, but one property (p_{28}) could not be preserved.

Thus, our system suggests as the best possible compatible set $rs_1 = \{R1,$ $R3, R8, R9, R10, R11, R13, R14, R16, R17, R18\}$ and $rs_2 = \{R3, R8, R9, R10,$ $R11, R13, R14, R15, R16, R17, R18\}$, in which the $R2$ is not considered. These two sets have the same scores 1.0 based on our proposed method. Thus, given the user-selected GMRs, there is a superset of compatible GMRs that can be fulfilled simultaneously. The next possible compatible set is when $R16$ is not considered and $R2$ will be kept. Thus, the system suggests the set $rs_3 = \{R2,$ $R3, R5, R7, R8, R10, R12, R13, R14, R19, R20\}$ with score 0.986. For the given $\mathcal{U}$, the 3^C-Cliques are $\{R3, R8, R16\}, \{R2, R8, R16\}$, and $\{R2, R3, R8\}$, and a 2^C-Clique is $\{R3, R8\}$. In Table 5, all $\mathcal{K}^C$-max-Cliques are shown, which are all possible maximal compatible sets for the user-selected GMRs. rs_1-rs_6, rs_8, and rs_9 are 11^C-max-Cliques, while rs_7, rs_{10}-rs_{16} are 10^C-max-Cliques, and rs_{17} and rs_{18} are 8^C-max-Clique and 7^C-max-Clique, respectively.

Table 5. All possible maximum compatible sets for user-selected GMRs $\mathcal{U} = \{R2, R3, R8, R16\}$. Green (no-line): user-selected compatible GMRs; Red (double-underline): user-selected incompatible GMRs; Orange (underline): extra compatible GMRs.

$\mathcal{RS}$	$\mathcal{K}$	Compatible	Incompatible	Score
rs_1	11	$\{R1, R3, R8, R9, R10, R11, R13, R14, R16, R17, R18\}$	$\{R2\}$	1.0
rs_2	11	$\{R3, R8, R9, R10, R11, R13, R14, R15, R16, R17, R18\}$	$\{R2\}$	1.0
rs_3	11	$\{R2, R3, R5, R7, R8, R10, R12, R13, R14, R19, R20\}$	$\{R16\}$	0.986
rs_4	11	$\{R2, R3, R5, R7, R8, R9, R10, R11, R12, R13, R14\}$	$\{R16\}$	0.975
rs_5	11	$\{R1, R2, R3, R5, R7, R8, R10, R13, R14, R19, R20\}$	$\{R16\}$	0.973
rs_6	11	$\{R2, R3, R5, R7, R8, R10, R13, R14, R15, R19, R20\}$	$\{R16\}$	0.973
rs_7	10	$\{R3, R6, R8, R9, R10, R11, R15, R16, R17, R18\}$	$\{R2\}$	0.97
rs_8	11	$\{R1, R2, R3, R5, R7, R8, R9, R10, R11, R13, R14\}$	$\{R16\}$	0.963
rs_9	11	$\{R2, R3, R5, R7, R8, R9, R10, R11, R13, R14, R15\}$	$\{R16\}$	0.963
rs_{10}	10	$\{R1, R3, R6, R8, R9, R10, R11, R16, R17, R18\}$	$\{R2\}$	0.957
rs_{11}	10	$\{R2, R3, R5, R6, R7, R8, R10, R15, R19, R20\}$	$\{R16\}$	0.944
rs_{12}	10	$\{R2, R3, R5, R6, R7, R8, R10, R12, R19, R20\}$	$\{R16\}$	0.943
rs_{13}	10	$\{R2, R3, R5, R6, R7, R8, R9, R10, R11, R15\}$	$\{R16\}$	0.934
rs_{14}	10	$\{R2, R3, R5, R6, R7, R8, R9, R10, R11, R12\}$	$\{R16\}$	0.933
rs_{15}	10	$\{R1, R2, R3, R5, R6, R7, R8, R10, R19, R20\}$	$\{R16\}$	0.931
rs_{16}	10	$\{R1, R2, R3, R5, R6, R7, R8, R9, R10, R11\}$	$\{R16\}$	0.921
rs_{17}	8	$\{R3, R4, R8, R9, R10, R11, R13, R14\}$	$\{R2, R16\}$	0.719
rs_{18}	7	$\{R3, R4, R6, R8, R9, R10, R11\}$	$\{R2, R16\}$	0.676

Second Use Case: $\mathcal{U} = \{R3, R6, R13\}$. In $\mathcal{O}_{M_1}$, $R3$ is fulfilled. $R13$ applies one type restriction. So, only one type for property p_6p_{16}:has_id should be preserved. But, applying $R13$ will cause that $R6$ will not be fulfilled, because not all values of property p_6p_{16} are preserved. Thus, $R6$ and $R13$ have a conflict with each other and cannot be fulfilled simultaneously in $\mathcal{O}_{M_1}$. Given the user-selected GMRs, there are two 2^C-Cliques as $\{R3, R13\}$ and $\{R3, R6\}$.

Our method suggests as $\mathcal{K}^C$-max-clique $rs_1 = \{R2,\ R3,\ R5,\ R7,\ R8,\ R10,\ R12,$ $R13,\ R14,\ R19,\ R20\}$ in which $R6$ is not include. The next two maximum compatible sets are $rs_2 = \{R2, R3, R5, R7, R8, R9, R10, R12, R13, R14\}$, $rs_3 = \{R1, R2, R3, R5, R7, R8, R10, R13, R14, R19, R20\}$, respectively.

Third Use Case: $\mathcal{U} = \{R1, R2, R3, R8, R10, R19\}$. In $\mathcal{O}_{M_1}$, classes c_3, c_{13}-c_{15} are missing. By applying $R1$, these classes will be added to the $\mathcal{O}_{M_1}$. Moreover, properties p_{11}, p_{13}, p_{18}-p_{22}, p_{24}, and p_{25} are missing. Thus, applying $R2$ will cause that these properties will be added to the $\mathcal{O}_{M_1}$. $R3$ will add the missing instance I_2 to the $\mathcal{O}_{M_1}$. $R8$, $R10$, and $R19$ are fulfilled in $\mathcal{O}_{M_1}$. In $\mathcal{O}_{M_2}$, class c_{15} and properties p_{15}, p_{24}, and p_{25} are missing. Applying $R1$ and $R2$ will add the missing classes and properties in $\mathcal{O}_{M_2}$. $R3$, $R8$, and $R10$ are fulfilled in $\mathcal{O}_{M_2}$. However, in the origin $\mathcal{O}_{M_2}$, the class c_{14} was unconnected. But, applying $R1$ and $R2$ caused that now c_{14} be connected. Thus, $R19$ is fulfilled. In this case study, the user-selected GMRs are compatible with each other, however, a superset of other compatible GMRs with $\mathcal{U}$ is suggested. The maximum compatible sets are $rs_1 = \{R1, R2, R3, R5, R7, R8, R10, R13, R14, R19, R20\}$ and $rs_2 = \{R1, R2, R3, R5, R6, R7, R8, R10, R19, R20\}$.

6   Conclusion

Various ontology merging systems have been proposed. Each covers a group of Generic Merge Requirements (GMRs). Since not all GMRs can be fulfilled at the same time, we proposed a graph-based framework to systematically determine the GMRs compatibility interaction. The framework allows users to specify the most important GMRs for their specific task at hand and detects a maximal compatible superset. This result can then be used to select a proper merge method or to parameterize a generic merge method. The intuition behind using the graph theory is to facilitate the encoding of the GMRs' compatibility via the graph presentation and reveal the other possible compatible requirements. GMRs embedded in the proposed framework can be easily extended, in which building the GMR interaction's graph and obtaining their compatibility can be performed in the same procedure for the new adapted GMRs. We have analyzed the GMRs within the $\mathcal{C}o\mathcal{M}erger$ system, where the users can access to the logged information of applying GMRs on their merged ontologies. Through the proposed framework, potential conflicts between GMRs can be found. Not all of these potential conflicts will actually materialize in each concrete merged ontology. In future work, we will investigate how the approach can be extended to take this into account. Our second future plan is a user study about the extent to which the users agree with the ranked suggested sets.

Acknowledgments. S. Babalou is supported by a scholarship from German Academic Exchange Service (DAAD).

References

1. Pottinger, R.A., Bernstein, P.A.: Merging models based on given correspondences. In: VLDB, pp. 862–873 (2003)
2. Raunich, S., Rahm, E.: Target-driven merging of taxonomies with ATOM. Inf. Syst. **42**, 1–14 (2014)
3. Jiménez-Ruiz, E., Cuenca Grau, B., Horrocks, I., Berlanga, R.: Ontology integration using mappings: towards getting the right logical consequences. In: Aroyo, L., Traverso, P., Ciravegna, F., Cimiano, P., Heath, T., Hyvönen, E., Mizoguchi, R., Oren, E., Sabou, M., Simperl, E. (eds.) ESWC 2009. LNCS, vol. 5554, pp. 173–187. Springer, Heidelberg (2009). https://doi.org/10.1007/978-3-642-02121-3_16
4. Chiticariu, L., Kolaitis, P.G., Popa, L.: Interactive generation of integrated schemas. In: ACM SIGMOD, pp. 833–846 (2008)
5. Thau, D., Bowers, S., Ludäscher, B.: Merging taxonomies under RCC-5 algebraic articulations. In: ONISW, pp. 47–54. ACM (2008)
6. Ju, S.P., et al.: CreaDO-a methodology to create domain ontologies using parameter-based ontology merging techniques. In: MICAI, pp. 23–28. IEEE (2011)
7. Mahfoudh, M., Thiry, L., Forestier, G., Hassenforder, M.: Algebraic graph transformations for merging ontologies. In: Ait Ameur, Y., Bellatreche, L., Papadopoulos, G.A. (eds.) MEDI 2014. LNCS, vol. 8748, pp. 154–168. Springer, Cham (2014). https://doi.org/10.1007/978-3-319-11587-0_16
8. Noy, N.F., Musen, M.A.: The prompt suite: interactive tools for ontology merging and mapping. Int. J. Hum.-Comput. Stud. **59**(6), 983–1024 (2003)
9. Makwana, A., Ganatra, A.: A known in advance, what ontologies to integrate? for effective ontology merging using k-means clustering. IJIES, **11**(4) (2018)
10. Saleem, K., Bellahsene, Z., Hunt, E.: Porsche: performance oriented schema mediation. Inf. Syst. **33**(7), 637–657 (2008)
11. Radwan, A., Popa, L., Stanoi, I.R., Younis, A.: Top-k generation of integrated schemas based on directed and weighted correspondences. In: SIGMOD (2009)
12. El-Gohary, N.M., El-Diraby, T.E.: Merging architectural, engineering, and construction ontologies. J. Comput. Civil Eng. **25**(2), 109–128 (2011)
13. Stumme, G., Maedche, A.: FCA-Merge: bottom-up merging of ontologies. In: IJCAI, pp. 225–230 (2001)
14. Priya, M., Kumar, C.A.: An approach to merge domain ontologies using granular computing. Granular Comput. 1–26 (2019). https://doi.org/10.1007/s41066-019-00193-3
15. Priya, M., Cherukuri, A.K.: A novel method for merging academic socialnetwork ontologies using formal concept analysis and hybrid semanticsimilarity measure. Libr. Hi Tech (2019)
16. Guzmán-Arenas, A., Cuevas, A.-D.: Knowledge accumulation through automatic merging of ontologies. Expert Syst. Appl. **37**(3), 1991–2005 (2010)
17. Babalou, S., König-Ries, B.: GMRs: reconciliation of generic merge requirements in ontology integration. In: SEMANTICS Poster and Demo (2019)
18. Babalou, S., Grygorova, E., König-Ries, B.: CoMerger: a customizable online tool for building a consistent quality-assured merged ontology. In: In ESWC, Poster and Demo Track June 2020
19. Zhang, L.-Y., Ren, J.-D., Li, X.-W.: OIM-SM: a method for ontology integration based on semantic mapping. J. Intell. Fuzzy Syst. **32**(3), 1983–1995 (2017)
20. Fahad, M., Moalla, N., Bouras, A.: Detection and resolution of semantic inconsistency and redundancy in an automatic ontology merging system. JIIS **39**(2), 535–557 (2012)

21. Mahfoudh, M., Forestier, G., Hassenforder, M.: A benchmark for ontologies merging assessment. In: Lehner, F., Fteimi, N. (eds.) KSEM 2016. LNCS (LNAI), vol. 9983, pp. 555–566. Springer, Cham (2016). https://doi.org/10.1007/978-3-319-47650-6_44
22. Raunich, S., Rahm, E.: Towards a benchmark for ontology merging. In: Herrero, P., Panetto, H., Meersman, R., Dillon, T. (eds.) OTM 2012. LNCS, vol. 7567, pp. 124–133. Springer, Heidelberg (2012). https://doi.org/10.1007/978-3-642-33618-8_20
23. Duchateau, F., Bellahsene, Z.: Measuring the quality of an integrated schema. In: Parsons, J., Saeki, M., Shoval, P., Woo, C., Wand, Y. (eds.) ER 2010. LNCS, vol. 6412, pp. 261–273. Springer, Heidelberg (2010). https://doi.org/10.1007/978-3-642-16373-9_19
24. Noy, N.F., et al.: Ontology development 101: A guide to creating your first ontology (2001)
25. Poveda-Villalon, M., Suarez-Figueroa, M.C., Gomez-Perez, A.: Validating ontologies with oops!, pp. 267–281 (2012)
26. Rector, A., et al.: Owl pizzas: practical experience of teaching owl-dl: common errors & common patterns. In: EKAW, pp. 63–81. Springer (2004)
27. Grygorova, E., Babalou, S., König-Ries, B.: Toward owl restriction reconciliation in merging knowledge. In: In ESWC, Poster and Demo Track, June 2020
28. Tomita, E., Tanaka, A., Takahashi, H.: The worst-case time complexity for generating all maximal cliques and computational experiments. TCS **363**(1), 28–42 (2006)

Capturing and Querying Uncertainty in RDF Stream Processing

Robin Keskisärkkä[1]([✉])[ID], Eva Blomqvist[1][ID], Leili Lind[1,2][ID],
and Olaf Hartig[1][ID]

[1] Linköping University, Linköping, Sweden
{robin.keskisarkka,eva.blomqvist,leili.lind,olaf.hartig}@liu.se
[2] RISE Research Institutes of Sweden/Division Digital Systems, Linköping, Sweden
leili.lind@ri.se

Abstract. RDF Stream Processing (RSP) has been proposed as a candidate for bringing together the Complex Event Processing (CEP) paradigm and the Semantic Web standards. In this paper, we investigate the impact of explicitly representing and processing uncertainty in RSP for the use in CEP. Additionally, we provide a representation for capturing the relevant notions of uncertainty in the RSP-QL* data model and describe query functions that can operate on this representation. The impact evaluation is based on a use-case within electronic healthcare, where we compare the query execution overhead of different uncertainty options in a prototype implementation. The experiments show that the influence on query execution performance varies greatly, but that uncertainty can have noticeable impact on query execution performance. On the other hand, the overhead grows linearly with respect to the stream rate for all uncertainty options in the evaluation, and the observed performance is sufficient for many use-cases. Extending the representation and operations to support more uncertainty options and investigating different query optimization strategies to reduce the impact on execution performance remain important areas for future research.

Keywords: RSP · CEP · Uncertainty · RSP-QL

1 Introduction

Complex Event Processing (CEP) provides techniques for continuously analyzing streaming data to detect patterns of interest. A *simple event* is used to denote anything that happens, or is contemplated as happening, while a *complex event* summarizes, represents, or denotes a set of simple events [17]. Existing CEP systems are generally not well-suited for integrating background data, supporting data interoperability, and reasoning [3]. Previous research has therefore proposed RDF Stream Processing (RSP) as a candidate for bringing together the CEP paradigm and Semantic Web standards [3,6,8,10], specifically targeting information integration and reasoning.

© Springer Nature Switzerland AG 2020
C. M. Keet and M. Dumontier (Eds.): EKAW 2020, LNAI 12387, pp. 37–53, 2020.
https://doi.org/10.1007/978-3-030-61244-3_3

Representing and reasoning with uncertainty has been recognized as a critical aspect for dealing with imprecise, incomplete, and noisy data in CEP [1,4,5]. However, to the best of our knowledge, no RSP system or model exists that provides any support for representing, processing, or propagating uncertainty. Hence, little is known about how uncertainty can be incorporated into RSP and what the properties of possible approaches to do so would be. The goal of this paper is to close this gap by addressing the following overall research question.

RQ: *What is the performance impact of incorporating uncertainty into RSP?*

To address this question, we focus on different ways of explicitly managing uncertainty using probabilistic approaches. The main contribution of our paper is an evaluation of the performance impact of uncertainty in RSP processing. Additionally, we provide a representation for capturing relevant notions of uncertainty, a formal description of the query operations that can operate on the proposed representation, and a prototype implementation.

In Sect. 2, we describe the use-case scenario that is used in the evaluation of the prototype system. Section 3 presents background and related work, and Sect. 4 describes how uncertainty is represented, while Sect. 5 describes the query operations that can operate on this representation. Section 6 describes how the query operations are leveraged to support different uncertainty options. Section 7 presents an evaluation on the prototype implementation. Finally, Sect. 8 summarizes the main conclusions of this work.

2   Use-Case Scenario

This section describes a scenario originating from the recent research project E-care@home[1]. The goal of the project was to develop technical solutions to improve the care of elderly patients in their homes. The E-care@home system uses Semantic Web standards, and RSP provides a way of bridging the gap between heterogeneous background data, and the detection of complex events from streaming data.

The requirements of different stakeholders have been documented in a project deliverable, which covers a number of personas and use case scenarios based on interviews with healthcare professionals, patients and next-of-kin [16]. We use one of these scenarios as the basis for the running examples and the evaluation of performance impact. The scenario focuses on the multi-morbid persona Farida who suffers from heart failure and advanced chronic obstructive pulmonary disease (COPD):

"After her latest hospital visit a month ago the elderly, multi-morbid patient Farida was offered to be remotely monitored from the primary healthcare center [...] by use of various body and environmental sensors (the E-care@home system). Her healthcare providers also want her to assess symptoms daily and report on intake of as-needed medications. [...] During the last two weeks Farida's heart

---
[1] http://ecareathome.se/.

failure and COPD have been rather stable due to medication changes. [...] Now, the system registers a rapidly rising body temperature and increase in heart and respiration rate. Also, her pulse is more irregular than usual." [16]

Based on the scenario above, we identify a need for the E-care@home system to be able to draw conclusions based on uncertain information, stemming from the domain itself, electronic health records (EHRs), and sensor data. For example, a patient's reported physical health parameters are affected by both the quality of the sensors, how well the sensors model a given feature, and how the sensors are used.

The changes in physical health parameters described in the scenario may point at a number of different diagnoses, such as a worsening of the heart failure, an infection, and/or COPD exacerbation (i.e., worsening of a patient's COPD condition). In the evaluation (c.f. Sect. 7), we focus on detecting potential COPD exacerbation events, which are often characterized by high heart rate, increased breathlessness (which leads to increased breathing rate), and low oxygen saturation levels.

3 Background and Related Work

In this section, we present the relevant background and related work. We describe the different uncertainty types that have been identified within CEP, the various ways in which uncertainty has been modeled in existing CEP systems, and briefly describe the RSP-QL* model on which we base our work.

3.1 Types of Uncertainty in CEP

Uncertainty has been recognized as a critical aspect in CEP [1,4,5], and can generally be classified based on three main types: *occurrence uncertainty, attribute uncertainty,* and *pattern uncertainty* [1,4,18].

Occurrence uncertainty refers to whether an event has actually occurred or not. All events in the real world are not necessarily reported, and some of the events that are reported may not have occurred at all. Occurrence uncertainty can be caused by unreliable or noisy sources, or when events are inferred from other events. For example, we may be uncertain about whether a report on a patient's heart rate should be classified as a high heart rate event.

We shall model occurrence uncertainty as a probability associated with *event type assertions*, i.e., statements that specify the type of an event. The occurrence uncertainty of an event is therefore defined with respect to a specific event type.

Attribute uncertainty refers to uncertainty in the content of events. Attributes can be incomplete, imprecise, vague, contradictory, or noisy [1,18]. Values that stem from physical phenomena always contain a degree of uncertainty that originates from, e.g., inaccuracy, imprecision, or noise in the source [5]. For example, the value reported by a heart rate sensor may be associated with a uniform distribution, representing the precision of the sensor. This means that we may have to take into consideration the probability that the true unobserved value is within some specific interval.

We shall model attribute uncertainty using continuous probability distributions, where the distribution of a given attribute value is described by a probability density function (PDF).

Pattern uncertainty relates to uncertainty about the matching and combination of events in queries or rules. It is generally impractical, or even impossible, to list all the preconditions and consequences that should apply to a given event pattern [1]. Additionally, the causal relationships and correlations between events in a given pattern may not be certain. By supporting pattern uncertainty, the fact that we have incomplete knowledge about the system under observation can be made explicit. For example, while high heart rate is a common symptom of COPD exacerbation it can also be caused by something else entirely.

We shall model pattern uncertainty using Bayesian Networks (BNs) to encode the conditional dependencies between event types. Uncertain observations of events are supported using Pearl's method [20], where probabilistic observations are represented using *virtual nodes* added as children to the event types being observed. The conditional probability tables of the virtual nodes are defined as likelihood ratios based on the probabilities of the observed events.

The incorporation of such types of uncertainty into RSP requires two main ingredients: a representation for capturing relevant notions of uncertainty, presented in Section 4, and query operations that can operate on this representation, presented in Sect. 5.

3.2   Approaches to Represent Uncertainty in CEP

Probability theory provides a powerful framework for reasoning with uncertainty and is the most commonly applied framework for dealing with uncertainty within CEP [1,5]. In probability theory, statements are either true or false in some world, but the world that should be considered the correct one is uncertain. If statements are assumed to be independent, the probability of a given *world* is simply the product of the probabilities of all the statements of that world.

Cugola et al. [5] extended the rule-based event specification language TESLA to support attribute uncertainty based on this principle. The extension was created to support probability distributions as a way of expressing measurement errors, and to support uncertain matches in filters. By assuming independence between all event attributes, the probability of a detected event was calculated as the product of the uncertain matches in the query.

Automata-based CEP systems have also been extended to deal with uncertainty, but typically focus on occurrence uncertainty [1]. Generally, each rule deployed gives rise to a single automaton. An incoming event matching a sequence constraint gives rise to a state transition, and when a rule is triggered the probability of the event is calculated based on its event history.

In the approach proposed by Kawashima et al. [13], which assumes independence between all simple events, the probability of a matching rule is calculated by summing the probabilities of all combinations that satisfy the rule.

The independence assumption enables various optimization strategies that make the summation of probabilities more efficient. Other approaches, like the system proposed by Wang et al. [21], relax the assumption of independence and instead allow transitions to follow first-order Markov processes.

One of the main challenges with the automata-based approaches is the lack of an efficient mechanism to take into account background information [1]. Gillani et al. [10] partially addressed this problem in an RSP system, where the graph pattern matching was used for enriching events, and non-deterministic automata were used for temporal event pattern matching.

Probabilistic graphical models are also popular alternatives for dealing with uncertainty in CEP [1]. The two most common classes include Markov networks and BNs [5,22,23]. In both cases, the nodes of the networks represent *random variables*, and edges encode their probabilistic dependencies.

In BNs, the structure of the network encodes probabilistic dependencies, which means that domain expert knowledge can be encoded as part of the network [1]. Cugola et al. [5] implemented support for BNs in their extension of the TESLA language to support pattern uncertainty. In their approach, a BN was automatically generated for every rule deployed, with event types representing nodes in the network. Domain knowledge was then manually added to each BN by a domain expert, who would then modify and enrich the resulting network.

3.3   RSP-QL*

Several RSP models and implementations have been proposed in the past decade, each of which have included different syntax and semantics. Based on the work of the RSP community group[2], Dell'Aglio et al. defined the first version of a common RSP query model and language, referred to as RSP-QL [7,9]. As an extension of RSP-QL, in our earlier work we proposed RSP-QL* [14] to provide an intuitive and compact way for representing and querying statement-level annotations in RDF streams by leveraging RDF* and SPARQL* [11].

RDF* and SPARQL* provide an alternative to RDF reification for annotating RDF triples with metadata and querying these annotations. In RDF*, enclosing a triple using the strings '<<' and '>>' allows the triple to be used as the subject or object in other triples. For example, the triple *:bob :knows :alice* can be annotated with the source *:wikipedia* as _<<_:bob :knows :alice>> :source :wipedia. Similarly, SPARQL* is an extension of SPARQL for querying RDF* data.

4   Capturing Uncertainty in RSP

In this paper, we use the RSP-QL* model [14] to capture the different notions of uncertainty discussed in Sect. 3.1. While there are several ways of representing uncertainty, in this paper we limit ourselves to attribute uncertainty represented using probability distributions, occurrence uncertainty represented as probability

---

[2] https://www.w3.org/community/rsp/.

annotations on event type assertions, and pattern uncertainty captured using BNs. The usage of these uncertainty types are covered further in the context of extensions for querying in Sect. 5.

In this section, we describe the three uncertainty types in more detail and introduce a way of representing uncertainty in RSP-QL*. For brevity, we omit URI prefix declarations for the remainder of the paper. We use the prefixes rspu, ecare, and sosa to refer to https://w3id.org/rsp/rspu#, http://example.org/ecare#, and http://www.w3.org/ns/sosa/, respectively.

4.1 Attribute Uncertainty as Probability Distributions

There is no standardized approach to represent probability distributions in RDF. Here we introduce an approach that uses RDF literals to represent attribute uncertainty. To this end, we define a new literal datatype, denoted by the URI *rspu:distribution*. The lexical space defining the set of valid literals for this datatype consists of all strings of the form $f(p_1, p_2, ..., p_n)$, where f is an identifier for a probability distribution type, and every p_i is a floating point number that represents a parameter value. Two such literals are considered equivalent only if they have the same identifier f and the same parameter values.

We do not specify how declarations of new probability distribution types are expressed. However, we assume that every probability distribution type specifies a probability density function (PDF), and a description of the list of parameters required by the distribution.

We here consider the normal and uniform distributions. For instance, the literal "Normal(85, 10)" would represent a normal distribution with a mean μ of 85, and a variance σ^2 of 10, whereas "Uniform(30, 40)" would represent a uniform distribution between 30 and 40.

We also provide an option for values to be annotated with probability distributions as meta data, by leveraging RDF* for statement-level annotations. We introduce the property *rspu:error* to annotate triples with measurement errors. Listing 1.1 shows an example where uncertainty is either reported directly as part of a literal, or as an annotation on a triple. A more fine-grained modeling approach for statistical distributions could potentially impact querying performance, and we consider this as part of future work.

```
1  <e1> sosa:hasSimpleResult "Normal(85,10)"^^rspu:distribution .
2  << <e1> sosa:hasSimpleResult 85 >> rspu:error "Normal(0,10)"^^rspu:distribution .
```

Listing 1.1. Attribute uncertainty represented as a literal (line 1) and as an annotation on a triple (line 2).

4.2 Occurrence Uncertainty as Probabilities

We leverage RDF* to provide a compact representation for annotating event type assertions with occurrence uncertainty. The property *rspu:hasProbability* is used to annotate an event type assertion with a probability. Listing 1.2 illustrates an example of an event type assertion annotated with an occurrence probability of 0.95.

```
1  <el> a ecare:HeartRate .
2  << <el> a ecare:HighHeartRate >> rspu:hasProbability 0.95 .
```

Listing 1.2. Occurrence probability as an annotation on an event type assertion.

An event type assertion that is not explicitly annotated with an occurrence probability is assumed to be certain, i.e., have a probability of 1. Intuitively, annotating an event with a probability of 0 would be equivalent to being certain that the event has not occurred (i.e., an explicit negation).

4.3 Pattern Uncertainty as Bayesian Networks

We identify BNs using URIs and each node in such a BN corresponds to a binary random variable, where the set of possible outcomes is limited to being true or false. An event type may be a node in a such a BN.

Adding evidence to a BN is equivalent to assigning a specific outcome to one of its nodes. However, in the presence of uncertain evidence, rather than simply assigning a state to a node, we use Pearl's method [20] to incorporate uncertain evidence by adding virtual nodes. The probability associated with the uncertain evidence is used to define the conditional probability table of the virtual node, which is expressed as a likelihood ratio in relation to the variable being observed.

For example, in Fig. 1 we represent an observation of a high heart rate as a virtual node that depends on high heart rate. The conditional probability table of this virtual node represents the uncertainty of our evidence, which then indirectly affects the probability of COPD exacerbation.

Fig. 1. Example illustrating how an observation of high heart rate is added as a virtual node (dashed line) that depends on the high heart rate variable.

5   Extensions for Querying

We now introduce functions for RSP-QL* queries that can operate on the representation of uncertainty described in the previous section. RSP-QL, which is based on SPARQL, is extensible and URIs can be introduced to represent custom functions in the query processor. The SPARQL specification provides no guidelines for how new functions should be defined, shared, or registered, and many RDF stores therefore provide their own methods for adding user-defined extensions (e.g., ARQ[3], RDF4J[4], and Virtuoso[5]). Our functions for dealing with uncertainty are captured by such custom functions to support operations on both probability distributions and BNs.

5.1 Operating on Probability Distributions

We define operations over probability distributions represented as literals of the aforementioned datatype *rspu:distribution* (see Sect. 4.1). For these definitions, let L_{dist} be the set of all *rspu:distribution* literals and *val* be a function that maps every $x \in L_{dist}$ to the probability distribution represented by x.

Definition 1. *The URI **rspu:add** denotes the function that, for every $x \in L_{dist}$ and $k \in \mathbb{R}$, returns a literal $z \in L_{dist}$ such that $val(z)$ is the probability distribution obtained by adding the constant k to the probability distribution $val(x)$.*

Definition 2. *The URI **rspu:subtract** denotes the function that, for every $x \in L_{dist}$ and $k \in \mathbb{R}$, returns a literal $z \in L_{dist}$ such that $val(z)$ is the probability distribution obtained by subtracting k from the probability distribution $val(x)$.*

Definition 3. *The URI **rspu:greaterThan** denotes the function that, for every $x \in L_{dist}$ and $a \in \mathbb{R}$, returns a floating point number such that this number is the probability that a random sample from $val(x)$ is greater than a.*

Definition 4. *The URI **rspu:lessThan** denotes the function that, for every $x \in L_{dist}$ and $b \in \mathbb{R}$, returns a floating point number such that this number is the probability that a random sample from $val(x)$ is less than b.*

Definition 5. *The URI **rspu:between** denotes the function that, for every $x \in L_{dist}$, $a \in \mathbb{R}$, and $b \in \mathbb{R}$, returns a floating point number that is the probability that a random sample from $val(x)$ is greater than a and less than b.*

The functions listed above support some of the most common operations on probability distributions. Examples of how these functions can be used in RSP-QL* queries follow in Sect. 6.

5.2 Operating on Bayesian Networks

We define operations for performing Bayesian inference and while supporting uncertain evidence in BNs (see Sect. 4.3). We assume a collection of BNs that are available to be invoked by the query processor, where each such BN is identified by a unique URI. Each node in such a BN represents a boolean variable that is also identified by a unique URI.

---

[3] https://jena.apache.org/documentation/query/writing_functions.html.

[4] https://rdf4j.eclipse.org/documentation/custom-sparql-functions/.

[5] http://vos.openlinksw.com/owiki/wiki/VOS/VirtTipsAndTricksGuideCustom SPARQLExtensionFunction.

An *evidence pair* for such a BN is a pair $(id, value)$ where id is a URI that denotes a node in the BN and $value \in [0, 1]$. If $value = 0$ or $value = 1$, the observed event is interpreted as an observation of the state of the node identified by id, otherwise the value is interpreted as an observation on a virtual node with id as the parent.

Definition 6. *The URI **rspu:belief** denotes a function that takes as input a URI bn denoting a BN, a URI θ denoting a node in that BN, a possible outcome $o \in \{true, false\}$, and an optional list of evidence pairs for the BN. The function returns a literal with a floating point number such that this number is the probability that the outcome of the node θ is o, where this probability is inferred by from the BN with the given evidence pairs.*

Definition 7. *The URI **rspu:mle** (maximum likelihood estimation) denotes a function that takes as input a URI bn denoting a BN, a URI θ denoting a node in that BN, and an optional list of evidence pairs for the BN. The function returns a boolean literal that represents the most likely outcome of the node θ, where the outcome is inferred from the BN with the given evidence pairs.*

Definition 8. *The URI **rspu:map** (maximum a posteriori probability) denotes a function that takes as input a URI bn denoting a BN, a URI θ denoting a node in that BN, and an optional list of evidence pairs for the BN. The function returns a boolean literal that represents the most likely outcome of the node θ, where the outcome is inferred from the BN with the given evidence pairs and weighted by the prior probability of θ.*

Now that we have defined the necessary operations for dealing with uncertainty, we are ready to apply them to support different uncertainty approaches.

6   Implementation of Uncertainty Approaches

The types of uncertainty introduced in Sect. 3.1, and the uncertainty operations described in the previous sections, can be combined with one another in different ways. We focus on a subset of the options for such a combination. That is, we consider options with each uncertainty type in isolation (Options 1–3 below), as well as a combination of pattern uncertainty with either occurrence uncertainty (Option 4) or attribute uncertainty (Option 5). We illustrate how these options are implemented using the extensions for querying from Sect. 5. To this end, we use the scenario outlined in Sect. 2, with the goal of detecting potential COPD exacerbation events based on heart rates, breathing rates, and oxygen saturation levels. For brevity, only the first example is written using RSP-QL*, while the remaining have been simplified and are expressed using SPARQL* (see the project repository for full examples).

Option 1.   Attribute uncertainty can be used to support uncertain matches based on event attributes. For example, rather than specifying a *hard* limit above which a heart rate should be considered high, we can define *soft* limits and determine the probability that the limit is exceeded. Under the assumption that attributes are independent, the probability of a query result is the product of all uncertain matches in the query. The option is illustrated in Listing 1.3.

```
REGISTER STREAM <stream/copd_exacerbation> COMPUTED EVERY PT1S AS
SELECT (?p1*?p2*?p3 AS ?confidence)
FROM NAMED WINDOW <w1> ON <stream/hr> [RANGE PT1S STEP PT1S]
FROM NAMED WINDOW <w2> ON <stream/br> [RANGE PT1S STEP PT1S]
FROM NAMED WINDOW <w3> ON <stream/ox> [RANGE PT1S STEP PT1S]
WHERE {
    WINDOW <w1> {
        GRAPH ?g1 { ?e1 a ecare:HeartRate ; sosa:hasSimpleResult ?hr . }
    }
    WINDOW <w2> {
        GRAPH ?g2 { ?e2 a ecare:BreathingRate ; sosa:hasSimpleResult ?br . }
    }
    WINDOW <w3> {
        GRAPH ?g3 { ?e3 a ecare:OxygenSaturation ; sosa:hasSimpleResult ?ox . }
    }
    BIND( rspu:greaterThan(?hr, 100) AS ?p1 )
    BIND( rspu:greaterThan(?br, 30) AS ?p2 )
    BIND( rspu:lessThan(?ox, 90) AS ?p3 )
}
```

Listing 1.3. Query illustrating attribute uncertainty (option 1), where attributes are reported as rspu:distribution literals.

Option 2. Occurrence uncertainty can be used to calculate the probability of a result based on the events captured. Under the assumption that events are independent, the probability of a given result is the product of the event type assertion probabilities of all matched events. The option is illustrated in Listing 1.4.

```
SELECT ( ?p1*?p2*?p3 AS ?confidence )
WHERE {
    << ?e1 a ecare:HighHeartRate >> rspu:hasProbability ?p1 .
    << ?e2 a ecare:HighBreathingRate >> rspu:hasProbability ?p2 .
    << ?e3 a ecare:LowOxygenSaturation >> rspu:hasProbability ?p3 .
}
```

Listing 1.4. Query illustrating occurrence uncertainty (option 2).

Option 3. Pattern uncertainty is captured by conditional dependencies between events, where the dependencies are represented in an underlying BN. We assume that events are certain by rounding off probabilities to the nearest integer (i.e., observations are simplified to true or false). The probability of a complex event is found from the BN after setting the observations of the captured events. The option is illustrated in Listing 1.5.

```
SELECT ?confidence
WHERE {
    << ?e1 a ecare:HighHeartRate >> rspu:hasProbability ?p1 .
    << ?e2 a ecare:HighBreathingRate >> rspu:hasProbability ?p2 .
    << ?e3 a ecare:LowOxygenSaturation >> rspu:hasProbability ?p3 .
    BIND(rspu:belief(ecare:COPDExacerbation,
            ecare:HighHeartRate, IF(?p1 > .5, 1, 0),
            ecare:HighBreathingRate, IF(?p2 > .5, 1, 0),
            ecare:LowOxygenSaturation, IF(?p3 > .5, 1, 0)) AS ?confidence)
}
```

Listing 1.5. Query illustrating pattern uncertainty (option 3).

Option 4. Pattern uncertainty can be combined with occurrence uncertainty to support uncertain evidence. Unlike the approach mentioned above (option 3), which assumes that all matched events are certain, the occurrence uncertainty of each matched event is used as part of the evidence. The option is illustrated in Listing 1.6.

```
SELECT ?confidence
WHERE {
    << ?e1 a ecare:HighHeartRate >> rspu:hasProbability ?p1 .
    << ?e2 a ecare:HighBreathingRate >> rspu:hasProbability ?p2 .
    << ?e3 a ecare:LowOxygenSaturation >> rspu:hasProbability ?p3 .
    BIND(rspu:belief(ecare:COPDExacerbation, true,
            ecare:HighHeartRate, ?p1,
            ecare:HighBreathingRate, ?p2,
            ecare:LowOxygenSaturation, ?p3) AS ?confidence)
}
```

Listing 1.6. Query illustrating pattern uncertainty combined with occurrence uncertainty (option 4).

Option 5. Pattern uncertainty can also be combined with attribute uncertainty, where the probability of an event type is derived as part of the query itself based on uncertain matches on event attributes. The option is illustrated in Listing 1.7.

```
SELECT ?confidence
WHERE {
    ?e1 a ecare:HeartRateEvent ; sosa:hasSimpleResult ?hr .
    ?e2 a ecare:BreathingRateEvent ; sosa:hasSimpleResult ?br .
    ?e3 a ecare:OxygenSaturationEvent ; sosa:hasSimpleResult ?ox .
    BIND(rspu:belief(ecare:COPDExacerbation, true,
            ecare:HighHeartRate, rspu:greaterThan(?hr, 100),
            ecare:HighBreathingRate, rspu:greaterThan(?br, 30),
            ecare:LowOxygenSaturation, rspu:lessThan(?ox, 90)) AS ?confidence)
}
```

Listing 1.7. Query illustrating pattern uncertainty combined with attribute uncertainty (option 5).

7 Impact Evaluation

Now we are ready to study the impact that integrating uncertainty in RSP may have in terms of query execution performance. We first validate the output of the prototype implementation with respect to the different uncertainty options described in the previous section. We then evaluate the performance overhead of these uncertainty options with respect to different input stream rates.

7.1 Experiment Setup

For the evaluation, we introduce a *test driver* responsible for generating event streams. The test driver generates the complex events to be detected (i.e., the ground truth) and the set of low-level events from which these complex events are to be detected. The test driver allows the stream rate and the uncertainty in the generated streams to be varied.

The experiments are based on the use-case described in Sect. 2, with the goal of detecting potential COPD exacerbation events based on heart rates, breathing rates, and oxygen saturation levels. The thresholds considered for these parameters are typically patient and context specific. For the experiments, we simplify the scenario by fixing these bounds as follows. Heart rates are considered high if they exceed 100, breathing rates are considered high if they exceed 30, and oxygen saturation levels are considered low if they are below 90.

The streams generated by the driver correspond to the types of preprocessed sensor streams that would be expected in the E-care@home system.

The test driver generates events based on the BN shown in Fig. 2. The event generation starts from the complex event that is to be detected. A COPD exacerbation event is created and assigned a truth value sampled from a Bernoulli distribution based on its prior probability. The truth value of the event constitutes the ground truth. For each COPD exacerbation event, the test driver then generates three reference events: a high heart rate event, a high breathing rate event, and a low oxygen saturation event. Each of these events are assigned truth values sampled from Bernoulli distributions based on their conditional probabilities, given the state of the COPD exacerbation event.

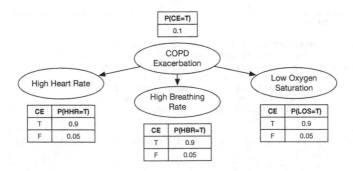

Fig. 2. The BN used by the test driver in the generation of event streams.

The test driver then samples attribute values for each event based on a *degree of attribute uncertainty*. The degree of attribute uncertainty is defined as the probability that a random sample does not match the expected threshold value. For example, for a true high heart rate event and an attribute uncertainty of 10%, the value is sampled from a normal distribution such that there is a 10% probability that the sample is below 100.

For occurrence uncertainty, the test driver assigns new truth values to the events. The *degree of occurrence uncertainty* is defined as the probability that a reported event type assertion does not match the reference truth value. For example, for a true high heart rate event and an occurrence uncertainty of 5%, the truth value is (re-)sampled such that there is a 5% probability that the event will be reported as false, and the event type assertion is annotated with a probability of 95%. The queries used in the evaluation have been excluded for brevity but are available in the project repository[6].

We base the experiments on the RSPQLStarEngine[7], which is a prototype system implementing the RSP-QL* model [14]. The query engine was extended to support SPARQL value functions along with the extensions described in Sect. 5. Operations on probability distributions were implemented using the library Commons Math[8], which provides support for operations on the most common probability distributions. Support for Bayesian inference was provided by using the library jSMILE (v.1.4.0) developed by BayesFusion[9]. All experiments were performed on a MacBook Pro 2015, with a quad-core 2.8 GHz Intel Core i7 processor, 16 GB of 1600MHz DDR3, and 8 GB of memory allocated to the JVM. The prototype, along with the experiment files and queries, is available under the MIT License.

7.2 Validation

The validation of the prototype implementation follows a design similar to that of Moreno et al. [19] and Cugola et al. [5]. The original set of COPD exacerbation events generated by the test driver is used as the basis for an *oracle* that can be used to check if an event occurred within a given time interval.

Due to uncertainty, a large number of detected events will have small but non-zero probabilities. The probability associated with a detected event can be interpreted as the confidence we have in it. In the validation, we apply a *confidence threshold* below which detected events are assumed to be false. Regardless of the uncertainty option used, both the true positive rate (i.e., the ratio of correctly detected events) and the false positive rate (i.e., the ratio of wrongly detected events) is expected to go down when the threshold increases. Higher degrees of uncertainty are expected to reduce the overall area under the resulting ROC curve.

For the validation, the stream rate was fixed at 1,000 events/sec per event stream, and the confidence thresholds were varied between 0 and 0.99. We illustrate the observed trade-off between true positives and false positives for two of

---

[6] https://www.w3id.org/rsp/rspu.
[7] https://github.com/keski/RSPQLStarEngine.
[8] https://commons.apache.org/proper/commons-math/ (version 3.6.1).
[9] https://www.bayesfusion.com/.

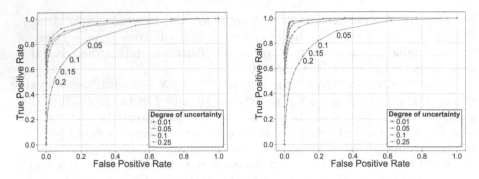

Fig. 3. ROC curves for option 1 (left) and option 5 (right), with labels showing a subset of the confidence threshold values.

the uncertainty options in Fig. 3, where each point on a line represents a specific confidence threshold for accepting a detected event. The top left corner of the ROC box represents a perfect system. The trade-off between true positives and false positives follows the expected pattern for all uncertainty options and degrees of uncertainty.

7.3 Performance Impact

We evaluate the impact of the different uncertainty options in terms of query execution times. The queries used for the evaluation are similar to those used for the validation in the previous section, but do not check the results against the oracle. Notably, the degree of uncertainty does not impact the overall query complexity, since the confidence for each result needs to be assessed for every potential COPD exacerbation event. For the experiments, we therefore fix the degree of uncertainty at 0.05.

In the experiments, we vary the stream rates between 100 and 3,000 events/sec per input stream, which corresponds to a total of 300–9000 events/sec (equivalent to 2,100–63,000 quads/sec). These stream rates are similar to those previously used in the testing of RSP systems [2,15]. Table 1 shows the average query execution times for different stream rates, and the relative overhead compared to a baseline query in which uncertainty is ignored completely.

Option 2 only adds an overhead of around 50%, whereas option 1 and option 3 increase overall execution time by a factor of 3 and 4 respectively. Option 4 increases query execution time by a factor of 7, while option 5 adds an overhead that is in the order of one magnitude.

The stream rates that can realistically be supported are difficult to generalize, due to aspects such as query and data complexity, number of parallel streams, and technical implementation details. However, the results show that the average query execution time increases linearly as a function of the stream rate, and that the cost of the uncertainty operations remain constant. This means that while the impact of explicitly considering uncertainty can have noticeable impact on

Table 1. Average query execution times (ms) for each of the uncertainty options with respect to stream rates (events/second per stream). The added overhead relative to the baseline query (where uncertainty is ignored) is given in parentheses.

Rate	Option 1	Option 2	Option 3	Option 4	Option 5
100	3.07 (2.73)	1.11 (0.35)	4.37 (4.32)	6.48 (6.88)	9.97 (11.13)
500	12.69 (3.20)	4.82 (0.60)	18.23 (5.04)	25.59 (7.48)	38.88 (11.88)
1000	25.84 (2.49)	10.32 (0.39)	36.07 (3.87)	52.81 (6.12)	82.89 (10.18)
1500	37.99 (2.25)	15.22 (0.30)	55.04 (3.70)	80.69 (5.90)	123.59 (9.56)
2000	51.65 (2.79)	19.70 (0.45)	74.44 (4.47)	110.72 (7.13)	166.03 (11.20)
2500	69.22 (3.07)	26.85 (0.58)	98.95 (4.82)	146.04 (7.59)	208.74 (11.28)
3000	86.80 (2.93)	35.08 (0.59)	130.55 (4.91)	194.53 (7.81)	286.89 (11.99)

query execution performance, the evaluation suggests that the performance is still sufficient for many use-cases.

8   Conclusions

To the best of our knowledge, this paper presents the first work on investigating the impact of incorporating uncertainty in the RSP context. We have defined s representation for capturing relevant notions of uncertainty in RSP, provided a formal description of the query operations that can operate on this representation, and evaluated the impact on query execution performance in a prototype implementation.

The cost of the different uncertainty options was shown to vary greatly, but the results show that continuous query execution could be supported at realistic stream rates even for the computationally expensive uncertainty options. Explicitly managing uncertainty in RSP also provides a lot of flexibility, since the user can choose when and where a given uncertainty option should be applied.

The representation of uncertainty used does not require any modifications to the underlying RSP-QL* query semantics. This means that the extensions could be supported in any engine that supports RSP-QL, since RDF* and SPARQL* can be viewed simply as syntactic sugar on top of RDF and SPARQL [12].

Extending the representation to support additional uncertainty options, such as fuzzy logic, and investigating query optimization strategies to reduce the impact on execution performance remain important areas for future research.

References

1. Alevizos, E., Skarlatidis, A., Artikis, A., Paliouras, G.: Probabilistic complex event recognition: a survey. ACM Comput. Surv. **50**, 1–31 (2017)
2. Ali, M.I., et al.: Real-time data analytics and event detection for IoT-enabled communication systems. Semant. Web J. **42**, 19–37 (2017). https://doi.org/10.1016/j.websem.2016.07.001

3. Anicic, D., Rudolph, S., Fodor, P., Stojanovic, N.: Stream reasoning and complex event processing in ETALIS. Semant. Web J. **3**(4), 397–407 (2012)
4. Artikis, A., Etzion, O., Feldman, Z., Fournier, F.: Event processing under uncertainty. In: Proceedings of the 6th ACM International Conference on Distributed Event-Based Systems (2012)
5. Cugola, G., Margara, A., Matteucci, M., Tamburrelli, G.: Introducing uncertainty in complex event processing: model, implementation, and validation. Computing **97**(2), 103–144 (2015)
6. Dao-Tran, M., Le-Phuoc, D.: Towards enriching CQELS with complex event processing and path navigation. In: Proceeding of the 1st Workshop on High-Level Declarative Stream Processing (2015)
7. Dell'Aglio, D., Calbimonte, J.-P., Della Valle, E., Corcho, O.: Towards a unified language for RDF stream query processing. In: Gandon, F., Guéret, C., Villata, S., Breslin, J., Faron-Zucker, C., Zimmermann, A. (eds.) ESWC 2015. LNCS, vol. 9341, pp. 353–363. Springer, Cham (2015). https://doi.org/10.1007/978-3-319-25639-9_48
8. Dell'Aglio, D., Dao-Tran, M., Calbimonte, J.-P., Le Phuoc, D., Della Valle, E.: A query model to capture event pattern matching in RDF stream processing query languages. In: Blomqvist, E., Ciancarini, P., Poggi, F., Vitali, F. (eds.) EKAW 2016. LNCS (LNAI), vol. 10024, pp. 145–162. Springer, Cham (2016). https://doi.org/10.1007/978-3-319-49004-5_10
9. Dell'Aglio, D., Della Valle, E., Calbimonte, J.P., Corcho, O.: RSP-QL semantics: a unifying query model to explain heterogeneity of RDF stream processing systems. Int. J. Semant. Web Inf. Syst. **10**(4), 17–44 (2014)
10. Gillani, S., Zimmermann, A., Picard, G., Laforest, F.: A query language for semantic complex event processing: syntax, semantics and implementation. Semant. Web J. **10**, 53–93 (2019)
11. Hartig, O.: Foundations of RDF* and SPARQL* - an alternative approach to statement-level metadata in RDF. In: Proceeding of the 11th AMW Workshop (2017)
12. Hartig, O., Thompson, B.: Foundations of an alternative approach to reification in RDF. CoRR abs/1406.3399 (2014)
13. Kawashima, H., Kitagawa, H., Li, X.: Complex event processing over uncertain data streams. In: Proceeding of 3PGCIC (2010)
14. Keskisärkkä, R., Blomqvist, E., Lind, L., Hartig, O.: RSP-QL*: enabling statement-level annotations in RDF streams. In: Proceeding of SEMANTiCS (2019)
15. Le-Phuoc, D., Dao-Tran, M., Pham, M.-D., Boncz, P., Eiter, T., Fink, M.: Linked stream data processing engines: facts and figures. In: Cudré-Mauroux, P., et al. (eds.) ISWC 2012. LNCS, vol. 7650, pp. 300–312. Springer, Heidelberg (2012). https://doi.org/10.1007/978-3-642-35173-0_20
16. Lind, L., Prytz, E., Lindén, M., Kristoffersson, A.: Use cases unified description. E-care@home project Milestone Report MSR5.1b (Project Internal) (2017)
17. Luckham, D., Schulte, R.: Event Processing Glossary Version 2.0. Event Processing Society (2011)
18. Margara, A., Urbani, J., van Harmelen, F., Bal, H.: Streaming the web: reasoning over dynamic data. J. Web Semant. **25**, 24–44 (2014)
19. Moreno, N., Bertoa, M., Burgueno, L., Vallecillo, A.: Managing measurement and occurrence uncertainty in complex event processing systems. IEEE Access **7**, 88026–88048 (2019)
20. Pearl, J.: Probabilistic Reasoning in Intelligent Systems: Networks of Plausible Inference. Morgan Kaufmann Publishers, San Francisco, California (1988)

21. Wang, Y.H., Cao, K., Zhang, X.M.: Complex event processing over distributed probabilistic event streams. Comput. Math. Appl. **66**(10), 1808–1821 (2013)
22. Wasserkrug, S., Gal, A., Etzion, O.: A model for reasoning with uncertain rules in event composition systems. In: 21st Conference on Uncertainty in Artificial International (2005)
23. Wasserkrug, S., Gal, A., Etzion, O., Turchin, Y.: Complex Event Processing over Uncertain Data. In: 2nd International Conference on Distributed Event-based Systems (2008)

Effective Use of Personal Health Records
to Support Emergency Services

Alba Catalina Morales Tirado$^{(\boxtimes)}$ (iD), Enrico Daga$^{(\boxtimes)}$ (iD), and Enrico Motta$^{(\boxtimes)}$ (iD)

Knowledge Media Institute, The Open University, Milton Keynes, UK
{alba.morales-tirado,enrico.daga,enrico.motta}@open.ac.uk

Abstract. Smart City systems capture and exchange information with the aim to improve public services. Particularly, healthcare data could help emergency services to plan resources and make life-saving decisions. However, the delivery of healthcare information to emergency bodies must be balanced against the concerns related to citizens' privacy. Besides, emergency services face challenges in interpreting this data; the heterogeneity of sources and a large amount of information available represent a significant barrier. In this paper, we focus on a case study involving the use of personal health records to support emergency services in the context of a fire building evacuation. We propose a methodology involving a knowledge engineering approach and a common-sense knowledge base to address the problem of deriving useful information from health records and, at the same time, preserve citizens' privacy. We perform extensive experiments involving a synthetic dataset of health records and a curated gold standard to demonstrate how our approach allows us to identify vulnerable people and interpret their particular needs while avoiding the disclosure of personal information.

Keywords: Health records · Smart City · Emergency services · Privacy · Knowledge engineering · ConceptNet

1 Introduction

The Smart City paradigm has been adopted to deliver technology-driven solutions, designed and built to enhance the management of city services, such as transportation, energy and water supply, health and emergency management, among others [1]. Smart City systems are designed as distributed cyber-physical systems in which the data exchange across different enterprises is of paramount importance to the success of their proposition. Generally, in the Smart City environment data is gathered by different means and from different sources; it could be very detailed and collected in real-time. An area of application in Smart Cities pertains to the use of health information to support emergency events. Just like smart systems for traffic management can help in reducing emergency services response time [2], an intelligent healthcare system could also continuously gather physiological signs (e.g., heart rate, body temperature) from patients [3], thus making data immediately available to hospitals and emergency medical services [4]. Besides, there is a promising trend towards fast, agile access to health records, for

© Springer Nature Switzerland AG 2020
C. M. Keet and M. Dumontier (Eds.): EKAW 2020, LNAI 12387, pp. 54–70, 2020.
https://doi.org/10.1007/978-3-030-61244-3_4

instance, the Emergency Care Summary (ECS) system implemented by the Scotland Government [5] aims to provide patient's useful information to healthcare staff. However, this summary is accessible only under the patient express consent and does not include detailed information of the patient. For example, recent diseases, surgeries or disabilities are not part of the summary. Also, ECS is an opt-out scheme; it means that not all the patients will have an ECS if they decide not to participate.

In recent years, research highlighted significant obstacles to effective data sharing between organisations and emergency services [6]. For example, a report from the UK government referring to the emergency response to the 7 July 2005 London Bombings points out that the *"Limitation on the initial collection and subsequent sharing of data"* was due to the concerns on sharing personal data [7]. The issues related to privacy that hamper the effective reuse of data can be summarised as follows:

- Disclosure or dissemination of sensitive information (such as health conditions, disabilities, sexual orientation, location, among others).
- Use of data for purposes other than the one stated initially (such as advertising).
- The exchange/sharing of personal data with other parties (insurance companies, the government, including emergency bodies) [8].
- Breaches of regulations, such as the EU General Data Protection Regulation (GDPR) and the UK Data Protection Act, leading to unlawful personal data exchange during emergency response.

Therefore, emergency responders must assess how to handle personal data just as any other organisation [9]. However, emergency response is exceptional in nature. Let us consider the role of health records in the following scenario. In a large organisation, employees use their access cards to enter the building and visitors must register as they enter or leave the premises. A fire starts on the fourth floor of the building, and emergency services are alerted. Having information about people in the building can help emergency services. However, additional information about vulnerable people could assist emergency responders to intervene and make effective decisions promptly. Crucially, this information can be retrieved from Health Records of the national health service. However, there are two significant problems. First, a person's health record can contain a large amount of very specific information. Therefore, finding a way to detect relevant information is essential. Second, health records contain very sensitive information and, therefore, the exchange of such data constitutes a privacy violation. Preventing the disclosure of personal data while providing emergency services with usable information is an important and difficult problem [10]. In this work, we focus on the following research questions:

- RQ1: How to use health records to support emergency services to identify *who* is in need of special assistance during an evacuation?
- RQ2: How to process health records in order to derive information about *why* the person needs assistance?

To answer these questions, we propose an approach based on knowledge engineering, semantic technologies, and the use of a common-sense knowledge base (ConceptNet

[11]). First, we analyse the regulations that large organisations in the UK are required to apply in relation to vulnerable people during a fire emergency. We performed our experiments relying on a synthetic healthcare dataset, encoded using the healthcare standards, such as, the Fast Healthcare Interoperability Resources (FHIR), for the exchange of electronic health records [12] and the Systematized Nomenclature of Medicine, Clinical Terms (SNOMED CT) [13]. Next, we analyse the data schema and annotate it according to its relevance and sensitivity. From the resulting dataset, we review features related to the description of health conditions (represented with SNOMED CT) and the time-validity of data. To enable querying over the data schema, we take a Linked Data approach and use RDF to characterise the information and SPARQL to query a schema-less representation of the data source. By doing this, we achieve a significant reduction of the data points and identify the persons with current medical conditions, therefore, potentially in need of special assistance. To answer the second research question, we match the identified data points with a categorisation of different types of disabilities relevant to building evacuation, according to the governmental guidelines of the UK [14], with the aid of a common-sense knowledge base (ConceptNet). The output of our system is a list of persons requiring assistance and the reason for their needs, without disclosing sensitive information. Our contributions[1] are:

- A novel approach to developing a data pipeline that allows the use of personal health records to derive relevant information and support emergency services;
- A synthetic dataset of annotated FHIR schema elements, according to their sensitivity and utility with respect to a fire evacuation emergency;
- A gold standard dataset developed on the healthcare dataset for evaluating systems in deciding who needs assistance and the reason for it;
- Extensive experiments to demonstrate the effectiveness of our method and to define a baseline for further research on the topic.

The remainder of this paper is organised as follows. We begin by presenting the scenario analysed in this paper in Sect. 2. After describing the related work in Sect. 3, we present the proposed methodology in Sect. 4 and its application in Sect. 5. Section 6 describes the implementation of the system. In Sect. 7, we present the results. Finally, we discuss future work and conclusions in Sect. 8.

2   Scenario

We consider a fire event in a large organisation, analysing the case of The Open University in the UK. The employees use their access cards to enter the building, and visitors must register as they enter or leave the premises. As stated in the organisation's procedures, all employees should inform the Health and Safety Department (HSD) if they have a long-term condition or a temporary disability. Following this notification, the HSD must assure that each employee has an emergency evacuation plan tailored to their needs. To record the evacuation plan, the HSD follows governmental guidelines and internal regulations.

---

[1] https://doi.org/10.5281/ZENODO.3862336.

Generally, a person designated by the HSD interviews the employee and evaluates his/her capacity to perform the plan. Typically, factors to take into account and negotiate a suitable evacuation plan are a) type of disability, b) the employee's capacity to perform a plan, and c) the means of escape available in the building. For the elaboration of a plan, the UK governmental guidelines [14] provide a comprehensive list of disabilities and recommended options for escape as well as important guidance for assessing and arranging the appropriate means of evacuation for the employee. Once identified the type of assistance required, the following action is to register a tailored Personal Emergency Evacuation Plan (PEEP). The PEEP collects employee's identity information (e.g., name, telephone number, staff number), a description of the conditions and disabilities that may affect his/her ability to evacuate the building, according to the categories identified in the governmental guidelines. Additionally, a step by step description of the actions an employee must perform in case of evacuation, as well as any aid equipment or assistance needed. This information must be shared with the nominated *fire wardens*.

A fire starts on the fourth floor of a building, it is spreading quickly, and emergency services are alerted. The HSD may be able to identify people with special needs by retrieving the PEEP record. However, a number of issues reduce the effectiveness of this approach. In the absence of digital infrastructure, PEEP files may be impossible to retrieve efficiently. But also, in the case of a database, the completeness and accuracy of the data are questionable. Compiling the PEEP requires the sharing of health information that could be considered very sensitive by employees. Many people may not want to share this type of information with the line manager or the colleagues appointed as fire wardens. For example, anxiety or other mental health conditions can be typically hard to disclose. In addition, the information included in the PEEP may be outdated. Crucially, visitors may not be included in the records. Having precise information about vulnerable people could help emergency services react promptly and take the right decisions when planning resources. In this context, accessing the health records of the National Health Service (NHS) by a Smart City system constitutes a substantial opportunity to retrieve up to date information and recognise accurately people requiring support. However, obtaining such amount of fine-grained and specialised data could be overwhelming for firefighters and fire wardens because:

- Healthcare data is highly specialised and may be difficult to interpret by the personnel involved in supporting the evacuation (e.g., firefighters).
- A large amount of data makes it difficult to find relevant information.
- Exchange of sensitive information might put citizens' privacy at risk.

Therefore, it is imperative to find a solution that can access healthcare data, filter out the relevant information and process it to deliver meaningful, *fit for purpose* summaries, while preserving citizens' privacy. In principle, an Intelligent System could act as a mediator between the healthcare data provider and the emergency services to balance the trade-off between utility and sensitivity.

3 Related Work

We consider related work in the areas of intelligent systems for emergency response, with particular attention to the use of healthcare data. A considerable amount of literature has been published on the use of healthcare data and personal health records [15, 16] in Smart Cities. In recent years, attention has also focused on the use of health records to assist emergency services [17]. For instance, solutions facilitating confidential access to health records during emergency events [18]. Another example is the implementation of smart home solutions that monitor the elderly's health and provide emergency services with accurate information [3].

The information represents a life-saving resource for first responders, who require data that is well structured, pertinent to their needs and readily available [19]. In this context, information management to support emergency services embraces diverse approaches, for example, decision support systems for data integration and utilisation of provenance data [20], and the use of semantics for the integration of heterogeneous knowledge [21].

Although these works focus on supporting emergency services by using healthcare-related data, they only focus on solving issues related to heterogeneous semantic data integration and organisation. For instance, in [22], the authors propose a similar scenario of a fire evacuation in a University, for which they developed a solution that queries different data sources (such as, an employee management system). The system allows emergency responders access to fire event-related information (hazardous materials, building information, among others) and employees' 'medical status' which is limited to indicate whether an employee has or not a disability. However, they do not consider the use of healthcare data or provide details about the type of disability. In our work, we focus on using health records and rely on the use of semantic web technologies to extract relevant information facilitating the interpretation of health data while providing emergency services details about vulnerable people and the type of assistance required.

Studies also raise privacy concerns when using healthcare data [23–25]. Research to date presents different approaches to tackle these concerns; for instance, a proposed framework for deriving security and privacy requirements [24]. Other solutions propose protocols to enable anonymous data exchange between stakeholders in cloud environments [25]. To the best of our knowledge, none of these approaches undertake the problem of optimising the trade-off between sensitivity and utility while accessing health records during emergency events, hence minimise data sensitivity before it is exchanged.

Several studies apply Knowledge Graphs as a solution for heterogeneous data integration in domains such as disaster management [20, 26] and health monitoring [21, 27]. In our work, Semantic Web technologies are used as part of the approach to managing healthcare data, in particular, representing a synthetic healthcare record dataset [28]. As healthcare records are increasingly becoming digitised, we use FHIR to structure and standardise its content. Our proposed solution uses annotations to identify relevant and sensitive data within the health records dataset. To make these resources available, we use RDF which addresses the requirements to perform meta-queries over the schema, using the utility and sensitivity annotations.

In summary, healthcare data is undoubtedly a paramount source of information for emergency services [17, 18]. Different applications make use of healthcare data implementing approaches concentrated on semantic integration of heterogeneous data sources [15, 16, 22]. Although integration is relevant, it is equally important to devise a method which extracts meaningful data to meet emergency services' requirements. Ultimately it will lead to exchange only useful data, minimising the amount of personal information and protecting citizens' privacy.

4 Methodology

As stated in Sect. 1, our research focuses on assisting emergency services to make use of healthcare data while preserving citizens' privacy. This methodology has the aim of supporting a data engineer in developing a privacy-aware pipeline for effective reuse of health records. Therefore, the methodology (Fig. 1) is generic and portable across similar scenarios where data sources contain extremely sensitive data. Throughout this paper, the term 'datapoint' refers to the smallest piece of information, and it is associated with one or more dimensions of the data schema—for example, a cell in a spreadsheet.

The first activity of our methodology is to identify the data requirements according to the emergency. The task is to represent the knowledge requirement in terms of a closed Competency Question (CQ), therefore formalising the information needs and facilitating the identification and extraction of required data. For instance, if the CQ is "Would the person be able to manipulate small objects?", then the relevant information constitutes the attributes that answer this question (e.g., conditions and procedures related to upper limbs).

Step 2 concentrates on identifying structured or unstructured data sources that could help to answer the CQ. These may include observations as well as reference taxonomies or domain ontologies.

Step 3 performs an exhaustive analysis and annotation of the data sources. The objective is to have a clear understanding of the role that each one of them may have in the pipeline. For example, analysing the content, its data schema (attributes and relationships) and identifying criteria for selecting useful information (for example, filtering out outdated information). Specifically, we inspect the data schema and annotate the properties according to two dimensions: *utility and sensitivity*. By assigning annotations, it is possible now to filter the data points that do are not useful to answer the CQ. The final result is a reduced collection of health records, leading to the extraction of relevant data.

The fourth Step in the methodology takes as input the subset of data points resulting from the analysis in Step 3. Data identified as useful, but not sensitive can be exchanged or used directly. On the other hand, data considered somehow sensitive has to be processed to reduce its degree of sensitivity. Building on these considerations, in Step 4 the objective is for the data engineer to transform the data, by applying privacy-preserving techniques, for example, using standard classification systems in substitution of the specific data point. The final output is a set of tailored information that satisfies the CQ, hence enabling effective use of personal health records.

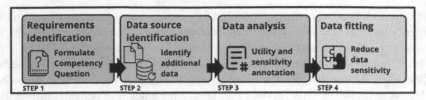

Fig. 1. Step by step methodology

5   Application of the Methodology

To illustrate the use of the methodology, we use the scenario set up from Sect. 2; we focus on a fire event in a large organisation and use a healthcare data source.

5.1   Requirements Identification

From the scenario in Sect. 2, we define the knowledge requirements of the emergency services. Specifically, firefighters need to be informed if any of the occupants of the building need assistance evacuating the premises and the type of support they may provide. Following our methodology, we start by formulating the CQ:

Who among the occupants in the building is in need of assistance in case of a fire evacuation, and what type of need?

5.2   Data Source Identification

To satisfy the need for information, we review the CQ formulated previously and identify specific or additional information that could contribute to answering the CQ. Specifically, the notification of a disability or a temporary condition triggers the creation of a PEEP. Therefore, we explore data sources and regulations about diseases and chronic conditions as well as types of assistance or disabilities regarding an impediment to performing an evacuation plan. About disabilities and risk for disabled people, the guidelines of the UK Government [14] provide a comprehensive list of types of disabilities and means of escape for people with special needs. Our synthetic dataset of health records uses SNOMED CT, a standard terminology for clinical content in electronic health records. Additionally, the NHS website[2] is a useful source of information for non-experts; it provides details about the impact of diseases and recovery times.

Health Dataset. Health-related data is considered highly sensitive information. Hence, to prevent any disclosure of private information, in our research we make use of synthetic healthcare data. Synthea [28] is an open-source software that generates synthetic electronic health records. The software models the medical history of synthetic patients. The health record of each patient is generated independently and simulates the health registers from birth to death through modular representations of various diseases. The synthetic electronic health records are deep and extensive as they include demographic

---

[2] https://www.nhs.uk/conditions/.

data, appointments, patient conditions, procedures, care plans, medication, allergies, and observations. We decided to represent the data using FHIR (Fast Healthcare Interoperability Resources) standard specification for exchanging healthcare information electronically. Specifically, we took a Linked Data approach and used the FHIR RDF ontology as the most suitable option to describe the dataset. From the generated dataset, we identify 155 attributes grouped into 14 different types of information, and we focus on these in the subsequent analysis.

5.3 Data Analysis

This step of the methodology is dedicated to analysing the content of the dataset, its data schema and to the production of annotations related to its sensitivity and utility.

We inspect the content of our health record dataset and its data schema to reason over the features of the data that can help to answer the CQ. Crucially, we want to distinguish data features that are useful and their degree of sensitivity. Particularly, we observe that data points describing health conditions have a temporal validity, since a condition may be valid for a specific amount of time. Therefore, we produced a set of annotations to identify the temporal validity of SNOMED CT codes. Separately, two of the authors annotated the time validity of the 417 SNOMED CT codes of our synthetic health dataset, using as support the NHS public information. For example, the NHS web page specifies that 'Pneumonia' disease may require six months to recover; thus, the annotations include the stated recovery time and the source of information. Next, they discussed each annotation and agreed on the time validity representation, including comments to describe the condition where possible.

Utility and Sensitivity Annotation. First, we define two custom RDF predicates that represent *utility* and *sensitivity*. Then, we annotate each attribute manually according to its utility to answer the CQ. For the sensitivity assessment, the task is to identify the attributes in the data schema that are considered personal data. To annotate attributes as sensitive, we use regulations that govern personal data (for instance, GDPR, data protection act) and define personal data and its impact on privacy. The result is a dataset annotated according to its utility and sensitivity. Applying a Linked Data approach allows us to perform *meta-queries* in SPARQL hence making it easy to filter data points by means of the annotations on their properties. For example, one data point of the health record could be represented in the following query (see Fig. 2). By using the annotations, we extract relevant data points and distinguish sensitive information. As shown in Table 1, this already translates into a significant reduction of the data to be processed. However, not all relevant data points describe a health condition nor a disability useful to answer our CQ. For instance, a data point describing an appointment, or a general procedure may not be relevant. Instead, one describing a recent fracture of the ankle certainly will. Thus, the next task is to derive the valid data points from the subset of relevant information.

Time-Validity Annotations. In our synthetic dataset, the description of any situation (for instance, care plans, appointments, procedures, allergies) gives us an idea of possible illness, disabilities and current health condition of a person. Therefore, to extract the valid data points, we use the time validity annotations assigned to each SNOMED CT code according to the following considerations (see Fig. 3):

property	subproperty	value	utility	sensitivity
fhir:Condition.codeableConcept	fhir:CodeableConcept.coding	58150001	epront:useful	epront:sensitive
fhir:Condition.codeableConcept	fhir:CodeableConcept.text	Fracture of clavicle	epront:useful	epront:sensitive
fhir:Condition.period	fhir:Period.start	2018-03-12T00:00:00.000Z	epront:useful	epront:sensitive
fhir:Condition.period	fhir:Period.end	2018-09-12T00:00:00.000Z	epront:useful	epront:sensitive
snomed:Validity.months		6	epront:useful	epront:sensitive

Fig. 2. Data point representation

Table 1. Reduction of data to be processed. One-person example

	All data points	Only relevant data points	Relevant & sensitive
# of data points	32,608	9,326	6,399

snomed code	description	validity	comment	source
82078001	Take blood sample	0	General procedure, never valid	https://www.nhs.uk/conditions/blood-tests/
232717009	Coronary artery bypass grafting	3	Up to 3 months to recover	https://www.nhs.uk/conditions/coronary-artery-bypass-graft-cabg/
180030006	Amputation of foot	*	Long term condition, always valid	https://www.nhs.uk/conditions/amputation/

Fig. 3. Time-validity annotation examples

- Never valid - for SNOMED CT codes that do not describe specific conditions or refer to general procedures
- Specific time validity - for SNOMED CT codes that describe the recovery time in months and could range from one to several months according to the condition.
- Always valid - for SNOMED CT codes that describe long-term conditions.

5.4   Data Fitting

We have now a reduced collection of data points only including useful and valid information, classified according to their sensitivity. Specifically, we observe how all data points usable for answering our CQ are sensitive data! In addition, we should take into consideration how healthcare data is generated and read by health professionals; this means that the interpretation of such information may represent a challenge for emergency services (e.g., fire wardens). To solve the problems of sensitivity and interpretation of health records, we use the categories that represent disabilities according to [14]. In order to bridge the gap between the categories in the classification and the description of the health records, we use a common-sense knowledge base: ConceptNet. First, for each category in the list of disabilities, we find a key concept in ConceptNet that represents it (see Table 2). Second, to match the health record data points with the most related type of disability, we use the ConceptNet API[3]. The API compares two terms and returns a 'relatedness value' indicating how connected the two terms are; the higher the value, the more related each pair of terms are. Hence, we query the API to obtain the relatedness

---

[3] https://github.com/commonsense/conceptnet5/wiki/API#relatedness-of-a-particular-pair-of-terms.

value between each valid data point and each key concept. After comparing all valid data points against the types of disabilities, our system calculates the average score, and this allows us to deliver a ranked list of the most related types of disabilities associated with the time-valid condition extracted from the health record. The result is a ranked list of possible reasons for assistance, answering the second part of our CQ (see Table 3).

Table 2. Types of disabilities and correspondent key concept

Category description	Key concept
Electric wheelchair and wheelchair user	*wheelchair_user*
Mobility impaired person	*movement_disorder*
Asthma and breathing issues	*respiratory_disease*
Visually impaired person	*visual_impairment*
Dyslexic and orientation disorders	*disorientation*
Learning difficulty and autism	*learning_difficulty*
Mental Health problems	*mental_health_problem*
Dexterity problems	*indexterity*
Hcaring impaired person	*hearing_impaired*

Table 3. Ranked top 3 reasons for assistance

Rank	Category	Score
1	Asthma and breathing issues	0.368
	/relatedness?node1 =/c/en/respiratory_disease&node2 = /c/en/injury_of_tendon_of_the_rotator_cuff_of_shoulder	0.126
	/relatedness?node1 =/c/en/respiratory_disease&node2 = /c/en/pulmonary_emphysema	0.610
2	Electric Wheelchair and wheelchair user	0.201
	/relatedness?node1 =/c/en/wheelchair_user&node2 = /c/en/injury_of_tendon_of_the_rotator_cuff_of_shoulder	0.371
	/relatedness?node1 =/c/en/wheelchair_user&node2 = /c/en/pulmonary_emphysema	0.031
3	Mobility impaired person	0.198
	/relatedness?node1 =/c/en/movement_disorder&node2 = /c/en/injury_of_tendon_of_the_rotator_cuff_of_shoulder	0.103
	/relatedness?node1 =/c/en/movement_disorder&node2 = /c/en/pulmonary_emphysema	0.293

6 System

In order to apply the proposed methodology, we developed a system which takes as input the annotated data source. Then it processes the data points following our approach to finally deliver the number of people requiring assistance and the type of help required. In what follows, we describe in detail the implementation of the system.

Input: As input, our system uses the types of disabilities, taken from the UK government guidelines for fire evacuation and tailored for our use case. The main data input is the annotated health record dataset according to its utility and sensitivity.

Process: First, our system identifies the people in the building at the moment the fire starts. For each person in the building, our system queries only the data points annotated as relevant. From this collection of relevant data points, our system now identifies the valid data points; this implies an evaluation of each data point according to its temporal validity. Each data point that represents a health condition has a time validity according to the type of disease, and its recovery time, thus, a data point is valid if the time validity and the data point start date overlap. If a person has at least one valid data point, it means that this person requires assistance.

On the contrary, if the person has no valid data points, then no assistance is required. Hence, our system identifies all the people that require assistance and the health records that support this result. Next, the system evaluates the type of disability, which defines the reason for the assistance. Our system uses the ConceptNet API to query the relatedness between each data point and each key concept of the type of disabilities. The query returns a 'relatedness value', the higher the value, the more related the pair of terms are. Thus, for each type of disability, our system registers an average score that allows us to obtain a ranked list of the most related types of disabilities.

Output: As exemplified in Fig. 4, the system returns a list of people requiring help and the best matching type of assistance needed according to their medical conditions.

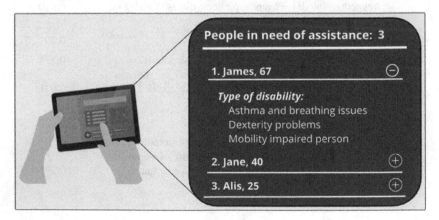

Fig. 4. Information provided by the system

7 Evaluation

In this section, we present the results of our system. We developed a well-curated Gold Standard Dataset that is the point of reference to measure the validity of our results.

Experiment Settings. For our study, we generated a sample of 10,000 patients, intending to create a large sample of health records and including as many diseases as possible. From the experiments, we focus on randomly selected 1,012 patients' health records. The age of the patients ranges from 20 to 80 years old, as we try to simulate the ages of employees of a large organisation such as The Open University.

7.1 Gold Standard Dataset

To evaluate the results of our experiments, we developed a Gold Standard Dataset (GSD) based on a collection of annotated patients health records answering the following questions:

- Q1: Who needs special assistance in case of a fire evacuation?
- Q2: What type of assistance the person needs?

The GSD was developed by two of the authors independently, and they are referred as the reviewers. It is worth mentioning that the authors are members of a large organisation (The Open University), and their competence is comparable to that of a fire warden.

To support the reviewers in building the GSD, we developed a web interface that for each sample displays: *a)* the question to be answered, *b)* the patient's details (name, last name, age) and *c)* a section with the whole patient's health record (description, reason, type of record, start date, end date). For GSDQ1, we present the reviewer with the option to answer 'Yes' or 'No' to the question if the person needs assistance. The reviewer should read the health records and detect any condition that could reveal that a person has an impediment to evacuate the building. For GSDQ2, we display the list of the type of disabilities and ask the reviewers to choose at least one item from the list. It is essential to mention that we used the same list of disabilities as our system. Additionally, GSDQ2's sample is composed only of the samples annotated as 'Yes' in GSDQ1. The GSD was initially built by two of the authors, using the following process:

- Annotate the GSD individually.
- Identify discrepancies by reviewing the differences between their answers.
- Discuss each difference, explanations and evidence for answering 'Yes' or 'No', including external sources, such as the NHS website.
- Take a motivated decision: evaluate the evidence and reach an agreement.
- Annotate the reasons for the agreement: write down any comments and reasons to ensure consistency across decisions.

The resulting GSD is an account of how a person typically involved in supporting a fire evacuation may interpret the content of health records, having sufficient time and resources.

7.2 Baselines

We compared the approach described in Sect. 5, with several baselines developed considering alternative hypotheses.

Baseline (1 M) - One-Month Time Frame Validity. Baseline 1 M applies the hypothesis that most recent health records reflect conditions that affect an individual's capacity to perform an evacuation plan. Therefore, to find valid conditions, we experiment with a time frame of one month.

Baseline (2 M) - Two-Months' Time Frame Validity. Baseline 2 M applies the assumption that valid data points occur in a two-month time frame.

Baseline (1 M+BLC) – Block-List For Non-Descriptive Conditions. Usually, the health records include data points that do not represent a health condition, for example, 'Medical Reconciliation'. Hence, this Baseline applies a block-list to filter out non-descriptive SNOMED CT codes, in combination with the 1 M time validity.

Baseline (1 M+BLC+CHR) - List of Chronic Conditions. We detect that long-term conditions usually are excluded when considering short time frames (1 M and 2 M). For example, amputation of foot or heart conditions are not identified. By including long-term conditions, our system may correctly identify more people. This Baseline uses an allow-list of long-term conditions from SNOMED CT valid at any time.

7.3 Results

In what follows, we present the evaluation of the two research questions formulated in Sect. 1.

Research Question 1(RQ1). For RQ1, the objective is to identify who requires special assistance during an evacuation. To measure the performance of our system, we use the following metrics:

- We use accuracy to evaluate our system as a boolean classifier and measure its ability to distinguish whether an individual needs assistance or not.
- Precision, to measure the percentage of people identified as vulnerable that were correctly classified.
- Recall, to measure the percentage of actual people in need of assistance that were correctly classified. Recall is a particularly relevant measure for our system as we want to minimise the risk of missing a person in need.
- F-Measure, for measuring the performance of the system considering both precision and recall.

We compare the decisions of our system against the GSDQ1; the results obtained from its analysis are summarised in Table 4.

Our approach reported accuracy of 0.91; therefore, our system correctly identifies 91% of the people that either need or not assistance. Precision and Recall prove to be

Table 4. Identification of people requiring assistance (RQ1)

Experiment	Accuracy	Precision	Recall	F-score
Our approach	**0.91**	**0.69**	**0.82**	**0.75**
Baseline (1 M)	0.85	0.54	0.35	0.43
Baseline (2 M)	0.82	0.44	0.48	0.45
Baseline (1 M+BLC)	0.86	0.65	0.32	0.43
Baseline (1 M+BLC+CHR)	0.81	0.43	0.47	0.45

significantly better results compared with alternative approaches. The main aim of our system is to maximise the possibility of identifying people in need of help, and thus in our study, we consider Recall the most important indicator. We managed to identify 82% of the cases as people that actually need help. There was a significant difference between the F-score of our approach and the other hypotheses. Our system outperforms the baselines in all the measures.

Research Question 2 (RQ2). For RQ2, we focus on *why* people need assistance. We compare the results of our system against the results from GSDQ2. In order to evaluate the capacity of our system of providing a precise ranking of the most relevant categories of disabilities, we use Precision at K. The results obtained are summarised in Table 5. The results show that overall our approach attains a high precision on identifying the first three more likely reasons concerning a disability. In Table 5, we show the results also using the other baselines with the purpose of demonstrating how a more accurate selection of relevant data points leads to a better-quality classification. It is also important to mention that for the GSDQ2, we asked participants to select at least one type of disability and the one they consider most important. Therefore, our approach also should find a way to give each type of disability a degree of impact or a level of importance besides finding the most related types of disability according to a person's health records.

Table 5. Classification of type of assistance (RQ2). Precision at 3.

Experiment	1st category	2nd category	3rd category
Our approach	**0.47**	**0.52**	**0.73**
Input from Baseline (1 M)	0.11	0.13	0.32
Input from Baseline (2 M)	0.16	0.17	0.40
Input from Baseline (1 M+BLC)	0.10	0.01	0.18
Input form Baseline (1 M+BLC+CHR)	0.13	0.18	0.35

8 Discussion and Conclusions

In this paper, we have introduced a methodology designed to make use of sensitive data in the context of a fire building evacuation. We developed a system that follows the proposed methodology and uses synthetic healthcare data to answer our research questions. We demonstrate that our approach allows us to identify people that require special assistance during a fire evacuation without the need of disclosing personal information. Specifically, we applied a knowledge engineering approach and used a common-sense knowledge base to categorise health conditions and transform the data for the convenience of non-expert users, for example, fire wardens and emergency responders.

Although results show a considerable high accuracy and recall, there is still work to be done in order to improve the precision. Possible directions could be reasoning over the combination of conditions and procedures. This hypothesis opens interesting challenges in relation to analysing and annotating large knowledge bases such as SNOMED CT in order to fit specific needs such as those of the emergency services.

Another important point is related to the experiment setting. Synthetic data is very accurate with respect to statistical considerations (e.g., the number of persons with a specific condition). However, there are also limitations. For example, we recognise that the synthetic dataset we used did not include explicit descriptions on the use of aid equipment, although these are contemplated in SNOMED CT. This information could definitely help on defining better strategies to automatically respond to why a person is in need of special assistance.

One aspect we consider relevant to explore concerns the different methodologies to support the implementation of systems compliant with data regulations, especially important for emergency services that should exchange sensitive data during exceptional situations. Further experiments could usefully explore the application of our proposed methodology in a different use case and include other sensitive datasets such as location or biometric data. Additionally, we recognise that a natural progression of this work will explore further the use of common-sense knowledge in order to support the interpretation of health records for timely emergency response in the Smart City.

References

1. Caird, S.: City approaches to smart city evaluation and reporting: case studies in the United Kingdom. Urban Res. Pract. **11**, 159–179 (2018). https://doi.org/10.1080/17535069.2017.1317828
2. Rego, A., Garcia, L., Sendra, S., Lloret, J.: Software defined network-based control system for an efficient traffic management for emergency situations in smart cities. Future Gener. Comput. Syst. **88**, 243–253 (2018). https://doi.org/10.1016/j.future.2018.05.054
3. Hussain, A., Wenbi, R., da Silva, A.L., Nadher, M., Mudhish, M.: Health and emergency-care platform for the elderly and disabled people in the Smart City. J. Syst. Softw. **110**, 253–263 (2015). https://doi.org/10.1016/j.jss.2015.08.041
4. Gharaibeh, A., et al.: Smart cities: a survey on data management, security, and enabling technologies. IEEE Commun. Surv. Tutor. **19**, 2456–2501 (2017). https://doi.org/10.1109/comst.2017.2736886
5. Scottish Government S.: Your Emergency Care Summary: What does it mean for you? https://www.gov.scot/publications/emergency-care-summary-mean/

6. Yüksel, B., Küpçü, A., Özkasap, Ö.: Research issues for privacy and security of electronic health services. Future Gener. Comput. Syst. **68**, 1–13 (2017). https://doi.org/10.1016/j.fut ure.2016.08.011
7. HM Government: Addressing lessons from the emergency response to the 7 July 2005 London bombings (2016)
8. Bertino, E.: Data security and privacy: concepts, approaches, and research directions. In: 2016 IEEE 40th Annual Computer Software and Applications Conference (COMPSAC), pp. 400–407. IEEE, Atlanta (2016). https://doi.org/10.1109/COMPSAC.2016.89
9. HM Government: Data protection and sharing guidance for emergency planners and responders (2007). https://www.gov.uk/government/publications/data-protection-and-sharing-gui dance-for-emergency-planners-and-responders
10. Morales, A., Motta, E., Daga, E.: Towards a privacy aware information system for emergency response. In: Proceedings of the 16th International Conference on Information Systems for Crisis Response and Management (ISCRAM), p. 4 (2019)
11. Speer, R., Chin, J., Havasi, C.: ConceptNet 5.5: an open multilingual graph of general knowledge. In: Proceedings of AAAI, vol. 31 (2017)
12. HL7.org: HL7FHIR. https://www.hl7.org/fhir/overview.html
13. SNOMED International. http://www.snomed.org/snomed-ct/five-step-briefing
14. HM Government: Fire safety risk assessment: means of escape for disabled people (2007). https://www.gov.uk/government/publications/fire-safety-risk-assessment-means-of-escape-for-disabled-people
15. Majumder, S., et al.: Smart homes for elderly healthcare—recent advances and research challenges. Sensors **17**, 2496 (2017)
16. Boyi, X., Da Li, X., Cai, H., Xie, C., Jingyuan, H., Fenglin, B.: Ubiquitous data accessing method in IoT-based information system for emergency medical services. IEEE Trans. Ind. Inform. **10**, 1578–1586 (2014). https://doi.org/10.1109/tii.2014.2306382
17. Abu-Elkheir, M., Hassanein, H.S., Oteafy, S.M.A.: Enhancing emergency response systems through leveraging crowdsensing and heterogeneous data. In: 2016 International Wireless Communications and Mobile Computing Conference (IWCMC), pp. 188–193. IEEE (2016)
18. Thummavet, P., Vasupongayya, S.: A novel personal health record system for handling emergency situations. In: 2013 International Computer Science and Engineering Conference (ICSEC), pp. 266–271. IEEE (2013). https://doi.org/10.1109/icsec.2013.6694791
19. Nunavath, V., Prinz, A., Comes, T.: Identifying first responders information needs: supporting search and rescue operations for fire emergency response. Int. J. Inf. Syst. Crisis Response Manag. IJISCRAM (2016). https://doi.org/10.4018/ijiscram.2016010102
20. McNeill, F., Bental, D., Missier, P., Steyn, J., Komar, T., Bryans, J.: Communication in emergency management through data integration and trust: an introduction to the CEM-DIT system. In: Proceedings of ISCRAM, p. 12, Valencia, Spain (2019)
21. Shi, L., Li, S., Yang, X., Qi, J., Pan, G., Zhou, B.: Semantic health knowledge graph: semantic integration of heterogeneous medical knowledge and services. Biomed. Res. Int. **2017**, 1–12 (2017). https://doi.org/10.1155/2017/2858423
22. Nunavath, V., Prinz, A.: LifeRescue: a web based application for emergency responders during fire emergency response. In: 2016 3rd International Conference on Information and Communication Technologies for Disaster Management (ICT-DM), pp. 1–8. IEEE (2016)
23. Kaelber, D.C., Jha, A.K., Johnston, D., Middleton, B., Bates, D.W.: A research agenda for personal health records (PHRs). J. Am. Med. Inform. Assoc. **15**, 729–736 (2008)
24. Oladimeji, E.A., Chung, L., Jung, H.T., Kim, J.: Managing security and privacy in ubiquitous eHealth information interchange. In: Proceedings of the 5th International Conference on Ubiquitous Information Management and Communication, p. 1. ACM Press (2011)

25. Rahman, S.K.M.M., Masud, M.M., Hossain, M.A., Alelaiwi, A., Hassan, M.M., Alamri, A.: Privacy preserving secure data exchange in mobile P2P cloud healthcare environment. Peer-to-peer Netw. Appl. **9**(5), 894–909 (2015). https://doi.org/10.1007/s12083-015-0334-2
26. Chehade, S., Pothin, J.-B., Matta, N., Cogranne, R.: Situation representation and awareness for rescue operations. In: Proceedings of the 16th International Conference on Information Systems for Crisis Response and Management (ISCRAM), p. 12 (2019)
27. Gyrard, A., Gaur, M., Shekarpour, S., Thirunarayan, K., Sheth, A.: Personalized health knowledge graph. In: ISWC2018 Contextualized KG Workshop, p. 7 (2018)
28. Walonoski, J., et al.: Synthea: an approach, method, and software mechanism for generating synthetic patients and the synthetic electronic health care record. J. Am. Med. Inform. Assoc. **25**, 230–238 (2018). https://doi.org/10.1093/jamia/ocx079

Analysis of Term Reuse, Term Overlap and Extracted Mappings Across AgroPortal Semantic Resources

Amir Laadhar[✉], Elcio Abrahão[ID], and Clement Jonquet[✉][ID]

Laboratory of Informatics, Robotics and Microelectronics of Montpellier (LIRMM),
University of Montpellier & CNRS, Montpellier, France
{amir.laadhar,elcio.abrahao,clement.jonquet}@lirmm.fr

Abstract. Ontologies in agronomy facilitate data integration, information exchange, search and query of agronomic data, and other knowledge-intensive tasks. We have developed AgroPortal, an open community-based repository of agronomy and related domains semantic resources. From a corpus of ontologies, terminologies, and thesauri taken from Agro-Portal, we have generated, extracted and analyzed more than 400,000 mappings between concepts based on: (i) reuse of the same URI between concepts in different resources –term reuse; (ii) lexical similarity of concept names and synonyms –term overlap; and (iii) declared mappings properties between concepts –extracted mappings. We developed an interactive visualization of each mapping construct separately and combined which helps users identify most prominent ontologies, relevant thematic clusters, areas of a domain that are not well covered, and pertinent ontologies as background knowledge. By comparing the size of the semantic resources to the number of their mappings, we found that most of them have under 5% of their terms mapped. Our results show the need of an ontology alignment framework in AgroPortal where mappings between semantic resources will be assembled, compared, analysed and automatically updated when semantic resources evolve.

Keywords: Ontology alignment · Term reuse · Term overlap ·
Extracted mappings · Mapping analysis · Visualization

1 Introduction

By reusing the NCBO BioPortal technology [16], we have designed AgroPortal (http://agroportal.lirmm.fr), an ontology repository for agronomy, plant and food sciences and originally biodiversity-ecology [9]. As of August 2020, AgroPortal includes 126 ontologies, terminologies and thesauri encoded in different formats like RDFS, OWL, OBO, UMLS-RRF and SKOS. AgroPortal stores reference resources such as the Plant Ontology or Agronomy Ontology or AGROVOC. The need for interconnecting these resources i.e., ontology alignment [3], has been explicitly expressed by almost all of our partners and collaborators to achieve

© Springer Nature Switzerland AG 2020
C. M. Keet and M. Dumontier (Eds.): EKAW 2020, LNAI 12387, pp. 71–87, 2020.
https://doi.org/10.1007/978-3-030-61244-3_5

interoperability among their semantic resources. But the need goes beyond the sole ability to automatically generate alignment between ontologies, it includes being able to store, compare, evaluate the mappings. Therefore, AgroPortal offers a mapping repository to store mappings between its semantic resources. To build this mapping repository, we currently consider three mappings constructs:[1] term reuse, term overlap and extracted mappings. By *term reuse*, we mean the situation in which a term of an ontology is explicitly reused inside another ontology using the same URI.[2] Term reuse is a good practice in ontology/terminology development as it facilitates semantic interoperability and reduce ontology engineering efforts [1]. However, for many reasons, it is not a common practice when semantic resources are not developed under the same umbrella or by the same group or simply when an ontology developer likes to add statements to an object which he/she does not want to conflict with statements in other ontologies. By *term overlap*, we mean the situation in which two classes/concepts use the same labels or synonyms in different semantic resources. Lexical matches are clearly known not to be fully reliable as semantic mappings simply because of the polysemic aspects of labels. However, they are also very well perceived as a useful and quick way of finding relevant similar concepts/ontologies [5]. By *extracted mapping*, we mean being able to extract and load in the repository mappings explicitly declared inside the ontology source files (typically using `owl:sameAs` or SKOS mapping properties) to reify them into first-class objects with provenance information. Contrary to expectations, the process of extracting mappings is not trivial considering the heterogeneity of means to encode mappings and the predominant use of ambiguous constructs like OBO XRefs for instance.

AgroPortal's mapping repository is valuable to our community, since it allows ontology developers and users to identify similar terms across ontologies and it facilitates data integration in systems relying on different semantic resources. Mappings help the identification of prominent ontologies that can serve as a common denominator or hub for data interoperability. If AgroPortal easily detects term reuse between ontologies, the identification of correct term overlap is harder because of polysemic labels and can bring to incoherences [4,17]. However, these "overlaps" are very useful as they can be used by developers to identify similar or equivalent terms to manually enrich their ontologies by declaring formal and rigorous mappings. Today, term reuse and term overlap are automatically detected by AgroPortal when an ontology is uploaded. However, we are currently working to automate mapping extraction from files during the ontology parsing routine.

In this article, we present an analysis of the mapping repository on a corpus of 109 ontologies built from AgroPortal's content in March 2020. Such analysis of the mappings between semantic resources is important as it tells us about the

---

[1] We prefer here the term "construct" to "type" which is used in our work with another meaning: to quality the mapping (exact match, close match, same as, etc.).

[2] The most frequent case of reuse concern classes/concepts, however any object identified by an URI can be reused from one semantic resource to the other (e.g., `owl:Class`, `owl:Individual`, `rdfs:Property`, `skos:Concept`).

landscape of semantic resources, the structure of the ontology repository, and the ways mappings can help in the process of ontology design and evaluation. The contributions of this work are the following:

- A dataset of multiple mappings constructs between semantic resources in agronomy and related domains which is in large part curated;
- An openly available tool called Ontology Mapping Harvester Tool (OMHT), which automatically extracts mappings declared inside ontology source files and represent them into classic mapping formats;
- An interactive visualization of the mapping dataset to display mapping constructs individually and combined;
- A descriptive analysis for each mapping construct.

The rest of the paper is organized as follows: the next section presents related work. In Sect. 3, we introduce the methodology used for each of the three mapping constructs for the generation the mappings dataset. In Sect. 4, we describe the analysis and introduce the visualization. Finally, in Sect. 5, we discuss our results and conclude in Sect. 6.

2   Related Work

Ontology alignment is a key aspect for ontologies: it makes them more interoperable and interconnect the ones on overlapping domain of interests [3]. There is lack of reference mapping repositories that would serve mappings as FAIR data [21]. Such mappings repositories should support representation, extraction, harvesting, generation, validation, merging, evaluation, visualization, storage and retrieval of mappings between the ontologies they host and other ones [8]. Mappings are handled differently within ontology repositories: Ontohub [19], for instance, allows browsing, searching, and aligning ontologies. To the best of our knowledge, only the repositories in the OntoPortal family[3] offers an integrated mapping repository, where different kind of mappings are stored with provenance and are accessible (read/write) through the user interface or via API calls. BioPortal [16] automatically detects term reuse and generates term overlap mappings (with a method called LOOM [5]), however, the technology does not embed any state-of-the-art automatic ontology matching systems and does not extract mappings declared inside the ontologies to reify them inside the mapping repository. Other initiatives, such as the UMLS Metathesaurus includes a specific table to store mappings between the medical terminologies (MRMAP). The European Bioinformatics Institute develops OxO (Ontology Xref Service) to visualize cross-references mappings (i.e., declared with the `oboInOwl:hasDbXref` property) extracted from ontologies inside the Ontology Lookup Service [10]. To disambiguate the prefix of XRefs targets and identify data sources, OxO uses

---

[3] The NCBO BioPortal technology can be reused and customized for deploying other ontology repositories e.g., AgroPortal or EcoPortal. Since 2019, the generic technology is branded as OntoPortal (https://ontoportal.org).

Identifiers.org, the OBO Library, and Prefixcommons.org. Whereas in our work, we semi-automatically curate the declared cross-references to keep only explicit valid mappings between ontology terms [13].

Mapping repositories are useful for several applications such as modules extraction, ontology partitioning, ontology alignment using background knowledge resources and mappings visualization. For instances: Amina et al. [2] proposed a background knowledge-based ontology matching system using as background knowledge a graph, build-out of external mappings, to interconnect the source and target ontologies and identify mapping candidates. Ghazvinian et al. [6] used mappings to extract modules from large ontologies. The YAM++ ontology matching system [15] defined a machine learning classifier trained on a set of reference external mappings. Kamdar et al. [12] proposed a visualization for mappings extracted from BioPortal but it was not maintained in sync with the ontology repository after publication.

Similar mappings analysis work to the one presented in this article are: In 2009, Ghazvinian et al. [7] analyzed more than four million term overlap mappings between 200 ontologies or terminologies in BioPortal (including 67 terminologies from the UMLS Metathesaurus). The mappings were generated with a simple lexical matching method to identify classes with same labels preferred terms and synonyms, over normalised strings. Although their approach was technically simple, they have demonstrated the value of the mappings extracted [5]. They performed term overlap analysis to learn more about the characteristics of the ontologies and the relationships between them e.g., identify hubs and clusters over the ontologies. They used network analysis methods to answer practical questions and to reason about the distribution of mappings among the ontologies. In 2012, Poveda et al. [18] analyzed the landscape of reuses in the 196 semantic resources included in the Linked Open Vocabularies (LOV) registry [20]. In 2015, Kamdar et al. [11] investigated term reuse and overlap in 377 biomedical ontologies from BioPortal. However, in this study, XRef mappings were mixed with other term reuses whereas in our work we distinguish them and consider them as extracted mappings. The authors highlighted the need for a sophisticated term recommendation mechanisms that support consistent term reuse. Later, the authors extend their study to 509 ontologies in BioPortal and reported a term reuse of 9% and a term overlap of 22.23% [12].

3   Methodology: Mapping Dataset Creation

We used for this study a set of 109 distinct agri-food and biodiversity-ecology semantic resources, hosted in AgroPortal in March 2020. These semantic resources include 9 ontologies in the OBO format (e.g., SOY, GR-TAX), 88 OWL ontologies (e.g., FOODON, ATOL), 10 SKOS thesauri (e.g., AGROVOC, NALT). 103 and 104 semantic resources (95%) show respectively term reuse and overlap; 28 semantic resources (25,68%) contain declared mappings in their source files.

In AgroPortal, term overlap and reuses are automatically detected but the system does not explicitly materialize these mappings with provenance and a mapping relation.[4] However, when we build our corpus, we represent these mappings as any other mappings in the repository and assign them provenance information and relevant relations: `owl:sameAs` for term reuse and `skos:relatedMatch` for term overlap. Indeed, `skos:relatedMatch` is in SKOS the "weaker" mapping relation which is appropriate, we believe, for non-curated lexical mappings even if in some case `skos:exactMatch` or `skos:closeMatch` would be more appropriate. Extracted mappings already have a mapping property chosen by the ontology developer when he/she created the mapping. In our dataset, each mapping is also described with some metadata information using a BioPortal specific JSON mapping format e.g., creation date, creator/tool, comment. More detail about the creation of our dataset is provided in the next subsections.

We consider term overlap mappings as symmetric because when there is a match between two labels of two different ontologies, this match is independent of the source and target ontologies. Therefore, term overlap mappings are bidirectional. Even if the URI of the mapped entity is the same, we do not consider term reuse mappings symmetric since they explicitly state that an ontology reuses another one but not the other way around. Therefore, term reuse mappings are unidirectional. Similarly, extracted mappings can be considered symmetric or not depending on their semantics; but in this study, those mappings are being explicitly declared in one ontology source file and not necessarily in the other, we thus consider them unidirectional.

3.1 Term Reuse Mappings Harvesting

We define term reuse as the situation in which an URI from one ontology is explicitly reused inside another ontology. This situation occurs when the developers of semantic resources decide to rely on knowledge described in other resources. It increases the reusability between ontologies and reduces development time and the proliferation of equivalent terms. A developer can either decide to reuse specific terms one by one by simply identifying them with their URIs in a statement or by (re)declaring them locally using the original URI. Or he/she can import all the objects and statements of an ontology (or ontology module) into another one. The later is only possible with OWL ontologies using the construct `owl:imports`. Ontology developers typically use this construct to import ontology modules. Among 88 OWL ontologies, we found 15 of them that use `owl:imports`. For instance, the Food Ontology (FOODON) imports some modules from ENVO or ChEBI. The imported modules may themselves contain any kind of mappings like term overlap, term reuse and extracted mappings. Therefore, we include the set of imported mappings in our mappings dataset.

We obtain term reuse mappings from AgroPortal's REST API.[5] AgroPortal creates mappings between any two classes or concepts explicitly declared or

---

[4] See https://github.com/agroportal/documentation/wiki/Mappings for details.
[5] E.g., the following call returns all the mappings between the Agronomy and Plant Ontology: http://data.agroportal.lirmm.fr/mappings?ontologies=AGRO,PO.

imported from one ontology to another using the same URI. Those "same URI mappings" are not materialized in the repository but generated on-the-fly. Several ontologies (especially in the OBO community) reuse multiple terms from one another, thus, from all these "same URI mappings", we keep only the ones corresponding to direct reuses from one ontology to the other. For example, AGRO's term "life of whole plant stage" originally defined in the Plant Ontology (PO:0025337) is same URI-mapped in AgroPortal to any other ontology using this term (e.g., PO, FLOPO, ENVO), however, we only retain as a term reuse the AGRO-PO, FLOPO-PO, ENVO-PO mappings. In addition, when an ontology reuses a term from another ontology, not in our corpus, we ignore this reuse. From our corpus of ontologies, we harvested a total of 16,958 term reuse mappings (over a total of more than 53,000 "same URI mappings").

3.2   Term Overlap Mappings Harvesting

We define term overlap as the situation in which two terms use the same labels or synonyms in different semantic resources. LOOM is an automatic ontology matching system [5] implemented in the OntoPortal technology thus –available in AgroPortal– to generate lexical matches between all the semantic resources independently of their original formats. To identify the correspondences, LOOM compares preferred names and synonyms of the terms in source and target ontologies and create a match, if and only if their labels are equal based on a modified-string comparison function. The tool first removes all delimiters from both strings (e.g., spaces, underscores, parentheses, etc.) and the accents. Then it uses an approximate matching technique to compare the strings, allowing for a mismatch of at most one character in strings with length greater than four and no mismatches for shorter strings.

We also obtain term overlap mappings from AgroPortal's REST API. Those "LOOM mappings" are also not materialized in the repository but generated on-the-fly. In AgroPortal, term overlaps are identified for any terms, being it reused from another ontology or not. Thus, from all these "LOOM mappings", we remove the ones corresponding to direct reuses from one ontology to the other. For example, AGRO's term "life of whole plant stage" originally defined in the Plant Ontology (PO:0025337) is Loom-mapped in AgroPortal to any other ontology using the same label (e.g., PO, FLOPO, ENVO), however, we only retain as a term overlap the AGRO-FLOPO, AGRO-ENVO and FLOPO-ENVO mappings. From our corpus of ontologies, we harvested a total of 246,348 term overlap mappings. Due to the large size of the harvested tern overlap mappings, we did not curate these mappings.

3.3   Extracted Mappings Harvesting

We mean by extracted mapping the ones explicitly declared inside the ontology source files and extracted to be to reified into a first-class objects with provenance information in a mapping repository or in our case included in our dataset. Extracted mappings are very valuable as they are usually manually created or curated by the ontology developers and because they are semantically well described with an explicit mapping property. Therefore, there is an obvious need to make these mappings available to the community in a repository, avoiding external users the burden of extracting them ontology per ontology.

We have extracted the declared mappings from the source files using OMHT[6], developed as a standalone Java program that works with one ontology source file pulled out from an ontology repository. The standard properties used by OMHT to identify declared mappings inside a source file are the following: `owl:sameAs`, `oboInOwl:hasDbXref`, SKOS mapping properties and optionally `rdfs:seeAlso`. OMHT processes semantic resources in XML/RDF syntax an relies on the ontology repository to deal with different representation languages. OMHT takes as input a set of AgroPortal ontology acronyms and returns a JSON file for each input ontology that stores extracted mappings along with their metadata. Sometime, the target ontology and term are not explicit (especially with OBO XRefs which do not use URIs) therefore, OMHT relies on a manually curated file to resolve ambiguous targets.

In the dataset, we have removed extracted mappings for which source and target ontology are the same e.g., AFO contains 421 `oboInOwl:hasDbXRef` mappings to concepts in the same ontology; similarly, PO contains 40 internal XRefs. Surprisingly, this situation happens quite often: we have found a total of 2,230 such internal mappings all of them using the `oboInOwl:hasDbXef` property. The use of `oboInOwl:hasDbXRef` for representing ontology mappings is controversial as this property is used in the OBO community to capture several pieces of information including mappings between ontologies e.g., cross-references to database or database entries, curators of terms, references to publications, etc. In this study, we have carefully curated only the XRefs that correspond to ontology mappings (11% of them) to build our corpus as explained in another publication [13]. For instance, we have excluded XRefs to URLs or databases. Finally, we distinguish internal, inter-portal, and external mappings respectively if the target ontology is in AgroPortal, another repository of the OntoPortal family or simply identified by its URI.

3.4   Final Mapping Dataset

The total number of mappings of this dataset is 444,496 as described by Fig. 1 (left). Term reuse and term overlap mappings represent (59,2%) of the total number of mappings, whereas explicit usage of mapping properties inside the ontology source files represent 40,8%.[7] Fig. 1 (right) represents the overlap between the three mappings constructs. This diagram shows also the number of unique mappings for each mapping construct. We found two sets of 1,278 and 49,563 of overlapping mappings, which represent 11,43% of the dataset. The first intersection is an uncommon and odd situation where ontology developers have declared

---

[6] https://github.com/agroportal/ontology_mapping_harvester.
[7] Our mapping dataset is publicly available at https://bit.ly/3gFJ2DD.

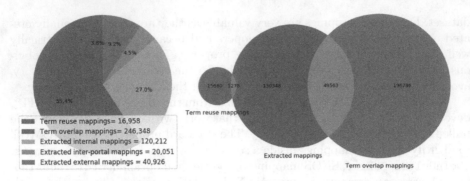

Fig. 1. Number of mappings (left). Venn diagram of the mapping dataset (right). (Color figure online)

an explicit mapping to a class being explicitly reused. The second intersection is more interesting: it shows how much the number of lexical match in our corpus are explicitly identified as declared mappings by ontology developers. One would like to see this intersection grows.

4   Mapping Dataset Analysis

Our goal in this study is to investigate the occurrence of patterns from the collected mappings. Therefore, we have built several mapping graphs that represent semantic resources and their alignments (i.e., set of mappings) respectively as nodes and edges. We can visualize these graphs based on the percentage of alignment, as described hereafter and provide an individual and a combined visualization for each mapping construct. Thus, we can identify hubs and clusters of semantic resources in our dataset. We expect such visualization will help ontology developers to better understand the ontology landscape in their domain of interest and possibly improve their semantic resources.

Similar to Ghazvinian et al. [7] percent-normalized link, we compute the percentage of mappings $\mathcal{P}$ by dividing the number of mappings $\mathcal{M}$ between a pair of ontologies $\mathcal{O}_s$ and $\mathcal{O}_t$ by the total number of concepts $|\mathcal{V}_s|$ of the source ontology based on the following formula: $\mathcal{P} = |\mathcal{M}(\mathcal{O}_s, \mathcal{O}_t)| \, / \, |\mathcal{V}_s|$. For instance, if an ontology $\mathcal{O}_1$ has 1000 terms, and 500 of these terms are mapped to terms in an ontology $\mathcal{O}_2$, then $\mathcal{P}(\mathcal{O}_1 \, \mathcal{O}_2) = 50\%$. If one ontology is much larger than another, a large fraction of the small ontology may be mapped to the large one, but the set of mappings still constitutes a small percentage of the large ontology. This formula helps to investigate the level of mappings compared to the size of source ontologies.

4.1   Term Reuse Analysis

Out of a total number of 3,725,495 declared classes or concepts in our corpus, we found 16,958 term reuse mappings, with an average percentage $\mathcal{P}$ of 18,28%

between pairs of semantic resources where at least one URI was explicitly shared between at least a pair of semantic resources. Out of 109 AgroPortal resources, 39 do not reuse any term from another ontology in the corpus which means that 70 does; but the number of distinct pairs of semantic resources is 174, which is quite low. The percentage of reuse is mostly under 5%, however, we found 42 pairs of ontologies with a term reuse above 10% and 8 pairs exhibit term reuse between 95% and 100% which illustrates a situation where an ontology almost completely reuse another one.

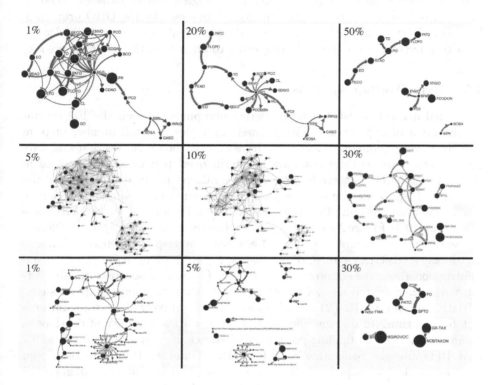

Fig. 2. The three mappings construct with different values of $\mathcal{P}$, arrows read as "is mapped to". Thickness of nodes and edges are respectively proportional to the sizes of the semantic resources and the percentage of mappings between them. Row 1: term reuse; Row 2: term overlap; Row 3: extracted mappings.

Figure 2's raw 1 represents the term reuse graphs at different percentages. In other words, we display an arrow between a pair of semantic resources, if at least P% of the source is reused in the target e.g., terms from BFO are being reused within ENVO. We can conclude from Fig. 2: (**1**) In the family of ontologies relying on the Basic Formal Ontology (BFO) upper level ontology –a total of 17 in our corpus– we distinguish important differences in the degree of reuses: from 2,77% (for CDAO) to 97,77% (for FOODON). (**2**) Some ontologies within the same area or build by the same group highly reuse one another e.g., the Plant Ontology (PO), Plant Trait Ontology (TO), Plant Experimental Conditions Ontology (PECO) and Plant Environment Ontology (EO) all developed in the Planteome project form a cluster. (**3**) Some ontologies are mostly built from reuse e.g., PECO reuses all the URIs of EO. (**4**) We can visualize different clusters often built around reference upper level ontologies (BFO) or reference standards (SSN or PO). Different values of $\mathcal{P}$ lead to different clusters. For instance, at $\mathcal{P} = 20\%$, we can distinguish a cluster around the SSN ontology being reused by a number of ontologies such as CASO and SOSA. (**5**) We only find term reuses in OBO and OWL ontologies. These ontologies tend to reuse URIs from each other as encouraged for instance by the OBO principles. However SKOS vocabularies or reference thesauri tend to systematically declare their own URIs and use mapping properties to align with the other ontologies.

4.2 Term Overlap Analysis

We found a total of 246,348 term overlap mappings between the 109 semantic resources of our corpus. With related ontologies, a small number of term overlap is very common: 6,204 pairs have at least one term overlap and only 12 semantic resources did not have any term overlap with any other ones in the corpus. Therefore, there is good lexical similarity in our dataset, even if the majority of the pairs contains less than 5% of term overlap with an average of 2.05%. We found 98 pair of semantic resources having a term overlap percentage more than 10%. Figure 2's raw 2 represents the term overlap graphs at different percentages. For example, there is 51 806 term overlap between the Gramene Taxonomy (GR-TAX) and NCBI Taxonomy. Figure 2 reveals other practices and information about the ontologies in our corpus: (**1**) Some resources strongly overlap with other related ones, without explicitly using mappings properties e.g., TRIPHASE and ATOL. (**2**) Some resources are definitely about the same area but have nothing to do one another with respect to community of developers, common practices, or funding project. For instance, we can visualize at $\mathcal{P} = 20\%$ that BFO and the Semanticscience Integrated Ontology (SIO) are two upper level ontologies developed for different purposes and by different communities but unsurprisingly contains a certain level of overlap. The same observation can be made for the Biological Collections Ontology (BCO) and the Darwin Core vocabulary (DSW) which are two resources developed to facilitate biodiversity data interoperability. (**3**) Term overlap allow us to discover cases where a thesaurus relies on an upper level ontology but without explicitly reusing its objects. For instance, the ANAEE Thesaurus's design is inspired from OBOE but the thesaurus being exclusively developed in SKOS cannot explicitly relies on OBOE developed in OWL. We observe 38% term overlap between them. (**4**) At $\mathcal{P} = 30\%$, we visualize several clusters e.g., between FLOPO, TO and PEAO. This cluster is visible for both term overlap and term reuse but through the PO hub in the case of term reuse. Despite these strong connections, we will see after, that we do not find any usage of mapping properties between these ontologies.

4.3   Extracted Mappings Analysis

Out of 109 semantic resources, we found 81 (74,31%) do not declare any mappings. From the 28 other resources, we have extracted 181,189 mappings from source files and found 174 pairs. Figure 1 (left) shows the majority of extracted mappings are internal i.e., between AgroPortal resources, which tends to corroborate the thematic coherence of the repository. 11% of these mappings pointing to target semantic resources in the NCBO BioPortal reveals the thematic proximity with biology and life sciences (e.g., environment, nutrition). Among the important targets in the NCBO BioPortal are the Foundational Model of Anatomy (FMA) with 3,431 mappings or the ChEBI ontology with 745 mappings from 11 ontologies. External mappings target semantic resources that are not yet hosted in an ontology repository which denotes: (i) the willingness of ontology developers to map to semantic resources beyond the original domain captured within an ontology – this is a good practice for linked open data; (ii) integration of semantic resources in domain-specific repositories is not over. Among the most important external targets, we can cite 20,699 mappings from AGROVOC to the Chinese Agricultural Thesaurus (CAT) not yet integrated in AgroPortal.

Figure 2's raw 3 reveals practices and information about extracted mappings in our corpus: (1) Every important reference thesaurus in AgroPortal (AGROVOC, ANNAETHES, NALT, GEMET) is strictly aligned to other ones in the domain, which seems to be a better practice than for ontologies in the wild. (2) Some semantic resources lexically very close (term overlap) are also formally aligned, like the case of GR-TAX being aligned to NCBITAXON. Indeed, when designed GR-TAX employed a lot of terms from NCBITAXON but the developers have decided to create new URIs and declared mappings between them. (3) At different levels of $\mathcal{P}$, we visualize some clusters different from the ones observed before e.g., around PO, a cluster is formed with different ontologies such as the TOP thesaurus which is developed by a different project. (4) We can observe a surprisingly low count of `owl:sameAs` in our dataset (3,255/181,189). Whereas this property was originally proposed explicitly for mappings, its strong logic entailment results in ontology developers not using it at the benefit of SKOS properties that do not have any logical entailment.

4.4   Combined Mappings Visualization and Analysis

Using an interactive visualization, we can see links between semantic resources for any mapping constructs and identify prominent hubs and clusters with variation of $\mathcal{P}$. It is available online with the ObservableHQ Web application: https://observablehq.com/@amirlad?tab=collections. Interested users can visualize each mapping construct individually and combined and dynamically change the percentage threshold. We believe, such visualization could be useful to ontology developers to select semantic resources for reuse or alignment.

Figure 3 (right) shows two hubs identified in our dataset: (i) PO, with mappings from and to 10 semantic resources; (ii) BFO, with terms being reused by many ontologies. Based on the combined visualization in Fig. 3 (left), we can also visualize other prominent hubs. NCBITAXON, with a set of 59,186 mappings coming from 6 other semantic resources (PECO, TO, CL, FOODON, GR-TAX, EO) counts for 47% of the total number of internal mappings in the dataset. Figure 3 (left) depicts a combined graph at different values of $\mathcal{P}$ for each mapping construct. In this graph, we easily visualize several clusters and how they involve different constructs. For instance, we can visualize a 5-resource cluster (SSN, SOSA, CASO, IRRIG, SAREF) in which a mix of term reuse and term overlap mappings interconnect the ontologies but no explicit declared mappings. We can also visualize a cluster of ontologies around AGROVOC.

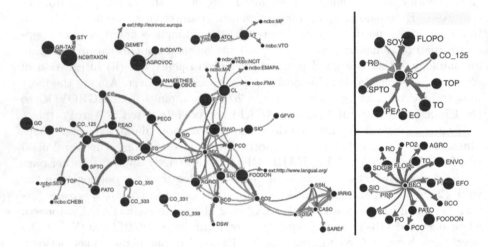

Fig. 3. (left) Combined graph of the three mapping constructs with $\mathcal{P}=$ 20% for term reuse, $\mathcal{P}=$ 35% for term overlap and $\mathcal{P}=$ 10% for extracted mappings. (right) Plant Ontology and Basic Formal Ontology hubs for all constructs at $\mathcal{P}=15\%$.

5   Discussion

Observations Specific to Ontologies in the OBO Foundry. For the 22 OBO Foundry ontologies in our corpus, there are 13,340 term reuses, 45,907 term overlaps mappings, and 2,799 extracted mappings. We found an average term reuse percentage of 15,06% between 73 pairs of OBO Foundry ontologies. Indeed, favoring term reuse is one principle of the OBO Foundry community. We found an average term overlap percentage of 4,92% between 345 pairs of OBO Foundry ontologies. In complement, we find an average percentage of extracted mappings of 1,73% between 48 pairs of OBO Foundry ontologies. Only two pairs of ontologies exhibit a percentage over 10%: EO-PO and EO-NCBITAXON with respectively a percentage of 15,65% and 21,53%.

Observations Specific to the Crop Ontology Project. The Crop Ontology project [14] counts 22 ontologies in our corpus. We did not find any term reuse or extracted mappings between them. However, these ontologies often rely on a set of terms, especially for upper-level entities, described in a namespace that corresponds to no ontology e.g., http://www.cropontology.org/rdf/Measurement. With the mapping visualization, at different levels of $\mathcal{P}$, we can observe a term overlap cluster made by several of the ontologies in the Crop Ontology projects. These ontologies define similar traits of different crops, so it is normal they display a strong overlap. We found a total of 31,368 term overlap mappings between 640 pairs with an average percentage of 3,85%. The term overlap percentage for the crop ontologies is slightly higher than the term overlap percentage in the corpus. However, the crop ontologies are not well reused or mapped by other ontologies in AgroPortal.

Observations Specific to SKOS Thesauri. Over 10 SKOS thesauri in our corpus, we did not find any term reuse mappings. We found 1,792 term overlap mappings and 41,932 of extracted mappings which tend to say the thesauri do not strongly overlap, even if they are well aligned with one another. There is an average percentage of 1.05% of term overlap between 52 pairs of the 10 SKOS thesauri of AgroPortal. We only found the use of mapping properties between 8 pairs with an average percentage of 10,35%. Reference thesauri developed by large organizations (e.g., FAO, USDA) do not reuse URIs from other semantic resources even if they overlap. But, they tend to declare explicit mappings using the SKOS mappings property more than the rest of the semantic resources in the corpus. For instance, AGROVOC, which is a controlled vocabulary covering all areas of interest of the Food and Agriculture Organization, do not reuse any terms from other semantic resources; however, it is explicitly aligned to GEMET and NALT. Thesauri tend to develop their URIs rather than reusing other URIs then aligning the copied terms to the original thesaurus. Unlike OBO Foundry ontologies, there is a lack of collaborative effort to develop SKOS thesauri that employ the same terms. But, when mappings are explicitly declared, they are well encoded and fully reusable as not in the XRefs, which are semantically ambiguous and need to be curated.

To the best of our knowledge, there is no other analysis of mappings in the domain covered by AgroPortal. However, in the following, we compare our results to the three most relevant mapping analysis studies identified in the related work.

Analogy with Ghazvinian et al. 2009 [7]. They analyzed a set of 4 million term overlap mappings for 207 biomedical ontologies stored in BioPortal and UMLS. Their dataset contained more than 4 million concepts. Here, we studied term reuse mappings, term overlap mappings, and extracted mappings from 3,735,344 concepts of 109 ontologies stored in AgroPortal. The total number of mappings is 444,496 with 246,348 term overlap mappings. We can deduce there is less term overlap in agri-food ontologies than biomedical ontologies. Indeed, Ghazvinian et al. reported that biomedical ontologies are very closely connected, with 33% of them having at least half of their concepts mapped to concepts in other ontologies. Whereas, in our dataset only 20 ontologies (18,34%) have at least 50% of their terms mapped to terms in some other ontologies. Therefore, there is less term overlap in our agronomy and biodiversity dataset than in the biomedicine dataset. Ghazvinian et al. stated that in biomedicine there is a little bit of overlap in everything, resulting in the extremely connected graph at $\mathcal{P} = 1\%$. At $\mathcal{P} = 20\%$, however, they report a meaningful power-law distribution. In our corpus, we visualize a similar observation for the term overlap mappings construct. With 2268 ontology pairs at $\mathcal{P} = 1\%$ and 132 ontology pairs at $\mathcal{P} = 20\%$. However, for term reuse mappings and extracted mappings, the power-law distribution is lower than for term overlap mappings. For term reuse mappings, we found 61 ontology pairs at $\mathcal{P} = 1\%$ and18 ontology pairs at $\mathcal{P} = 20\%$. Dealing with extracted mappings, we found 68 ontology pairs at $\mathcal{P} = 1\%$, and 18 at $\mathcal{P} = 20\%$. Ghazvinian et al. visualized only term overlap mappings, however in our case, we can generate a combined visualization of the three mapping constructs. They stated term overlap mappings can be employed to identify prominent ontologies in a domain. This is true in our study too plus, the combination of the mapping constructs helps to have a better overview of the existing prominent ontologies.

Analogy with Poveda et al. 2012 [18]. They reported a percentage of 40% of term reuse in 196 semantic resources in the Linked Open Vocabularies (LOV) registry, which do not contain agri-food or biodiversity-ecology semantic resources. This percentage is higher than the average percentage (18,28%) of term reuse in AgroPortal ontologies.

Analogy with Kamdar et al. 2015 and 2017 [11,12]. They first reported an average percentage of term overlap of 14.4% across 377 biomedical ontologies then in 2017, they reported a higher term overlap percentage (22.23%). For 109 AgroPortal ontologies, we found an average term overlap percentage of 2.05%, which is much lower than reported for BioPortal. This is mostly due to the method used to find lexical similarity. With a lower threshold and with the removal of stopwords, Kamdar et al.'s method keeps more term overlap mappings than LOOM (higher recall). However, our method can result in a better precision, even if we acknowledge it has certain limitation: lexically-similar labels in different ontologies may represent totally different concepts. Kamdar et al. considered XRefs as term reuse mappings, however, they do not consider other mapping properties. In our study, we extracted mappings with all the mapping properties available in the ontologies (including XRefs) and kept for term reuse only entities using the same URIs. This approach allows us to derive better insights from our dataset. Similarly to Kamdar et al., we found that most ontologies reuse less than 5% of their terms. This is contrary to the orthogonality principle encouraged in ontology engineering [1].

6   Conclusions and Perspective

We have built and analyzed a dataset of three mapping constructs based on a corpus of 109 semantic resources from AgroPortal. We have gathered more than 400,000 mappings either generated from AgroPortal or contained in the ontology source files. Our finding shows that most ontologies overlap with, reuse, or map less than 5% of their terms to other ontologies. Some communities have adopted certain good practices that it would be valuable to share with others. For instance, term reuse is more common in ontologies from the OBO Foundry, however the way these ontologies encode declared mappings is bad. On the other hand, term reuse is nonexistent in reference to SKOS thesauri, however these thesauri have a clear and consistent use of SKOS mapping properties for their declared mappings.

Despite the recent promotion of the FAIR data principles [21], which apply to semantic resources as any other data, some efforts are still necessary to interconnect them. Overall, ontology developers sometimes copy terms from other semantic resources or define terms without checking reusable ontologies–which result in term overlap– or without explicitly reusing them or explicitly mapping them to the source ontology. Coming back to Fig. 1 (right), a better situation would be to have a blue circle (term reuse) as big as possible, which would consequently decrease the size of the orange circle (extracted mappings) in which most of the green circle would be included (term overlap) making the yellow intersection (overlap with explicitly declared mappings) much of it.

The main contribution of our paper is the analysis and the visualization of these three mapping constructs which we hope will serve ontology developers to improve their practices and build semantic resources that will be as much as possible interoperable, reusable, and reused. This analysis can lead to relevant insights on the characteristics of the mappings repository. Since the use of ontologies, thesauri, and taxonomies expands, this visualization and its analysis can play an important role in understanding the relationships between semantic resources, and to identify clusters and hubs. We hope that these findings will be used to develop better guidelines, enhance term reuse and the use of mappings properties, and minimize term overlap.

The number of ontologies in AgroPortal increase and they are constantly updated. As future work, we plan to automate the analysis and visualization of term reuse, term overlap, and extracted mappings directly in AgroPortal. So that the subsequent version of the dataset used in this study could be automatically produced and exported from AgroPortal. We also plan to include an analysis and visualization of mappings for each ontology in the repository, which means that a developer will have an analysis, specific to his/her ontology. We are currently working on a new ontology alignment framework inside AgroPortal. This framework will contain a revised version of the ontology repository which shall generate term overlap mappings, identify term reuse mappings, extract declared mappings and also use external automatic matching systems to generate new mappings. Then each source of mappings will be merged into a unique alignment where each merged mappings will be scored and described with provenance.

Acknowledgements. This work was achieved with support of the AGRO Labex (ANR-10-LABX-0001), the NUMEV Labex (ANR-10-LABX-20) and the Data to Knowledge in Agronomy and Biodiversity (D2KAB – www.d2kab.org) project that received funding from the French National Research Agency (ANR-18-CE23-0017).

References

1. Ghazvinian, A., Noy, F.N., Musen, M.A.: How orthogonal are the OBO Foundry ontologies? J. Biomed. Semant. **2**(2), S2 (2011). https://doi.org/10.1186/2041-1480-2-S2-S2
2. Annane, A., Bellahsene, Z., Azouaou, F., Jonquet, C.: Building an effective and efficient background knowledge resource to enhance ontology matching. Web Semant. **51**, 51–68 (2018)
3. Euzenat, J., Shvaiko, P.: Ontology Matching. Springer, Heidelberg (2013). https://doi.org/10.1007/978-3-642-38721-0
4. Faria, D., Jiménez-Ruiz, E., Pesquita, C., Santos, E., Couto, F.M.: Towards annotating potential incoherences in bioportal mappings. In: Mika, P., et al. (eds.) ISWC 2014. LNCS, vol. 8797, pp. 17–32. Springer, Cham (2014). https://doi.org/10.1007/978-3-319-11915-1_2
5. Ghazvinian, A., Noy, N.F., Musen, M.A.: Creating mappings for ontologies in biomedicine: simple methods work. In: American Medical Informatics Association Annual Symposium, AMIA'09, Washington, USA, pp. 198–202 (2009)
6. Ghazvinian, A., Noy, N.F., Musen, M.A.: From mappings to modules: using mappings to identify domain-specific modules in large ontologies. In: 6th International Conference on Knowledge Capture, K-CAP'11, Banff, Canada, pp. 33–40 (2011)
7. Ghazvinian, A., Noy, N.F., Jonquet, C., Shah, N., Musen, M.A.: What four million mappings can tell you about two hundred ontologies. In: Bernstein, A., et al. (eds.) ISWC 2009. LNCS, vol. 5823, pp. 229–242. Springer, Heidelberg (2009). https://doi.org/10.1007/978-3-642-04930-9_15
8. Jonquet, C.: Ontology repository and ontology-based services – challenges, contributions and applications to biomedicine & agronomy. HDR Manuscript,University of Montpellier, Montpellier, France (2019)
9. Jonquet, C., et al.: AgroPortal: a vocabulary and ontology repository for agronomy. Computers and Electronics in Agriculture, pp. 126–143 (2018)
10. Jupp, S., Liener, T., Sarntivijai, S., Vrousgou, O., Burdett, T., Parkinson, H.: OxO a gravy of ontology mapping extracts. In: 8th International Conference on Biomedical Ontology, ICBO'17, Newcastle, UK, **2137**, p. 2 (2017)
11. Kamdar, M.R., Tudorache, T., Musen, M.A.: Investigating term reuse and overlap in biomedical ontologies. In: 6th International Conference on Biomedical Ontology, ICBO'15 (2015)
12. Kamdar, M.R., Tudorache, T., Musen, M.A.: A systematic analysis of term reuse and term overlap across biomedical ontologies. Semant. web **8**(6), 853–871 (2017)
13. Laadhar, A., Abrahao, E., Jonquet, C.: Investigating one million XRefs in thirthy ontologies from the OBO world. In: 11th International Conference on Biomedical Ontologies, ICBO'20. Bozen-Bolzano, Italy (2020)
14. Matteis, L., et al.: Crop ontology: vocabulary for crop-related concepts. In: 1st International Work. on Semantics for Biodiversity, Montpellier, France, pp. 37–46 (2013)
15. Ngo, D.H., Bellahsene, Z.: YAM++ : a multi-strategy based approach for ontology matching task. In: Teije, A., et al. (eds.) EKAW 2012. LNCS (LNAI), vol. 7603, pp. 421–425. Springer, Heidelberg (2012). https://doi.org/10.1007/978-3-642-33876-2_38
16. Noy, N.F., et al.: BioPortal: ontologies and integrated data resources at the click of a mouse. Nucleic Acids Res. **37**(ws), 170–173 (2009)

17. Pathak, J., Chute, C.G.: Debugging mappings between biomedical ontologies: preliminary results from the NCBO bioportal mapping repository. In: International Conference on Biomedical Ontology, Buffalo, USA, pp. 95–98 (2009)
18. Poveda Villalón, M., Suárez-Figueroa, M.C., Gómez-Pérez, A.: The landscape of ontology reuse in linked data. Ontology Engineering in a Data-driven World, OEDW'12 (2012)
19. Till, M., Kutz, O., Codescu, M.: Ontohub: a semantic repository for heterogeneous ontologies. In: Theory Day in Computer Science, DACS'14, Bucharest, Romania, p. 2 (2014)
20. Vandenbussche, P.Y., Atemezing, G.A., Poveda-Villalón, M., Vatant, B.: Linked Open Vocabularies (LOV): a gateway to reusable semantic vocabularies on the Web. Semant. Web 8(3), 437–452 (2014)
21. Wilkinson, M.D., et al.: The FAIR guiding principles for scientific data management and stewardship. Sci. Data 3(1), 1–9 (2016)

Ontologies Supporting Research-Related Information Foraging Using Knowledge Graphs: Literature Survey and Holistic Model Mapping

Viet Bach Nguyen[1]([✉]) [iD], Vojtěch Svátek[1] [iD], Gollam Rabby[1] [iD],
and Oscar Corcho[2] [iD]

[1] University of Economics, Prague, Czech Republic
{nguv03,svatek,rabg00}@vse.cz
[2] Ontology Engineering Group, Universidad Politécnica de Madrid, Madrid, Spain
ocorcho@fi.upm.es

Abstract. We carried out a literature survey on ontologies dealing with the scholarly and research domains, with a focus on modeling the knowledge graphs that would support information foraging by researchers within the different roles they fulfill during their career. We identified 43 relevant ontologies, of which 35 were found sufficiently documented to be reusable. At the same time, based on the analysis of extensive CVs and activity logs of two senior researchers, we formulated a structured set of competency questions that could be answered through information foraging on the web, and created a high-level conceptual model indicating the data structures that would provide answers to these questions via a holistic knowledge graph. We then studied the retrieved ontologies and mapped them on the entities and relationships from our conceptual model. We identified many overlaps between the ontologies, as well as a few missing features. Preliminary proposals for dealing with some of the overlaps and gaps were formulated.

Keywords: Scholarly ontology · Literature survey · Competency questions · Knowledge graph · Information foraging

1 Introduction

On a daily basis, researchers find themselves in situations where they need to acquire information from resources on the Web. The nature of such information needs differs based on the specific academic role of the researcher at the given moment, such as that of a paper writer, event organizer, scientific evaluator, advisor of other researchers, or project coordinator. Yet, many of these information needs revolve around a small set of generic entity types and their relationships on which information is sought, such as people, institutions, publications, scientific venues, projects, topics, problems, arguments, or research artifacts.

© Springer Nature Switzerland AG 2020
C. M. Keet and M. Dumontier (Eds.): EKAW 2020, LNAI 12387, pp. 88–103, 2020.
https://doi.org/10.1007/978-3-030-61244-3_6

This common basis is relatively generic across research fields and makes it possible to proceed from textual search to the exploitation of structured databases on the web. Further, the rise of RDF-based knowledge graphs (KGs) may help overcome the rigidity of traditional database schemas; information from independent resources could nowadays be integrated and searched with less overhead. Yet, academic KGs spanning over many different entity types are still scarce; most published RDF datasets are only restricted to a few of these entity types, e.g., publications and their authors, paper citations, or projects and the institutions involved. Researchers who look for research-related information thus still have to either deal with multiple databases or delve into unstructured textual search. In any case, the process can be characterized as *information foraging*, the term having been originally coined in the narrower context of following web hyperlinks [6]. Namely, given the limited amount of time the researchers can devote to the search (this not being the prime activity they are paid for), they have to follow often unreliable 'information scent', and sometimes even to sacrifice a valid 'prey' as the 'energy cost' of locating it would be too high.

Holistic academic KGs could ease research information foraging both by making the 'information scent' more reliable (leveraging on integrated ontological underpinning) and by reducing the 'energy cost' associated to switching between different web database environments and keyword search. However, a prerequisite of the development of such KGs is a solid understanding of the currently available 'eco-system' of reusable, well documented ontologies that could underlie these KGs, including the awareness of the overlaps and gaps in this system. While the existence of overlaps implies the need of some decision support in the choice among the overlapping ontologies, the gaps, in turn, ask for the development of new ontologies.

Many papers published in the last two decades contained some surveys of existing scholarly ontologies, whether standalone or in comparison with a newly introduced model. We are however unaware of either a survey or a comprehensive ontology aiming to cover the concepts referenced by the *daily activities* of an (especially, senior) researcher. For such activities, a researcher takes on multiple 'hats' (roles), including such that directly relate to research–for example, not just to undergraduate education or to the general course of a working contract valid for any position and organization. Most previous papers and models restrict the analyzed activities to 'doing research' proper (methods, experiments, tools, etc.) and/or to attributes of research publications. This is the case, e.g., for the previous standalone survey by Ruiz & Corcho [25], focused on modeling scientific documents. Similarly, the recent requirements analysis for an Open Research KG by Brack et al. [4] is confined to the 'literature-oriented' tasks of scientists. Even the Scholarly Ontology [23], which comprehensively covers 'scholarly practices' (using thorough modeling with the help of foundational ontologies) including entities such as projects, courses, or information resources, focuses on a use case related to scientific activities tied to experiments and paper writing.

In this paper we aim not only at updating the previous scholarly/research ontology surveys by covering some newly developed models, but, in particular, at aligning them with a systematic analysis of information needs triggered by *different research-related roles* played by researchers. The information needs are expressed using *high-level competency questions*, giving rise to entity type paths from which a *holistic conceptual graph* was eventually built. Entities and relationships from the graph were approximately (manually, in a lightweight manner) *matched* with those of the surveyed ontologies, thus providing insights into what is covered and what is not, as well as where the overlaps are the strongest. The full coverage table of 73 model concepts and 35 ontologies can be found in our research repository on GitHub[1], where we also include the set of competency questions and all other relevant resources. By opting for a semi-informal model (instead of a new formal ontology) we wanted to avoid pre-mature optimization and aspiration to a 'new standard ontology', that would certainly suffer from arguable commitments. We deemed the chosen kind of conceptual model adequate as a step directly associated with the literature survey undertaken.

The main content of this paper is structured in the following way. Section 2 describes the process of literature search through which the relevant ontologies were identified and selected. Section 3 explains how the competency questions were formulated and the corresponding high-level model constructed. Section 4 presents the alignment between the model and the surveyed ontologies. Last, section 5 wraps up and outlines the directions for future research.

2   Literature Survey Methodology and Results

The first step of our survey was to obtain a list of candidate ontologies that could potentially include entities related to researcher information needs and its context. Given the fact that most ontologies and relevant projects are reported in papers, a major source to be searched were high-coverage bibliographic/citation databases, of which we considered *Scopus,*[2] *Web of Science*[3] and *Google Scholar.*[4] Additionally, we also directly asked the generic *Google search engine*, to also cater for ontologies not accompanied with a paper for some reason. The different resources are complementary. While the (top) Google/Scholar search should lead to popular resources with many inlinks/citations, the traditional bibliographic databases primarily return respectful academic publications (even those with a lower citation response) and can be searched using more sophisticated means, thus reducing the amount of noise for the subsequent manual scan of results. While there are, obviously, a number of other possible databases to consider (such as DBLP, or the IEEE/ACM libraries), we assumed that sufficient coverage can already be obtained via the four we chose. Finally, for directly retrieving ontologies, an obvious choice was the *Linked Open Vocabularies* (LOV) portal.[5]

Using Google as the initial baseline, we searched for the most obvious phrases only, to keep the precision acceptable: *scholar/ly ontology, academic ontology, research/er ontology,* and *bibliography/ic ontology*. For each Google query, we

---

[1] https://github.com/nvbach91/iga-knerd.
[2] https://www.scopus.com/.
[3] https://webofknowledge.com.
[4] https://scholar.google.com/.
[5] https://lov.linkeddata.es/.

examined the first 10 pages of results, which consisted in a mix of publications, projects, and actual ontology documentations. Overall we identified, this way, a total of 9 relevant ontologies.

We then used the Google Scholar search engine with the same search terms. Google Scholar returned, in all cases, publications, from which we collected 5 further relevant ontologies.

Next, we used the Scopus bibliographic database. The advantage of searching in a specialized database was the higher degree of relevance. To make a better use of the search tools provided by Scopus, we used our search terms to search for papers by titles and keywords, while limiting the scope to the Computer Science and Engineering fields. The following snippet represents our Scopus search query, which we used for searching in the title; analogous queries were applied on the abstract and keywords:

```
TITLE ((academic OR scholarly OR researcher OR bibliography)
    AND  ontology) AND (SUBJAREA("COMP") OR  SUBJAREA("ENGI"))
```

The search in the titles (TITLE) yielded 57 results, the search in abstracts (ABS) yielded 2829 results, and the search in keywords (KEY) yielded 279 results, all sorted by relevance. In the case of abstract-related results, we browsed the first 10 pages (approx. 100 results). Among these results, we found a total of 22 additional ontologies.

Our last bibliographic database of choice was the Web of Science. First, we searched for each term one by one. The term *scholarly ontology* yielded 32 results, the term *academic ontology* yielded 87 results, the term *researcher ontology* yielded 182 results (all with the refinement to the 'article' document type and to the 'computer science and information systems' category). Next, we used a query equivalent to the one used on Scopus, for searching in the title (and, analogously, in the topic) as follows:

```
TI = ((academic OR scholarly OR researcher OR bibliography)
    AND ontology) AND SU = (Computer Science OR Engineering)
```

This query returned 22 results for the title filter (TI) and 423 results for the topic (TS) filter. Among these results, we found 2 additional ontologies.

Aside the keyword-based search, we also benefited from the availability of *citation links* in Google Scholar, Scopus and Web of Science. We followed some promising incoming citation links to the papers on ontologies found so far. Using this technique, we identified 3 further ontologies.

For each ontology found through a paper reporting on it, we as much information as possible, including its metadata, source code and full texts of the referencing papers (when available).

Last, we directly searched for ontologies on the LOV portal. We found a considerable amount of relevant resources using the keywords *research, academic, scholar* and *bibliography*, of which most had already been covered by the previous bibliographic database or Google results. However, two new relevant ontologies were still found this way.

We then used the LOV results as a referencing resource to find related literature that described them (and possibly escaped the previous literature search), projects that used them, as well as to complete the missing information such as the namespaces and links to the source code.

To facilitate running a similar process in the future, we briefly summarize our literature search protocol for finding state-of-the-art ontology data:

1. determine search engines and relevant online databases,
2. define search criteria for optional filtering which include the top-level field, topic or domain, and keywords including their combinations,
3. execute initial search and iterate through an adequate amount of results,
4. exclude duplicate articles among the initial results,
5. manually include relevant articles based on title, keywords and abstract,
6. since search by keyword can miss some papers, try reverse citation tracking, even if paper is weak (has not been cited many times), forward tracing, reverse tracking of citations, since a later work could include a comparison of such papers,
7. look for ontologies in online specialized catalogs such as LOV.

In Fig. 1, we provide an overview of this literature survey procedure.

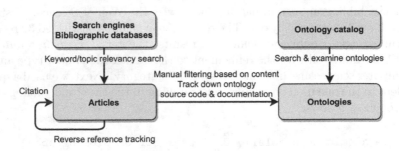

Fig. 1. Procedure for retrieving ontology related resources.

The result of our survey is a comprehensive table of metadata related to the ontologies. However, there are some incomplete records due to unavailable or missing information. Content-level analysis also revealed some ontologies that were likely irrelevant for practical information search, e.g., an 'Ontology for describing academic mental state'. From the totality of 43 ontologies found, we thus eventually chose 35 for which: 1) we deemed the availability of source code and/or metadata sufficient for effective reuse; and 2) the ontology content was indeed relevant to researcher information needs. Table 1 shows the final list of ontologies[6] used in our subsequent analysis.

---

[6] Some acronyms in this table are unofficial, e.g. OAD or RPO, and are only introduced for convenient referencing within this research.

Table 1. Research-related ontologies

Acronym	Name	
SO	Scholarly Ontology	[23]
OLOUD	Ontology for Linked Open University Data	[11]
VIVO	VIVO-ISF Ontology	[3]
CCSO	Curriculum, Course, and Syllabus Ontology	[17]
AIISO	Academic Institution Internal Structure Ontology	[16]
FRAPO	Funding, Research Administration and Projects Ontology	[29]
ORKG	Open Research Knowledge Graph	[18]
ESO & EAO	Education Standards & Education Application Ontology	[24]
SEDE	Ontology for Scholarly Event Description	[14]
OAD	Ontology for Academic Department	[36]
AcademIS	AcademIS Ontology	[35]
CSO	The Computer Sciene Ontology	[27]
BIBO	The Bibliographic Ontology	[8]
FOAF-Academic	FOAF-Academic Ontology	[16]
SemSur	Semantic Survey Ontology	[10]
RO	Research Object Ontology	[2]
SWRC	Semantic Web for Research Communities	[33]
ABET	Ontology for Academic Program Accreditation	[26]
RPO	Researcher Profile Ontology for the Academic Environment	[5]
CERIF	Common European Research Information Format Ontology	[15]
FaBiO	FRBR-aligned Bibliographic Ontology	[20]
CiTO	Citation Typing Ontology	[20]
BiRO	Bibliographic Reference Ontology	[13]
C4O	Citation Counting and Context Characterisation Ontology	[19]
DoCO	Document Components Ontology	[7]
PSO	Publishing Status Ontology	[22]
PRO	Publishing Roles Ontology	[22]
PWO	Publishing Workflow Ontology	[12]
SCoRO	Scholarly Contributions and Roles Ontology	[30]
DataCite	DataCite Ontology	[31]
BiDO	Bibliometric Data Ontology	[34]
FiveStars	Five Stars of Online Research Articles Ontology	[32]
FR	FAIR* Reviews Ontology	[28]
OCO	OpenCitations Ontology	[21]
AIDA	Academia Industry Dynamics OWL schema	[1]

3   Roles, Competency Questions and Conceptual Model

As mentioned, our starting point for examining the required coverage for scholarly knowledge graphs were the researcher needs associated with their research-related activities. Our approach is thus more 'human-centric', compared to 'data-centric' approaches to scholarly KG requirement analysis, which primarily look at what is already available in structured databases and KGs.

We started with identifying the *roles* fulfilled by researchers and entailing information foraging from external sources. For this purpose, the two senior co-authors (VS and OC) went through their comprehensive CVs and/or daily activity log, and distilled from the activities and achievements a set of distinct roles. The following roles (partially grouped, for brevity) have been identified:

- Researcher (general) - researching and publishing
- Leader of a research group (or of a more formal unit such as a Department)
- Advisor (of PhD students, or generally, more junior colleagues)
- Event organizer / Volume editor / Journal board member
- Evaluator of publications, researchers, organizations/groups, projects, and funding programs
- Research project proposer / manager
- Industry transfer mediator / recruiter.

For each researcher role, we formulated several verbal *competency questions* (CQs) and equipped them with *paths* of high-level concepts and relationships (corresponding to focal terms appearing in the CQs) whose instantiations should provide answers to the questions in a hypothetical KG. An example of path is RESEARCHER - ORGANIZATION - EVENT. This way, we created a set of paths from which we then constructed a holistic, highly abstract *conceptual model* presented in Fig. 3. We also gathered the terms in these paths into a separate collection. These terms were later put into a logical hierarchy, as shown in Fig. 2. To reduce the complexity of the conceptual model, we only show ten top-level terms in it. In Table 2 we showcase several chosen CQs and associated paths. (To demonstrate the wider scope of the conceptual model, we omit the roles of 'general' researcher and publication writer, as these have been the main focus of most previous initiatives surveying scholarly ontologies/KGs. They are however also part of our complete CQ set.)

The hierarchy in Fig. 2 shows six of the top-level concepts, further broken down to subtypes. The scope and purpose of each concept are as follows:

- The *Topic* concept may refer to research areas, research problems, methods etc.; namely, to anything that can be referred to as the subject of publications, of activities by research projects, research groups, funding programs, events, etc. Even 'tangible' assets used for research, including software and datasets, may be considered as a research topic in this context.
- The *Event* concept refers to scientific events such as conferences or seminars, and relates, e.g, to the on what kind of events can an organization organize or and which researchers have been involved in it through their publications.

Table 2. Examples of high-level competency questions and entity type paths

Research Group Leader / Advisor CQ	
What positions (in projects, or general) in other organizations may attract junior researchers as an alternative to working in my group?	• Topic - Project - Organization • Topic - Position - Organization

Research Event Organizer / Volume Editor / Journal Board Member CQ	
Who should I invite as keynote speaker or reviewer (based on thematic relevance, research quality, and history of engagement in this or similar events)?	• Topic - Publication - Researcher - Assessment • Topic - Researcher - Assessment • Publication Venue - Publication - Researcher - Assessment

Evaluator of publications CQ	
What has been researched / written on the topic this publication deals with?	• Publication - Topic - Publication • Publication - Topic - Project
What has the author previously published on this topic? What is the overlap with the current paper?	• Publication - Researcher - Publication - Topic
How does the paper comply with the standard criteria of scientific writing? What argument is used by an author or a reviewer in a publication/review?	• Publication - Assessment • Publication - Review - Argument

Evaluator of researchers CQ	
How important are the venues where the researcher publishes?	• Researcher - Publication Venue - Assessment
How much technology transfer activity (to industry) does a researcher do?	• Researcher - Organization

Evaluator of projects CQ	
How topical are the goals of the project, in terms of problems addressed? Do people often write on these problems? Are they encouraged by funding programs?	• Project - Goal/Problem - Publication - Researcher • Project - Goal/Problem - Program

Project proposer CQ	
What are the preferred topics of the program/call? What are the topical problems in the field?	• Program - Topic - Problem
Who has experience with previous projects in the chosen program?	• Program - Project - Researcher
What partners should be invited for such a kind of project, based on the problem addressed?	• Problem - Publication - Researcher - Organization • Problem - Method - Researcher - Organization
What is the usual budget of projects in this program?	• Program - Project

Industry transfer promotor CQ	
Which company or other organization is active in the given field, as a potential transfer target?	• Project - Topic - Organization

- The *Assessment* concept refers to various evaluations of the quality of organizations, researchers, research projects, research publications (i.e. peer- or
  professional reviewing) and publication venues. The quality can be represented by metrics, rankings, certifications, textual reviews, etc.
- The *Organization* concept is a parent concept to the types of organizations
  or working units that a researcher might be engaged in; some types of organizations can also offer funding programs and support the research projects of
  researchers, or be the recipients of the academic know-how. We identified 6
  subtypes as follows: *NGO, Foundation, Academic Institution, Research Group,
  Company, Government Body*. The important concept of *Research Spin-off* is
  a special type of *Company*.
- The *Publication* concept has 5 subtypes, which distinguish between different
  publication purposes and publishing formats. For example, an *Edited Collection* can be a book, proceedings, a journal special issue, or any other thematically coherent collection of individual publications, typically with a preface
  or editorial (its writing is a part of authoring this kind of publication). An
  Outreach Publication's purpose is to connect science with the society. It can
  be a magazine article, a press release, etc.
- The *Publication Venue* concept refers to different parts of types of publication
  venues can researchers submit their manuscripts to.

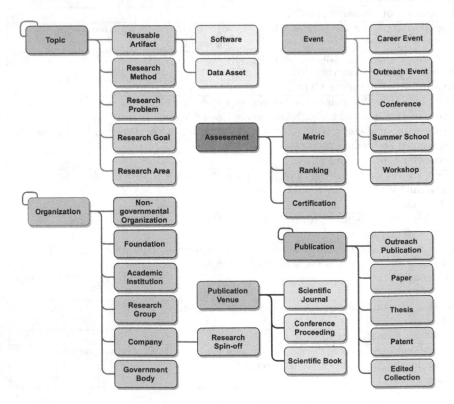

Fig. 2. Natural concept hierarchy

All mentioned relationships in the previous descriptions of top-level concepts are captured in Fig. 3. In this model, there are 3 other top-level concepts that do not have a further breakdown. We describe them as follows:

– A *Researcher* can, e.g., be a member of organizations and can contribute to research projects and publications. The researcher may also be engaged in an *Event* or a *Publication Venue*.
– The *Position* concept is used to describe possible positions or roles of a researcher within an organization.
– The *Funding Program* concept models a source of funding for research projects, possibly assigned across multiple calls.
– A *Project* may be proposed and undertaken by researchers (in some positions) or organizations, supported by funding programs, and associated with publications.

Note that the paths are not disambiguated, and in many cases may correspond to semantically different kinds of relationships, e.g., Researchers may provide assessments on something, but can also be assessed by other researchers. Some paths also link entities of the same type (e.g., one publication citing another, one researcher supervising another, or one topic being thematically close to another); this is indicated by the 'self-loops'.

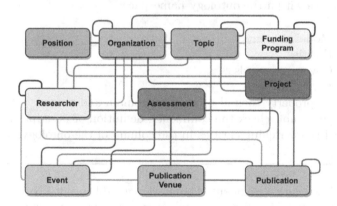

Fig. 3. High-level relationship model

4   Mapping the Ontologies to the Holistic Model

Our high-level conceptual model consists of concepts and of relationships that hold between them. It can be broken down into individual elements and fragments of concepts. This is needed to map existing ontologies onto the model and to identify their coverage. For this reason, we created a spreadsheet listing concepts, their subtypes and entity-relationship paths in the first column. Then, for each examined ontology, we noted down which concept is (at least, partially) covered by which entities in those ontologies. The detailed (manual) steps can be approximately described in the form of an algorithm:

Algorithm 1. Ontology coverage

Result: Coverage table
input : Latest versions of ontologies
output: Entities
foreach *Ontology* **do**
  if *Ontology documentation exists* **then**
    Check documentation;
    if *Ontology documentation has descriptive figures* **then**
      | Use entities in figures;
    else
      | Use entities listed in documentation;
  else if *Ontology source code exists* **then**
    | Use entities described in source code;
  else if *Paper has entity descriptions* **then**
    | Use entities described in the paper;
end
foreach *Entity* **do**
  | Keep only classes, their instances, object properties and datatype
  | properties within the ontology namespace;
end
input : Model elements
input : Entities
output: Coverage records
foreach *Entity* **do**
  | If it is a property then also check its domain and range;
  | When in doubt, check the comments, definition or description;
  | Record the matching entities in the column of the ontology;
end

In Table 3, we show a fragment of our coverage table results. Numerical values in row **Terms covered** indicate how many concepts or relationship paths in the model are covered by the given ontology. Numeric values in column **C** indicate how many ontologies have positive coverage for the given term from the model. Positive coverage means that an ontology concept corresponds to the naming and/or context of a term in our model, providing a similar or same semantics. In many cases, the coverage was not apparent and some manual approximation had to be made. For example, in this table, the model term *Research Group* was considered to be covered by *Group* in the Scholarly Ontology despite its specificity. Other cases include relationships being covered by classes, such as *Researcher – Position* vs. *vivo:contributionRole*.

Table 3. Ontology coverage – table excerpt

Terms covered	C	SO	OLOUD	VIVO core	...
		15	6	34	...
Position	12	:ActorRole	:Role	:Position, :Faculty Position	...
Position – Project	5	:ActorRole		:contributingRole	...
Org	10		:Organization	:ResearchOrganization	...
NGO	0				...
Foundation	1			:Foundation	...
Academic Institution	8			:Faculty, :Institute	...
Research Group	3	:Group			...
Company, Spin-off	1			:Company, :Private Company	...
Government Body	1			:GovernmentAgency	...
Org – Assessment	2				...
Org – Org	2				...
Org – Position	4		:roleAt, :role		...
Org – Topic	1			:hasResearchArea	...
Org – Event	1				...
Org – Project	6	:ActorRole		:supportedBy, :sponsoredBy	...
Org – Fund Prog	4			:FundingOrganization	...
Topic	7	:Topic	:Specialization		...
Reuseable Artifact	9	:Tool, :Information-Resource		:Dataset	...
Research Method	8	:Method, :Assertion		:CaseStudy	...
Research Problem	4	:Proposition, :ResearchQuestion			...
Research Goal	5	:Assertion, :Goal			...
Research Area	6	:Discipline		:hasResearchArea, :subjectAreaOf, :researchAreaOf	...
Topic – Topic	4	:hasPart, :Step			...
...	...	...	...	...	...

The coverage table indicates that even if the roles played by researchers during their career, and the associated CQs, are numerous, the relevant concepts and relationships are mostly well covered by available ontologies. Presumably, a proper (but still relatively large) subset of them might be found that would still cover all considered CQs. For such a set of ontologies, the abstract concept-relationship paths could be instantiated by constellations of OWL entities that could become part of *guidelines* for researcher data publishers. Possibly several alternative ontologies can be recommended for the parts of the domain where multiple of them *overlap*; these are, for example, the parts dealing with publications or organizations. More detailed criteria describing these choices in terms of ontology design patterns and their impact should be formulated.

As a likely gap in the existing ontology eco-system, we perceive, for example, the sub-domain of *spin-offs*. (In fact, even beyond the scope of the current survey, we were unable to find any ontology devoted to start-ups in general.) Underdeveloped also seems to be the conceptualization of, e.g., *funding programs* or some forms of *assessment*. In some cases, notions belonging to one 'bag' are dispersed across several ontologies, lacking a unifying super-concept, e.g. a *reusable artifact*.

The ontologies with highest coverage of different terms, in the table, are VIVO (34), BIBO (22) and SCoRO (21). There are however differences in their coverage pattern. While VIVO covers concepts from nearly any term group (associated with high-level terms from the conceptual model), BIBO's entities deal nearly exclusively with terms related to publications, events and venues, and SCoRO has a wider span, but almost exactly complementary to that of BIBO. Overall, of the 34 ontologies there are 22 that cover each at least five terms.

5   Conclusions and Future Work

The presented research adds to the current vivid motion around scholarly KGs the perspective of a wider scope of (senior) researcher daily activities as well as that of ontology reuse. The comparison between a model extracted from a collection of researcher information needs and KG competence questions on one side and existing ontologies on the other side reveals that in many areas a huge number of models overlap while some others are nearly untouched.

Obviously, a semi-informal conceptual graph does not provide the kind of operationality that would have been offered by a *formal* ontology. Creation of a holistic formal model of the researcher information needs, primarily focusing on the alignment with existing ontologies, should come as a next step.

The presented survey is also focused on ontologies alone. The most imminent future work then consists in extending the survey, in an integrated manner, to actual KGs as well as to existing thesauri. Although any ontology can be reused in the future, their actual usage in datasets may vary; this represents another dimension that could be added to our analysis. We have been collecting, in parallel, links to scholarly KGs, roughly partitioned according to the concepts from the model presented in this paper.

The mapping of the ontologies to the holistic model could be used, among other, as a supportive resource for aligning the ontologies among themselves. It would be interesting to see to what degree the application of state-of-the-art ontology matching [9] techniques would return similar results.

The research has been partially supported by the VSE IGS project no. 43/2020, "Knowledge Engineering of Researcher Data (KNERD)".

References

1. Angioni, S., Salatino, A., Osborne, F., Recupero, D.R., Motta, E.: AIDA: a knowledge graph about research dynamics in academia and industry (2020) http://aida.kmi.open.ac.uk/
2. Belhajjame, K., et al.: The research object suite of ontologies: sharing and exchanging research data and methods on the open web. CoRR abs/1401.4307 (2014) http://arxiv.org/abs/1401.4307
3. Börner, K., Conlon, M., Corson-Rikert, J., Ding, Y.: VIVO: a semantic approach to scholarly networking and discovery. Synthesis Lectures on the Semantic Web, Morgan & Claypool Publishers. **7**(1), 1–178, (2012) https://doi.org/10.2200/S00428ED1V01Y201207WBE002

4. Brack, A., Hoppe, A., Stocker, M., Auer, S., Ewerth, R.: Requirements analysis for an open research knowledge graph. CoRR abs/2005.10334 (2020)
5. Bravo, M., Reyes-Ortiz, J.A., Cruz, I.: Researcher profile ontology for academic environment. In: Arai, K., Kapoor, S. (eds.) CVC 2019. AISC, vol. 943, pp. 799–817. Springer, Cham (2020). https://doi.org/10.1007/978-3-030-17795-9_60
6. Budiu, R.: Information foraging: a theory of how people navigate on the web
7. Constantin, A., Peroni, S., Pettifer, S., Shotton, D.M., Vitali, F.: The document components ontology (DoCO). Semant. Web 7(2), 167–181 (2016). https://doi.org/10.3233/SW-150177
8. D'Arcus, B., Giasson, F.: Bibliographic Ontology Specification, http://bibliontology.com/. Accessed 10 April 2020
9. Euzenat, J., Shvaiko, P.: Ontology Matching. Springer, Heidelberg (2013). https://doi.org/10.1007/978-3-642-38721-0
10. Fathalla, S., Vahdati, S., Auer, S., Lange, C.: SemSur: a core ontology for the semantic representation of research findings. In: Fensel, A., et al. (eds.) Proceedings of the 14th International Conference on Semantic Systems, SEMANTICS 2018, Vienna, Austria, September 10–13, 2018. Procedia Computer Science, 137, 151–162. Elsevier (2018) https://doi.org/10.1016/j.procs.2018.09.015
11. Fleiner, R., Szász, B., Micsik, A.: OLOUD-an ontology for linked open university data. Acta Polytech. Hung. 14, 63–82 (2017). 10.12700/APH.14.4.2017.4.4
12. Gangemi, A., Peroni, S., Shotton, D.M., Vitali, F.: The publishing workflow ontology (PWO). Semant. Web 8(5), 703–718 (2017). https://doi.org/10.3233/SW-160230
13. Iorio, A.D., Nuzzolese, A.G., Peroni, S., Shotton, D.M., Vitali, F.: Describing bibliographic references in RDF. In: Castro, A.G., Lange, C., Lord, P.W., Stevens, R. (eds.) Proceedings of the 4th Workshop on Semantic Publishing co-located with the 11th Extended Semantic Web Conference (ESWC 2014), Anissaras, Greece, May 25th, 2014. CEUR Workshop Proceedings, CEUR-WS.org, 1155 (2014) http://ceur-ws.org/Vol-1155/paper-05.pdf
14. Jeong, S., Kim, H.: SEDE: an ontology for scholarly event description. J. Inf. Sci. 36(2), 209–227 (2010). https://doi.org/10.1177/0165551509358487
15. Jörg, B.: CERIF: the common european research information format model. Data Sci. J. 9, CRIS24–CRIS31 (2010). https://doi.org/10.2481/dsj.CRIS4
16. Kalemi, E., Martiri, E.: FOAF-academic ontology: a vocabulary for the academic community. In: Xhafa, F., Barolli, L., Köppen, M. (eds.) 2011 Third International Conference on Intelligent Networking and Collaborative Systems (INCoS), Fukuoka, Japan, November 30 - Dec. 2, 2011, Computer Society, pp. 440–445. IEEE (2011) https://doi.org/10.1109/INCoS.2011.94
17. Katis, E., Kondylakis, H., Agathangelos, G., Vassilakis, K.: Developing an ontology for curriculum and syllabus. In: Gangemi, A., et al. (eds.) ESWC 2018. LNCS, vol. 11155, pp. 55–59. Springer, Cham (2018). https://doi.org/10.1007/978-3-319-98192-5_11
18. Oelen, A., Jaradeh, M.Y., Farfar, K.E., Stocker, M., Auer, S.: Comparing research contributions in a scholarly knowledge graph. In: Garijo, D., Markovic, M., Groth, P., Santana-Pérez, I., Belhajjame, K. (eds.) Proceedings of the Third International Workshop on Capturing Scientific Knowledge co-located with the 10th International Conference on Knowledge Capture (K-CAP 2019), Marina del Rey, California, November 19th, 2019. CEUR Workshop Proceedings, CEUR-WS.org, 2526, pp. 21–26 (2019) http://ceur-ws.org/Vol-2526/paper3.pdf

19. Osborne, F., Peroni, S., Motta, E.: Clustering citation distributions for semantic categorization and citation prediction. In: Zhao, J., van Erp, M., Keßler, C., Kauppinen, T., van Ossenbruggen, J., van Hage, W.R. (eds.) Proceedings of the 4th Workshop on Linked Science 2014 - Making Sense Out of Data (LISC2014) co-located with the 13th International Semantic Web Conference (ISWC 2014), Riva del Garda, Italy, October 19, 2014. CEUR Workshop Proceedings, CEUR-WS.org, **1282**, 24–35 (2014) http://ceur-ws.org/Vol-1282/lisc2014_submission_9.pdf

20. Peroni, S., Shotton, D.M.: FaBiO and CiTO: ontologies for describing bibliographic resources and citations. J. Web Semant. **17**, 33–43 (2012). https://doi.org/10.1016/j.websem.2012.08.001

21. Peroni, S., Shotton, D.M.: Open citations, an infrastructure organization for open scholarship. Quant. Sci. Stud. **1**(1), 428–444 (2020). https://doi.org/10.1162/qss_a_00023

22. Peroni, S., Shotton, D.M., Vitali, F.: Scholarly publishing and linked data: describing roles, statuses, temporal and contextual extents. In: Presutti, V., Pinto, H.S. (eds.) I-SEMANTICS 2012–8th International Conference on Semantic Systems, I-SEMANTICS '12, Graz, Austria, September 5–7, 2012, pp. 9–16. ACM (2012) https://doi.org/10.1145/2362499.2362502

23. Pertsas, V., Constantopoulos, P.: Scholarly ontology: modeling scholarly practices. Int. J. Digit. Libr. **18**(3), 173–190 (2017). https://doi.org/10.1007/s00799-016-0169-3

24. Rashid, S.M., McGuinness, D.L.: Creating and using an education standards ontology to improve education. In: Waterman, K.K. (ed.) Proceedings of the Workshop on Semantic Web for Social Good co-located with 17th International Semantic Web Conference, SW4SG@ISWC 2018, Monterey, California, USA, October 9, 2018, Monterey, California, USA, October 9, 2018. CEUR Workshop Proceedings, CEUR-WS.org, **2182** (2018) http://ceur-ws.org/Vol-2182/paper_5.pdf

25. Ruiz-Iniesta, A., Corcho, O.: A review of ontologies for describing scholarly and scientific documents. In: Castro, A.G., Lange, C., Lord, P.W., Stevens, R. (eds.) SePublica. CEUR Workshop Proceedings, CEUR-WS.org, **1155** (2014) http://ceur-ws.org/Vol-1155/paper-07.pdf

26. Sabri, J.: Ontology for academic program accreditation. Int. J. Adv. Comput. Sci. Appl. **7**(7), 123–127 (2016) https://doi.org/10.14569/IJACSA.2016.070717

27. Salatino, A.A., Thanapalasingam, T., Mannocci, A., Osborne, F., Motta, E.: The computer science ontology: a large-scale taxonomy of research areas. In: Vrandečić, D., et al. (eds.) ISWC 2018. LNCS, vol. 11137, pp. 187–205. Springer, Cham (2018). https://doi.org/10.1007/978-3-030-00668-6_12

28. Santana-Pérez, I., Poveda-Villalón, M.: FAIR* Reviews Ontology. http://fairreviews.linkeddata.es/def/core/index.html. Accessed 13 May 2020

29. Shotton, D., Peroni, S.: FRAPO, the Funding, Research Administration and Projects Ontology. https://sparontologies.github.io/frapo/current/frapo.html. Accessed 13 May 2020

30. Shotton, D., Peroni, S.: SCoRO, the Scholarly Contributions and Roles Ontology. https://sparontologies.github.io/scoro/current/scoro.html. Accessed 13 May 2020

31. Shotton, D., Peroni, S., Barton, A.J., Gramsbergen, E., Ashton, J., Jacquemot, M.C.: The DataCite Ontology. https://sparontologies.github.io/datacite/current/datacite.html. Accessed 13 April 2020

32. Shotton, D.M.: The five stars of online journal articles–a framework for article evaluation. D-Lib Mag. **18**(1), 1 (2012). https://doi.org/10.1045/january2012-shotton

33. Sure, Y., Bloehdorn, S., Haase, P., Hartmann, J., Oberle, D.: The SWRC ontology–semantic web for research communities. In: Bento, C., Cardoso, A., Dias, G. (eds.) EPIA 2005. LNCS (LNAI), vol. 3808, pp. 218–231. Springer, Heidelberg (2005). https://doi.org/10.1007/11595014_22
34. Tapia-León, M., Santana-Perez, I., Poveda-Villalón, M., Espinoza-Arias, P., Chicaiza, J., Corcho, O.: Extension of the BiDO ontology to represent scientific production. In: Proceedings of the 2019 8th International Conference on Educational and Information Technology, pp. 166–172 (2019) https://doi.org/10.1145/3318396.3318422
35. Triperina, E., Sgouropoulou, C., Tsolakidis, A.: AcademIS: an ontology for representing academic activity and collaborations within HEIs. In: Ketikidis, P.H., Margaritis, K.G., Vlahavas, I.P., Chatzigeorgiou, A., Eleftherakis, G., Stamelos, I. (eds.) 17th Panhellenic Conference on Informatics, PCI 2013, Thessaloniki, Greece - September 19–21, 2013. pp. 264–271. ACM (2013), https://doi.org/10.1145/2491845.2491884
36. Yuan, A.: An Ontology for Academic Department. http://www.cs.toronto.edu/~yuana/researchCenter/yuanaOnto.html. Accessed 10 April 2020

A Unified Nanopublication Model for Effective and User-Friendly Access to the Elements of Scientific Publishing

Cristina-Iulia Bucur[1]($^{\boxtimes}$) (iD), Tobias Kuhn[1] (iD), and Davide Ceolin[2] (iD)

[1] Vrije Universiteit Amsterdam, Amsterdam, The Netherlands
{c.i.bucur,t.kuhn}@vu.nl
[2] Centrum Wiskunde & Informatica, Amsterdam, The Netherlands
davide.ceolin@cwi.nl

Abstract. Scientific publishing is the means by which we communicate and share scientific knowledge, but this process currently often lacks transparency and machine-interpretable representations. Scientific articles are published in long coarse-grained text with complicated structures, and they are optimized for human readers and not for automated means of organization and access. Peer reviewing is the main method of quality assessment, but these peer reviews are nowadays rarely published and their own complicated structure and linking to the respective articles are not accessible. In order to address these problems and to better align scientific publishing with the principles of the Web and Linked Data, we propose here an approach to use nanopublications as a unifying model to represent in a semantic way the elements of publications, their assessments, as well as the involved processes, actors, and provenance in general. To evaluate our approach, we present a dataset of 627 nanopublications representing an interlinked network of the elements of articles (such as individual paragraphs) and their reviews (such as individual review comments). Focusing on the specific scenario of editors performing a meta-review, we introduce seven competency questions and show how they can be executed as SPARQL queries. We then present a prototype of a user interface for that scenario that shows different views on the set of review comments provided for a given manuscript, and we show in a user study that editors find the interface useful to answer their competency questions. In summary, we demonstrate that a unified and semantic publication model based on nanopublications can make scientific communication more effective and user-friendly.

1 Introduction

Scientific publishing is about how we disseminate, share and assess research. Despite the fact that technology has changed how we perform and disseminate research, there is much more potential for scientific publishing to become a more transparent and more efficient process, and to improve on the age-old paradigms of journals, articles, and peer reviews [3,28]. With scientific publishing often

© Springer Nature Switzerland AG 2020
C. M. Keet and M. Dumontier (Eds.): EKAW 2020, LNAI 12387, pp. 104–119, 2020.
https://doi.org/10.1007/978-3-030-61244-3_7

stuck to formats optimized for print such as PDF, we are not using the advances that are available to us with technologies around the Semantic Web and Linked Data [7,35].

In this work, following our "Linkflows" vision [5], we aim to address some of these problems by looking at the scientific publishing process at a more finer-grained level and recording formal semantics for the different elements. Instead of treating big bulks of text as such, we propose to represent them as small snippets — e.g. paragraphs — that have formal semantics attached and can be treated as independent publication units. They can link to other such units and therefore form a larger entity — such as a full paper or review — by forming a complex network of links.

With that approach, we can ensure that provenance of each snippet of information can be accurately tracked together with its creation time and author, and therefore allow for more flexible and more efficient publishing than the current paradigm. A process like peer-reviewing can then be broken down into small snippets and thereby take the specialization of reviewers and the detailed context of their review comments into account, and these review comments can formally and precisely link to exactly the parts of the paper they address. Each article, paragraph and each review comment thereby forms a single node in a network and is each identified by a dereferenceable URI.

We demonstrate here how we can implement such a system with the existing concept and technology of nanopublications, a Linked Data format for storing small assertions together with their provenance and meta-data. We then show how this approach allows us to build powerful and user-friendly interfaces to aggregate and access larger numbers of such small communication elements. In order to assess the concrete benefits, we zoom in to just one out of the countless scenarios in which we can expect substantial advantages from such fine-grained semantic representations. We chose here the concrete case of a system for editors to assess manuscripts based on a set of review comments, and based on this concrete case we demonstrate and assess our approach.

In this research we aim to answer the following research questions:

1. Can we use nanopublications as a unifying data model to represent the structure and links of manuscripts and their assessments in a precise, transparent, and provenance-aware manner?
2. Is a fine-grained semantic publishing and reviewing model able to provide us with answers to common competency questions that journal editors face in their work as meta-reviewers?
3. Can we design an intuitive and effective interface based on a fine-grained semantic publishing and reviewing model that supports journal editors in judging the quality of manuscripts based on the received reviews?

We address these research questions with the following contributions:

- A general scheme of how nanopublications can be used to represent and publish different kinds of interlinked publication elements

– A dataset of 627 nanopublications, implementing this scheme to represent exemplary articles and their open reviews
– A set of seven competency questions for the scenario of journal editors meta-reviewing a manuscript, together with SPARQL representations of these questions
– A prototype of a fine-grained semantic analysis interface for the above scenario and dataset, powered by nanopublications
– Results from a user study on the perceived importance of the above competency questions and the perceived usefulness of the above prototype for answering them

The rest of this article is structured as follows. In Sect. 2 we describe the current state of the art in the field of scientific publishing and the reviewing process in particular. In Sect. 3 we describe our approach with regard to performing the reviewing process in a fine-grained manner based on nanopublications. In Sect. 4.1 we describe in detail how we performed the evaluation of our approach, while we report and discuss the results of this evaluation in Sect. 4.2. Future work and conclusion of the present research are outlined in Sect. 5.

2   Background

Before we move on to describe our approach, we give here the relevant background on scientific publishing, semantic papers, and the specific concept and technology of nanopublications.

Scientific publishing is at the core of scientific research, which has moved in the last decades from print to online publishing [36]. It is, however, still mostly following the paradigm from the print age, with narrative articles being published in journals and assessed by peer reviewers, only the printed volumes having been replaced by PDF files that are made accessible via search engines [22]. Considering the ever increasing number of articles and the increasing complexity of research methods, this old paradigm of publishing seems to have reached its limit, and scientists are struggling to stay up to date in their specific fields [21]. Slowly but steadily, these old paradigms are shifting with open access publishing, semantically enriched content, data publication, and machine-readable metadata gaining momentum and importance [33,37]. Opposition is also growing against the use of impact factor [9,10,24] or h-index as metrics for assessment of the participants in this publication process, and it has been shown that these metrics can be tampered with easily [1,8,29,31].

Advances in Semantic Web technologies like RDF, OWL, and SPARQL have allowed for the semantic enhancement of scholarly journal articles when publishing data and metadata [32,34]. As such, semantic publishing was proposed as a way to make scholarly publications discoverable, interactive, open and reusable for both, humans and machines, and to release them as Open Linked Data [13,23,30]. In order to extract formal semantics from already published papers in an automated manner, sophisticated methods such as the compositional and iterative semantic enhancement method (CSIE) [25], conceptual frameworks for modelling contexts associated with sentences in research articles [2] and semantic lenses were developed [12]. Furthermore, HTML formats like RASH have been proposed to represent scientific papers that include semantic annotations [27], and vocabularies like the SPAR (Semantic Publishing and Referencing) suite of ontologies have been introduced to semantically model all aspects relevant to scientific publishing [26]. These approaches mostly work on already published articles, but it has been argued that scientific findings and their contexts should be expressed in semantic representations from the start by the researchers themselves, in what has been named *genuine semantic publishing* [18].

In our previous work [6], we applied the general principles of the Web and the Semantic Web to promote this kind of genuine semantic publishing [18] by applying it to peer reviews. We proposed a semantic model for reviewing at a finer-grained level called Linkflows and argued that Linked Data principles like dereferenceable URIs using open standards like RDF can be used for publishing small snippets of information, such as an individual review comment, instead of big chunks of text, such as an entire review. These small snippets of text can be represented as nodes in a network and can be linked with one another with semantically-annotated connections, thus forming distributed and semantically annotated networks of contributions. The individual review comments are semantically modeled with respect to what part of the paper they target, whether they are about syntax or content, whether they raise a positive or negative point, and whether they are a suggestion or compulsory, and what their impact on the quality of the paper is. We showed on this model that it is indeed beneficial if we capture these semantics at the source (i.e. the peer reviewer in this case).

Nanopublications [11] are a specific concept and technology based on Linked Data to publish scientific results and their metadata in small publication units. Each nanopublication has an assertion that contains the main content (such as a scientific finding), and comes with provenance about that assertion (e.g. what study was conducted to derive at the assertion; or which documents it was extracted from) and with publication information about the nanopublication as a whole (e.g. by whom and when it was created). All these three parts are represented in RDF and thereby machine-interpretable.

It has been shown how nanopublications can also be used for other kinds of assertions, including meta-statements about other nanopublications [15], and in order to make nanopublications verifiable and immutable, *trusty URIs* [17] can be used as identifiers, which include cryptographic hash values that are calculated on the nanopublication's content. A decentralized server network has been established based on this, through which anybody can reliably publish and retrieve nanopublications [19]. In order to group nanopublications into larger collections and versions thereof, index nanopublications have been introduced [20]. With these technologies, small interconnected Linked Data snippets can be published in a reliable, decentralized, provenance-aware manner.

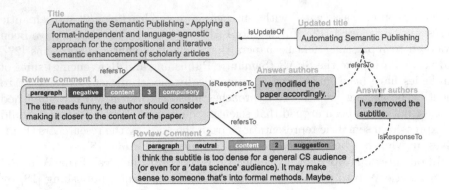

Fig. 1. An example of a nanopublication-style communication interaction.

3 Approach

Our general approach is to investigate the benefits of using the philosophy and technology of nanopublications as a unifying publishing unit to establish a new paradigm of scientific communication that is better aligned with the principles of the Web and Linked Data. We investigate how such an approach could allow us to communicate in a more efficient, more precise, and more user-friendly manner.

3.1 Semantic Model and Nanopublications

Our unifying semantic model based on nanopublications uses a number of existing ontologies like SPAR, PROV-O, FAIR* reviews, the Web Annotation Data Model, and our own Linkflows model [6] to break the big bulks of article and review texts into smaller text snippets. An example of a nanopublication-style communication interaction during the reviewing process is illustrated in Fig. 1, where the title of a paper is addressed by several review comments that come with semantic classes (e.g. *suggestion*), which are themselves referred to by the authors' answers that link them to the updated version. Each node in this network is represented as a separate nanopublication and all the attributes and relations are formally represented as Linked Data.

As we can see in Fig. 1, the properties *refersTo, isResponseTo, isUpdateOf* play the key role of linking different nodes in this network. *refersTo* is a property that links a review comment to the text snippet in the article it refers to. *isResponseTo* links the answer of the authors to the review comments of the reviewer and also to new versions of the text snippets that these review comments triggered. *isUpdateOf* links a version of the text snippet to another.

In our approach, snippets of scientific articles (mostly corresponding to paragraphs) as well as their review comments (corresponding to individual review comments) are semantically represented as nanopublications [11], and thereby they each form a node in the network described above. A complete example of such a nanopublication containing a review comment is shown in Fig. 2.

```
@prefix this: <http://purl.org/np/RA28QwaD22DK7U1Xq94UESAd3Y2jpGmVMCAk6_7aB_ivc> .
@prefix sub: <http://purl.org/np/RA28QwaD22DK7U1Xq94UESAd3Y2jpGmVMCAk6_7aB_ivc#> .
@prefix dcterms: <http://purl.org/dc/terms/> .
@prefix xsd: <http://www.w3.org/2001/XMLSchema#> .
@prefix prov: <http://www.w3.org/ns/prov#> .
@prefix pav: <http://purl.org/pav/> .
@prefix np: <http://www.nanopub.org/nschema#> .
@prefix linkflows: <https://github.com/LaraHack/linkflows_model/blob/master/Linkflows.ttl#> .

sub:Head {
    this: np:hasAssertion sub:assertion ;
        np:hasProvenance sub:provenance ;
        np:hasPublicationInfo sub:pubinfo ;
        a np:Nanopublication .
}

sub:assertion {
    sub:comment-7 a linkflows:ContentComment , linkflows:NegativeComment , linkflows:ReviewComment , linkflows:SuggestionComment ;
        linkflows:hasCommentText "In section 3.2) you give background information on the Find-Fix-Verify pattern (2nd paragraph). This information (in
which scenario it was used first, etc.) is not really necessary for the rest of the paper." ;
        linkflows:hasImpact "2"^^xsd:positiveInteger ;
        linkflows:refersTo <http://purl.org/np/RAoFc19T2f1F2j25Q6xBtfclZ1LyAZrlD5IU6F_yBozGE#paragraph> .
}

sub:provenance {
    sub:assertion prov:hadPrimarySource <http://www.semantic-web-journal.net/content/detecting-linked-data-quality-issues-crowdsourcing-dbpedia-study> ;
        prov:wasAttributedTo <https://orcid.org/0000-0001-7069-9804> .
}

sub:pubinfo {
    this: dcterms:created "2019-11-26T09:05:11+01:00"^^xsd:dateTime ;
        pav:createdBy <https://orcid.org/0000-0002-7114-6459> .
}
```

Fig. 2. Example nanopublication of a review comment.

Each of the three main parts of a nanopublication — assertion, provenance, and publication info — is represented as an RDF graph. In the example of Fig. 2, the assertion graph describes a review comment using the classes and properties of the Linkflows model[1]. It raises a negative point with an importance of 2 out of 5, and is marked as a suggestion for the authors. Furthermore, we see that this review comment refers to an external element, with a URI ending in `#paragraph`, as the target of this comment. This external element happens to be a paragraph of an article described in another nanopublication, which we can find out by following that trusty URI link.

Moreover, the nanopublication contains information regarding the creator of the assertion and the creator of the nanopublication that contains this assertion. These pieces of information can be found in the *provenance* and *publication info* graphs. As illustrated in Fig. 2, the author of the review comment is indicated by his ORCID identifier and the source of the original source of the review comment is indicated by the URL pointing to a link of the Semantic Web Journal. From the publication info graph, we can see who created the whole nanopublication together with the date and time of its creation.

As provenance and immutability of scientific contributions are crucial, we use trusty URIs [16] to enforce these properties. As such, for every nanopublication, in order for it to be published, a unique immutable URI is generated to refer to the node that holds the nanopublication. Any change of this nanopublication results in the generation of a new nanopublication, thus of a new node that is linked to the previous one. Such nanopublications can then be published in the existing decentralized nanopublication network [19].

---

[1] https://github.com/LaraHack/linkflows_model.

3.2   Use Case with Competency Questions

In the scientific publishing context, editors of journals play a key role, being an important link between content providers for journals (authors), the people who assess the quality of the content (peer reviewers) and the consumers of such content (the readers). While the peer reviewers are the ones that can recommend the acceptance or rejection of an article, it is up to the editors to make the final decision. We will look here into how our approach can benefit the specific scenario of editors assessing a manuscript based on given reviews and having to write a meta-review.

Performing such a meta-review is not a trivial task. As classical reviews are mainly comprised of a large bulks of text in natural language, it is hard to provide a tool with quantitative information about the reviews and their collective implications on the manuscript. As such, an editor needs to spend a lot of time just to read these reviews fully to even get an overview of the nature and range of the raised issues.

In order to apply our approach to this chosen use case, we first define a set of competency questions (CQs), which are natural language questions that are created with the objective to assess the practicality and coverage of an ontology or model [4]. After consulting with publishing experts at IOS Press[2] and the Netherlands Institute of Sound and Vision[3] during an informal session, we came up with the following seven quantifiable competency questions from an editor's point of view during meta-reviewing:

- **CQ1**: *What is the number of positive comments and the number of negative comments per reviewer?*
- **CQ2**: *What is the number of positive comments and the number of negative comments per section of the article?*
- **CQ3**: *What is the distribution of the review comments with respect to whether they address the content or the presentation (syntax and style) of the article?*
- **CQ4**: *What is the nature of the review comments with respect to whether they refer to a specific paragraph or a larger structure such as a section or the whole article?*
- **CQ5**: *What are the critical points that were raised by the reviewers in the sense of negative comments with a high impact on the quality of the paper?*
- **CQ6**: *How many points were raised that need to be addressed by the authors, as an estimate for the amount of work needed for a revision?*
- **CQ7**: *How do the review comments cover the different sections and paragraphs of the paper?*

3.3   Dataset

In order to evaluate our approach on the given use case, we need some data first. For this, we selected three papers that were submitted to a journal that

[2] https://www.iospress.nl/.
[3] https://www.beeldengeluid.nl/en.

has open reviews (Semantic Web Journal). Therefore, we could also access the full text of the reviews these papers received. We then manually modelled all the article, paragraphs, review comments, their interrelations, as well as their larger structures — in the form of sections and full articles and reviews — as individual nanopublications according to our approach. All these elements were thereby semantically modeled, and we could reuse part of our earlier dataset of manually assigned Linkflows categories [6]. Figure 2 above shows an example of a nanopublication that resulted from this manual modeling exercise. We would like to stress here that according to the vision underlying our approach, these semantic representations would in the future be generated as such from the start, and therefore this manual effort is only for evaluation purposes. This should be integrated in the future in smart tools, such that this approach does not come at an additional burden for reviewers but in fact leads to a more efficient way of reviewing.

Apart from nanopublications at the lowest level, such as the one shown in Fig. 2, higher-level ones combine them (by simply linking to them) to form larger structures, such as entire sections, papers, and reviews. Section nanopublications, for example, point to their paragraphs and define their order among other metadata. We also created a nanopublication index [20] that refers to this set of manually created nanopublications such that we can retrieve and even reuse parts of this dataset for new versions incrementally. All the nanopublications from our dataset are in an online repository[4].

3.4   Interface Prototype for Use Case

In order to apply and evaluate our approach on the chosen use case, we developed a prototype of an editor interface that accesses the nanopublications in the dataset presented above to provide a detailed and user-friendly interface to support editors in their meta-reviewing tasks.

This prototype comes with two views: one where the review comments are shown per reviewer in a bar chart broken down into the different dimensions and classes, as shown in Fig. 3 and another view that focuses on the distribution of the review comments to the different sections of the article, as shown in Fig. 4. The interface for an exemplary article with three reviews can be accessed online[5]. The shown content is aggregated from nanopublications stored in a triple store and displayed by showing color codes for the different Linkflows classes for the individual review comments.

In the reviewer-oriented view (Fig. 3), we can see in a more quantitative way the set of review comments and their types represented in different colors, where the checkboxes in the legend can be used to filter the review comments of the given category. To see the content of the review comments that are in a certain dimension, it is sufficient to just click on a bar in the chart.

---

[4] https://github.com/LaraHack/linkflows_model_implementation.
[5] http://linkflows.nanopubs.lod.labs.vu.nl.

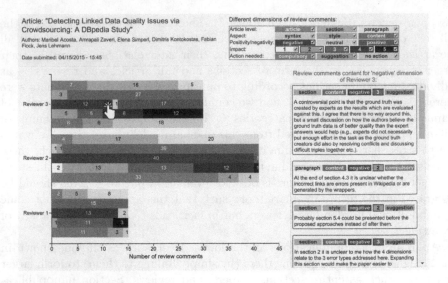

Fig. 3. The reviewer-oriented view for the editor study.

The section-oriented view (Fig. 4), aggregates all the finer-grained dimensions of the review comments at the level of sections in an article. Again, clicking on one cell in the table, thus selecting one specific dimension of the review comments, will show the content of those review comments underneath the table in the interface.

When data from the triple store is required, the server (implemented in NodeJS with the Express web application framework[6]) sends a request to the Virtuoso triple store where the nanopublications are stored. This request executes a SPARQL query on the stored nanopublications and returns the result to the server that, in turn, passes it further to the client, in the web browser, where the results are postprocessed and visualized. The code for the prototype can be found online[7].

4   Evaluation

Here we present the evaluation of our approach in the form of a descriptive analysis, the analysis of the SPARQL implementations of our competency questions, and a user study with editors on our prototype interface.

---

[6] https://nodejs.org, https://expressjs.com/.

[7] Interface: https://github.com/LaraHack/linkflows_interfaces
Backend application: https://github.com/LaraHack/linkflows_model_app
Data: https://github.com/LaraHack/linkflows_model_implementation.

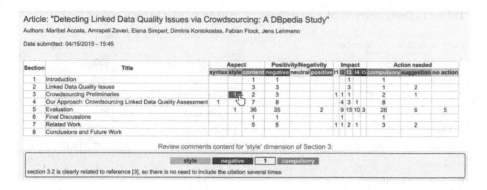

Fig. 4. The section-oriented view for the editor study.

4.1 Evaluation Design

First, we run a small descriptive analysis on the nanopublication dataset that we created. We can quantify the size and interrelation of the represented manuscripts and reviews in new ways, including the number of nanopublications, triples, paragraphs, review comments, and links between them.

As we are dealing with hundreds of individual nanopublications instead of just a hand-full of submission and review files, the performance of downloading them might pose a practical problem. For that reason, we also tested how long it takes to download all 627 nanopublications from the server network, using `nanopub-java` [14] as a command-line tool and giving it only the URI of the index nanopublication. This small download test was performed on a personal computer via a normal home network. For this, we retrieved them all via the library's `get` command and measured the time. We performed this 50 times, in five batches of 10 executions.

Next, we used our dataset to see if we are able to answer the seven competency questions that we defined above, in order to help editors in their meta-reviewing task. With this, we want to find out whether the combination of ontologies and vocabularies we used in our approach is sufficient to cover them, and then whether we can use the SPARQL query language to operationalize them and make them automatically executable on our nanopublication data.

Finally, we perform a user experiment involving editors to find out whether they indeed consider our competency questions important, and how useful they find our interface for getting an answer to these questions. For this study, we created a form that had two parts corresponding to the two parts of the study. We chose an article from our dataset that had a large number of review comments. For the first part, we asked for the importance of the competency questions using a Likert scale (from 1 to 5). For the second part, we provided static screenshots of our tool (the reviewer-oriented or the section-oriented view, depending on the question) together with a link to the live demo and asked about how useful the participants would find such a tool to answer the given competency question. The answers were on the same kind of a Likert scale from 1 to 5. We sent this

Table 1. Descriptive statistics dataset

Part of article	Number
Articles	3
Sections	89
Paragraphs	279
Figures	11
Tables	10
Formula	8
Footnote	2
Review comments	213

Table 2. Statistics nanopublications.

	Number	Average
Nanopublications	627	
Head triples	2508	4.00
Assertion triples	5420	8.64
Provenance triples	1254	2.00
Publication info triple	1255	2.00
Total triples	10 437	16.65

questionnaire (details online[8]) to a total of 401 editors of journals that support open reviews, specifically Data Science, the Semantic Web Journal and PeerJ Computer Science.

4.2 Evaluation Results

We can now turn to the results of these three parts of our evaluation. Details about the dataset and how it was generated and further queries and results can be found online[9].

Descriptive Analysis. Our representation of the three papers of our dataset together with their reviews leads to a total of 10 437 triples in 627 nanopublications, 279 text snippets and 213 review comments (85 for article 1, 59 for article 2 and 69 for article 3). Each of the three articles had three reviews: first article - 17, 18 and 50 review comments provided by the three reviewers, second article - 16, 21, 22 review comments each and third article - 11, 42, 16 review comments each.

In Table 1 some general statistics of the dataset are presented, while Table 2 shows general statistics about the nanopublications corresponding to the three articles and their reviews. Overall, this demonstrates the working of our approach of representing the elements of scientific communication in a fine-grained semantic manner. Of course, more complex analyses are possible, including network analyses of the complex interaction structure, and the queries for the competency questions that we defined above, to which we come back below.

Our small test on the performance of retrieving all nanopublications from the decentralized nanopublication network showed an average download time of 11.66s overall (with a minimum of 8.39s and a maximum of 13.34s). This operation retrieves each of the 627 nanopublications separately and then combines them in a single output file. The time per nanopublication is thereby just 18.6 milliseconds, which is achieved by executing the request in parallel to several servers in the network at the same time.

---

[8] https://github.com/LaraHack/linkflows_editor_survey/.
[9] https://github.com/LaraHack/linkflows_model_implementation.

Competency Question Execution. In order to answer the competency questions in Sect. 3.2, we managed to implement each of them as a concrete SPARQL query. We can't go into them here in detail due to space limitations, but the complete queries and all the required data and code can be found online[10].

This shows that our model is indeed able to capture the needed aspects for our competency questions, but we still need to find out whether these competency questions are indeed considered important by the editors, and whether the results from the SPARQL queries allow us to satisfy these users' information needs. These two aspects are covered in our user study.

User Study Results. Out of the total 401 questionnaire requests sent, we received a total of 42 answers (10.5%). The importance of the seven competency questions for editors and the usefulness of the interface presented to answer these competency questions, assessed on a Likert scale from 1 to 5 where 1 is *not important at all* and 5 is *very important* can be seen in Table 3. We marked with * the competency questions that had a significant p-value (< 0.05) and without, the ones that were not significant. We calculate significance with a simple binomial test by splitting the responses into the ones that assign at least medium importance or usefulness (≥ 3) and the ones that assign low importance or usefulness (< 3).

We see the respondents declared high importance to five of the seven competency questions in a significant manner with average values from 3.05 to 4.58 (CQ1, CQ3, CQ4, CQ5 and CQ6), while the remaining two (CQ2 and CQ7) were not considered important in the editors' view (average values of 2.36 and 2.79, respectively). Apparently, the number of positive and negative comments per section of the article (CQ2) and how the review comments cover the different parts of the article such as sections (CQ7), seem to have mixed reviews from editors, not being considered significantly important. The critical points that were raised by the reviewers (negative comments with a high impact on the paper) seems to be considered the most important competency question for the editors that responded (CQ5) with an average value of 4.58. Also important, in decreasing order, are the distribution of review comments with respect to whether they address the content or the presentation (syntax and style) of the article (CQ3), the number of points raised to be addressed by authors as an estimate for the amount of work needed for a reviewer (CQ6), the number of positive and negative comments per reviewer (CQ1), and the nature of the review comments with respect to whether they refer to a paragraph or a larger structure such as a section or the whole article (CQ4). For CQ2 and CQ7, we can say that editors did find it on average less important which sections of the article the reviews comments addressed. In general, however, we can conclude that most of competency questions are found to be important by most editors. However, we also observe a quite large standard deviation (SD) as seen in Table 3, ranging from 0.93 to 1.36 on our Likert scale that has a maximum distance of 4.0.

---

[10] https://github.com/LaraHack/linkflows_model_implementation/tree/master/queries.

Table 3. Results of the user study with editors.

Question	Importance of question						Usefulness of interface					
	AVG	MED	SD	Count <3 ≥3		Δcount p-value	AVG	MED	SD	Count <3 ≥3		Δcount p-value
CQ1	3.17	3	1.36	15	27	0.044 *	3.48	4	1.17	9	33	1.36e−4 *
CQ2	2.36	2	1.10	24	18	0.860	3.83	4	1.03	5	37	2.22e−7 *
CQ3	3.64	4	0.93	5	37	1.36e−4 *	3.40	3.5	1.04	9	33	1.47e−3 *
CQ4	3.05	3	1.19	14	28	0.022 *	3.26	3	1.20	14	28	0.022 *
CQ5	4.58	5	0.63	0	42	< e−12 *	3.21	3	1.16	9	33	1.36e−4 *
CQ6	3.57	4	1.02	6	36	1.41e−6 *	3.43	4	1.06	8	34	3.44e−5 *
CQ7	2.79	3	1.12	18	24	0.220	3.62	4	1.03	5	37	2.22e−7 *

Next, we evaluated the usefulness of our prototype interface. Here the Likert scale went from 1 standing for *not useful at all* to 5 standing for *very useful*. As we can see from Table 3, this interface was on average considered useful for all of the seven competency questions, with averages ranging from 3.21 to 3.83. The preference for scores of 3 or larger is clearly significant for all of them. A substantial minority of respondents, however, didn't find our interface useful leading again to relatively large standard deviation values between 1.06 and 1.19.

The free-text feedback field at the end of the questionnaire, finally, gave us a variety of suggestions for improvement (some of the editors argued that the interface used too many colors, others suggested other ways of grouping the data) but without clear overall tendencies. These responses also did not hint at any competency questions they found to be missing.

5 Discussion and Conclusion

Our results show that we can practically represent the different elements of scientific communication, such as articles and reviews, in a fine-grained and semantic way with nanopublications. We could show that we thereby can automatically answer a wide range of competency questions in the concrete scenario of editors in their meta-reviewing task. We found, however, that some of these were not found to be important, on average, by the editors who participated in our user study. Specifically, the questions about how well the review comments cover the different parts of the paper were not found to be important by a majority of editors. This could indicate that the article structure in terms of its different sections is not a good target for measuring the coverage of reviews. For all the questions, a relatively high variation is observed, which might be hinting at a lack of agreement among editors with respect to how scientific manuscripts should be assessed. This in turn could highlight the importance of more structured and more open reviewing processes. Irrespective of whether the competency questions are important, the majority of editors found our prototype to be useful to answer them, although again with a large variation. With our approach focusing on interoperability and openness, however, it is not necessary to design a single interface that suits everybody, but we could allow editors to choose from several alternatives in the future.

In summary, we could show that nanopublications might be a suitable format not just for scientific findings but also for their reviewing processes. Their open and semantic nature can moreover allow other participants outside of the assigned editor and invited reviewers to contribute with their suggestions and comments, both before and after publication, while all the provenance needed to understand the context of each contribution is recorded. In this way, publication and reviewing as a whole might become more fluid, more inclusive, and more powerful.

Acknowledgements. This research was partly funded by IOS Press and the Netherlands Institute for Sound and Vision. The authors would like to thank Stephanie Delbeque, Maarten Fröhlich, Erwin Verbruggen, Johan Oomen, and Jacco van Ossenbruggen for providing their insight and expertise.

References

1. Alberts, B.: Impact factor distortions. Science **340**, 787 (2013). https://doi.org/10.1126/science.1240319
2. Angrosh, M., Cranefield, S., Stanger, N.: Contextual information retrieval in research articles: semantic publishing tools for the research community. Semant. Web **5**, 261–293 (2014). https://doi.org/10.3233/SW-130097
3. Berners-Lee, T., Hendler, J.: Publishing on the semantic web. Nat. **410**, 1023–1024 (2001). https://doi.org/10.1038/35074206
4. Bezerra, C., Freitas, F., Santana, F.: Evaluating ontologies with competency questions. In: 2013 IEEE/WIC/ACM International Joint Conferences on Web Intelligence (WI) and Intelligent Agent Technologies (IAT). **3**, 284–285 (2013) https://doi.org/10.1109/WI-IAT.2013.199
5. Bucur, C.I.: Linkflows: enabling a web of linked semantic publishing workflows. In: Gangemi, A., et al. (eds.) ESWC 2018. LNCS, vol. 11155, pp. 262–271. Springer, Cham (2018). https://doi.org/10.1007/978-3-319-98192-5_45
6. Bucur, C.I., Kuhn, T., Ceolin, D.: Peer reviewing revisited: assessing research with interlinked semantic comments. In: In K-CAP 2019: Proceedings of the 10th International Conference on Knowledge Capture, pp. 179–187 (2019). https://doi.org/10.1145/3360901.3364434
7. Clark, T.: Next generation scientific publishing and the web of data. Semant. Web **5**, 257–259 (2014). https://doi.org/10.3233/SW-140139
8. Dong, P., Loh, M., Mondry, A.: The "impact factor" revisited. Biomed. Digit. Libr. **2**, 1–8 (2005). https://doi.org/10.1186/1742-5581-2-7
9. Garfield, E.: Journal impact factor: a brief review. CMAJ **161**, 979–980 (1999)
10. Garfield, E.: The history and meaning of the journal impact factor. JAMA **295**, 90–93 (2006). https://doi.org/10.1001/jama.295.1.90
11. Groth, P., Gibson, A., Velterop, J.: The anatomy of a nanopublication. Inf. Serv. Use **30**, 51–56 (2010). https://doi.org/10.3233/ISU-2010-0613
12. Iorio, A.D., Peroni, S., Vitali, F., Zingoni, J.: Semantic lenses to bring digital and semantic publishing together. In: Proceeding of 4th International Conference Linked Science@ISWC, vol. 128, pp. 12–23 (2014)
13. Jacob, B., Ortiz, J.: Data.world: a platform for global-scale semantic publishing. In: Proceedings of the ISWC posters & demonstrations and industry tracks co-located with 16th International Semantic Web Conference (ISWC) (2017)

14. Kuhn, T.: nanopub-java: a java library for nanopublications. In: Proceedings of the 5th Workshop on Linked Science (LISC 2015), vol. 1572, pp. 19–25 (2015)
15. Kuhn, T., Barbano, P.E., Nagy, M.L., Krauthammer, M.: Broadening the scope of nanopublications. In: Cimiano, P., Corcho, O., Presutti, V., Hollink, L., Rudolph, S. (eds.) ESWC 2013. LNCS, vol. 7882, pp. 487–501. Springer, Heidelberg (2013). https://doi.org/10.1007/978-3-642-38288-8_33
16. Kuhn, T., Dumontier, M.: Trusty URIs: verifiable, immutable, and permanent digital artifacts for linked data. In: Presutti, V., d'Amato, C., Gandon, F., d'Aquin, M., Staab, S., Tordai, A. (eds.) ESWC 2014. LNCS, vol. 8465, pp. 395–410. Springer, Cham (2014). https://doi.org/10.1007/978-3-319-07443-6_27
17. Kuhn, T., Dumontier, M.: Making digital artifacts on the web verifiable and reliable. IEEE Trans. Knowl. Data Eng. **27**, 2390–2400 (2015). https://doi.org/10.1109/TKDE.2015.2419657
18. Kuhn, T., Dumontier, M.: Genuine semantic publishing. Data Sci. **1**, 139–154 (2017). https://doi.org/10.3233/DS-170010
19. Kuhn, T., et al.: Decentralized provenance-aware publishing with nanopublications. PeerJ Comput. Sci. **2**, e78 (2016). https://doi.org/10.7717/peerj-cs.78
20. Kuhn, T., Willighagen, E., Evelo, C., Queralt-Rosinach, N., Centeno, E., Furlong, L.I.: Reliable granular references to changing linked data. In: d'Amato, C., et al. (eds.) ISWC 2017. LNCS, vol. 10587, pp. 436–451. Springer, Cham (2017). https://doi.org/10.1007/978-3-319-68288-4_26
21. Landhuis, E.: Scientific literature: information overload. Nat. **535**, 457–458 (2016). https://doi.org/10.1038/nj7612-457a
22. Lippi, G., et al.: Scientific publishing in the "predatory" era. Clin. Chem. Lab. Med. (CCLM) **56**(5), 683–684 (2018). https://doi.org/10.1515/cclm-2017-1079
23. Mirri, S., et al.: Towards accessible graphs in html-based scientific articles. In: 4th IEEE Annual Consumer Communications & Networking Conference (CCNC), pp. 1067–1072 (2017) https://doi.org/10.1109/CCNC.2017.7983287
24. Opthof, T.: Sense and nonsense about the impact factor. Cardiovasc. Res. **33**, 1–7 (1997). https://doi.org/10.1016/S0008-6363(96)00215-5
25. Peroni, S.: Automating semantic publishing. Data Sci. **1**, 155–173 (2017). https://doi.org/10.3233/DS-170012
26. Peroni, S., Shotton, D.: The SPAR ontologies. In: Vrandečić, D., et al. (eds.) ISWC 2018. LNCS, vol. 11137, pp. 119–136. Springer, Cham (2018). https://doi.org/10.1007/978-3-030-00668-6_8
27. Peroni, S., et al.: Research articles in simplified html: a web-first formatfor html-based scholarly articles. PeerJ Comput. Sci. **3**, e132 (2017). https://doi.org/10.7717/peerj-cs.132
28. Priem, J.: Beyond the paper. Nat. **495**, 437–440 (2013). https://doi.org/10.1038/495437a
29. Saha, S., Saint, S., Christakis, D.A.: Impact factor: a valid measure of journal quality? JMLA **91**, 42–46 (2003)
30. Sateli, B., Witte, R.: From papers to triples: an open source workflow for semantic publishing experiments. In: González-Beltrán, A., Osborne, F., Peroni, S. (eds.) SAVE-SD 2016. LNCS, vol. 9792, pp. 39–44. Springer, Cham (2016). https://doi.org/10.1007/978-3-319-53637-8_5
31. Seglen, P.O.: Why the impact factor of journals should not be used for evaluating research. BMJ **314**, 498–502 (1997). https://doi.org/10.1136/bmj.314.7079.497
32. Shotton, D.: Semantic publishing: the coming revolution in scientific journal publishing. Learn. Publ. **22**, 85–94 (2009). https://doi.org/10.1087/2009202

33. Shotton, D.: The five stars of online journal articles-a framework for article evaluation. D-Lib Mag. **18**, 457–458 (2012). https://doi.org/10.1045/january2012-shotton
34. Shotton, D., Portwin, K., Klyne, G., Miles, A.: Adventures in semantic publishing: exemplar semantic enhancements of a research article. PLoS Comput. Biol. **5**(4), e1000361 (2009). https://doi.org/10.1371/journal.pcbi.1000361
35. Sikos, L.F.: Knowledge representation with semantic web standards. Description Logics in Multimedia Reasoning, pp. 11–49. Springer, Cham (2017). https://doi.org/10.1007/978-3-319-54066-5_2
36. Stern, B.M., O'Shea, E.K.: A proposal for the future of scientific publishing in the life sciences. PLoS Biol. **17**(2), 683–684 (2019). https://doi.org/10.1371/journal.pbio.3000116
37. Wang, P., Rath, M., Deike, M., Qiang, W.: Open peer review: An innovation in scientific publishing. In: IConference 2016 Proceedings (2016) https://doi.org/10.9776/16315

Concept Extraction Using Pointer–Generator Networks and Distant Supervision for Data Augmentation

Alexander Shvets[1]([✉])[iD] and Leo Wanner[1,2][iD]

[1] NLP Group, Pompeu Fabra University, Roc Boronat 138, Barcelona, Spain
{alexander.shvets,leo.wanner}@upf.edu
[2] Catalan Institute for Research and Advanced Studies (ICREA), Barcelona, Spain

Abstract. Concept extraction is crucial for a number of downstream applications. However, surprisingly enough, straightforward single token/nominal chunk–concept alignment or dictionary lookup techniques such as DBpedia Spotlight still prevail. We propose a generic open domain-oriented extractive model that is based on distant supervision of a pointer–generator network leveraging bidirectional LSTMs and a copy mechanism and that is able to cope with the *out-of-vocabulary* phenomenon. The model has been trained on a large annotated corpus compiled specifically for this task from 250K Wikipedia pages, and tested on regular pages, where the pointers to other pages are considered as ground truth concepts. The outcome of the experiments shows that our model significantly outperforms standard techniques and, when used on top of DBpedia Spotlight, further improves its performance. The experiments furthermore show that the model can be readily ported to other datasets on which it equally achieves a state-of-the-art performance.

Keywords: Open-domain discourse texts · Concept extraction · Pointer-generator neural network · Distant supervision

1 Introduction

In knowledge discovery and representation, the notion of *concept* is most often used to refer to *sense*, i.e., 'abstract entity' or 'abstract object' in the Fregean dichotomy of *sense* vs. *reference* [10]. In Natural Language Processing (NLP), the task of detection of surface forms of concepts, namely *Concept Extraction* (CE), deals with the identification of the language side of the concept coin, i.e., Frege's *reference*. Halliday [16] offers a syntactic interpretation of *reference*. In his terminology, it is a "classifying nominal group". For instance, *renewable energy* or *nuclear energy* are classifying nominal groups: they denote a class (or type) of energy, while, e.g., *cheap energy* or *affordable energy* are not: they do not typify, but rather qualify *energy* (and are thus "qualifying nominal groups").

CE is crucial for a number of downstream applications, including, e.g., language understanding, ontology population, semantic search, and question answering; it is also the key to entity linking [22]. In generic open domain subject-neutral discourse across different (potentially unrelated) subjects, indexing the

© Springer Nature Switzerland AG 2020
C. M. Keet and M. Dumontier (Eds.): EKAW 2020, LNAI 12387, pp. 120–135, 2020.
https://doi.org/10.1007/978-3-030-61244-3_8

longest possible nominal chunks and their head words located in sequences of tokens between specified "break words" [34] and special dictionary lookups such as *DBpedia Spotlight* [6] and *WAT* [28] are very common techniques. They generally reach outstanding precision, but low recall due to constant evolvement of the language vocabulary. Advanced deep learning models that already dominate CE in specialized closed domain discourse on one or a limited range of related subjects, e.g., biomedical discourse [14,33], and that are also standard in keyphrase extraction [2,25] are an alternative. However, such models need a tremendous amount of labeled data for training.

We present an operational CE model that utilizes pointer–generator networks with bidirectional long short-term memory (LSTM) units [12,30] to retrieve concepts from general discourse textual material.[1] Furthermore, since for a generic, open domain concept extraction model we need a sufficiently large training corpus that covers a vast variety of topics and no such annotated corpora are available, we opt for distant supervision to create a sufficiently large and diverse dataset. Distant supervision consists in automatic labeling of potentially useful data by an easy-to-handle (not necessarily accurate) algorithm to obtain an annotation which is likely to be noisy but, at the same time, to contain enough information to train a robust model [26]. Two labeling schemes are considered. Experiments carried out on a dataset of 250K+ Wikipedia pages show that copies of our model trained differently and joined in an ensemble significantly outperform standard techniques and, when used on top of DBpedia Spotlight, further improve its performance by nearly 10%.

2   Related Work

In this section, we focus on the review of generic discourse CE; for a comprehensive review of the large body of work on specialized discourse CE, and, in particular, on biomedical CE; see, e.g., [15]. We also do not discuss recent advances in keyphrase extraction [2] because their applicability to generic concept extraction is limited due to the specificity of the task.

The traditional CE techniques interpret any single and multiple token nominal chunk as a concept [34] or do a dictionary lookup, as, e.g., *DBpedia Spotlight* [6], which matches and links identified nominal chunks with DBpedia entries (6.6M entities, 13 billion RDF triples)[2], based on the Apache OpenNLP[3] models for phrase chunking and named entity recognition (NER). Given the large coverage of DBpedia, the performance of DBpedia Spotlight is rather competitive. However, obviously, the presence of an entry cannot always be ensured. Consider, e.g., a paper title "Natural language understanding with Bloom embeddings, convolutional neural networks and incremental parsing", where DBpedia Spotlight does not detect "Bloom embeddings" or "incremental parsing", as there are no such entries in DBpedia.

---

[1] We adopt Halliday's notion of classifying nominal group as definition of a concept.
[2] https://wiki.dbpedia.org/develop/datasets/dbpedia-version-2016-10.
[3] https://opennlp.apache.org/.

As DBpedia Spotlight, AIDA [35] relies on an RDF repository, YAGO2. WAT and its predecessor TagMe [28] use a repository of possible spots made of wiki-anchors, titles, and redirect pages. Both TagMe and WAT rely on statistical attributes called *link probability* and *commonness*; WAT draws furthermore on a set of statistics to prune a set of mentions using an SVM classifier. Wikifier [4] focuses on relation extraction, relying on a NER, which uses gazetteers extracted from Wikipedia and simple regular expressions to combine several mentions into a single one. All of them are used for state-of-the-art entity linking and (potentially nested) entity mention detection and typing [17,36]. FRED [11] also focuses on extraction of relations between entities, with frames [9] as the underlying theoretical constructs. Unlike Wikifier and FRED, e.g., OLLIE [24] does not rely on any precompiled repository. It outperforms its strong predecessors REVERB [8] in relation extraction by expanding the set of possible relations and including contextual information from the sentence from which the relations are extracted.

A number of works focus on the recognition of named entities, which are the most prominent concept type. NERs work at a sentence level and aim at labeling all occurred instances. Among them, Lample et al. [20] provide a state-of-the-art NER model that avoids traditional heavy use of hand-crafted features and domain-specific knowledge. The model is based on bidirectional LSTMs and Conditional Random Fields (CRFs) that rely on two sources of information on words: character-based word representations learned from an annotated corpus and unsupervised word representations learned from unannotated corpora. Another promising approach to NER is fine-tuning of a language representation model such as, e.g., BERT [7]. The pre-trained BERT model can be fine-tuned with just one additional output layer to create state-of-the-art models for a wide range of tasks, including NER, without substantial task-specific architecture modifications.

Pointer-generator networks, which are generally applied in summarization contexts, are also experimented with in information extraction; cf., e.g., [27], where they have been successfully applied to the detection of term definitions in sentences with a specific structure and their translation into Description Logics formulæ using syntactic transformation. As a matter of fact, this similar task partially motivated our choice to use pointer-generator networks for CE.

3 Description of the Model

We implement a deep learning model and a large-scale annotation scheme for distant supervision to cope autonomously with dictionary-independent generic CE and to complement state-of-the-art lookup-based approaches in order to increase their recall. In addition, we would like our model to perform reasonably well on pure NER tasks with a small gap to models specifically tuned for the NER datasets. The model follows the well-established tendency in information extraction adopted for NER and extractive summarization and envisages CE as an attention-based sequence-to-sequence learning problem.

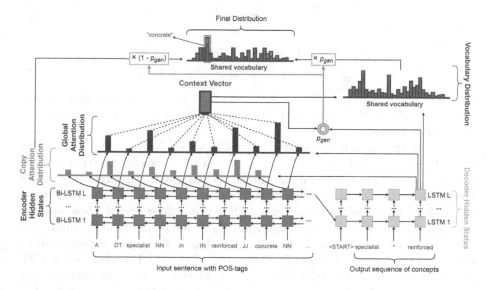

Fig. 1. The neural architecture for concept extraction

3.1   Overview of the Model

As basis of our model, we use the pointer–generator network proposed in [30], which aids the creation of summaries with accurate reproduction of information. In each generation step t, the *pointer* allows for copying words w_i from the source sequence to the target sequence using the distribution of the attention layer a^t, while the *generator* samples tokens from the learned vocabulary distribution P_{vocab}, conditioned by a context vector h_t^* produced by the same attention layer, which is built based on hidden states h_i of an encoder (a bidirectional LSTM [12]) and states s_t of a decoder (a unidirectional LSTM). In addition, a coverage mechanism is applied to modify a^t using a coverage vector c^t to avoid undesirable repetitions in the output sequence. Specifically, to produce a word w, the above-mentioned distributions are combined into a single final probability distribution, which is weighted using the *generation probability* $p_{gen} \in [0,1]$:

$$P(w) = p_{gen}P_{vocab}(w) + (1 - p_{gen})\sum\nolimits_{i:w_i=w} a_i^t \qquad (1)$$

where $P_{vocab}(w)$ is the vocabulary distribution, which is zero if w is an out-of-vocabulary (OOV) word; a^t is the attention distribution; w_i - tokens of the input sequence; $\sum_{i:w_i=w} a_i^t$ is zero if w does not appear in the source sequence. In accordance with [30], the individual vectors, distributions, and probability p_{gen} are defined as follows:

$$c^t = \sum\nolimits_{t'=0}^{t-1} a^{t'} \qquad (2)$$

$$e_i^t = v^T tanh(W_h h_i + W_s s_t + w_c c_i^t + b_{attn}) \qquad (3)$$

$$a^t = softmax(e^t) \qquad (4)$$

$$h_t^* = \sum_i a_i^t h_i \tag{5}$$

$$P_{vocab} = softmax(V'(V[s_t, h_t^*] + b) + b') \tag{6}$$

$$p_{gen} = \sigma(w_{h*}^T h_t^* + w_s^T s_t + w_x^T x_t + b_{ptr}) \tag{7}$$

where v, W_h, W_s, w_c, b_{attn}, V, V', b, b', w_{h*}, w_s, w_x, b_{ptr} are learnable parameters, T stands for the transpose of a vector, x_t is the decoder input, and σ is the sigmoid function.

To adapt this basic model to the task of CE, we applied several modifications to it (cf., Fig. 1[4]): (i) following Gu et al. [13], we use separate distributions for copy attention and global attention, instead of one for both; (ii) experiments have shown that encoders and decoders with several LSTM layers perform better than with a single layer, such that we work with multiple layer LSTMs; how many is determined using a development dataset; (iii) we adapt the forms of input and target sequences to the specifics of the task of CE. The input is comprised of tokens and their part-of-speech (PoS) tags (e.g., 'The DT President NN is VBZ elected VBD by IN a DT direct JJ vote NN'). The target sequence concatenates concepts in the order they appear in the text and separates them by a token "*" especially introduced to partition the output (e.g., 'President * direct vote').

This model is naturally applicable to the task of CE since it facilitates the selection and transfer of subsequences of tokens that form classifying nominal groups (= concepts) from a given source sequence of tokens (= text input) to the target sequence (= partitioned sequence of concepts). The pointer mechanism implies the ability to cope with OOV words, which is crucial for open domain CE, while the generator implies the ability to adjust vocabulary distribution for selecting the next word (which might be a termination token "*") based on a given context vector, which allows us to implicitly take into account the domain specifics and linguistic features that facilitate the task of CE. Furthermore, the vocabulary distribution update adds the possibility to vanish or strengthen the copy effect and thus learn to distinguish concepts with outer modifiers (such as, e.g.,"hot *air*", "[fully] crewed *aircraft*", "reinforced *group*") from multiword concepts (such as, e.g., *"hot air balloon"*, *"unmanned aerial vehicle"*, *"reinforced concrete"*).

3.2   Training and Applying the Model

For training, token sequences are taken from annotated sentences (see the compilation of the annotated training dataset in Sect. 4.2 below) with a sliding overlapping window of a fixed maximum length (see the Experiments section), which is minimally expanded if needed in order not to deal with incomplete concepts at the borders. The trained model is applied to unseen sentences, which are also split into sequences of tokens with an overlapping window of the same size, without any expansion. Finally, the corresponding mentions in the plain text

---

[4] We use a similar layout as in [30] for easier comparison of our extension with the original model.

are determined since the output format does not include offsets. In particular, following [17], we find all possible matches for all detected concepts and then successively select non-nested concepts from the beginning to the end of the sentence, giving priority to the longest, in case of a multiple choice.

4 Datasets

In what follows, we describe the data and the procedure for their weak annotation to create extensive training and test datasets.

4.1 Data

We take a snapshot of the WordNet synset-typed[5] Wikipedia [29], from which we use the raw texts of the Wikipedia pages and text snippets of the links to other pages as ground truth concepts regardless their type; cf., Fig. 2[6]. These links often share the headings of anchor pages, which are in most cases some real-world entities, cf., e.g., "Arthur Heurtley House", "Price Tower", etc. Sometimes, they are also lexical variations of terms behind the link, as, e.g., the highlighted link in the fragment "the two small *coastal battleships* General-Admiral Graf Apraxin and Admiral Senyavin" leads to the page named "Coastal defence ship".

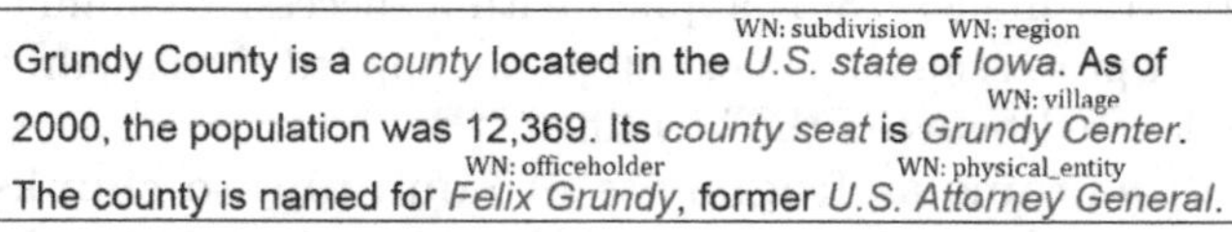

WN: subdivision WN: region
Grundy County is a *county* located in the *U.S. state* of *Iowa*. As of
WN: village
2000, the population was 12,369. Its *county seat* is *Grundy Center*.
WN: officeholder   WN: physical_entity
The county is named for *Felix Grundy*, former *U.S. Attorney General*.

Fig. 2. Ground truth concept annotation

The manual annotation of multi-word expressions in 100 randomly selected sentences with at least one multi-word link in each by a professional linguist showed that at least 63% of such phrases are indeed concepts (cf., e.g., "punctuated equilibrium", "chief of staff", "2004 presidential election"). For our work, we selected several data subsets from the collection of Wikipedia pages: 250K pages to be weakly, but *densely* annotated.[7] Out of these 250K pages, 220K are used for training and 30K for validation. In addition, we use 7K Wikipedia pages with

---

[5] https://wordnet.princeton.edu/.

[6] Wikipedia does not contain self-links, therefore the concept *"Grundy County"* in a text from the self-titled page is not a link.

[7] Henceforth, we refer to the link snippet-based annotation of the pages as a *sparse* gold standard annotation since it covers by far not all concepts encountered in a page. Our distant supervision-based annotation is referred to as *dense* annotation since it (supposedly) covers all concepts on a given page. As usual, distant supervision-based annotation is also referred to as *weak* since it is an automatic annotation.

the sparse gold standard annotation as development set for choosing parameters of distant supervision and selecting the best model among several models trained with different parameters, and 7K pages with the sparse gold standard annotation as test set. The test set does not allow an exhaustive evaluation of the model since it does not contain many generic concepts. However, given the lack of a large manually annotated dataset, this is still the best choice. Furthermore, in view of the fact that one third of the concepts in the test set are unseen during training, allows for the assessment of the ability of our model to handle OOV concepts.

4.2   Compilation of the Training Corpus

We automatically create a (noisy) training corpus using two various annotators over a large unlabeled dataset: DBpedia Spotlight with the value of its confidence coefficient, which gains the highest recall, and our own algorithm, which uses a number of rules and heuristics. Our labeling is based on the sentence-wise analysis of statistical and linguistic features of sequences of tokens. First, named entities and multiple token concepts and then single token concepts are identified. The algorithm covers the following tasks:

1. Application of a statistical NER model. A significant number of concepts in Wikipedia are capitalized terms, which can be captured by statistical named entity recognizers (NER); see Sect. 2 above. Therefore, at first, SpaCy's state-of-the-art NER model [18] is applied with a successive elimination of used tokens for further processing. The next steps are applied then separately to fragments of texts located between the identified NEs.

2. Selection of n-grams as fragments of noun phrase chunks that can form part of multiple token concepts. For this task, we define PoS-patterns based on Penn Treebank tagset[8], which were inherited from the patterns for multiword expression detection introduced in [5] and expanded here, resulting in the following set: $P = \{$N_N, J_N, V_N, N_J, J_J, V_J, N_of_N, N_of_DT_N, N_of_J, N_of_DT_J, N_of_V, N_of_DT_V, CD_N, CD_J$\}$, where N stands for "noun", i.e., NN|NNS|NNP|NNPS, J stands for "adjective", i.e., JJ| JJR|JJS, V – "verb" but limited to VBD|VBG|VN, CD – "cardinal number", DT – "determiner", and "of" is an exact pronoun. Each pattern matches an n-gram with two open-class lexical items and at most two auxiliary tokens between them.

3. Assessment of the distinctiveness of each selected n-gram. The distinctiveness of the selected n-grams is assessed using word co-occurrences from the Google Books N-gram Corpus [21]. Let us assume a given n-gram $T_1 A_1 A_2 T_2 \in c_k$, where T_1 and T_2 are open class lexical items and A_1 and A_2 are optional auxiliary tokens, and c_k is a set of all n-grams of a particular kind of pattern $p_k \in P$. We use $T_1 A_1 A_2 T_2$ as a point of a function that passes through normalized document frequencies of a set of similar n-grams $T_1 A_1 A_2 T_j$, $j \in \{i \mid T_1 A_1 A_2 T_i \in c_k\}$ arrayed in ascending order, to find a tangential angle at this point $\alpha_1 \in [0°; 90°)$. As an illustration, one may think of Zipf curves built from the tail to the head individually for each set of n-grams. Similarly, $\alpha_2 \in [0°; 90°)$,

---

[8] https://www.ling.upenn.edu/courses/Fall_2003/ling001/penn_treebank_pos.html.

is a tangential angle at the point $T_1A_1A_2T_2$ on a curve of ordered frequencies of n-grams $T_hA_1A_2T_2$, $h \in \{i \mid T_iA_1A_2T_2 \in c_k\}$. We leverage these angles to check how prominent an n-gram is, i.e., to what extent it differs from its neighbors by overall usage. In case an n-gram is located among equally prominent n-grams with a tangential angle close to $0°$, we do not consider it as a potential part of a concept since it does not show a notable distinctiveness inherent in concepts, especially in common idiosyncratic concepts. The thresholds α_{min_1} and α_{min_2} ($\alpha_{min_1} \geq \alpha_{min_2}$) for minimally allowed tangential angles such as $\max(\alpha_1, \alpha_2) \geq \alpha_{min_1}$, $\min(\alpha_1, \alpha_2) \geq \alpha_{min_2}$ are predermined in development experiments. We calculate tangential angles through central difference approximation with a coarse-grained grid:

$$\alpha = \arctan(\frac{f(x+h) - f(x-h)}{2h}) \cdot \frac{180}{\pi} \tag{8}$$

where h was chosen large enough ($h = 50$ in general, and it is maximum possible on the borders) for smoothing the curve to eliminate numerous abrupt changes in document frequency with relatively low amplitude. Thus, the approximation is intentionally carried out less accurately to result in such values that in practice form a curve with longer monotonous sections. Cf., Fig. 3 for an example of assessing the prominence of an n-gram "prestressed concrete"; in the above notation, T_1 equals "prestressed_ADJ", A_1 and A_2 are omitted, and T_2 equals "concrete_NOUN".

Table 1. Tangential angles of concept candidates

Candidate	Angle	Wiki-term
reinforced_ADJ concrete_NOUN	89.77	YES
mixed_ADJ concrete_NOUN	89.07	NO
prestressed_ADJ concrete_NOUN	88.40	YES
pre-cast_ADJ concrete_NOUN	83.66	YES
first_ADJ concrete_NOUN	33.12	NO
original_ADJ concrete_NOUN	16.63	NO
massive_ADJ concrete_NOUN	9.85	NO
resistant_ADJ concrete_NOUN	8.08	NO
special_ADJ concrete_NOUN	5.66	NO
polymer_ADJ concrete_NOUN	4.03	YES
tall-wall_ADJ concrete_NOUN	1.90	NO
large_ADJ concrete_NOUN	1.75	NO
open_ADJ concrete_NOUN	0.75	NO
. . .	. . .	. . .
unusual_ADJ concrete_NOUN	OOV	NO
raised_ADJ concrete_NOUN	OOV	NO
. . .	. . .	. . .

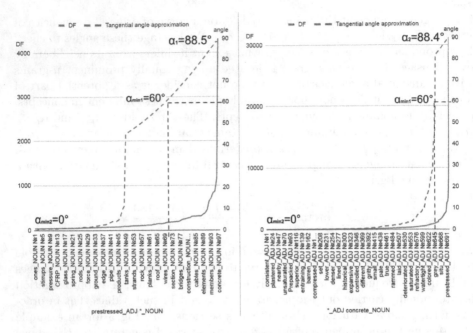

Fig. 3. Relation between document frequency and coarse-grained tangential angle approximation

Table 1 illustrates how the approximations of tangential angles differentiate classifying nominal groups from qualifying nominal groups. The most of the candidates with a large tangential angle have a separate article in Wikipedia (i.e., they are likely to be concepts), while candidates with a small tangential angle or without an entry in Google Books (and belong thus to OOV) in general do not have a Wikipedia article. This shows that the chosen criterion for differentiating the concepts is suitable for weak annotation within distant supervision.

Grid search was applied to find the best combination of parameters α_{min_1} and α_{min_2} from the three possible tangential angles: 85°, 60°, and 0°. These angles correspond to various levels of the distinctiveness of a concept and therefore give dissimilar annotations. As a result, $\alpha_{min_1} = 60°$ and $\alpha_{min_2} = 0°$ gave the best scores on the development set and were used for annotation of the training set.

4. Combination of intersected highly distinctive parts as concepts. We combine those distinctive n-grams that share common tokens and iteratively drop the last token in each group if it is not a noun, in order to end up with complete noun phrase candidate concepts (e.g., "value of the played card" is a potential concept corresponding to the patterns {N_of_DT_V; V_N}). Some single-word concepts already might appear at this point.

5. Recovery of missed single-word concepts. To enrich the set of candidate concepts, we consider all unused nouns and numbers in a text as single-word concept candidates.

The obtained training corpus contains moderate amount of noise: the proposed annotation algorithm outperforms some baselines and might be used for CE by itself; cf. setup (A) in Tables 2 and 3 with results of evaluation in the following section.

5   Experiments

5.1   Setup of the Experiments

For our experiments, we use the realization of See et al. [30]'s pointer–generator model in the OpenNMT toolkit [19], which allows for the adaptation of the model to the task of CE along the lines described in Sect. 3.1 above. We use the default OpenNMT attention proposed in [23], which simplifies and generalizes the attention mechanism of [3] used in [30]. Furthermore, the default types of the alignment functions are used: *general* for copy attention and *dot* for global attention, as suggested in [23].

The model has 512-dimensional hidden states and 256-dimensional word embeddings shared between encoder and decoder. We use a vocabulary of 50k words as we rely mostly on a copying mechanism that uses dynamic vocabulary made up of words from the current source sequence. We train the CE-adapted pointer–generator networks of two and three bi-LSTM layers with 20K and 100K training steps on the two training datasets (obtained using Google Books and DBpedia Spotlight, respectively; see above) using the Stochastic Gradient Descent on a single GeForce GTX 1080 Ti GPU with a batch size of 64. Validation and saving of checkpoint models has been performed at each one-tenth of the number of training steps.

In order to compare our extended pointer–generator model with state-of-the-art techniques, several efficient entity extraction algorithms were chosen as baselines: OLLIE [24], AIDA [35], AutoPhrase+ [31], DBpedia Spotlight [6], WAT [28],[9] and several state-of-the-art NER models, namely SpaCy NER [18], FLAIR NER [1] and two deep learning-based NER models [7,20][10];[11]. AutoPhrase+ was used in combination with the StanfordCoreNLP PoS-tagger (as it was reported to show better performance with PoS-tags) and trained separately on its default DBLP dataset and on the above-mentioned raw Wikipedia texts our training dataset is composed of. Its output was slightly modified by removing auxiliary tokens from the beginning and the end of the phrase to make it more competitive with the rest of the algorithms. OLLIE's and SpaCy's outcomes were also modified the same way, which improved their performance. DBpedia Spotlight was applied with two different values of confidence coefficient: 0.5 (default value) and 0.1, which increased the recall.

---

[9] FRED [11] was not used as baseline as it is not scalable enough for the task: its REST service has a strong limitation on a number of possible requests per day, and it fails on processing long sentences (approximately more than 40 tokens).

[10] https://github.com/glample/tagger

[11] https://github.com/kyzhouhzau/BERT-NER

The performance is measured in terms of precision, recall, and F_1-score, aiming at high recall, first of all. Since positive ground truth examples are sparse, and there are no negative examples, we treated only the detected concepts that partially overlapped the ground truth concepts as false positives. Concepts that have the same spans as the ground truth concepts are counted as true positives, and missed ground truth concepts as false negatives. This perfectly meets our goal to detect the exact match. It also allows us to penalize brute force high-recall algorithms that produce a large number of nested concepts, which are of limited use in real-world applications. Table 2 shows the reached performance on the domain-specific datasets, and Table 3 on the open domain set. The sign "*" stands for modifications made on cutting some first and last words of detected concepts in order to present them as "canonic" noun phrases, and "**" stands for removing nested concepts when this procedure gave better scores.

Table 2. Results on the domain-specific datasets

Setup	Model	"Architecture"			"Terrorist groups"		
		P	R	F_1	P	R	F_1
	FLAIR (Akbik et al. 2019)	0.79	0.74	0.76	0.77	0.66	0.71
	BERT NER (Delvin et al. 2019)	0.78	0.74	0.76	0.78	0.67	0.72
	AutoPhrase+$_{DBLP}^{**}$ (Shang et al. 2018)	0.38	0.44	0.41	0.31	0.34	0.33
	AutoPhrase+$_{WIKI}^{**}$ (Shang et al. 2018)	0.42	0.52	0.46	0.36	0.45	0.40
	SpaCy NER (Honnibal and Montani 2017)	0.59	0.51	0.55	0.5	0.41	0.45
	SpaCy NER* (Honnibal and Montan 2017)	0.71	0.61	0.66	0.59	0.49	0.54
	NER Tagger (Lample et al. 2016)	0.78	0.71	0.75	0.76	0.65	0.7
	WAT** (Piccinno and Ferragin 2014)	0.66	0.53	0.59	0.64	0.5	0.56
	Spotlight$_{0.5}$ (Daiber et al. 2013)	**0.85**	0.74	0.79	**0.8**	0.7	**0.75**
	Spotlight$_{0.1}$ (Daiber et al. 2013)	0.7	0.79	0.74	0.65	0.77	0.7
	OLLIE* (Schmitz et al. 2012)	0.46	0.2	0.28	0.41	0.22	0.28
	AIDA (Yosef et al. 2011)	0.76	0.57	0.65	0.74	0.54	0.62
(A)	$DSA_{(60,0)}$	0.63	0.74	0.68	0.5	0.64	0.56
(B)	$PG_{(3L,80K)}(DSA_{DICT})$	0.67	0.77	0.72	0.61	0.73	0.66
(C)	$PG_{(2L,18K)}(DSA_{(60,0)})$	0.7	0.8	0.75	0.59	0.72	0.65
(D)	(B) + (C)	0.75	0.83	0.79	0.66	0.77	0.71
(E)	(B) + (C) + Spotlight$_{0.1}$	0.78	0.85	0.81	0.7	**0.8**	**0.75**
(F)	(B) + (C) + Spotlight$_{0.5}$	0.78	0.85	0.81	0.7	**0.8**	**0.75**
(G)	(C) + Spotlight$_{0.5}$	0.79	**0.86**	**0.82**	0.69	0.79	0.74

Table 3 displays the scores of two different experiment runs. In the first, only concepts with an assigned WordNet type label in our typed Wikipedia dataset (in their majority, named entities; cf. [29] for details of the typification) were considered as positive examples (from about 276K nouns in the test set, only 83K nouns, i.e., about 30%, were part of ground truth concepts); in the second, all text snippets of the links were taken as ground truth concepts (from about 390K nouns in the test set, 141K nouns, i.e., about 36%, were part of ground truth concepts). Setups A – H display the performance of different variants of our model. When several outcomes are merged to check if one can benefit from a combination of various models (as in D-H), we follow "first the earliest, then the longest" strategy as in Sect. 3.2. 'DSA_{DICT}' stands for the distant supervision annotation obtained using DBpedia Spotlight, i.e., a dictionary lookup, while '$DSA_{(60,0)}$' – for the proposed token-cooccurrence frequency-based method (cf. Step 3 of the compilation of the training corpus), where the values in parentheses correspond to α_{min_1} and α_{min_2}, which gave the best scores on the development set. $PG_{(2L,18K)}$ and $PG_{(3L,80K)}$ stand for pointer–generator networks with parameters shown in parentheses chosen using the development set (2 layers, $18K/20K$ training steps and 3 layers, $80K/100K$ training steps).

Table 3. Results on a large-scale open-domain dataset

Setup	Model	Only WordNet-typed concepts			All ground truth concepts		
		P	R	F_1	P	R	F_1
	FLAIR (Akbik et al. 2019)	**0.8**	0.74	0.77	**0.79**	0.59	0.67
	AutoPhrase+$^{**}_{DBLP}$ (Shang et al. 2018)	0.42	0.45	0.43	0.4	0.43	0.41
	AutoPhrase+$^{**}_{WIKI}$ (Shang et al. 2018)	0.46	0.52	0.49	0.43	0.49	0.46
	NER Tagger (Lample et al. 2016)	0.78	0.72	0.75	0.77	0.58	0.66
	WAT** (Piccinno and Ferragina, 2014)	0.72	0.55	0.62	0.68	0.42	0.52
	Spotlight$_{0.1}$ (Daiber et al. 2013)	0.73	0.76	0.75	0.69	0.73	0.71
	OLLIE* (Schmitz et al. 2012)	0.45	0.19	0.27	0.44	0.18	0.26
	AIDA (Yosef et al. 2011)	**0.8**	0.6	0.68	0.77	0.45	0.57
(A)	$DSA_{(60,0)}$	0.68	0.75	0.71	0.65	0.72	0.68
(B)	$PG_{(3L,80K)}(DSA_{DICT})$	0.71	0.74	0.73	0.68	0.72	0.7
(C)	$PG_{(2L,18K)}(DSA_{(60,0)})$	0.71	0.81	0.76	0.68	0.76	0.72
(D)	(B) + (C)	0.76	0.84	0.8	0.72	0.8	0.76
(H)	(C) + Spotlight$_{0.1}$	0.78	**0.85**	**0.81**	0.75	**0.81**	**0.78**

To compare the performance of our model with state-of-the-art NER, we applied it to two common public datasets for NER (CoNLL-2003 and GENIA). Table 4 shows the results on the CoNLL-2003 dataset for two variants of our model (Setups B and C) trained on our large training set, without any further NER adaptation, as well as for their updated versions (Setups I, J, and K), which were fine-tuned with the training set of the shared task $CoNLL_T$, contrasted with the results of the two genuine state-of-the-art NE recognizers [20] and [7] and DBpedia Spotlight. It should be noted that NER is a concept extraction subtask which aims at detecting less generic concepts. Consider the following statistics that highlight the difference of NER with generic CE: from about 69K nouns in the CoNLL-2003 training set, only 31K nouns are part of NEs (e.g., S&P, BAYERISCHE VEREINSBANK, London Newsroom, Lloyds Shipping Intelligence Service), while the remaining 38K nouns (as in "air force", "deposit rates", "blue collar workers") are not part of NEs; as far as GENIA is concerned, from about 132K nouns, only 93K form NEs (e.g., "tumor necrosis factor", "terminal differentiation", "isolated polyclonal B lymphocytes"), while the remaining 39K do not (as "colonies", "interpretation", "notion", "circular dichroism", "differential accumulation").

Table 4. Results on the CoNLL-2003 datasets

		CoNLL-2003 (test-a)			CoNLL-2003 (test-b)		
Setup	Model	P	R	F_1	P	R	F_1
	BERT NER (Delvin et al. 2019)	0.95	0.96	0.95	0.94	0.94	0.94
	NER Tagger (Lample et al. 2016)	0.97	0.97	**0.97**	0.97	0.96	**0.96**
	Spotlight$_{0.5}$ (Daiber et al. 2011)	0.9	0.63	0.74	0.9	0.65	0.75
	Spotlight$_{0.1}$ (Daiber et al. 2011)	0.77	0.77	0.77	0.76	0.77	0.77
(B)	$PG_{(3L,80K)}(DSA_{DICT})$	0.81	0.78	0.8	0.81	0.79	0.8
(C)	$PG_{(2L,18K)}(DSA_{(60,0)})$	0.82	0.82	0.82	0.79	0.81	0.8
(I)	$FineTune((B), CoNLL_T)$	0.95	0.92	0.93	0.95	0.92	0.94
(J)	$FineTune((C), CoNLL_T)$	0.94	0.91	0.93	0.96	0.92	0.94
(K)	(I) + (J)	0.94	0.93	0.93	0.95	0.93	0.94

Table 5 shows the results of our models fine-tuned with GENIA along with the results of concept identification by the recently published model [32],[12] which provides the most promising scores on different GENIA tasks.

Table 5. Results on the GENIA dataset

		GENIA		
Setup	Model	P	R	F_1
	seq2seq (Straková et al. 2019)	0.86	0.79	0.82
(L)	$FineTune((B), GENIA_T)$	0.85	0.8	0.82
(M)	$FineTune((C), GENIA_T)$	0.84	0.77	0.81
(N)	(L) + (M)	0.85	0.8	**0.83**

5.2   Discussion

Tables 2 and 3 show that a combination of the different variants of the proposed pointer-generator model, which do not rely on external dictionaries after being trained (cf. Setup D), outperforms in terms of recall and F_1-score nearly all other models, including the dictionary lookup-based DBpedia Spotlight, which is a hard to beat as it was applied to "known" data. However, a combination of

---

[12] https://github.com/ufal/acl2019_nested_ner.

the pointer–generator model with DBpedia Spotlight is even better; it outperforms DBpedia Spotlight by 10%. In other words, a deep model combined with
a DBpedia-lookup is the best solution for generic CE. This applies to both runs
displayed in Table 3, while all tested models show a lower performance in the
discovery of non-named entities. In particular, the NER models expectedly suffer
a dramatic drop in recall. In terms of precision, DBpedia Spotlight on its own
is considerably better than any other proposal on the two small domain-specific
test sets, while AIDA is best on the open domain test set. This is to be expected
for dictionary lookup-based strategies. Also, as expected, DBpedia Spotlight,
applied with its confidence coefficient $= 0.1$, showed significantly better recall
than with the default value of 0.5, although the F_1-score was lower. The experiment on the CoNLL-2003 dataset shows that our model for generic CE performs
well even without any special adjustment ($F_1 = 0.8 - 0.82$). It can be further
fine-tuned to the specific dataset resulting in scores comparable to state of the
art, even if not designed specifically for the NER task ($F_1 = 0.93 - 0.94$), while
its overall CE performance is better than of the targeted NER models (compare,
e.g., (B)+(C) with Lample et al. (2016)'s NER in Tables 2 and 3.

We also assessed the ability of our model to detect OOV concepts taking
Setup C as an example. We found out that it detected correctly 87% of known
concepts and roughly 50% of the concepts unseen during the training phase.
The latter include such entities as "bertsolaritza", "rotary table", "oil refin-
ing complex", "rope ferry", "Lake of Two Mountains", "Gyrodyne Company of
America", etc. Concepts that were missed often have unusual structures in terms
of PoS-tag sequences or ways of capitalization; cf., e.g., "As the Rush Comes"
(detected as "Rush Comes"), and "New York Times Co. v. Sullivan" (detected
as "New York Times Co.", "v.", "Sullivan").

6   Conclusions

We presented an adaptation of the pointer–generator network model [30] to
generic open domain concept extraction. Due to its capacity to cope with
OOV concept labels, the model outperforms dictionary lookup-based CE such
as DBpedia Spotlight or AIDA in terms of recall and F_1-score. It also shows
an advantage over deep models that focus on NER only since it also covers
non-named concept categories. However, a combination of the pointer–generator
model with DBpedia Spotlight seems to be the best solution since it takes advantage of both the neural model and the dictionary lookup. In order to facilitate a
solid evaluation of the proposed model and compare it to a series of baselines, we
utilized Wikipedia pages with text snippet links as a sparsely concept-annotated
dataset. To ensure that our model is capable of extracting all generic concepts
instead of detecting only texts of the page links, we ignored this sparse annotation
during training. Instead, we compiled a large densely concept-annotated dataset
for leveraging it within the distant supervision using the algorithm described
above. To the best of our knowledge, no such dataset was available so far. In the
future, we plan to address the problem of multilingual concept extraction, using

pre-trained multi-lingual embeddings and compiling another large dataset that contains a higher percentage of non-named entity concepts.

The code for running our pretrained models is available in the following GitHub repository: https://github.com/TalnUPF/ConceptExtraction/.

Acknowledgments. The work presented in this paper has been supported by the European Commission within its H2020 Research Programme under the grant numbers 700024, 700475, 779962, 786731, 825079, and 870930.

References

1. Akbik, A., Bergmann, T., Blythe, D., Rasul, K., Schweter, S., Vollgraf, R.: FLAIR: an easy-to-use framework for state-of-the-art NLP. In: Proceeding of NAACL (2019)
2. Al-Zaidy, R., Caragea, C., Giles, C.L.: Bi-LSTM-CRF sequence labeling for keyphrase extraction from scholarly documents. In: Proceeding of WWW (2019)
3. Bahdanau, D., Cho, K., Bengio, Y.: Neural machine translation by jointly learning to align and translate. In: 3rd International Conference on Learning Representations (2015)
4. Cheng, X., Roth, D.: Relational inference for wikification. In: Proceeding of the EMNLP, pp. 1787–1796 (2013)
5. Cordeiro, S., Ramisch, C., Villavicencio, A.: UFRGS&LIF at semeval-2016 task 10: rule-based MWE identification and predominant-supersense tagging. In: Proceeding of SemEval-2016, pp. 910–917 (2016)
6. Daiber, J., Jakob, M., Hokamp, C., Mendes, P.: Improving efficiency and accuracy in multilingual entity extraction. In: Proceeding of the 9th International Conference on Semantic Systems (I-Semantics) (2013)
7. Devlin, J., Chang, M.W., Lee, K., Toutanova, K.: BERT: Pre-training of deep bidirectional transformers for language understanding. In: Proceeding of the NAACL-HLT, pp. 4171–4186 (2019)
8. Fader, A., Soderland, S., Etzioni, O.: Identifying relations for open information extraction. In: Proceeding of the EMNLP, pp. 1535–1545 (2011)
9. Fillmore, C., Baker, C.: Frame semantics for text understanding. In: Proceeding of the JWordNet and Other Lexical Resources Workshop at NAACL (2001)
10. Frege, G.: Ueber Sinn und Bedeutung. Zeitschrift fuer Philosophie und philosophische Kritik **100**, 25–50 (1892)
11. Gangemi, A., Presutti, V., Reforgiato Recupero, D., Nuzzolese, A., Draicchio, F., Mongiovì, M.: Semantic web machine reading with fred. Semant. Web **8**(6), 873–893 (2017)
12. Graves, A., Schmidhuber, J.: Framewise phoneme classification with bidirectional LSTM and other neural network architectures. Neural Netw. **18**(5–6), 602–610 (2005)
13. Gu, J., Lu, Z., Li, H., Li, V.O.: Incorporating copying mechanism in sequence-to-sequence learning. In: Proceeding of the ACL, pp. 1631–1640 (2016)
14. Habibi, M., Weber, L., Neves, M., Wiegandt, D.L., Leser, U.: Deep learning with word embeddings improves biomedical named entity recognition. Bioinformatics **33**(14), i37–i48 (2017)
15. Hailu, N.G.: Investigation of Traditional and Deep Neural Sequence Models for Biomedical Concept Recognition. Ph.D. thesis, University of Colorado (2019)

16. Halliday, M.: Halliday's Introduction to Functional Grammar. Routledge, London & New York (2013)
17. Hasibi, F., Balog, K., Bratsberg, S.: Entity linking in queries: tasks and evaluation. In: Proceeding International Conference on The Theory of Information Retrieval, pp. 171–180. ACM (2015)
18. Honnibal, M., Montani, I.: spaCy 2: natural language understanding with bloom embeddings, convolutional neural networks and incremental parsing (2017). https://spacy.io/
19. Klein, G., Kim, Y., Deng, Y., Nguyen, V., Senellart, J., Rush, A.: Opennmt: neural machine translation toolkit. In: Proceeding of the 13th Conference of the AMTA, vol. 1, pp. 177–184 (2018)
20. Lample, G., Ballesteros, M., Subramanian, S., Kawakami, K., Dyer, C.: Neural architectures for named entity recognition. Proc. NAACL-HLT (2016)
21. Lin, Y., Michel, J.B., Aiden Lieberman, E., Orwant, J., Brockman, W., Petrov, S.: Syntactic annotations for the Google books NGram corpus. In: Proceeding of the ACL 2012 System Demonstrations, pp. 169–174, July 2012
22. Logeswaran, L., Chang, M.W., Lee, K., Toutanova, K., Devlin, J., Lee, H.: Zero-shot entity linking by reading entity descriptions. Proc. ACL, 3449–3460, July 2019
23. Luong, T., Pham, H., Manning, C.: Effective approaches to attention-based neural machine translation. Proc. EMNLP, 1412–1421 (2015)
24. Mausam, Schmitz, M., Soderland, S., Bart, R., Etzioni, O.: Open language learning for information extraction. In: Proceeding of the 2012 Joint EMNLP and CoNLL Conferences, pp. 523–534 (2012)
25. Meng, R., Zhao, S., Han, S., He, D., Brusilovsky, P., Chi, Y.: Deep keyphrase generation. Proc. ACL, 582–592 (2017)
26. Mintz, M., Bills, S., Snow, R., Jurafsky, D.: Distant supervision for relation extraction without labeled data. In: Proceeding of the ACL, pp. 1003–1011 (2009)
27. Petrucci, G., Rospocher, M., Ghidini, C.: Expressive ontology learning as neural machine translation. J. Web Semant. **52**, 66–82 (2018)
28. Piccinno, F., Ferragina, P.: From TagME to WAT: a new entity annotator. In: Proceeding of the First International Workshop on Entity Recognition and Disambiguation, pp. 55–62. ERD '14, ACM, New York, NY, USA (2014)
29. Schenkel, R., Suchanek, F., Kasneci, G.: Yawn: a semantically annotated wikipedia xml corpus. Datenbanksysteme in Business, Technologie und Web, -12 (2007)
30. See, A., Liu, P.J., Manning, C.D.: Get to the point: summarization with pointer-generator networks. Proc. ACL, 1073–1083 (2017)
31. Shang, J., Liu, J., Jiang, M., Ren, X., Voss, C., Han, J.: Automated phrase mining from massive text corpora. IEEE Trans. Knowl. Data Eng. **30**(10), 1825–1837 (2018)
32. Straková, J., Straka, M., Hajic, J.: Neural architectures for nested NER through linearization. Proc. ACL, 5326–5331 (2019)
33. Tulkens, S., Šuster, S., Daelemans, W.: Unsupervised concept extraction from clinical text through semantic composition. J. Biomed. Inform. **91**, 103–120 (2019)
34. Woods, W.A.: Conceptual Indexing: A Better Way to Organize Knowledge. Technical Report SMLI, TR97-61, Sun Microsystems Laboratories (1997)
35. Yosef, M., Hoffart, J., Bordino, I., Spaniol, M., Weikum, G.: Aida: an online tool for accurate disambiguation of named entities in text and tables. Proc. VLDB Endowment **4**(12), 1450–1453 (2011)
36. Zhang, Z., Han, X., Liu, Z., Jiang, X., Sun, M., Liu, Q.: ERNIE: enhanced language representation with informative entities. Proc. ACL, 1441–1451 (2019)

Entity-Based Short Text Classification Using Convolutional Neural Networks

Mehwish Alam[1,2(✉)], Qingyuan Bie[2], Rima Türker[1,2], and Harald Sack[1,2]

[1] FIZ Karlsruhe, Leibniz Institute for Information Infrastructure,
Karlsruhe, Germany
{mehwish.alam,rima.turker,harald.sack}@fiz-karlsruhe.de
[2] Karlsruhe Institute of Technology (KIT), Karlsruhe, Germany
qingyuan.bie@fiz-karlsruhe.de

Abstract. It is beyond human capabilities to analyze a huge amount of short text produced on the World Wide Web in the form of search queries, social media platforms, etc. Due to many difficulties underlying short text for automated processing, i.e, sparsity and insufficient context, the traditional text classification approaches cannot easily be applied to short text. This study discusses a Convolutional Neural Network (CNN) based approach for short text classification. Given a short text, the model generates the text representation by leveraging words together with the entities. To validate the effectiveness of the model, several experiments have been conducted on different datasets. The results suggest that the proposed model is capable of performing short text classification with a high accuracy and outperforms the baseline.

Keywords: Short text classification · Convolutional Neural
Networks · Text classification

1 Introduction

Recently, with the advent of the World Wide Web (WWW) and the digitization of all areas an explosive growth of globally available textual data has been observed. Additionally, short text has become one of the fundamental ways to express and share opinions over different online platforms. A huge amount of such a content is generated each second such as tweets, search queries, snippets, blogs, news feeds, product reviews, etc. Performing analytics over these data is beyond human capability. Consequently, there is a special need to automatically process and analyze these data for many downstream Natural Language Processing (NLP) tasks such as text classification, text summarization and recommendation [19], fake news detection [10,12], etc.

To-date many text classification algorithms have been proposed [5]. However, different kinds of challenges are encountered while handling short text, i.e., (i) short texts such as search queries do not follow proper syntax rules of a written natural language. Slang language is very frequent in tweets along with many

C. M. Keet and M. Dumontier (Eds.): EKAW 2020, LNAI 12387, pp. 136–146, 2020.
https://doi.org/10.1007/978-3-030-61244-3_9

typing errors. In such cases, the algorithms based on syntactic parsing fail. (ii) Short text has limited context, e.g., search queries, limited characters in a tweet, etc. which makes the text more ambiguous.

Search engines are usually able to handle the search queries, however, this is mainly due to the fact that a user clicks through the relevant links which helps in resolving the ambiguity that the selected links might be the preferred meaning of what the user is searching for. Now, the question arises, how does the human mind understand the information contained in this short text? The human mind makes use of external information in order to make sense of this limited and ambiguous content. One of the ways to make this short text machine understandable is conceptualization [13], where the short text is mapped to the concepts defined in a taxonomy or a knowledge base (external). Such approaches can be classified under explicit representation models. On the other hand, many methods use implicit representation models, i.e., deep learning techniques to generate latent semantic representations of short-text [15]. Following these lines, this study combines implicit as well as explicit representation models by making use of the information provided by entities in the external knowledge base as well as the latent representations of the words and the entities. The study proposes a Convolutional Neural Network (CNN) based model due to its outstanding empirical performance on short text classification. In order to enrich the text representation, the model utilizes both words and entities together from the content of the documents for their representation. After entity linking is performed over the short text, the proposed model exploits several language models such as Word2Vec, Doc2Vec, BERT, Wikipedia2Vec, etc. An experimental evaluation was performed over several datasets for short text classification belonging to different genres such as twitter, news articles, etc. The proposed model outperforms the baseline with high accuracy.

This paper is organized as follows: Sect. 2 gives an insight into the existing methods for short text classification while Sect. 3 details the proposed approach. In order to prove the feasibility of our approach, several experiments were conducted which are given in Sect. 4. Finally, Sect. 5 concludes this study and discusses the future work.

2   Related Work

Text classification is one of the fundamental tasks in NLP. A huge amount of literature on text classification has been summarized in [5]. This section further dives into the existing approaches for short text classification. In [14], the authors combine the implicit and explicit representations, i.e., they introduce a method which in the first step conceptualizes, i.e., annotates the short text with concepts from a knowledge base (explicit representation) and then uses implicit representation, i.e, their corresponding embeddings along with the character level features for short text classification. In [2], the authors use Convolutional Neural Networks along with attention mechanism for sentiment-aware short text classification, however, the approach proposed in this study is applied for short text classification in general without targeting a specific task. The authors in [19] exploit topic memory networks for short text classification. [17] propose a model, which consists of two modules. The first module extracts the concepts and context features then applies an attention mechanism to find the context relevant features. Then the second module leverages a convolutional neural network with the high-level features along with the context relevant features. To alleviate the data sparsity problem [1] leverages knowledge from an external source. In other words, the model utilizes conceptual information from a KB to enhance the text representation. Moreover, the approach utilizes an attention mechanism to measure the importance of the information for classifying the input text.

3   Short Text Classification Using Words and Entities

This section dives into the proposed framework for short text classification by combining both the explicit and implicit representation model.

3.1   Entity Linking and Vector Representations

Entity Linking and Entity Embeddings. Given a sentence, TagMe[1] [3] is used for entity identification. It is a tool which augments the plain text with the hyperlinks from Wikipedia, i.e., connecting it to Wikipedia entities. TagMe was chosen because it proves to have good performance over short text. For vector representations of entities Wikipedia2Vec [18] was used. It is a python based tool which jointly learns word and entity embeddings where similar words and entities are close to one another in the vector space.

Word and Contextual Embeddings. The vector representations of words is obtained with the help of two embedding methods, i.e., (i) Word2Vec [8], (ii) Doc2Vec [6]. In order to incorporate contextual information in the embedding spaces the contextual embedding approach, BERT [11] was used.

3.2   Entity Convolutional Neural Networks

The overall workflow of the proposed approach, i.e., Entity Convolutional Neural Networks (EntCNN) is shown in Fig. 1. The input layer takes a word and an entity matrix. The second layer uses 3 sets of convolution kernels with width of 2, 3 and 4, each size has 2 kernels. Each of the convolution kernels slides over the whole sentence to generate a feature map.

Input (Embedding) Layer. As a first step, an embedding matrix is created from the preprocessed sentence. This word embedding matrix maps vocabulary word indices into low-dimensional vector representations. The vectors for out of vocabulary words were randomly initialized. Similarly, an entity embedding matrix was created by using Wikipedia2Vec. This entity embedding matrix

---

[1] https://tagme.d4science.org/tagme/.

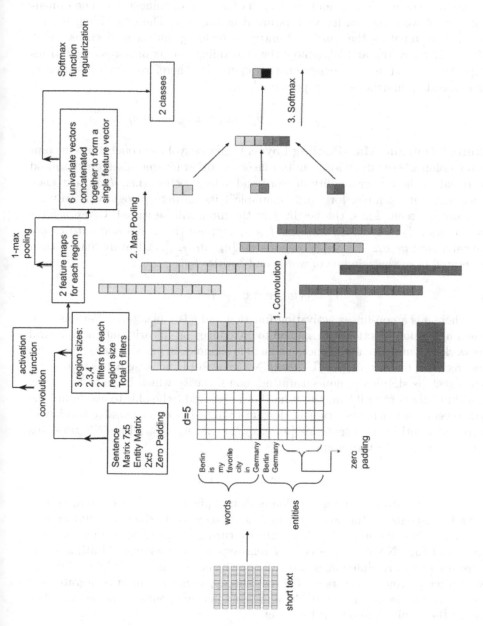

Fig. 1. Overall architecture of EntCNN

should have the same length as the word embedding matrix hence the matrix is zero padded. Zero-padding strategy was adopted for the entities which don't have entity embeddings in the pre-trained model.

Assume the maximum sentence length of a given document is l. The dimensionality of word and entity vectors are denoted as d. The embedding matrix W by concatenating the word and entity embedding matrix is given as: $W = W_w \oplus W_e$, where W_w and W_e denote the embedding matrix of words and entities respectively. $\oplus$ stands for concatenation operator. Therefore, given a sentence, its embedding matrix can be represented as:

$$W = v_1^w \oplus v_2^w \oplus \cdots \oplus v_l^w \oplus v_1^e \oplus v_2^e \oplus \cdots \oplus v_l^e$$

Convolution and Max-Pooling Layer. Unlike convolution operations in computer vision where filter width can be one or any other integer, filter width should be equal to the dimensionality of word and entity vectors (i.e., d) in text classification. For example, for word "example", its hard to recognize if only xa or $ampl$ are seen. Thus, the height f of the filter will be varied. Given a filter (convolution kernel) which has size $f \times d$, suppose the words and entities are concatenated $v_i, v_{i+1}, \ldots, v_{i+j}$, denoted as $[v_i : v_{i+f-1}]$. A feature map is then generated from this window of words and entities by:

$$c_i = g(w \cdot [v_i : v_{i+f-1}] + b)$$

where g is a non-linear activation function and b is a bias term. Various non-linear activation functions are applied to introduce non-linearity into deep neural networks. Commonly used functions include sigmoid, hyperbolic tangent (tanh) and rectified linear unit (ReLU). EntCNN uses ReLU because it has characteristics such as simplicity, non-saturating, non-linearity which helps to avoid the vanishing gradient problem, and it has been observed to be able to accelerate the convergence of stochastic gradient descent (SGD). For every possible window of words and entities in a sentence $\{x_{1:f}, x_{2:f+1}, \ldots, x_{n:f+1:n}\}$ EntCNN uses this filter to produce feature maps:

$$c = [c_1, c_2, \ldots, c_{n-f+1}]$$

A max-over-time pooling function is then applied to this feature map to create a fixed length vector. Max-pooling is a strategy where the maximum value is taken, reducing its dimensionality while capturing the most important features. Note that EntCNN uses filters of different region sizes (heights). Multiple filters were used to learn different features for the same region size (height). Because each filter produces vectors of different shapes, there is a need to iterate over them, create a layer for each of them, adopt the same pooling scheme, and then merge the results into one feature vector.

Dropout Layer. This feature vector is then passed to a dropout layer. A dropout layer stochastically disables a fraction of its neurons during training by setting them to zero, which prevents neurons from co-adapting and forces them to learn individually useful features, thus significantly reduces over-fitting. The output of the dropout layer is denoted as h.

Softmax Layer. The feature vector from dropout layer is finally passed to a fully connected layer. Label predictions are generated by performing matrix multiplication and picking the class with the highest score. Softmax function was applied to convert raw scores into a probability distribution over labels.

$$p = softmax(w \cdot h + b)$$

$$\hat{p} = argmax(p)$$

Training. The goal of training is to minimize the loss function. The cross-entropy error is the standard loss function for categorization problems. Compared with cross-entropy error, the mean squared error (MSE) and classification error are not suitable loss functions for classification. For binary classification, cross-entropy error can be calculated as:

$$L = -(ylog(p) + (1 - y)log(1 - p))$$

In the case of multi-class classification, a separate loss for each class per observation is calculated and the sum of the result is taken. L2-regularization is used to prevent over-fitting.

4   Experimental Results

This section discusses details about the datasets used for evaluation along with their statistics. In order to show that the applicability of the proposed framework, an empirical analysis over the results was performed.

4.1   Datasets

The experiments are conducted on four widely used datasets for different text classification task, i.e., (i) Twitter, (ii) Movie Review, (iii) TREC, and (iv) AG-News. Table 1 shows the statistics of the datasets used for evaluation.

- **Twitter.** The current study specifically uses the *Sentiment Analysis in Twitter* (task [9]) from SemEval 2013 and more specifically the dataset related to polarity classification (subtask B)[2]. The noisy nature of the natural language in tweets makes it a good candidate for the evaluation.
- **Movie Review** is a widely used dataset for evaluating the algorithms for polarity detection[3]. The dataset does not have a standard test set, therefore, 10% of the training data have been selected as the development set.

---

[2] https://www.cs.york.ac.uk/semeval-2013/task2/.
[3] http://www.cs.cornell.edu/people/pabo/movie-review-data/.

- **TREC** was first introduced for evaluating question classification method [7]. The dataset is freely available online[4]. It includes the following six different question labels: *Abbreviation, Entity, Description, Human, Location,* and *Numeric count.*
- **AG News** was first introduced in [20]. The original dataset consists of news title and their description[5]. From this dataset, four largest categories were chosen, i.e., world, sports, business, sci/tech. The current experiment only uses news titles.

During the preprocessing step the sentences were converted to lower case and then tokenization, stop-words removal, stemming and lemmatization were performed. In case of Twitter dataset all the URLs as well as user mentions were removed and retweets were retained by removing *"RT:"*. The hashtags were replaced with the corresponding words in the hashtag.

Table 1. $|S|$ represents the max. sentence length, $|V|$ represents the vocabulary size, $|V_{pre}|$ represents the number of words present in pre-trained model. CV stands for cross-validation, i.e., there is no standard train/test split, thus 10-fold cross validation is used.

Datasets	#classes	#labels	$|S|$	#train set	#test set	$|V|$	$|V_{pre}|$	Avg. Len
TREC	6	10	33	5452	500	8602	7223	10
Twitter	3	19	35	9684	3547	20755	12140	19
AG News	4	7	23	120000	7600	38916	25310	7
Movie Review	2	21	59	10662	CV	19897	16394	20

4.2   Experimental Setup

All the experiements were conducted on a workstation having 3.60GHz Intel Xeon 4 Cores CPUs, 1 single NVIDIA GeForce GTX 1060 GPU with CUDA 10.0.130, cuDNN 7.3.0 and TensorFlow 1.3. The pre-trained word2vec model trained on Google News was used. The model contains 300 dimensional vectors for 3 million words and phrases. For the out of vocabulary words the vectors were randomly initialized from a uniform distribution [-0.25,0.25]. The pre-trained Wikipedia2Vec[6] model trained on English Wikipedia dump was used. Doc2Vec model was trained on the latest English Wikipedia dump with 300 dimensions and 5 epochs. The model exploits different feature combinations as shown in Table 2. In the first set of experiments, only word vectors (Word(Word2Vec), Word(Doc2Vec), Word(BERT)) from the respective

---

[4] http://cogcomp.cs.illinois.edu/Data/QA/QC/.
[5] http://groups.di.unipi.it/~gulli/AG_corpus_of_news_articles.html.
[6] https://wikipedia2vec.github.io/wikipedia2vec/pretrained/.

embedding model and entity vectors (Entity(Wikipedia2vec)) were utilized separately for the classification task. In the second set of experiments, combination of word and entity vectors (Word(Word2Vec) + Entity(Wikipedia2Vec), Word(Wikipedia2Vec) + Entity(Wikipedia2Vec, etc.) were leveraged as a feature set.

The following hyper-parameters were used for the experiments (here we state the optimal parameters):

- filter sizes; lower:[3, 4, 5], upper:[3, 4, 5, 6],
- number of filters; lower:16, upper:256,
- dropout rate; 0.5,
- batch size; 64,
- l2 regularization; 3.0,
- embedding dimension; lower:100, upper:300,
- learning rate; 0.005.

4.3   Evaluation Results

The baseline used for the experimentation was Knowledge Powered Convolutional Neural Network (KPCNN) [14]. It uses external knowledge from Probase [16] along with the character, word and concept embeddings. It finally uses a CNN based model for short-text classification. KPCNN was chosen because the method is very close to our proposed approach. The method is also compared against TextCNN [4] which uses only word vectors with CNN.

The results of the experiments are illustrated in Table 2. The results show that the entities play an important role in classifying short text. It can be seen that the best classification accuracy, i.e., TREC 93.0%, Movie Review 83.0% and AG News 88.1% has been achieved by including words as well as entities in the classification process. In one of the experiments with the Movie Review dataset, where only words have been utilized, the achieved accuracy is 83.0% which is equivalent to the results based on entities leading to the fact that entities have not played a role in the classification performance. The reason here can be attributed to the characteristics of the dataset. The proportion of entities in the Movie Review dataset (83.5%) is less in comparison to other two datasets (92%). Additionally, it can be seen that for all the datasets our method outperforms the baseline. Interestingly, for each dataset a different embedding model helps to obtain the best performance but all of them use entities. Overall, it can be concluded that no single word embedding or entity embedding works best for all datasets and combination of word and entity features can help to improve the overall performance of short text classification.

The accuracy on Twitter 68.1% is much lower than three other datasets. It can be attributed to the fact that tweets contain more complicated language such as slang language and short-hand language as well as noisy or faulty sentences. When compared with TREC and AG News, it is obviously more difficult to analyze and label the sentences. In the original SemEval task [9], the best result of Twitter Task 2 subtask B is 69% which is closer to our results (Figs. 2 and 3).

Table 2. Classification accuracy of proposed model against the baseline

Methods	Twitter	TREC	MR	AG News
Baseline: KPCNN	57.24	89.3	81.5	86.1
Word(Word2Vec) (TextCNN)	68.1	89.4	**83.0**	87.4
Word(Doc2Vec)	**69.3**	91.6	81.5	87.6
Word(BERT)	**69.3**	90.2	79.3	87.4
Entity(Wikipedia2vec)	46.4	61.4	51.8	79.3
Word(Word2Vec) + Entity(Wikipedia2Vec)	68.2	90.4	**83.0**	87.9
Word(Wikipedia2Vec) + Entity(Wikipedia2Vec)	68.8	89.8	82.8	87.9
Word(Word2Vec) + Entity(Doc2Vec)	**69.3**	89.0	82.0	**88.1**
Word(Doc2Vec) + Entity(Doc2Vec)	**69.3**	**93.0**	81.3	87.4

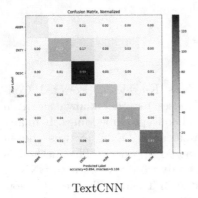
TextCNN

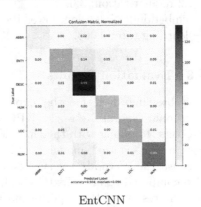
EntCNN

Fig. 2. Normalized confusion matrix on TREC

From the confusion matrices shown in Fig. 4, it can be seen that our model EntCNN (i.e., text classification using words and entities) improves the classification accuracy on label HUM from 91% to 95%, ENTY from 73% to 77% respectively, and has overall higher accuracy than TextCNN. Another observation about the classification results is that labels ABBR and ENTY have much lower accuracy than other labels. One possible explanation is that label ABBR and ENTY lack training data. The confusion matrices presented for other datasets can also be interpreted in the same way.

Finally, in order to take advantage of the sequential information contained in a sentence, methods such as Bi-LSTM and Recurrent Convolutional Neural Networks (RCNN) were used. The results are shown in Table 3. It can be observed that TextCNN outperforms RCNN and BiLSTM. In Table 2, it can be seen that the entity based methods outperform TextCNN.

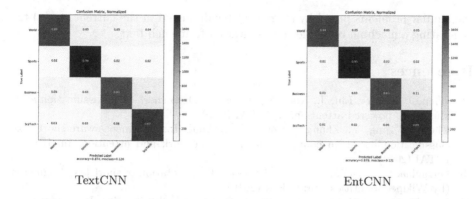

TextCNN   EntCNN

Fig. 3. Normalized confusion matrix on AGNews

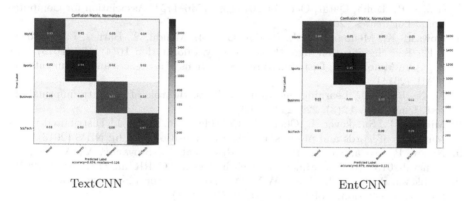

TextCNN   EntCNN

Fig. 4. Normalized confusion matrix on Twitter

Table 3. Comparison to RCNN and Bi-LSTM

Model	Twitter	TREC	Movie Review	AG News
TextCNN	68.1	89.4	83.0	87.4
RCNN	67.6	90.4	82.3	88.3
Bi-LSTM	63.6	88.4	83.7	88.2

5   Conclusion and Future Work

In this study, a CNN based model has been utilized to perform short text classification. In contrast to traditional classification models, our approach utilizes both words and entities together from the documents to represent documents as well as for dealing with the problem of ambiguity accompanied by short text. The experimental results illustrate that entities play an important role for short text classification, especially when the available context is rather limited. As future perspective, short text understanding would be exploited by targeting the similar problems posed by short text (as discussed in the current study) for generating a machine readable representation from such text.

References

1. Chen, J., Hu, Y., Liu, J., Xiao, Y., Jiang, H.: Deep short text classification with knowledge powered attention. In: AAAI (2019)
2. Chen, Z., Tang, Y., Zhang, Z., Zhang, C., Wang, L.: Sentiment-aware short text classification based on convolutional neural network and attention. In: IEEE - ICTAI (2019)
3. Ferragina, P., Scaiella, U.: TAGME: on-the-fly annotation of short text fragments (by Wikipedia entities). In: CIKM (2010)
4. Kim, Y.: Convolutional neural networks for sentence classification. In: Proceedings of the 2014 Conference on Empirical Methods in Natural Language Processing (EMNLP), Doha, Qatar, October 2014, pp. 1746–1751. Association for Computational Linguistics (2014)
5. Kowsari, K., Meimandi, K.J., Heidarysafa, M., Mendu, S., Barnes, L.E., Brown, D.E.: Text classification algorithms: a survey. Information **10**(4), 150 (2019)
6. Le, Q.V., Mikolov, T.: Distributed representations of sentences and documents. In: ICML (2014)
7. Li, X., Roth, D.: Learning question classifiers: the role of semantic information. Nat. Lang. Eng. **12**(3), 229–249 (2006)
8. Mikolov, T., Sutskever, I., Chen, K., Corrado, G.S., Dean, J.: Distributed representations of words and phrases and their compositionality. In: NIPS (2013)
9. Nakov, P., Kozareva, Z., Ritter, A., Rosenthal, S., Stoyanov, V., Wilson, T.: Semeval-2013 task 2: sentiment analysis in Twitter. CoRR, abs/1912.06806 (2019)
10. Oshikawa, R., Qian, J., Wang, W.Y.: A survey on natural language processing for fake news detection. CoRR, abs/1811.00770 (2018)
11. Peters, M.E., Neumann, M., Iyyer, M., Gardner, M., Clark, C., Lee, K., Zettlemoyer, L.: Deep contextualized word representations. In: NAACL-HLT (2018)
12. Rashkin, H., Choi, E., Jang, J.Y., Volkova, S., Choi, Y.: Truth of varying shades: analyzing language in fake news and political fact-checking. In: EMNLP (2017)
13. Song, Y., Wang, H., Wang, Z., Li, H., Chen, W.: Short text conceptualization using a probabilistic knowledgebase. In: IJCAI. IJCAI/AAAI (2011)
14. Wang, J., Wang, Z., Zhang, D., Yan, J.: Combining knowledge with deep convolutional neural networks for short text classification. In: Sierra, C. (ed.) IJCAI (2017)
15. Wang, Z., Wang, H.: Understanding short texts. In: The Association for Computational Linguistics (ACL) (Tutorial), August 2016
16. Wu, W., Li, H., Wang, H., Zhu, K.Q.: Probase: a probabilistic taxonomy for text understanding. In: ACM SIGMOD (2012)
17. Xu, J., Cai, Y.: Incorporating context-relevant knowledge into convolutional neural networks for short text classification. In: AAAI (2019)
18. Yamada, I., et al.: Wikipedia2Vec: an efficient toolkit for learning and visualizing the embeddings of words and entities from Wikipedia. arXiv preprint 1812.06280v3 (2020)
19. Zeng, J., Li, J., Song, Y., Gao, C., Lyu, M.R., King, I.: Topic memory networks for short text classification. In: EMNLP (2018)
20. Zhang, X., LeCun, Y.: Text understanding from scratch. CoRR, abs/1502.01710 (2015)

What2Cite: Unveiling Topics and Citations Dependencies for Scientific Literature Exploration and Recommendation

Davide Giosa and Luigi Di Caro[✉]

University of Turin, Turin, Italy
giosa.davide@gmail.com, luigi.dicaro@unito.it

Abstract. The continuous evolution of research has led to an exponential growth of the scientific literature. This engenders difficulties for researchers to entirely capture the most salient efforts related to their own research. In this paper, we propose a novel knowledge model for unveiling meaningful and labeled relations among articles based on both topics and latent citation dependencies. An experimentation on the whole literature in the Computer Science field allowed us to validate our approach by bridging the gap between few lines of textual content (e.g., an abstract) to the most relevant papers to be included in the bibliography.

Keywords: Citation modeling · Topic modelling · Document semantic

1 Introduction

The search and the exploration of relevant information within large amounts of scientific papers is becoming more and more laborious. While there is an obvious connection between articles through the content that they express (i.e., their semantics), other dynamics related to the citational aspect of the scientific literature are also involved. In the light of this, in this work we aim at modeling relations among articles based on both their thematic information and the latent structure of the referenced citations within the entire literature of a generic domain (Computer Science, in our case).

Generally speaking, we started from the main goal of associating few lines of textual content (e.g., an abstract) with a set of papers that should be considered for inclusion as references. A first and standard view on this problem, which is indeed utilized by several online services, is that of providing (or suggest, recommend, etc.) articles which reflect similar content. However, it is known that a simple abstract may have an incredible large set of very similar documents, whereas the decision of what to include is completely left to the complex reasoning and knowledge of researchers, who may know highly deep details about fine-grained information and perspective contained in each single article. While

© Springer Nature Switzerland AG 2020
C. M. Keet and M. Dumontier (Eds.): EKAW 2020, LNAI 12387, pp. 147–157, 2020.
https://doi.org/10.1007/978-3-030-61244-3_10

we may consider such semantic depth as too complex to unravel for any Artificial Intelligence mechanism so far, we can utilize the *output* of such scientists' reasoning for going back up to it. This basis, in our view, is represented by the already-existing choice of references each article in literature carries within its bibliography. In other words, the co-occurrence of citations within the literature is an evidence of reasoning processes which relate the specific content of a paper to other articles irrespective of their surface lexical semantics (or topics).

When an article A is related to another article B, it usually happens when A and B share some features, possibly regardless of the similarity between their topics. For instance, article B may use the data of A although for different goals.

In this paper, we propose a citation-centered modeling approach which creates a semantic knowledge of both topics and clusters of citations (which we name *citopics* from now on) which allows a fair connection between a short textual summary with the most relevant references in the literature. Section 2 goes through the related works on the topic, while Sect. 3 presents the method[1] and its technicalities. Section 4 describes the evaluation of the proposal and Sect. 5 finally concludes the contribution highlighting critical points and possible future directions.

2   Related Work

Our contribution has similarities with several approaches related to the modeling and use of the citations within large scholar databases, such as *(i)* semantic modeling of citations (e.g., [5,12,17]), *(ii)* data analysis and extraction of relevant information (e.g., [6,7,15,18]), and *(iii)* exploration of the scientific literature by means of faceted search queries and visualization tools (e.g., [1,2,8,9,13]).

So far, part of the scientific literature is focused on the theoretical and top-down aspects of the citations. For example, *CiTo* [17] is focused on the modeling of possible citation intents. More in detail, they identified and formalized different types of possible citation meanings by proposing an ontology which includes a wide set of complex cases. However, this type of approach requires manual efforts of annotations and it is not suitable for large-scale analysis of a scientific domain.

On the other side, computational approaches to citation modeling have been presented, mostly based on clustering or classification tasks. In [10], the authors presented an unsupervised technique based on a clustering process, identifying and then manually labeling 11 classes of citations in a corpus. Differently, in [5] the authors proposed a classifier based on Scaffolds models [19] that was able to identify 6 classes of citations on the ACL-ARC dataset and 3 classes on a larger dataset named SciCite with high accuracy levels.

Our goal, conversely, is to focus on the association between the semantic content of papers and their bibliography, creating a dual space where to search for relevant candidate references to ascribe to short research descriptions.

---

[1] The code is publicly available at https://github.com/Dive904/What2Cite.

3   Data and Method

In this section we present the details of the proposed method and the utilized datasets and resources. We built our experimentation on the Semantic Scholar's dataset[2], filtering out non-English contributions[3], and reaching around 4 millions Computer Science papers associated with metadata such as *identifiers, years of publication, sources, titles, abstracts* and *out citations*.

3.1   Topic Modeling and Classification

The first phase of the approach consists in the extraction of the topics from the textual abstracts contained in the dataset. To this end, we employed the well known Latent Dirichlet Allocation (LDA) technique[4] [4] on half of the dataset, only considering articles from 2010 and applying standard text preprocessing steps such as lemmatization and stopwords removal[5].

We experimented with different numbers of topics, finally focusing on 35, 40 and 45. Then, after a careful qualitative analysis on the obtained results, we decided to opt for 40 topics. Below, we show some examples:

```
Topic #3: security attack scheme privacy protocol key secure
Topic #8: gene available tool analysis database file sequence
Topic #13: problem algorithm fuzzy solution set time optimization
Topic #27: patient medical health clinical disease treatment care
Topic #32: text word document task information semantic topic
```

Generally speaking, we consider the whole set of 40 topics as of very high quality, with high topic coherence and consistency.

After this phase, we used the trained LDA model to further train a Neural Network model for classifying new instances. In particular, we created a dedicated dataset by picking up 2000 random papers which were most highly-associated with each topic, then dividing it as follows: 60% for the training set, 30% for the test set, 10% for the validation set.

The employed Neural Network model is a Bidirectional LSTM [16]. This allows us the classification of new textual contents (e.g., new abstracts) based on stable LDA topics, also taking into account the sequential nature of the natural language and the recent advancement of neural-based word embedding technologies. The overall model architecture is shown in Fig. 1, and it is composed of a first embedding layer with 300 dimensions and a Bidirectional LSTM of 550 units, followed by a dropout of 0.4. We used GloVe embeddings [14] trained with 840 billion of entities and 2.2 million of words, with a vector size of 300.

---

[2] Dataset available at https://api.semanticscholar.org/corpus/download/.

[3] *langdetect* - https://pypi.org/project/langdetect/.

[4] *scikit-learn* - https://scikit-learn.org/0.16/modules/generated/sklearn.lda.LDA.html.

[5] *nltk* - https://www.nltk.org.

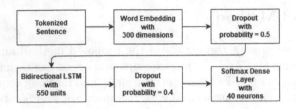

Fig. 1. The proposed Neural Network architecture.

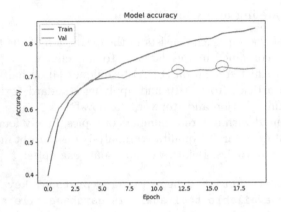

Fig. 2. Model accuracy during training.

Figure 2 shows the model accuracy during the training. We trained the network for 20 epochs, and selected the epoch 17 for the final model, reaching the accuracy scores shown in Tables 1 and 2.

3.2 Citation Topic Modeling: The Concept of *Citopics*

A *Citopic* (a.k.a. *Citation Topic*) is a set of paper IDs which, within the literature, are most often cited together. Thus, we considered this scenario as fitting a standard application of Topic Modeling where, instead of words, the input documents are composed of citations (IDs of papers). By treating every citation as a single word, a single bibliography of an input paper is transformed in a sentence-like sequence of cited papers where to apply a topic modeling exercise. In this particular case, the output is a set of topics (that we rename as *citopics*) containing paper IDs often cited together in the literature.

Since the dataset has some missing *OutCitations* information, we first made a scan of the entire dataset creating a new version where every paper has at least $\frac{2}{3}$ of its citations in the dataset. This new dataset counts approximately 800 K papers. As in the first (thematic) Topic Modeling on the abstracts, we run the LDA model on the citations trying different numbers of topics n. Due to the goal of unraveling many small sets of papers, we maximized n, reaching the value of $n = 750$ before encountering technical problems with the used library.

Table 1. Model scores at epoch 17.

Training		Validation		Test	
Loss	Accuracy	Loss	Accuracy	Loss	Accuracy
2.0715	0.8292	2.4107	0.7280	1.1776	0.7197

Table 2. Model scores with top 3 elements and using threshold

Set	Top 3	Using Threshold of 0.4
Training	0.922	0.735
Validation	0.98	0.893
Test	0.918	0.724

After obtaining 750 different citopics, we applied a *rank-and-filter* approach. In particular, we sorted the citopics words (i.e., citations) and kept those until summing up to the $\frac{2}{3}$ of the entire citopics scores[6]. Figure 3 shows a citopic example.

82266f6103bade9005ec555ed06ba20b5210ff22 **Gaussian processes for machine learning**	0c8413ab8de0c1b8f2e86402b8d737d94371610f **Gaussian Process Optimization in the Bandit Setting: No Regret and Experimental Design**
0a2586e0a5f8bb4e35aa0763a6b8bca428af6bd2 **Taking the Human Out of the Loop: A Review of Bayesian Optimization**	cd5a26b89f0799db1cbc1dff5607cb6815739fe7 **A Tutorial on Bayesian Optimization of Expensive Cost Functions, with Application to Active User Modeling and Hierarchical Reinforcement Learning**
93bc65d2842b8cc5f3cf72ebc5b8f75daeacea35 **Scalable Bayesian Optimization Using Deep Neural Networks**	2e2089ae76fe914706e6fa90081a79c8fe01611e **Practical Bayesian Optimization of Machine Learning Algorithms**

Fig. 3. An example of citation topic (*Citopic*), mostly belonging to Topic 38 (*algorithm search problem* ...) and Topic 1 (*network feature learning* ...).

3.3   Linking Topics and Citopics: The $L_t(x)$ Function

To relate *citopics* with *topics*, we define a function $L_t(x) : String \rightarrow List$ (where x is a paper ID) which returns a list of t elements, each one identifying one topic. In detail, each element i reports the number of times the paper x is cited by a paper of topic i. Algorithm 1 illustrates this dictionary creation process.

In our case, we can use the function $L_{40}(x)$, where x is a paper ID in one *citopic*, to get the list of frequencies. To make an example, we can call this function with a sample paper *id*:

$$L\_EXP = L_{40}(id)$$

---

[6] The score of a citopic is the sum of all the scores of a single ID in the citopic. We can get this score from the LDA while creating the clusters.

Algorithm 1. Create Dictionary

$D \leftarrow dataset$
$Dic \leftarrow initialize\_dictionary()$
for all paper p in D **do**
   $id \leftarrow get\_paper\_id(p, D)$
   $topic \leftarrow get\_paper\_topic(p, D)$
   $outcitations \leftarrow get\_paper\_outcitations(p, D)$
   for all citation c in $outcitations$ **do**
      $score\_list \leftarrow Dic.get(c)$
      $score\_list[topic] \leftarrow score\_list[topic] + 1$
      $Dic[c] \leftarrow score\_list$
   end for
end for

from which we get the following list:

```
[0, 36, 1, 0, 0, 0, 0, 0, 0, 1, 3, 0, 0, 1, 0, 0, 0, 0, 1, 0,
1, 0, 0, 1, 2, 0, 0, 0, 0, 1, 0, 106, 0, 0, 0, 0, 2, 61, 1, 0]
```

As we can notice, the result is a list of size 40 where every element is a number (e.g., L_EXP[31] = 106, meaning that the input paper has been cited 106 times by another paper of topic #31).

3.4 Linking Texts to Citopics: The $ScoreCitTopic_c(x)$ Function

Now, we can define a function that recommends *citopics* given an input abstract of a generic paper x. Let us define the $ScoreCitTopic_c(x) : String \rightarrow Int$ function with Algorithm 2.

Algorithm 2. Score Function

$cit \leftarrow cit\_topic$
$x \leftarrow paper$
$topic \leftarrow get\_paper\_topic(x)$
$final\_score \leftarrow 0$
for all id in cit **do**
   $score\_list \leftarrow L_{40}(id)$
   $score \leftarrow score\_list[topic]$
   $final\_score \leftarrow final\_score + score$
end for
return $final\_score$

The score function is based on the $L_t(x)$ function. We start from the topic of the input paper and we scan the input *citopic*. First, for each paper within the *citopic*, we obtain the frequency list through the $L_t(x)$ function. At this point, we then take the frequency related to the topic associated with the input paper x. In words, with this step we are answering the following question: "how many times a paper in the *citopic* has been cited by papers with the same topic of the input paper?". By answering this question for each paper in *citopic* we can obtain a global score. After this phase, we take the score of every available *citopic* for a specific paper.

Algorithm 3. Score All Citopics Function

$x \leftarrow paper$
$cit\_topics \leftarrow get\_cit\_topics()$
$score\_list \leftarrow empty\_list()$
for all cit in cit_topics **do**
    $score \leftarrow ScoreCitTopic_{cit}(x)$
    $score\_list.append(score)$
end for
return $score\_list$

In particular, Algorithm 3 returns a list with the same size of the total number of *citopics*, that is, in our case, 750. Using this function with a particular input paper x, we obtain the following list $[s_0, s_1, \ldots, s_{749}]$. Here, the generic element s_i represents the score for the i-th *citopic*. We then conclude with Algorithm 3 that relates a particular paper to different *citopics*, in particular by assigning a score to each of them. An immediate usage of this result is the possibility of sorting the list to obtain the final articles recommendation. In detail, from the list in 3.4, we can create a second list as follows: $[(0, s_0), (1, s_1), \ldots, (749, s_{749})]$, where every element is a pair (i, s_i). Now, by sorting the pairs through the scores s_i we reach a rank of *citopics* indices. From this, we may select the first k *citopics* with highest scores for recommendation. The overall architecture of the proposal is shown in Fig. 4.

4   Evaluation

4.1   Miss Set and Hit Set

Let us consider a paper x with a list O of out citations: $O = [o_0, \ldots, o_n]$, where each o_i is a paper cited by paper x. Similarly, if we pick up a *citopic* C, we have $C = [c_0, \ldots, c_m]$, where each c_j is a paper in that cluster. From these sets we can generate an H-set, also called *Hit Set*, in the following way: $H = C \cap O$, where H represents intersection between C and O. With the H-set, we can create the *Miss set* M, i.e. $M = C - H$. If we consider a function $out(x)$ which returns the *out citation* set of a paper x, we can define a function $hit_C(x)$, where $hit_C(x) = C \cap out(x)$. The $hit_C(x)$ function of a paper x with a *citopic* C returns a set containing all the papers within the *out citation* set of x that are actually in *citopic* C. Thus, it returns the H-set of a paper x with a *citopic* C.

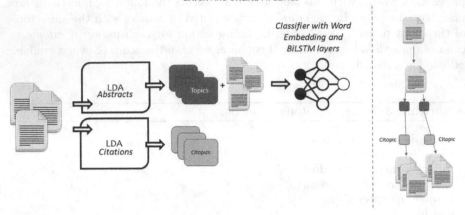

Fig. 4. Batch and online architecture of the proposal.

4.2   Accuracy Definition

We need to remember that the *citopics* are generated from an LDA run. Thus, it may happen that a paper ID does not appear in any *citopic*. Thus, to create a fair evaluation of our proposed method, we counted its obtained *hits* in relation with the total citations that have been covered by all *citopics* only.

Let us consider a function $ht(x)$ from where we can enumerate all the possible hits for a specific paper x. So, we can calculate the accuracy with:

$$A_C(x) = \frac{|hit_C(x)|}{ht(x)} \tag{1}$$

We can make things a little more complex, considering both different *citopics* and different papers at the same time. In particular, we may have a set of papers $P = [p_0, \ldots, p_n]$ and a set of different *citopics* for a particular paper p_i $C^{p_i} = [C_0^{p_i}, \ldots, C_m^{p_i}]$ where $C_j^{p_i}$ is a selected *citopic* for paper p_i. We can then suppose to make another set $C = [C^{p_0}, \ldots, C^{p_n}]$.

Finally, the general accuracy formula becomes:

$$A_C(P) = \frac{\sum_{p_i \in P} \sum_{C_j^{p_i} \in C^{p_i}} |H_{C_j^{p_i}}(p_i)|}{\sum_{p_i \in P} HT(p_i)} \tag{2}$$

In the numerator, the first sum loops on each input paper p_i, while the second one is used to loop on each *Citopic* $C_j^{p_i}$ in the selected list C^{p_i}. Then, we use the H function with $C_j^{p_i}$ and p_i as input, to calculate the *Hit Set* and, in particular, its cardinality. In the denominator, we have a single loop on every input paper p_i where we calculate the number of all possible hits that could be obtained. In conclusion, the $A_C(P)$ function calculates the percentage of obtained hits out of the total possible hits. Algorithm 4 shows the accuracy calculation process.

Algorithm 4. Accuracy with more papers and more *Citopics*

$P \leftarrow list\_of\_papers$
$n \leftarrow input\_number$
$C \leftarrow empty\_list()$
for all *paper* in P **do**
   $scores \leftarrow AllScoreFunction(paper)$
   $scores \leftarrow sort(scores)$
   $citopics \leftarrow get\_citopics\_with\_max\_scores(n)$
   $C.append(citopics)$
end for
$acc \leftarrow A_C(P)$
return acc

To have a precise idea on the accuracy of the entire system, we could use Algorithm 4 and with the n parameter equals to 750. In this way, we take all the *citopics* and calculate the accuracy on each individual *citopic*. The idea is that if the individual accuracy values calculated on each *citopic* have a decreasing trend as the scores drop, then the result may be considered as satisfactory.

In detail, let us imagine a simple score list $L = [s_0, \ldots, s_{749}]$. Then, we divide the scores list into further sublists (or portions). Taking as input a certain percentage p, we have to divide the list of scores into sublists composed of p percent of the total elements. If the percentage is 10%, each individual sublist will be composed of 10% of the elements (data binning). This way, we do not take into account top-ranked elements but top-ranked portions. Thus, the list will be $L = [[s_0, \ldots, s_{49}], \ldots, [s_{674}, \ldots, s_{749}]]$. With this combination of sublists, we can take a single sublist, then the *citopics* related to that sublist[7], and compute the cardinality of the Hit Set for each *citopic*. Finally, we can calculate the sum over all the citopics. Thus, if the percentage is e.g. 10%, we should have a partitioned list $PL = [l_0, \ldots, l_9]$ where every l_i is the number of hits from the *citopics* in portion i of the list L.

4.3   Results

We calculated the accuracy of the proposed method on a random set of 1000 input papers. It must be specified that the papers taken as input are papers that have not been used for the creation of the *citopics* (i.e., it can be considered as a test test). In this way, we also simulate the behaviour of our approach in the real case in which the input is a paper that does not yet exist in the literature. During this process, we take into account all the classified topics of a single paper with a probability higher than 40%. Results are shown in Fig. 5.

The decreasing trend of hits percentage ($P1 = 65.5\%$, $P2 = 14.9\%$, $P3 = 7.1\%$, $P4 = 4.3\%$, etc.) is a clear sign that the score-based metric is the right one, since we see a drop in the number of hits together with the decreasing of the *citopic* scores. This trend leaves complete freedom to the user (or application)

---

[7] Every score s_i is related to the *Citopic i*.

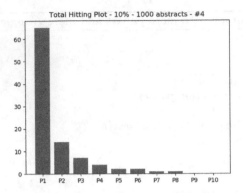

Fig. 5. Cumulative distribution of hits over the portions.

regarding the choice of the number of *citopics* to consider. For example, taking the first 2 portions and then the 4 portions, the method cumulatively reach around 80% and 91% of accuracy respectively (i.e., probability that the returned papers fit the input textual content or abstract).

5   Conclusions and Future Works

Linking an abstract to single citations can be very challenging, as the simple content-based similarity may end up with thousands of equally-relevant articles. For this reason, in this paper we proposed a method which includes information about citations dependencies through a topic modeling techniques applied on paper IDs, obtaining very promising results. At the moment, we based our efforts on some qualitative analysis (e.g., the choice of the number of topics) which can be certainly improved in future research. Another type of extension could be based on hierarchical topic modeling [11]. Indeed, topics are often correlated and standard topic modeling techniques are not able to capture these relationships [3]. Another future direction could focus on the used metrics for the accuracy evaluation. In this work, only frequencies have been used, whereas other types of statistical information might be employed.

References

1. Akujuobi, U., Zhang, X.: Delve: a dataset-driven scholarly search and analysis system. SIGKDD Explor. Newsl. **19**(2), 36–46 (2017). https://doi.org/10.1145/3166054.3166059. http://doi.acm.org/10.1145/3166054.3166059
2. Alexander, E., Kohlmann, J., Valenza, R., Witmore, M., Gleicher, M.: Serendip: topic model-driven visual exploration of text corpora. In: 2014 IEEE Conference on Visual Analytics Science and Technology (VAST), pp. 173–182. IEEE (2014)
3. Blei, D.M., Lafferty, J.D., et al.: A correlated topic model of science. Ann. Appl. Stat. **1**(1), 17–35 (2007)

4. Blei, D.M., Ng, A.Y., Jordan, M.I.: Latent dirichlet allocation. J. Mach. Learn. Res. **3**, 993–1022 (2003)
5. Cohan, A., Ammar, W., van Zuylen, M., Cady, F.: Structural scaffolds for citation intent classification in scientific publications. In: Proceedings of the 2019 Conference of the North American Chapter of the Association for Computational Linguistics: Human Language Technologies NAACL-HLT 2019, Minneapolis, MN, USA, June 2–7, 2019, Volume 1 (Long and Short Papers), pp. 3586–3596 (2019). https://www.aclweb.org/anthology/N19-1361/
6. Di Caro, L., Cataldi, M., Schifanella, C.: The d-index: discovering dependences among scientific collaborators from their bibliographic data records. Scientometrics **93**(3), 583–607 (2012)
7. Šubelj, L., van Eck, N.J., Waltman, L.: Clustering scientific publications based on citation relations: a systematic comparison of different methods. PLoS ONE **11**(4), e0154404 (2016)
8. van Eck, N.J., Waltman, L.: VOS: a new method for visualizing similarities between objects. In: Decker, R., Lenz, H.-J. (eds.) Advances in Data Analysis. SCDAKO, pp. 299–306. Springer, Heidelberg (2007). https://doi.org/10.1007/978-3-540-70981-7_34
9. van Eck, N.J., Waltman, L.: CitNetExplorer: a new software tool for analyzing and visualizing citation networks. J. Informetrics **8**(4), 802–823 (2014)
10. Ferrod, R., Schifanella, C., Caro, L.D., Cataldi, M.: Disclosing citation meanings for augmented research retrieval and exploration. In: Proceedings of the Semantic Web - 16th International Conference, ESWC 2019, Portorož, Slovenia, 2–6 June 2019, pp. 101–115 (2019). https://doi.org/10.1007/978-3-030-21348-0_7
11. Griffiths, T.L., Jordan, M.I., Tenenbaum, J.B., Blei, D.M.: Hierarchical topic models and the nested chinese restaurant process. In: Advances in neural information processing systems, pp. 17–24 (2004)
12. Kim, J., Kim, D., Oh, A.: Joint modeling of topics, citations, and topical authority in academic corpora. arXiv preprint arXiv:1706.00593 (2017)
13. Nagwani, N.: Summarizing large text collection using topic modeling and clustering based on MapReduce framework. J. Big Data **2**(1), 6 (2015)
14. Pennington, J., Socher, R., Manning, C.D.: Glove: global vectors for word representation. In: Proceedings of the 2014 Conference on Empirical Methods in Natural Language Processing (EMNLP), pp. 1532–1543 (2014)
15. Popescul, A., Ungar, L.H., Flake, G.W., Lawrence, S., Giles, C.L.: Clustering and identifying temporal trends in document databases. In: ADL, p. 173. IEEE (2000)
16. Schuster, M., Paliwal, K.K.: Bidirectional recurrent neural networks. IEEE Trans. Signal Proces. **45**(11), 2673–2681 (1997)
17. Shotton, S.P.D.: FaBiO and CiTO: ontologies for describing bibliographic resources and citations. Web Semant. Sci. Serv. Agent World Wide Web **17**, 33–43 (2012)
18. Strapparava, R.M.C.C.C.: Corpus-based and knowledge-based measures of text semantic similarity. In: Proceedings of the 21st National Conference on Artificial Intelligence AAAI 2006, Vol. 1, pp. 775–780 (2006)
19. Swayamdipta, S., Thomson, S., Lee, K., Zettlemoyer, L., Dyer, C., Smith, N.A.: Syntactic scaffolds for semantic structures. In: Proceedings of the 2018 Conference on Empirical Methods in Natural Language Processing, Brussels, Belgium, 31 October - 4 November 2018, pp. 3772–3782 (2018). https://www.aclweb.org/anthology/D18-1412/

Mining Latent Features of Knowledge Graphs for Predicting Missing Relations

Tobias Weller[(✉)], Tobias Dillig, Maribel Acosta, and York Sure-Vetter

Karlsruhe Institute of Technology, Englerstraße 11, Karlsruhe, Germany
{tobias.weller,maribel.acosta,york-sure-vetter}@kit.edu

Abstract. Knowledge Graphs (KGs) model statements as head-relation-tail triples. Intrinsically, KGs are assumed incomplete especially when knowledge is represented under the Open World Assumption. The problem of KG completeness aims at identifying missing values. While some approaches focus on predicting relations between pairs of known nodes in a graph, other solutions have studied the problem of predicting missing entity properties or relations even in the presence of unknown tails. In this work, we address the latter research problem: for a given head entity in a KG, obtain the set of relations which are missing for the entity. To tackle this problem, we present an approach that mines latent information about head entities and their relations in KGs. Our solution combines in a novel way, state-of-the-art techniques from association rule learning and community detection to discover latent groups of relations in KGs. These latent groups are used for predicting missing relations of head entities in a KG. Our results on ten KGs show that our approach is complementary state-of-the-art solutions.

1 Introduction

Knowledge graphs (KGs) have become an important foundation to represent knowledge exploited in, e.g, Question Answering, Entity Linking, and recommender systems. While current real-world KGs, such as DBpedia [3] and Wikidata [20], contain millions of facts, they still suffer from incompleteness which may hinder the effectiveness of the applications where they are consumed.

Motivating Example. Consider the KG depicted on Fig. 1 (left), representing facts about persons. However, in the KG, the entity *Paul_Sereno* is not described with the relation *placeOfBirth*. The question that arises is whether the relation *placeOfBirth* for this head entity is missing. Furthermore, it could be that the actual value (i.e., the tail entity) for *placeOfBirth* does not exist in the KG. This work aims at predicting missing relations for a given head entity, regardless of the existence of the tail entity in the KG.

To address the problem of KG completeness, approaches typically assume that two of the components in the triple are known a priori, e.g., when predicting relations, it is assumed that the head and tail entities are represented in the

© Springer Nature Switzerland AG 2020
C. M. Keet and M. Dumontier (Eds.): EKAW 2020, LNAI 12387, pp. 158–170, 2020.
https://doi.org/10.1007/978-3-030-61244-3_11

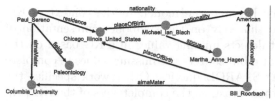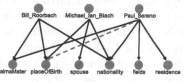

Fig. 1. Motivating Example. Consider the given subgraph of DBpedia on the left. We address the problem of predicting missing relations, based on a given head-entity. On the right we converted the graph into a bipartite graph by only considering the heads and the relations of the KG. The red dotted edge corresponds to the motivated scenario of predicting the missing relation *placeOfBirth* for entity *Paul_Sereno*.

KG. This is a typical assumption in approaches that rely on subsymbolic representations, e.g., KG embeddings [5,19]. However, predicting missing relations to estimate head entity completeness is not directly possible under this assumption, as shown in the following example. Following the motivating scenario from Fig. 1, assume that the entity *Paul_Sereno* was actually born in *Aurora (Illinois, USA)*, leading to the fact that current approaches cannot detect that the entity *Paul_Sereno* is incomplete with respect to the relation *placeOfBirth*, as they cannot establish an association between a head entity and an unknown tail entity. To overcome this limitation, we propose a solution to perform the prediction of missing relations associated with an entity in a KG even in the presence of unknown tail entities. Our solution comprises two main stages: the relation-centric stage and the prediction stage. In the relation-centric stage, we use a technique from association rule learning to reduce noise and mining groups of frequently occurring relations. Afterwards, the information from that analysis is represented as a graph. This graph is used to identify communities of relations, which represent clusters of latently related relations. In the prediction stage, the information from the interactions of the entities in the KG and the information about the latently related relations encoded in the communities are used to predict missing relations of head entities. Experimental results show that the evaluated approaches exhibit a complementary performance, and that our approach significantly outperforms the state-of-the-art in four out of the ten studied KGs.

2   Related Work

Knowledge Graph Completion. TransE [5] represents relation, head and tail entities as vectors. ComplEx [19] is based on the same concept as TransE, but uses complex-valued vectors for predicting relations in knowledge graphs. Both methods are transductive learning algorithms, making it possible to predict missing parts of triples, given that the individual entities and relations are known to the model in advance. In contrast to these methods, EDMAR [18] and RDF Shape Induction [10] are inductive methods that learn a general model from examples and are therefore applicable to all triples, even if entities and relations were not known in advance while learning the model. In the context of KG completion, there are approaches that rely on the symbolic representation of KGs. HARE [1] is an engine that detects missing values in a KG based on the Local-Closed World Assumption. It crowdsources the missing values to complete the KG and allows for answering SPARQL queries. Other work specifies the number of missing relations and thus measures the completeness of the KG [14]. The information about missing relations can be used to learn rules [8] for KG completion. All these methods predict relations between two given entity nodes in the KG.

Frequent Itemsets. High-utility Itemsets [7,9] is an extension to Highly-correlated itemset mining [2] in which the most frequent itemsets are to be found, which yield the highest profit. The utility of the transactions is the most important criteria. However, the problem of finding high-utility frequent itemsets is computational very expensive. Faster High-Utility Itemset Mining (FHM) is a very fast High-Utility Itemset Mining algorithm [7], which reduces the number of join operations and thus improves the runtime. However, utilizing utility results in many itemsets which yield a high utility but correlate only very weakly. Therefore, FHM was extended to guarantee that the itemsets correlate strongly, besides yielding a high utility [7].

Community Detection. The identification of communities is particularly prominent in the area of social network analysis [17]. Community detection, however, is not exclusively applicable to social networks. Network analyses in the field of co-authorship are also conceivable [12]. In general, a community is a dense subgraph. Detecting them is computationally very expensive. For this reason, random walks [15] or grouping methods [16] have been used to simplify and speed up the computations. However, a trade-off will arise here between the quality of the results and runtime for large networks. Nevertheless, there are also approaches that have returned reliable results on very large graphs while exhibiting a satisfying runtime [6].

3   Problem Definition

In this work, we define a knowledge graph G as $G = (H \cup T, R)$, where H denotes the set of head entities, T the set of tail entities, and R the set of labelled relations. The information in the knowledge graph G can be modeled as triples (h, r, t), with $h \in H$ denotes the head entity which has a relation $r \in R$ to a tail entity, denoted as $t \in T$. Furthermore, consider $R_h(G)$ the set of relations where the entity h appears in the head of a statement in G, i.e., $R_h(G) = \{r \mid \exists t \in T, (h, r, t) \in G, r \in R\}$.

Problem Statement. Given a knowledge graph G, consider G^* the ideal graph, containing all statements known about entities that should be in G, i.e., $G \subseteq G^*$. For a given head entity $h \in H$ in G, the research problem is to identify the set of missing relations of h, i.e., the set of relations defined as $R_h(G^*) \setminus R_h(G)$.

---

4   Our Approach

An overview of our proposed solution to predict missing relations is presented in Fig. 2. In our proposed solution, we distinguish two main stages: the *relation-centric stage* and the *prediction stage*. The *relation-centric stage* captures the latent features of the relations encoded in the KG. The outcome of this stage is then used in the *prediction stage* to predict missing relations of head entities.

Fig. 2. Proposed approach for the predictions of missing relations for head entities, based on a knowledge graph G. The relation-centric stage captures latent knowledge between the relations. The prediction stage predicts missing relations based on the communities detected in the previous stage and the KG G for a given head entity h.

4.1   Relation-Centric Stage: Mining Latent Interactions from Relations

This stage identifies groups of relations that are related based on the implicit knowledge encoded in G. The input of this stage is a KG G. To get a better view on the co-occurrence of relations we transform G into a bipartite graph. In this bipartite graph, nodes represent head entities and relations, while edges encode the head-relation interactions. We denote this graph the *head-relation graph.*

Definition 1 (Head-Relation Graph]). *Assume a KG $G = (H \cup T, R)$. A head-relation graph is a bipartite graph $I = (V, E)$, where $V = H \cup R$. An edge $(h, r) \in E$ denotes that the head entity $h \in H$ interacts with the relation $r \in R$ in G.*

To illustrate the concept of a head-relation graph I, consider the running example from Fig. 1 (right) of the graph. The head-relation graph corresponds to persons and their existing outgoing relations in the knowledge graph G. Based on I, we will identify highly-correlated relations. To this end, we propose the application of frequent itemsets mining. Frequent itemsets approaches rely on transactions to identify items that highly co-occur. In our approach, the set of all relations of one head entity represents one transaction. Therefore, all transactions can be determined by the union over the transaction of the individual head entities. A good side effect of using frequent itemsets, is the removal of noise in the data and filter out relations that occur very rarely. One important aspect to consider when applying frequent pattern mining is that many frequent patterns are not interesting and items cannot appear more than once in a transaction. This is for the usage of itemset mining in KGs not useful, since a head entity can have the same relation multiple times to different tail entities, e.g.

fields, and this might affect the computation of itemsets. At the same time some relations which occur very infrequent but are of high interest could be higher weighted than others that occur very frequently in a KG but are at the same time only of limited interest. Using the Apriori algorithm [2] would identify frequent itemsets, but could not overcome those limitations. To overcome those two limitations, the Fast Correlated high-utility itemset Miner (FCHM) [7] efficiently finds highly correlated itemsets, based on transaction data. FCHM prunes all itemsets that does not fulfill a minimum number of utility (*minutil*) and correlation (*minbond*). The bond measure indicates how items in a frequent itemset correlate and thus expresses the relative importance of a relationset [7,13]. This method allows for identifying relations that correlate and, therefore, occur very frequently with each other. In addition, we can identify and remove relations that occur only very rarely in the KG. These low occurring relations are noise in the KG and due to their low occurrence provide only very little information for the prediction of relations. The input for FCHM is a set of transactions. One transaction is the list of existing relations for a head entity h, i.e., R_h. Considering our motivating example in Fig. 1, the transaction for head entity *Paul_Sereno* is the following (*residence, fields, nationality, almaMater*). The computation of highly-correlated relationsets, using a head-relation graph is defined as follows:

Definition 2 (Highly-Correlated Relationsets). *Let* $I = (H \cup R, E)$ *be a head-relation graph, minbond* $\in \{x \in \mathbb{R} \mid 0 \leq x \leq 1\}$ *be a minimum bond threshold and minutility* $\in \mathbb{R}^+$ *be a minimum utility threshold. The set of interactions is* $D = \{T_1, T_2, \ldots, T_q\}$ *where each element is a tuple* $T_x := (X = \{r \in R \mid \exists h_x \in H, (h_x, r) \in E\}, |X|)$ *containing the relations of head entity* $h_x \in H$ *and the number of the relations as utility. FCHM receives minbond, minutility and* D *as input parameters and returns the set* $\mathcal{S}$. *The set* $\mathcal{S} = \{S_0, S_1, \ldots, S_m\}$ *is a set of highly-correlated relationsets where* $S_k \subseteq R$ *and* $B(S_k) \geq minbond$, *for each* $S_k \in \mathcal{S}$. $B(S_k)$ *denotes the bond measure of the highly-correlated relationset* S_k *and is defined as follows:*

$$B(S_k) = \frac{support(S_k)}{dissup(S_k)}, where$$

$$support(S_k) = |\{h \in H \mid \forall r \in S_k : (h, r) \in E\}|,$$

$$dissup(S_k) = \sum\nolimits_{r \in S_k} |\{h \in H \mid (h, r) \in E\}|.$$

The outcome of FCHM are sets of highly correlated relations, called relationsets. The returned relationsets in $\mathcal{S}$ are different in size and strongly overlapping. Thus, a relation $r \in R$ can occur in different relationsets. Due to the overlap and the differences in the sizes of these sets, the information from the relationsets will be grouped. To extract information from the relationsets, we will model the corresponding relations as nodes in an undirected, weighted graph, which we denote relation-bonding graph G'.

Definition 3 (Relation-Bonding Graph]). *Let $S = \{S_0, S_1, \ldots, S_m\}$ be a set of highly-correlated relationsets. An Relation-Bonding Graph is an undirected weighted graph $G' = (R', E', w)$, where $R' = \bigcup_{S_k \in S} S_k$, and for each $S_k \in S$, $r_x, r_y \in S_k \Rightarrow (r_x, r_y) \in E'$. The weights w are defined as a function $w : R' \times R' \to \mathbb{R}$ and computed as the sum of the corresponding bond measure, i.e.:*

$$w(r_x, r_y) = \sum_{r_x, r_y \in S_k} B(S_k).$$

The graph G' contains the relations from the relationsets as nodes. It should be noted that due to the computation of the highly-correlated relationsets, $R' \subseteq R$ applies, which means that not every item $r \in R$ of the original graph G must also be represented in G'. The edges of G' represent the common occurrence of relations in the same relationset. The weight of the edge between the relations is the sum of all bond values of the relationsets in which both relations occur. The weight of the edge thus expresses the strength of its tie across all relationsets. In the last step to determine the latent features from the relations, we will use the information represented in the relation-bonding graph G' to identify communities within. A community is a set of nodes in a graph such that each node of the set is densely connected to each other node in the set. The identification of communities in G' is used to group relations that are strongly related.

There are many community detection algorithms that use different methods, e.g., minimum cut method or modularity maximization. In particular, the modularity describes the strength of a network by dividing it into communities. We chose Fastgreedy algorithm [6] for detecting communities, which optimizes the metric modularity when discovering communities. A benefit of Fastgreedy is that there is no need to predefine the number of communities since this algorithm detects the best number of communities by itself. Fastgreedy is a non-overlapping community detection algorithm, which means that nodes in the graph are exactly assigned to one community. By using the Fastgreedy algorithm, communities will be detected in the relation-bonding graph G'. These communities represent a set of relations from G' that have a high density, with only a few connections to the other communities. The communities represent latent features mined from the KG and, in our work, are called relation communities.

Definition 4 (Relation Community Set). *Let G' be a relation-bonding graph. A relation community set is denoted $C = \{C_1, C_2, \ldots, C_p\}$, where $C_j \in C$ is a relation community defined as a dense sub-graph of G', and $C_i \cap C_j = \emptyset$, for each $C_i, C_j \in C$.*

4.2 Prediction Stage: Predicting Missing Relations in Knowledge Graphs

We use the information from the KG G and the information we mined from it and encoded in the relation community sets C, to predict missing relations

Table 1. Overview of experimental configurations per knowledge graph. At the top of the table, a summary of characteristics and at bottom of the table, parameters used for the computation of communities for our approach.

Metric	FB15k	WN18	Pers(DBp)	Pers(WD)	Comp(DBp)	Comp(WD)	Mov(DBp)	Mov(WD)	Songs(DBp)	Songs(WD)
#Entities	14,951	40,943	229,613	190,419	63,545	10,925	231,637	287,775	39,619	126,606
#Relations	1,345	18	2,239	1,509	1,189	304	959	382	332	321
#Train	483,142	141,442	313,296	229,059	142,887	12,103	396,834	390,295	95,833	184,542
#Valid	50,000	5,000	10,000	10,000	10,000	10,000	10,000	10,000	10,000	10,000
#Test	59,071	5,000	10,000	10,000	10,000	10,000	10,000	10,000	10,000	10,000
minbond	0.1	0	0.1	0.1	0.1	0.1	0.1	0.3	0.1	0.1
minutility	1.0	1.0	1.0	1.0	1.0	1.0	1.0	1.0	1.0	1.0

of head entities. In general, the number of possible relation candidates for predicting is, depending on the number of relations in the KG, usually very high. Therefore, in the following, we reduce the number of possible candidate relations. For this, we use the information from the community sets $\mathcal{C}$. We compute for a head entity h the relative number of its existing relations in the KG G to each community set. We sort the results in descending order. Exemplary sorted communities for a given head-entity is e.g. $C_1 = \frac{7}{10}, C_2 = \frac{3}{23}, C_3 = \frac{1}{10}, C_4 = 0$. We select the first community set C_1 with the highest relative frequency, unless the relative frequency is one. A relative frequency of one for a community means that the head entity h is already complete with respect to the relations from this community. Possible candidates for missing relations of a head entity h are now all relations in this community set that the entity h does not already have. In mathematical terms, this means that, starting from a fixed h and C_i, we check the following relations as possible candidates for prediction: $R_{cand} = \{r \mid r \in R : r \in C_i \wedge \neg \exists t \in T : (h, r, t) \in G\}$. For each of these candidates we compute a confidence of prediction. The confidence for predicting a relation $r \in R_{cand}$ for head entity $h \in H$ is computed as follows:

$$conf(h,r) = \frac{|\{h_j \mid h_j \in E \ \wedge \ \exists t \in T : (h_j, r, t) \in G \wedge \exists r_k \in R, r_k \neq r \exists s, t \in T : (h_j, r_k, s) \ \wedge \ (h, r_k, t)\}|}{|\{h_j \mid h_j \in H \wedge \exists t \in T : (h_j, r, t) \in G\}|}$$

The confidence divides the number of head entities that have relation r and share at least one relation with h by the number of entities that have relation r. We compute for each relation in R_{cand} its confidence and use the top-k relations as predictions.

5   Experiments

Datasets. We used DBpedia (DBp) [3] and Wikidata (WD) [20] for the evaluation. We used subgraphs related to the class Person (Pers), Company (Comp), Movie (Mov) and Song. In addition, we used FB15k [4] and WN18 [11] for evaluating our approach. An overview of the characteristics of the KGs used in this evaluation is given in Table 1.

Silver Standards. We constructed silver standards for each of the previously described KGs. We split the KGs into three disjunctive sets: training, validation, and test set. We call it silver standard, as the created test sets may suffer from incompleteness originated in the KG, thus, creating spurious false positives. In other words, a prediction may be correct but the relations might be missing in the KG and hence in the test set.

Configurations. We set the utility for computing frequent relationsets to a constant value of 1 ,i.e, each relation is considered equally important. The *minbond* where chosen such that the relations of the union of all highly-correlated relationsets covers 70%–90% of the relations in G. In this way, we make sure that the information loss is minimized and at the same time enable a sufficient removal of noise in the data. This resulted in *minbond* values from 0 to 0.3 for the different KGs. The used parameters of the entire experimental setup are given in Table 1.

Metrics. Following related KG completion studies, we use Hits@k as evaluation metric. Hits@k measures the proportion of correct relations in top-k ranked relations.

Preprocessing. For DBpedia and Wikidata, we removed regularly appearing relations for all head entities, e.g., *wikiPageID*, *wikiPageRevisionID*, and *P31*.[1] We removed them for making predictions more challenging by deleting regularly occurring relations.

Table 2. Comparison of our approach with state-of-the-art algorithms. Our approach (CPP) uses the head entity to predict missing relations. The compared methods uses head and tail entity to predict missing relations.

KG	Hits@1			Hits@3			Hits@10		
	CPP	TransE	ComplEx	CPP	TransE	ComplEx	CPP	TransE	ComplEx
FB15k	.389	.667	**.519**	.473	**.885**	.800	.698	**.974**	.940
WN18	.561	.924	**.945**	.650	.974	**.986**	.900	**.997**	.995
Pers(DBp)	**.438**	.085	.085	**.490**	.149	.233	**.655**	.246	.292
Pers(WD)	.253	**.328**	.273	.254	.431	**.468**	.367	.517	**.618**
Comp(DBp)	.275	.185	**.319**	.345	.326	**.699**	.580	.452	**.780**
Comp(WD)	**.635**	.483	.008	**.647**	.603	.017	.674	**.692**	.058
Mov(DBp)	.393	**.453**	.106	**.615**	.515	.222	**.900**	.582	.347
Mov(WD)	**.471**	.383	.205	**.567**	.450	.424	**.833**	.527	.553
Songs(DBp)	.398	**.444**	.409	.498	**.898**	.736	.811	**.980**	.887
Songs(WD)	.488	**.788**	.203	.654	**.941**	.359	.825	**.986**	.452

5.1 Comparison to Related Knowledge Graph Completion Approaches

We selected TransE [5] and ComplEx [19] for comparison, since they gained a lot of momentum in the area of KG completion and achieve very good results

---

[1] These are DBpedia- and Wikipedia-specific relations to denote information about the Wikipedia page and the class of an entity, respectively.

on prominent knowledge graph completion tasks. We used the default parameters for TransE and ComplEx for all KGs. It is import to note that, unlike our method, both methods use head and tail information to predict relations. The additional information about the tail entity for predicting the missing relation is not available to our approach. This must be taken into account when analysing the results, which are presented in Table 2. The results show that even without the information about the tail entity, our approach is competitive with state-of-the-art methods. For some KGs, our approach achieved higher values in the Hits@k metric than the compared methods. Our solution is superior to the other methods in KGs with a high number of relations, as is the case of Pers(DBp). At the same time, in Pers(DBp), the mean size of communities and the standard deviation is very low. This ensures that there are fewer relations in the individual communities and thus the predictions become more precise. Considering the Pers(WD) KG, the number of relations is also very high, but the structure of the computed communities is not as compact as the community structure of Pers(DBp) KG. The mean size of communities in Pers(WD) is higher (cf. Table 3), as well as the standard deviation. As a result, the Hits@k performance is lower, compared to the other methods. Another consideration in this evaluation is that not all the relations in the silver standard are covered by the communities computed by our approach. As can be observed in Table 3, except for the WN18, not all the relations are present in the detected communities. This coverage varies from 37.07% to 86.47%, which hinders the number of true positives achieved by our approach. Therefore, in the following experiment, we analyze the performance of our solution when the silver standard only contains relations from the communities.

Table 3. Overview of the structure of computed communities for the studied KGs.

Metric	FB15k	WN18	Pers(DBp)	Pers(WD)	Comp(DBp)	Comp(WD)	Mov(DBp)	Mov(WD)	Songs(DBp)	Songs(WD)
Relations	86.47%	100%	72.53%	84.84%	78.47%	71.38%	51.02%	37.07%	77.27%	44.59%
Communities	110	3	244	76	77	28	104	31	29	31
Mean Com.	10.57	6	6.52	16.58	12.12	7.75	4.55	4.48	8.21	4.52
Std. Com.	15.49	4	16.9	44.83	39.53	10.30	4.32	8.60	10.28	4.68
Max Com.	71	10	213	313	313	47	40	44	39	24
Min Com.	2	2	2	2	2	2	2	2	2	2

5.2 Comparison with Relations in Community

To demonstrate the relevance of the latent structures of the relations in the communities, the following are examples of relation communities for FB15k detected with our proposed approach: *Community 18 = {nominated_for, honored_for, award_nominee}*, and *Community 25 = {symptom_of, diseases, causes, risk_factors}*.

In this evaluation, we study the results of our approach if we only consider relations in the test set which are present in the communities. To this end, we will filter out triples that contain relations which are not present in the computed communities for the respective KGs. We report again on the Hits@k metric (cf. Table 4), since it allows for a better comparison with the results from the previous section. As expected, the overall performance of our approach increases, since now only known relations are now considered. For Hits@1, our approach now significantly improves for FB15k. With increasing k, however, the gain in Hits@k turns out not to be strong in the same proportion. The result of WN18 does not change at all, since all relations are covered in the communities. For the KGs Pers(DBp) and Pers(WD), the performance of our approach does not significantly increase. We hypothesize that the structure of the communities, more precisely the very large average size and standard deviation, is the reason for this. Similar observations apply to Comp(DBp). The largest improvement in Hits@k can be observed in Comp(WD), which has a moderate coverage of relations (71.38%, cf. Table 3). The standard deviation of the communities is slightly increased, but the dataset has a low average community size. The results of this KG increase significantly due to the reduction to known relations. The results for both Mov(DBp) and Mov(WD) do not increase significantly, although the average size of the communities is very small, and the coverage of the relations is moderate to low, respectively. However, our approach outperforms the state-of-the-art in these KGs in the previous evaluation (Hits@3, Hits@10), which indicates that the original silver standard already includes a high number of relations that are covered by the communities. Likewise, there is no strong effect on the results of Songs(DBp). However, Songs(WD) benefits from the adjustment of the test dataset. Both, the amount of covered relations in the communities is low, as well as the average number of relations per community. Restricting the data and the analysis to relations known in the communities leads to an improvement of the results.

5.3   Discussion of Experimental Results

While TransE and ComplEx exploit head and tail entity information to predict the missing relation information, our approach uses only the head entity to perform the predictions. Therefore, a direct comparison is difficult. However, in order to position our empirical results with respect to state-of-the-art solutions, we still compared against KG embedding methods despite the differences in the underlying assumptions. The experimental results show that the evaluated approaches exhibit complementary Hits@k performance, i.e., there is no single approach that outperforms the others in all the KGs. The advantage of our method is the usage of only head entity information. Therefore, missing relations, even to unknown tail entities, can be predicted. In general, we observe that the performance of our approach strongly depends on the structure of the computed communities and the number of relations in the KG. A small number of average relations per community and a small deviation from the average allows for achieving better results with our approach. This effect can be followed by looking at the average community size (cf. Table 3) and the results of the Hits@k (cf. Table 2).

Another important consideration is the original incompleteness of the KGs. Consider the movie *The_Naked_Gun* in the Mov(DBp) dataset. We predicted

Table 4. Performance of the proposed approach over the filtered test dataset. The datasets contain triples which have a relation that is present in a relation community.

KG	FB15k	WN18	Pers(DBp)	Pers(WD)	Comp(DBp)	Comp(WD)	Mov(DBp)	Mov(WD)	Songs(DBp)	Songs(WD)
Hits@1	.394	.561	.462	.254	.277	.733	.404	.486	.400	.502
Hits@3	.483	.650	.520	.257	.350	.775	.634	.599	.503	.675
Hits@10	.714	.900	.695	.371	.589	.803	.927	.886	.821	.852

among others *basedOn* as missing relation for this head entity. According to our silver standard, this prediction is considered to be a false positive because this head entity does not contain a *basedOn* relation in the KG. However, assuming complete knowledge, the prediction of our approach would be correct, because the film is based on the American television comedy *Police Squad!*. Similar cases of spurious false positives are encountered in other KGs, e.g. Pers(DBp). For example, the head entity *Deven_Marrero* describes an American professional baseball player. Our approach predicted *throws* as missing relation, which was wrongly considered a false positive. The above examples illustrate the problems involved in evaluating KG completeness. Although in some cases the predictions are correct, the evaluation classifies them as wrong since the information is not available in the KG. Due to the incompleteness of the KGs, the actual quality of the predictions cannot be assessed with absolute certainty.

6   Conclusions and Future Work

In this paper, we presented an approach to predict missing relations for head entities in Knowledge Graphs (KG). Our approach groups related relations by means of latent relationships encoded by the interactions of the head entities with their corresponding relations. These associations are exploited for detecting communities of frequent co-occurring relations in the KG. The experimental results show that our approach is competitive with existing KG embedding approaches (TransE and ComplEx), even if they use information about the tail entity for the prediction. We observed that our approach can keep-up and compete (for the metric Hits@k) with existing KG embedding methods that uses head and tail entities for predicting missing relations.

Future work could focus on further structures of communities, as these have a high impact on the performance of our solution. Furthermore, our approach could be integrated into a larger KG completion pipeline that is able to: (i) predict missing relations for head entities with our approach; (ii) identify tail candidates (for known entities), using for example TransE or ComplEx, based on the predictions from the previous step.

References

1. Acosta, M., Simperl, E., Flöck, F., Vidal, M.: Enhancing answer completeness of SPARQL queries via crowdsourcing. J. Web Semant. **45**, 41–62 (2017)
2. Agrawal, R., Srikant, R.: Fast algorithms for mining association rules in large databases. In: Proceedings of VLDB 1994, pp. 487–499. Morgan Kaufmann Publishers Inc. (1994)

3. Auer, S., Bizer, C., Kobilarov, G., Lehmann, J., Cyganiak, R., Ives, Z.: DBpedia: a nucleus for a web of open data. In: Aberer, K., et al. (eds.) ASWC/ISWC -2007. LNCS, vol. 4825, pp. 722–735. Springer, Heidelberg (2007). https://doi.org/10.1007/978-3-540-76298-0_52

4. Bollacker, K., Evans, C., Paritosh, P., Sturge, T., Taylor, J.: Freebase: a collaboratively created graph database for structuring human knowledge. In: Proceedings of ACM SIGMOD, pp. 1247–1250. ACM (2008)

5. Bordes, A., Usunier, N., Garcia-Durán, A., Weston, J., Yakhnenko, O.: Translating embeddings for modeling multi-relational data. In: Proceedings of NIPS, pp. 2787–2795 (2013)

6. Clauset, A., Newman, M.E.J., Moore, C.: Finding community structure in very large networks. Phys. Rev. E **70**, 066111 (2004)

7. Fournier-Viger, P., Wu, C.-W., Zida, S., Tseng, V.S.: FHM: faster high-utility itemset mining using estimated utility co-occurrence pruning. In: Andreasen, T., Christiansen, H., Cubero, J.-C., Raś, Z.W. (eds.) ISMIS 2014. LNCS (LNAI), vol. 8502, pp. 83–92. Springer, Cham (2014). https://doi.org/10.1007/978-3-319-08326-1_9

8. Galárraga, L.A., Teflioudi, C., Hose, K., Suchanek, F.: Amie: association rule mining under incomplete evidence in ontological knowledge bases. In: Proceedings of WWW, pp. 413–422. ACM (2013)

9. Liu, Y., Liao, W.k., Choudhary, A.: A fast high utility itemsets mining algorithm. In: Proceedings of UBDM 2005, pp. 90–99. ACM (2005)

10. Mihindukulasooriya, N., Rashid, M.R.A., Rizzo, G., García-Castro, R., Corcho, O., Torchiano, M.: RDF shape induction using knowledge base profiling. In: Proceedings of ACM SAC (SAC 2018), pp. 1952–1959. Association for Computing Machinery, New York (2018)

11. Miller, G.A.: WordNet: a lexical database for english. Commun. ACM **38**(11), 39–41 (1995)

12. Newman, M.E.J.: The structure of scientific collaboration networks. Proc. Nat. Acad. Sci. **98**(2), 404–409 (2001)

13. Omiecinski, E.R.: Alternative interest measures for mining associations in databases. IEEE TKDE **15**(1), 57–69 (2003)

14. Pellissier Tanon, T., Stepanova, D., Razniewski, S., Mirza, P., Weikum, G.: Completeness-aware rule learning from knowledge graphs. In: d'Amato, C., et al. (eds.) ISWC 2017. LNCS, vol. 10587, pp. 507–525. Springer, Cham (2017). https://doi.org/10.1007/978-3-319-68288-4_30

15. Pons, P., Latapy, M.: Computing communities in large networks using random walks. In: Yolum, I., Güngör, T., Gürgen, F., Özturan, C. (eds.) ISCIS 2005. LNCS, vol. 3733, pp. 284–293. Springer, Heidelberg (2005). https://doi.org/10.1007/11569596_31

16. Raghavan, U.N., Albert, R., Kumara, S.: Near linear time algorithm to detect community structures in large-scale networks. Phys. Rev. E **76**, 036106 (2007)

17. Rebhi, W., Yahia, N.B., Ben Saoud, N.B.: Hybrid modeling approach for contextualized community detection in multilayer social network. Procedia Comput. Sci. **112**(C), 673–682 (2017)

18. Tran, M.D., d'Amato, C., Nguyen, B.T., Tettamanzi, A.G.B.: An evolutionary algorithm for discovering multi-relational association rules in the semantic web. In: Proceedings of GECCO (GECCO 2017), pp. 513–520. ACM, New York (2017)
19. Trouillon, T., Welbl, J., Riedel, S., Gaussier, E., Bouchard, G.: Complex embeddings for simple link prediction. In: Proceedings of ICML, pp. 2071–2080. JMLR.org (2016)
20. Vrandečić, D., Krötzsch, M.: Wikidata: a free collaborative knowledgebase. Commun. ACM **57**(10), 78–85 (2014)

Comp-O: An OWL-S Extension for Composite Service Description

Grégory Alary, Nathalie Hernandez[(✉)][iD], Jean-Paul Arcangeli[iD],
Sylvie Trouilhet[iD], and Jean-Michel Bruel[iD]

Institut de Recherche en Informatique de Toulouse, University of Toulouse,
Toulouse, France
{gregory.alary,nathalie.hernandez,jeanpaul.arcangeli,
sylvie.trouilhet,jeanmichel.bruel}@irit.fr

Abstract. Component-based software engineering is a paradigm that fosters software flexibility and emphasizes composability and reuse of software components. These are runtime units that provide services and, in turn, may require other services to operate. Assembling components consists in binding components' required services to provided ones to deliver composite services with added value. Building a composite service is a challenging task as it requires identifying components and services that are compatible, binding them to implement the service, and describe it for discovery. For that, the vocabulary used to describe component-based services (i.e., services offered by components or assemblies) must support the description of required services, and descriptions must be combinable in order to automatically generate composite service descriptions. However, existing solutions are limited to the description and composition of provided (and not required) services. In this paper, we consider ontologies to describe component-based services implemented by component assemblies. After comparing existing service ontologies, we present an extension of OWL-S called Comp-O. Through a proof-of-concept, we demonstrate how the added semantics can be handled to automatically build composite service descriptions.

1 Introduction

Component-based software engineering consists in designing software as assemblies of reusable and versatile *software components*. Software components are building blocks that implement and provide services. As they exhibit the services they require at the same level as the services they provide, components are easily composable [1]. In order to make a component fully operational, i.e., actually provide its services, each of its required services must be bound to a service that is provided by another component. Composing components, that is to say building assemblies of components, means binding services based on their abstract specifications (e.g., signatures, pre- and post-conditions). Composition leads to complex *composite services* with added value whose behavior depends on the components that are involved in the assembly.

C. M. Keet and M. Dumontier (Eds.): EKAW 2020, LNAI 12387, pp. 171–182, 2020.
https://doi.org/10.1007/978-3-030-61244-3_12

To improve discoverability by third parties, *component-based services*(CBSs) must be semantically described. When they result from composition, their semantics depend on the ones of the components. The semantics of the services provided by a component depends on the semantics of the services required by this component. Since these required services are abstracted, the actual semantics depend on the semantics of the provided services they are bound to. In a way, the semantics of a composite service is distributed among the components.

The problem is to describe the services provided by components that have required services, both to enable assistance to the service developer when she/he assembles components and to combine such descriptions to automatically generate composite service descriptions. We propose to describe CBSs with ontologies in order to leverage the semantics of such knowledge representations regarding two issues : (i) support a detailed description of composite services; (ii) support the composition of services and produce a description of a composite service depending on the components participating to the assembly.

Considering ontologies in the description of services improves their discoverability [2] and their composition [2,3]. Several ontologies and approaches exploiting them have thus been proposed. However, existing solutions mainly consider Web services and are not suited for CBSs requiring specific services.

In this paper we propose Comp-O, an extension of the well-known OWL-S ontology in order to consider specific characteristics of CBSs and we demonstrate how the added semantics can be handled to automatically build composite service descriptions. The paper is organized as follows. Section 2 briefly introduces software components, component-based development, and CBSs, then the characteristics of CBSs are exposed. In Sect. 3, the requirements for a component-based service ontology are presented and tested against several existing ontologies. Comp-O, an extension of OWL-S complying with the requirements, is then presented and instantiated in Sect. 4. Section 5 proposes an approach to assist the developer in the building of Comp-O composite services and to generate their descriptions automatically. Last, Sect. 6 summarizes the contribution and discusses some future works.

2   Component-Based Services

2.1   Components and CBSs

Component-based software engineering is a paradigm that emphasizes composability and reuse of software components. *Software components* are loosely coupled self-contained runtime units that *provide* services specified by interfaces. To provide their services, they may *require* external services. Figure 1 shows the UML representation of the VoiceToTextConverter component, where the provided services (VoiceProcess) are pictured by a bullet and the required services (TextProcess) by a socket. Unlike objects, software components bring the required services at the same level as the provided ones. As a result, components are building blocks that can be *assembled* by *binding* required to provided services if their interfaces match, to deliver a composite service with added value.

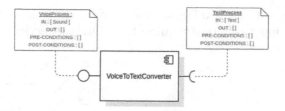

Fig. 1. UML representation of the VoiceToTextConverter component

Flexibility is one of the main advantages of component-based development. Components are versatile and reusable in different contexts. In an assembly, a component can be replaced at design or execution time by another component that offers an "equivalent" functionality, this equivalence being based on compatibility of the interfaces. Interfaces specify a contract of use containing the type of the inputs and outputs, pre-conditions to satisfy when invoking the service and guaranteed post-conditions. We call *component-based service* (CBS) a service that is provided by a software component. If the latter requires external services, the CBS is implemented by an assembly, and its actual semantics depends on the components that are involved in the assembly.

2.2 Illustrative Examples

The right side of Fig. 2 represents the TextPrinter component that provides the CBS called PrintText. PrintText takes a Text as the only input: when invoked, the text is printed and there is no result in return. Like a Web service, PrintText is ready to use since TextPrinter has no required interface.

The VoiceProcess service provided by the VoiceToTextConverter component is however not ready to use. To make it work, the TextProcess required service must be bound to a CBS that takes a text as input, e.g., PrintText of TextPrinter (assuming that PrintText matches TextProcess). Figure 2 represents an assembly that implements a component-based composite service that takes a voice record as input, converts it to a text, and prints it.

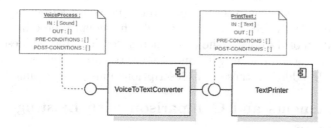

Fig. 2. Implementation of the VoiceProcess composite service

As components are replaceable, a TextTransformer component can be inserted between VoiceToTextConverter and TextPrinter (assuming the services match), to translate the text before printing it. The result is shown in

Fig. 3: when invoked, the TextTransformer component demands the translation in French of the input text then requires the PrintText service.

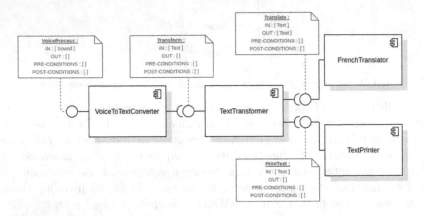

Fig. 3. Another implementation of the VoiceProcess composite service

2.3   Issues

In the previous section, two implementations of the VoiceProcess composite service have been presented in Fig. 2 and Fig. 3: although its interface does not change, the semantics vary from one implementation to another (print a speech, print a speech after its translation into French, ...). So, the true nature of a CBS depends on the components that compose the implementing assembly and what these components actually do. Thus, to determine this nature, it is necessary to inspect the different components. In a component, how a service is delivered depends on the services the component requires, the ordering of the requests and the internal operating process. Therefore, describing CBSs with interfaces only, i.e., as black boxes, is not enough. Interfaces support matching but do not make the behavior explicit. For example, they do not specify that the PrintText service of the TextPrinter component prints the text on paper or elsewhere. Maybe a human could guess this information from the service name, but a machine certainly could not.

Thus, to support efficient service discovery and composition, CBSs must be described semantically. The problem is to build the semantic description of a CBS by a combination of the ones of the components' services. Indeed, describing services provided by a component with one or more required services is fundamental for our work. In addition, these unit descriptions must be combinable.

3   Requirements and Comparison with Existing Ontologies

The development of the requirements of our ontology is compliant with the NeOn methodology [4]. We have specified the purposes and the scope of the ontology, the uses and the final users, and the competency questions the ontology should satisfy. Competency questions are used to evaluate existing ontologies.

3.1   Purposes and Scope

The motivation and final goal of this ontology is to offer a way to describe CBSs, in particular the service offered and the required interfaces that must be bound to make a service operational. Concomitantly, during the development of a new service built with CBSs, the description of each service can be used to automatically generate the description of the composite service.

We have identified two types of users : the service publishers and the service developers. A **service publisher** is an agent wishing to publish the description of CBSs or composite services that will be invokable and bindable. A **service developer** is an agent wishing to bind one or more published services to build a more complex application. In both cases, the services must be described as unambiguously as possible in order to automatize the tasks.

3.2   Competency Questions

These competency questions come from an analysis of the component-based software engineering domain and several use cases [1,5] similar to the one presented in Sect. 2.2. The use cases are not seen as an end *per se*, but as an instantiation of the general domain of component-based software engineering. Therefore, the competency questions presented in Table 1 represent the knowledge required for a reusable ontology, with no regard for the application domain. The answers are simplified for the sake of readability but should be represented thanks to corresponding resources.

In **CQ8**, the notion of service binding is only relevant for CBSs as it means that the service S1 invokes another service through one of its required interfaces. **CQ9** is crucial for the generation of composite service descriptions as the behavior of the internal orchestration will help deducing the operational aspects of the service. The expected answer is an ordered list of operations executed by the service such as invocations, variables operations and returns.

3.3   Comparison with Existing Ontologies

As recommended by NeOn, reusable ontologies that are compliant with parts of the requirements have been integrated in our design process. Therefore, we have used the competency questions to analyze which ontologies satisfy which part of the requirements. We compared six ontologies: SAREF [6], SOSA/SSN [7], MSM [8], OWL-S [9] (formerly DAML-S), WSML [10] and HRests [11]. For each competency question, the absence of star means that the corresponding ontology does not satisfy at all the question, one star means that the question is partially covered and two stars that the question is totally satisfied (Table 2).

All the studied ontologies cover the questions **CQ1**, **CQ2** and **CQ3** as they all provide a way to type a resource as a service and to define the types of its inputs and outputs. WSML also covers **CQ4**, **CQ5** and **CQ6** but not the others as WSML describes a service as black-box, without information about its internal working. SOSA/SSN only partially satisfies the questions **CQ7** and **CQ8** as

Table 1. Competency questions

ID	Competency questions	Answers
CQ1	What are all the available services?	(S1, S2, S3); ()
CQ2	What are the types of the inputs of the service *S1*?	(Boolean, Int); (String);
CQ3	What are the types of the outputs of the service *S1*?	(ON/OFF Command, Int); (ON/OFF State); ()
CQ4	What are the preconditions of the service *S1*?	(cond1; cond2); (cond1); ()
CQ5	What are the post-conditions of the service *S1*?	(cond1; cond2); (cond1); ()
CQ6	What is the service offered by the service *S3*?	Square root
CQ7	Does the service *S1* invoke any services?	Yes; No
CQ8	What services are invoked by the service *S1*?	(S2; S3); (S4); ()
CQ9	What is the internal orchestration of the service *S1*?	(invokeS2, invokeS3); (invokeS2); ()
CQ10	Is the service *S1* a component-based service?	Yes; No
CQ11	What are the required interfaces of the service *S2*?	(perform1, perform2); ()
CQ12	What are the types of the inputs of the service required by the required interface *perform1*?	(ON/OFF Command); (Int); ()
CQ13	What are the types of the outputs of the service required by the required interface *perform1*?	(Boolean); (String);
CQ14	What are the post-conditions of the service required by the required interface *perform1*?	(cond1, cond2); (cond1); ()
CQ15	What are the preconditions of the service required by the required interface *perform1*?	(cond2); ()
CQ16	Is the service *S1* already bound with any other services?	Yes; No

the invocation of a service by another should be described by using the *observes* and *detects* properties. However, by using these predicates, the semantics are different since the service S2 is not invoked by S1 *per se* but is self invoked when a new observation is detected, as SOSA/SSN is used to describe sensors and observations and is not dedicated to services. OWL-S totally satisfies

Table 2. Comparison between the competency questions and the ontologies

Competency question	CQ1	CQ2	CQ3	CQ4	CQ5	cQ6	CQ7	CQ8	CQ9	CQ10	CQ11	CQ12	CQ13	CQ14	CQ15	CQ16
SAREF	**	**	**	–	–	–	–	–	–	–	–	–	–	–	–	–
SOSA/SSN	**	*	*	–	–	–	*	*	–	–	–	–	–	–	–	*
MSM	**	**	**	–	–	–	–	–	–	–	–	–	–	–	–	–
OWL-S	**	**	**	**	**	**	**	**	**	–	–	–	–	–	–	*
WSML	**	**	**	**	**	**	**	–	–	–	–	–	–	–	–	–
HRests	**	**	**	–	–	–	–	–	–	–	–	–	–	–	–	–
Comp-O	**	**	**	**	**	**	**	**	**	**	**	**	**	**	**	**

CQ4, **CQ5**, **CQ6**, **CQ7**, **CQ8** and **CQ9**. Preconditions and post-conditions can be described in the profile of the service. Invocations of other services and internal orchestration are described in the service's process. Moreover, the service offered can be semantically described using the preconditions and post-conditions. SOSA/SSN and OWL-S partially cover **CQ16** as they both provide a mechanism to describe the invocation or actuation of a service by another but is not specific enough to describe the binding of an interface with a service. The binding of interfaces is a mechanism specific to CBSs where SOSA/SSN and OWL-S are used to describe Web services. No studied ontology satisfies questions **CQ10** to **CQ15**.

Based on the comparison, we conclude that OWL-S is the ontology that covers the best our requirements. We develop Comp-O, an extension for OWL-S that covers all the competency questions.

4 Comp-O, an OWL-S Extension for CBSs

Comp-O is a minimal ontology extending OWL-S that helps to efficiently describe CBSs. The ontology is available at https://github.com/comp-o. All the namespaces used in this paper are given in Table 3. This section presents the key concepts of OWL-S, an overview of Comp-O and an example of a CBS description using this ontology.

Table 3. Namespace prefixes used in this paper

Prefix	Namespace
Service	http://www.daml.org/services/owl-s/1.2/Service.owl#
Profile	http://www.daml.org/services/owl-s/1.2/Profile.owl#
Process	http://www.daml.org/services/owl-s/1.2/Process.owl#
Comp-o	https://comp-o.github.io/comp-o#

4.1   Key Concepts of OWL-S

As explained in [9], the description of a service with OWL-S is split in three parts, the service profile presents what the service does, the service grounding how to access it and the service model how to use it. We focus on the service profile as the purpose of our work is on the behavior of CBSs, their internal orchestrations and their interfaces.

A *service:ServiceProfile* presents the service's parameters (*process:Inputs* and *process:Outputs*), the *process:Precondition* and the *process:Results* (outputs and effects). The profile describes the service as a black-box as the description is dedicated to its contract and not to its behavior with the clients nor its orchestration. To describe the internal orchestration of a service, a *process:CompositeProcess* can be linked to the process resource which is defined in a service profile. A composite process is used to describe the choreography of messages between the client and the service but also to the invocation of others services. As explained in [9], *"any composite process can be considered a tree whose nonterminal nodes are labeled with control constructs, each of which has children specified using components. The leaves of the tree are invocations of other processes, indicated as instances of class process:Perform (an invocation of another service)"*. Based on this definition, we defined in Comp-O a new control construct used to describe the required interfaces of CBSs.

4.2   Comp-O: Concepts and Properties

An overview of Comp-O is presented in Fig. 4. The ontology defines three new concepts, and one object property.

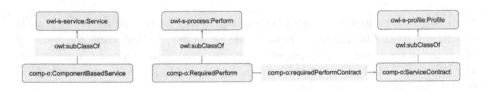

Fig. 4. Architecture of Comp-O

ComponentBasedService is the first and main concept: it is a service that can have no or several *RequiredPerform* (required interface) in its process, and that is not operational until all its *RequiredPerform* are replaced with an actual perform referencing another process.

A *Required perform* is a sub concept of the Perform control construct: it describes a required interface. It references a service interface through the *requiredPerformContract* predicate.

The third concept is the *Service contract*: it is a *ServiceProfile* that does not specify an implementation through the *has_process* predicate. Practically, this concept is used to define the types of the inputs and outputs and the pre/post-conditions specified by a required interface.

Finally, the *requiredPerformContract* predicate is used to link a *RequiredPerform* with the *ServiceContract* it requires.

4.3 Use Case and Instantiation

This section contains the descriptions of the CBSs presented in Sect. 2.2. We focus on the most original and key services that highlight the different uses of Comp-O.

A CBS with no required interface can be described as a Web service. Therefore, the *TextPrinter* service description does not need to use Comp-O at all but can rely on OWL-S only. Obviously, CBSs described with Comp-O can still be bound with traditional OWL-S services like *TextPrinter*.

As explained in Sect. 4.2, a required interface of a CBS is described with the *comp-o:RequiredPerform* concept. This concept is a special *Perform* that does not reference a concrete service but a service contract specifying the type of the inputs and outputs, the preconditions and the post-conditions. Therefore, to describe the *VoiceToTextConverter*, instead of referencing another service with a *Perform* as presented in Listing 1.1, we can now use the *comp-o:RequiredPerform* as shown in Listing 1.2.

```
:voice-to-text-converter-perform
   rdf:type            process:Perform ;
   process:process :the-other-process;
```
Listing 1.1. Invocation of another process with OWL-S

```
:voice-to-text-converter-req-interface
   rdf:type                      comp-o:RequiredPerform ;
   comp-o:requiredPerformContract :text-input-contract ;
   process:hasDataFrom       # ...

:text-input-contract
   rdf:type comp-o:ServiceContract ;
   profile:hasInput [
       rdf:type              process:Input ;
       process:parameterType "[...]#Text" .
   ] ;
```
Listing 1.2. Comp-O description of the VoiceToTextConverter required interface

Also, to describe a service with several required interfaces, the mechanism is the same as the one used to describe VoiceToTextConverter. A process can contain an unlimited number of *comp-o:RequiredPerform*.

5   Using Comp-O

5.1   Assisted Building of Composite Services

To assist the developer, we propose a multi-step approach synthesized in Fig. 5. In a first step, a list of the available CBSs is presented. To do so, all that is needed is to retrieve the set of resources typed by the *service:Service* class. Then, the service developer must choose the "root" service, i.e., the service to implement. Comp-O helps to determine whether the component that provides the chosen service has any required interface. A component has a required interface if one of the control constructs of the process of the service it provides is a *comp-o:RequiredPerform*. This property can be comprehensively checked considering the OWL-S control constructs using the SPARQL request of Listing 1.3.

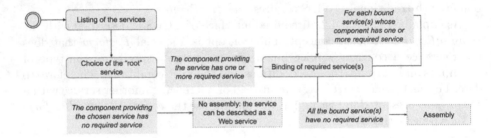

Fig. 5. Building of a Comp-O assembly

```
ASK {
    <service> service:presents/profile:has_process/process:composedOf/(
        process:then|process:else|process:whileProcess|process:untilProcess|
        process:components)*/(owl-list:rest*)/owl-list:first+ ?instruction .

    ?instruction a comp-o:RequiredPerform
}
```

Listing 1.3. SPARQL request to determine whether a service requires to be bound

If the component providing the chosen service does not require any service, it can be described as an OWL-S service, whose description is available and publishable as it is. Contrariwise, if the component has one or more required service, the latter must be bound to external CBSs.

If so, to ease the binding decisions, it is possible to determine if a provided service is compatible with a required one, i.e., if the two services match. This requires to check if the types of the inputs and outputs, the preconditions and the post-conditions match. The strategy used to determine whether there is a match depends on the application domain; it is not specified in our solution but several proposals have been made (see e.g., [2,12] and [13]).

Finally, when a required service is bound and if the provider also has one or more required services, this step must be repeated for these services until the assembly is closed, i.e., all the required interfaces in the assembly are bound. At this point, an assembly is available and its description can be generated.

5.2   Automatic Generation of Comp-O Composite Service Descriptions

We propose an algorithm that implements the generation of a composite service description from an assembly.

The first step consists in replacing every *comp-o:RequiredPerform* by a *process:Perform* referencing the process associated in the assembly, using the *process:process* predicate instead of referencing a *comp-o:ServiceContract* via the *comp-o:requiredPerformContract* predicate. The process of a CBS references as variables the inputs and outputs of a *comp-o:ServiceContract* it requires. For each service, the second step is therefore to replace the references to these variables by references to the equivalent variable of the associated service. This step can be easily accomplished by processing all the *process:fromProcess* predicates having as object a resource of the type *comp-o:ServiceContract*. After these steps, all the CBSs are now described as services with OWL-S since their required interfaces are bound with other services.

5.3   Proof of Concept

To ensure and show that the solution works, we have developed a proof of concept (POC) that implements it. It is available online at https://github.com/comp-o/comp-o-poc. It proposes a command line interface that helps the user to build the composition plan and outputs the OWL-S description of the assembly. The POC has been used to test the approach against twelve key CBSs chosen for their representativity of the recurrent topologies encountered in component-based software engineering. The description of these services also are available online and are not described in this paper due to space limitation.

6   Conclusion and Perspectives

This paper has introduced Comp-O, an extension of OWL-S for CBSs, which are services provided by software components. Comp-O has been developed following the principles of the Neon methodology. One of them is the reuse of ontologies that partially meet the requirements.

As OWL-S is the most compliant with our requirements, we have proposed to extend it: Comp-O supports the description of required services and a combination of descriptions in order to automatically generate the description of composite services. Beyond the semantic description of services for publication purposes and to facilitate their discovery, Comp-O helps the developer: at design time, based on Comp-O, the matching between required and provided interfaces can be controlled and the services (so, the components) that are available for the composition may be proposed. In addition, supplying the description of the composite services under construction gives the engineer useful feedback. Using a proof-of-concept prototype, we have demonstrated the ability to assist the service developer and to automatically generate composite descriptions from component unit descriptions that have required services.

Now, we plan to use Comp-O in an ongoing project carried out in our team, which aims to make user-oriented services emerge at runtime in ambient environments. There, an intelligent engine builds on the fly composite services from software components present at the time in the environment, without having been required by the user. As a consequence, composite services that emerge must be described to inform the user who can accept, modify or reject them. Then, a user-intelligible description is required for a sound understanding of the service, that could be computed from the Comp-O generated description.

References

1. Sommerville, I.: Component-based software engineering. In: Software Engineering, chapter 16, 10th edn., pp. 464–489. Pearson Education (2016)
2. Klusch, M., Kapahnke, P., Schulte, S., Lecue, F., Bernstein, A.: Semantic web service search: a brief survey. KI-Künstliche Intelligenz 30(2), 139–147 (2016)
3. Kurniawan, K., Ekaputra, F.J., Aryan, P.R.: Semantic service description and compositions: a systematic literature review. In: ICICoS, pp. 1–6 (2018)
4. Suárez-Figueroa, M.C., Gómez-Pérez, A., Fernández-López, M.: The NeOn methodology for ontology engineering. In: Suárez-Figueroa, M.C., Gómez-Pérez, A., Motta, E., Gangemi, A. (eds.) Ontology Engineering in a Networked World, pp. 9–34. Springer, Heidelberg (2012). https://doi.org/10.1007/978-3-642-24794-1_2
5. Koussaifi, M.: User-oriented description of emerging services in ambient systems. In: Yangui, S., et al. (eds.) ICSOC 2019. LNCS, vol. 12019, pp. 259–265. Springer, Cham (2020). https://doi.org/10.1007/978-3-030-45989-5_21
6. Daniele, L., den Hartog, F., Roes, J.: Created in close interaction with the industry: the smart appliances REFerence (SAREF) ontology. In: Cuel, R., Young, R. (eds.) FOMI 2015. LNBIP, vol. 225, pp. 100–112. Springer, Cham (2015). https://doi.org/10.1007/978-3-319-21545-7_9
7. Haller, A., et al.: The SOSA/SSN ontology: a joint W3C and OGC standard specifying the semantics of sensors, observations, actuation, and sampling. Semant. Web 1, 1–19 (2018)
8. MSM: Minimal Service Model (LOV) (2017). https://lov.linkeddata.es/dataset/lov/vocabs/msm
9. OWL-S: Semantic Markup for Web Services (2004). https://www.w3.org/Submission/2004/SUBM-OWL-S-20041122/
10. de Bruijn, J., Lausen, H., Polleres, A., Fensel, D.: The web service modeling language WSML: an overview. In: Sure, Y., Domingue, J. (eds.) ESWC 2006. LNCS, vol. 4011, pp. 590–604. Springer, Heidelberg (2006). https://doi.org/10.1007/11762256_43
11. Kopecký, J., Gomadam, K., Vitvar, T.: hRESTS: an HTML microformat for describing RESTful web services. In: 2008 IEEE/WIC/ACM, vol. 1, pp. 619–625. IEEE (2008)
12. Klusch, M., Fries, B., Sycara, K.: OWLS-MX: a hybrid semantic web service matchmaker for OWL-S services. J. Web Semantics 7(2), 121–133 (2009)
13. Fenza, G., Loia, V., Senatore, S.: A hybrid approach to semantic web services matchmaking. Int. J. Approx. Reason. 48, 808–828 (2008)

Perceptron Connectives in Knowledge Representation

Pietro Galliani[1], Guendalina Righetti[1], Oliver Kutz[1(✉)], Daniele Porello[2], and Nicolas Troquard[1]

[1] Conceptual and Cognitive Modelling Research Group (CORE), KRDB Research Centre for Knowledge and Data, Faculty of Computer Science, Free University of Bozen-Bolzano, Bolzano, Italy
Oliver.Kutz@unibz.it
[2] Laboratory for Applied Ontology, ISTC-CNR, Trento, Italy

Abstract. We discuss the role of perceptron (or threshold) connectives in the context of Description Logic, and in particular their possible use as a bridge between statistical learning of models from data and logical reasoning over knowledge bases. We prove that such connectives can be added to the language of most forms of Description Logic without increasing the complexity of the corresponding inference problem. We show, with a practical example over the Gene Ontology, how even simple instances of perceptron connectives are expressive enough to represent learned, complex concepts derived from real use cases. This opens up the possibility to import concepts learnt from data into existing ontologies.

Keywords: Description logic · Machine learning · Perceptrons · Linear classifiers · Threshold operators · Ontologies

1 Introduction

Weighted Threshold Operators are n-ary logical operators which compute a weighted sum of their arguments and verify whether it reaches a certain threshold. These operators have been extensively studied in the context of circuit complexity theory (see e.g. [22]), and they are also known in the neural network community under the alternative name of *perceptrons* (see e.g. [4]).[1]

In [19], threshold operators were studied in the context of Knowledge Representation, focusing in particular on Description Logics (DLs). We refer the reader to [3] for a more thorough introduction to DL. Adding threshold operators to DL is not hard. In brief, if $C_1 \ldots C_n$ are concept expressions, $w_1 \ldots w_n \in \mathbb{R}$ are weights, and $t \in \mathbb{R}$ is a threshold, we can introduce a new

---

[1] Under the modern understanding of the term, a 'Perceptron' may have an activation function different from the Step Function (in particular, a differentiable one which is more suited to learning via back-propagation in multi-layer networks). In this work, however, we concentrate on the single-layer, step-function case.

© Springer Nature Switzerland AG 2020
C. M. Keet and M. Dumontier (Eds.): EKAW 2020, LNAI 12387, pp. 183–193, 2020.
https://doi.org/10.1007/978-3-030-61244-3_13

concept $\mathbb{W}^t(C_1 : w_1 \ldots C_n : w_n)$ to designate those individuals d such that $\sum\{w_i : C_i \text{ applies to } d\} \geq t$. In the context of DL and concept representation, such threshold ("Tooth") expressions are natural and useful, as they provide a simple way to describe the class of the individuals that satisfy "enough" of a certain set of desiderata. For example, we may wish to state that a student must obtain at least three credits from attending courses $\mathbf{A}$, $\mathbf{B}$, $\mathbf{C}$ and $\mathbf{D}$, where courses $\mathbf{A}$ and $\mathbf{B}$ are worth one credit each and courses $\mathbf{C}$ and $\mathbf{D}$ are worth two credits each. This is naturally expressed by the TBox axiom

$$\mathbf{Student} \sqsubseteq \mathbb{W}^3(\exists \mathtt{Att}.\mathbf{A} : 1, \exists \mathtt{Att}.\mathbf{B} : 1, \exists \mathtt{Att}.\mathbf{C} : 2, \exists \mathtt{Att}.\mathbf{D} : 2)$$

where $\mathtt{Att}$ represents the "attends" role. Suppose now that course $\mathbf{A}$ became compulsory. This could be done in two distinct ways: we could explicitly demand that students attend course $\mathbf{A}$, thus turning the above axiom into

$$\mathbf{Student} \sqsubseteq (\exists \mathtt{Att}.\mathbf{A}) \sqcap \mathbb{W}^3(\exists \mathtt{Att}.\mathbf{A} : 1, \exists \mathtt{Att}.\mathbf{B} : 1, \exists \mathtt{Att}.\mathbf{C} : 2, \exists \mathtt{Att}.\mathbf{D} : 2),$$

or we could simply assign more credits to course $\mathbf{A}$ and increase the credits requirement, thus turning the above axiom to e.g.

$$\mathbf{Student} \sqsubseteq \mathbb{W}^{12}(\exists \mathtt{Att}.\mathbf{A} : 10, \exists \mathtt{Att}.\mathbf{B} : 1, \exists \mathtt{Att}.\mathbf{C} : 2, \exists \mathtt{Att}.\mathbf{D} : 2).$$

These last two possibilities are semantically equivalent: in either scenario, a student has to attend course $\mathbf{A}$ and at least two of the others. However, they convey subtly different situations, and would lead to different consequences should the ontology be modified further (e.g. by adding another course $\mathbf{E}$ that is worth 10 credits by itself).

For a less mundane example, consider the *Felony Score Sheet* used in the State of Florida[2], in which various aspects of a crime are assigned points, and a threshold must be reached to decide compulsory imprisonment. For example, possession of cocaine corresponds to 16 points if it is the primary offense and to 2.4 points otherwise, a victim injury describable as "moderate" corresponds to 18 points, and a failure to appear for a criminal proceeding results in 4 points. Imprisonment is compulsory if the total is greater than 44 points and not compulsory otherwise. A knowledge base describing the laws of Florida would need to represent this score sheet as part of its definition of its **CompulsoryImprisonment** concept, for instance as

$$\mathbb{W}^{44}(\mathbf{CocainePrimary} : 16, \mathbf{ModerateInjuries} : 18, \ldots).$$

While it would be possible to also describe it (or any other Boolean function) in terms of more ordinary logical connectives (e.g. by a DNF expression), a definition in terms of Tooth expressions is far simpler and more readable. As such, the definition is more transparent and more explainable.

We refer the interested reader to [19] and to [13] for a more in-depth analysis of the properties of this operator. The paper [13] also introduces a *knowledge-dependent* variant of the threshold operator, in which the individuals are not

---

[2] http://www.dc.state.fl.us/pub/scoresheet/cpc_manual.pdf (accessed: 20 May 2020).

scored with respect to the current interpretation but with respect to some knowledge base $\mathcal{K}$ (which, in the case of a felony score sheet, may describe for example the findings according to which the score is to be computed). Having Tooth expressions in a language of knowledge representation has notable advantages, from a cognitive point of view and from the practical point of view of knowledge acquisition. First, in psychology and cognitive science, the combination of two or more concepts has a more subtle semantics than set theoretic operations. As shown in [20], Tooth operators can be used to represent these new concepts more faithfully regarding the way in which humans think of them and combine them. Second, as illustrated in [13], since a Tooth expression is simply a linear classification model, it is possible to use standard linear classification algorithms (such as the Perceptron Algorithm, Logistic Regression, or Linear SVM) to learn its weights and its threshold given a set of assertions about individuals (that is, given an ABox).

Extensions of Description Logic involving threshold operators have also been discussed in [1] and [2]. The approaches presented in these two papers are, however, very different from the one summarized above: the former paper, indeed, changes the semantics of Description Logic by associating *graded membership functions* to models and requiring them for the interpretation of expressions, while the latter one extends the semantics of the Description Logic $\mathcal{ALC}$ by means of weighted alternating parity tree automata. The approach described above is, in comparison, more direct: no changes are made to the definitions of the models of the Description Logic(s) to which threshold operators are added, and the language is merely extended by means of the above-described operators, which as already pointed out in [19], can be easily seen not to increase the expressive power of any language that contains the ordinary Boolean operators.

Aside from these technical differences, we argue that the approach introduced in [19] is more adequate even from a cognitive point of view. Although the proposal of Baader *et al.* allows one to represent concepts in an approximate way, introducing weights in the language permits to represent in a more straightforward way the relative importances of the different features participating in the concept descriptions. Tooth operators are in fact in line with the classical definition of prototypes given in the Prototype Theory exploited in the cognitive sciences (see e.g. [17, chapter 3]). Moreover, threshold expressions of [19] are putatively more intuitive and readable for non logic-experts, making them more cognitively adequate and less error-prone.

Two questions, however, need to be answered in order to assess the viability of this proposed addition to the language(s) of Description Logic:

1. Given a Description Logic $\mathcal{L}$, let $\mathcal{L}(\mathbb{W})$ be the logic obtained by adding threshold operators to it. How does the inference problem for $\mathcal{L}(\mathbb{W})$ compare to that for $\mathcal{L}$? More specifically: let $\mathcal{K}$ be a $\mathcal{L}(\mathbb{W})$-knowledge base and let ϕ be a $\mathcal{L}(\mathbb{W})$ axiom. Can we reduce the problem of whether $\mathcal{K} \models \phi$ (that is, of whether every interpretation that satisfies $\mathcal{K}$ satisfies ϕ) to the problem of whether $\mathcal{K}_0 \models \phi_0$ for some $\mathcal{K}_0, \phi_0 \in \mathcal{L}$ with an at-most-polynomial overhead?

2. Can we find examples in which simple threshold expressions can be used to express, more shortly and readably than (but roughly as accurately as) alternative approaches, non-trivial concepts derived from real data? If so, this would validate the claim that such expressions are well-suited for representing complex concepts in a readable way [19,20].

In what follows, we will answer these two questions.

2   Translating Threshold Expressions

The key ingredient for our result will be the following Proposition:

Proposition 1. *Let* $\mathrm{T} = \mathbb{W}^t(C_1 : w_1 \ldots C_n : w_n)$ *be any* $\mathcal{L}(\mathbb{W})$ *threshold expression, where* $C_1 \ldots C_n$ *are* $\mathcal{L}$*-concepts and* $t, w_1 \ldots w_n$ *are positive integers. Furthermore, let* TOOTH *be an atomic concept symbol not appearing in* T.

Then we can build a knowledge base $\mathcal{K}(\mathrm{T} \mapsto \mathit{TOOTH})$ *in* $\mathcal{L}$*, containing expressions built out of the concepts expressions* $C_1 \ldots C_n$ *and of a number of fresh atomic symbols (including* TOOTH*) such that*

1. $\mathcal{K}(\mathrm{T} \mapsto \mathit{TOOTH}) \models \mathit{TOOTH} \equiv \mathrm{T}$*;*
2. *Every interpretation* I *whose signature contains the atoms contained in* T *but not the fresh atoms introduced by* $\mathcal{K}(\mathrm{T} \mapsto \mathit{TOOTH})$ *can be expanded in one and only one way into some* I' *that satisfies* $\mathcal{K}(\mathrm{T} \mapsto \mathit{TOOTH})$*;*
3. *The size of* $\mathcal{K}(\mathrm{T} \mapsto \mathit{TOOTH})$ *is polynomial in the size of* T.[3]

Before proving this, let us show that it leads to the intended conclusion. A consequence of Proposition 1 is the following:

Proposition 2. *Let* C *be any* $\mathcal{L}(\mathbb{W})$*-concept. Then we can find an* $\mathcal{L}$*-theory* $\mathcal{K}_C$*, of size polynomial in the size of* C *and containing the symbols occurring in* C *as well as a number of fresh atomic concept symbols, and a* $\mathcal{L}$ *concept expression* C' *of size smaller or equal than that of* C*, such that*

1. $\mathcal{K}_C \models C \equiv C'$*;*
2. *Every interpretation* I *whose signature contains the symbols of* C *but not the fresh symbols added by* $\mathcal{K}_C$ *can be expanded in one and only one way to an interpretation* I' *that satisfies* $\mathcal{K}_C$*.*

Then the desired theorem follows at once:

Theorem 1. *Let* $\mathcal{L}$ *be a Description Logic that contains all Boolean connectives, let* $\mathcal{K}$ *be a* $\mathcal{L}(\mathbb{W})$ *knowledge base and let* ϕ *be a* $\mathcal{L}(\mathbb{W})$ *axiom. Then, the problem of whether* $\mathcal{K} \models \phi$ *can be reduced, with polynomial overhead, to the problem of whether* $\mathcal{K}_L \models \phi_L$ *for some* $\mathcal{L}$ *knowledge base* $\mathcal{K}_L$ *and some* $\mathcal{L}$ *axiom* ϕ_L.

---

[3] For the purposes of this work, the size of a concept expression includes also the number of bits required to express the weights and thresholds eventually occurring in it.

Thus, the inference problem in $\mathcal{L}(\mathbf{W})$ can indeed be reduced efficiently to the inference problem in $\mathcal{L}$ whenever Boolean connectives are already in the language of $\mathcal{L}$.

It remains to verify that Proposition 1 holds. So let $\mathbf{W}^t(C_1 : w_1 \ldots C_n : w_n)$ be our threshold expression, let k be the number of binary digits required to write the threshold and the (positive) weights, and let us also assume the other premises of Proposition 1. What we ultimately will do is writing the specification of a ripple-carry adder[4] and of a digital number comparator in the syntax of Description Logic.

For the sake of clarity, we will do so in several steps:

2.1   Encoding the Weights

Let $W_{ij} : i \in 1 \ldots n, j \in 0 \ldots k-1$ and $T_j : j \in 0 \ldots k-1$ be fresh atoms. Then let $\mathcal{K}_0$ be the TBox containing

- $W_{ij} \equiv C_i$, for all $i \in 1 \ldots n$ and for all $j \in 0 \ldots k-1$ such that the j-th least significant digit of the binary representation of w_i is 1, and $W_{ij} \equiv \bot$ for all the others;
- $T_j \equiv \top$ for all $j \in 0 \ldots k-1$ such that the j-th least significant digit of the binary representation of t is 1, and $T_j \equiv \bot$ for the others.

Lemma 1. $\mathcal{K}_0$ *has size polynomial in the size of our original threshold expression. Moreover, any interpretation I in which $C_1 \ldots C_n$ can be interpreted and in which the fresh atoms W_{ij} and T_j do not appear has a unique extension to an interpretation I' such that $I' \models \mathcal{K}_0$. For that interpretation, we furthermore have that, for all individuals $d \in \Delta^{I'}$,*

$$\sum\{2^j : j = 0 \ldots k-1, d \in W_{ij}^{I'}\} = \begin{cases} w_i & \text{if } d \in C_i^I; \\ 0 & \text{otherwise.} \end{cases}$$

for all $i \in 1 \ldots n$. Likewise,

$$\sum\{2^j : j = 0 \ldots k-1, d \in T_j^{I'}\} = t.$$

2.2   Encoding the Sum

Summing the First Weight. We define[5] $\mathcal{K}_1$ as the union of $\mathcal{K}_0$ and the following axioms, for the fresh atomic symbols $\mathtt{SUM}_0^1 \ldots \mathtt{SUM}_{k-1}^1$:

- For all $j = 0 \ldots k-1$, we add the axiom $\mathtt{SUM}_j^1 \equiv W_{1j}$.

---

[4] Other, more efficient types of adder circuits are known and used in practice, and could be translated along similar lines; but ripple-carry adders have the advantage of simplicity and suffice for our purposes.

[5] This first sum is strictly speaking unnecessary, but we keep it for clarity of exposition.

Lemma 2. $\mathcal{K}_1$ *has size polynomial in the size of our original threshold expression. Let I be as in Lemma 1: then I has exactly one expansion to a model I' of $\mathcal{K}_1$, and for I' we have that $\sum\{2^j : j = 0 \ldots k-1, d \in (SUM_j^1)^{I'}\} = \sum\{w_i : 1 \leq i \leq 1, d \in C_i^I\}$.*

Summing the Other Weights. For $i = 2 \ldots n$, we define inductively $\mathcal{K}_i$ as $\mathcal{K}_{i-1}$ plus the following axioms (for fresh symbols $SUM_0^i \ldots SUM_{k-1}^i$ and $CARRY_0^i \ldots CARRY_{k-1}^i$) and $OVERFLOW^i$:

- The axiom $CARRY_0^i \equiv \bot$;
- For all $j = 0 \ldots k-1$, the axiom

$$SUM_j^i \equiv (CARRY_j^i \sqcap SUM_j^{i-1} \sqcap W_j^i) \sqcup (CARRY_j^i \sqcap \neg SUM_j^{i-1} \sqcap \neg W_j^i) \sqcup$$
$$(\neg CARRY_j^i \sqcap SUM_j^{i-1} \sqcap \neg W_j^i) \sqcup (\neg CARRY_j^i \sqcap \neg SUM_j^{i-1} \sqcap W_j^i);$$

- For all $j = 1 \ldots k-1$, the axiom

$$CARRY_j^i \equiv (CARRY_{j-1}^i \sqcap SUM_{j-1}^{i-1}) \sqcup (CARRY_{j-1}^i \sqcap W_{j-1}^i) \sqcup (SUM_{j-1}^{i-1} \sqcap W_{j-1}^i);$$

- The axiom

$$OVERFLOW^i \equiv (CARRY_{k-1}^i \sqcap SUM_{k-1}^{i-1}) \sqcup (CARRY_{k-1}^i \sqcap W_{k-1}^i) \sqcup (SUM_{k-1}^{i-1} \sqcap W_{k-1}^i).$$

Lemma 3. *For all $\ell = 1 \ldots n$, $\mathcal{K}_\ell$ has size polynomial in the size of our original threshold expression.*

Moreover, for every such ℓ, every interpretation I as in Lemma 1 can be extended in exactly one way to an interpretation I' which satisfies $\mathcal{K}_\ell$; and for this interpretation $SUM_{k-1}^\ell \ldots SUM_0^\ell$ is a binary encoding of the sum of the weights (up to w_ℓ) which correspond to concepts that apply to the current individual, in the sense that (for all $d \in \Delta^{I'}$) $\sum\{2^j : j = 0 \ldots k-1, d \in (SUM_j^\ell)^{I'}\} = \sum\{w_i : 1 \leq i \leq \ell, d \in C^I\}$ whenever that value is less than 2^k, and $d \in (OVERFLOW^\ell)^{I'}$ otherwise.

In particular, if $I \models \mathcal{K}_n$ then $\sum\{2^j : j = 0 \ldots k-1, d \in (SUM_j^n)^{I'}\} = \sum\{w_i : 1 \leq i \leq n, d \in C^I\} = v_T^I(d)$ is the value of our tooth expression $T = \mathbb{W}^t(C_1 : w_1 \ldots C_n : w_n)$ if that value is less than 2^k, and otherwise $d \in (OVERFLOW^i)^{I'}$ for at least one $i = 2 \ldots n$.

2.3   Comparing with the Threshold

Now define $\mathcal{K}$ as $\mathcal{K}_n$ plus the following axioms (for fresh atoms $EQ_{k-1} \ldots EQ_0$, $MAJ_{k-1} \ldots MAJ_0$, TOOTH:

- $EQ_{k-1} \equiv ((SUM_{k-1}^n \sqcap T_{k-1}) \sqcup (\neg SUM_{k-1}^n \sqcap \neg T_{k-1}))$;
- For $j = (k-2) \ldots 0$, the axiom

$$EQ_j \equiv EQ_{j+1} \sqcap ((SUM_j^n \sqcap T_j) \sqcup (\neg SUM_j^n \sqcap \neg T_j));$$

- $\mathtt{MAJ}_{k-1} \equiv \mathtt{SUM}^n_{k-1} \sqcap \neg T_{k-1}$;
- For $j = (k-2) \ldots 0$, the axiom

$$\mathtt{MAJ}_j \equiv \mathtt{EQ}_{j+1} \sqcap \mathtt{SUM}^n_j \sqcap \neg T_j;$$

- The axiom

$$\mathtt{TOOTH} \equiv \mathtt{OVERFLOW}^2 \sqcup \ldots \sqcup \mathtt{OVERFLOW}^n \sqcup$$

$$\mathtt{MAJ}_{k-1} \sqcup \ldots \sqcup \mathtt{MAJ}_0 \sqcup \mathtt{EQ}_0.$$

Lemma 4. *$\mathcal{K}$ has size polynomial in the size of our original threshold expression. Moreover, every interpretation I as in Lemma 1 can be extended in exactly one way to an interpretation I' that satisfies $\mathcal{K}$; and for this interpretation and for every individual $d \in \Delta^{I'}$,*

- *For all $j = k-1 \ldots 0$, $d \in EQ^I_j$ if and only if the binary encodings of $v^I_T(d)$ and of t agree from the most significant digit to the j-th least significant digit;*
- *For all $j = k-1 \ldots 0$, $d \in MAJ^I_j$ if and only if the binary encodings of $v^I_T(d)$ and of t disagree on the j-th least significant digit, which is greater for $v^I_C(d)$ than for t, but agree on all the digits on the left of it;*
- *$d \in TOOTH^{I'}$ if and only if we obtained an overflow when summing all the weights which apply to the individual d (remember that we assumed positive weights, so this implies at once that $v^I_T(d)$ is greater than the threshold), or if there is a digit that is greater for $v^I_R(d)$ than for t and all the digits to the left agree, or if all the digits of $v^I_T(d)$ and of t are the same - that is, if and only if $v^I_T(d) \geq t$.*

At this point, Proposition 1 follows at once by picking this $\mathcal{K}$ for $\mathcal{K}(\mathtt{T} \mapsto \mathtt{TOOTH})$.

3   Learning Simple Threshold Expressions

In order to evaluate the practical usefulness of threshold expressions, we are going to investigate whether simple non-nested threshold expressions suffice to represent adequately Gene Ontology concepts.

The Gene Ontology. The Gene Ontology [12] (GO) is a knowledge base consisting (by January 2020) of 44,700 different concepts ("terms") annotating more than one million gene products from 4,591 different species. Different concepts relate to each other not only via the usual subsumption ("is-a") relation, but also via other relations such as "part-of" or "regulates"; and they are partitioned into the three disjoint sub-ontologies of *Cellular Component*, for concepts relating to locations inside of a cell, like "nucleus" (term GO:0005634) or "Golgi Apparatus" (term GO:0005794); *Biological Process*, for concepts specifying "biological programs" to which a gene product participates, like "Asexual Reproduction" (term GO:0019954) or "Oxygen Transport" (term GO:0015671); and *Molecular Function*, for concepts relative to specific molecular-level roles performed by gene products such as "Enzyme Binding" (term GO:0019899) or "Structural Constituent of Ribosome" (term GO:0003735).

Datasets exist that associate gene products to Gene Ontology terms: for example, according to the Saccharomyces Genome Database [9,10],[6] the enzyme *ATP synthase* (ATP8) is located in the *mitochondrion* (GO:0005739), is involved in the biological processes of *ion transport* (GO:0006811) and *transmembrane transport* (GO:0055085), and more specifically *ATPase activity* (GO:0016887) and *hydrolase activity* (GO:0016787) are among its molecular functions.

Approach. For the purposes of this work, we decided to focus on the annotations of the Saccharomyces Genome Database and on the subset of the Gene Ontology (the "GO slim", in the terminology used by the Gene Ontology Consortium) that has been curated by it for the purpose of annotating yeast gene products. We likewise downloaded Gene Ontology annotations of yeast gene products from the website of the Saccharomyces Genome Database. Then we considered the following question: up to which degree is it possible to infer the Molecular Function annotations of a gene product from its Cellular Component and Biological Process ones? In other words, given the locations of a gene product inside of a yeast cell and the overall "cellular programs" it is involved in, can we infer (to some degree, at least) its specific molecular-level roles?

It is worth emphasizing here that our purpose is *not* to design and propose a novel state-of-the-art machine learning algorithm. Rather, our aim is to investigate the expressive potential of simple threshold expressions in real use scenarios. To this purpose, we designed a very basic evolutionary algorithm to extract threshold expressions from data. In brief, a population of one hundred random threshold expressions (with Gene Ontology concepts as arguments, integer weights, at most 10 arguments, and threshold fixed at 100) is generated, then they attempt to "copy" (concept, weight) pairs from randomly selected neighbours[7], keeping them if they improve the performance on the training data; weights are mutated randomly, and the mutation is likewise kept if it is an improvement; and every ten turns the half worst-performing threshold expressions are removed and replaced with random ones. After one thousand turns, we simply return the threshold expression that performs best over the training data. This is only a cursory description, but again, we wish to make it clear that this algorithm is merely a means to an end—the end being to verify whether simple threshold expressions can adequately capture complex concepts. No serious attempt was made to fine-tune its performance or refine its overall design.

As a baseline, we used a few state-of-the-art learning algorithms as implemented in the Waikato Environment for Knowledge Analysis (WEKA) [14], namely a Random Forest classifier [7], the Sequential Minimal Optimization

---

[6] The Saccharomyces Genome Database is available at https://www.yeastgenome.org/.

[7] While maintaining the maximum number of components of every threshold expression to 10: if that number has been reached, the copied weight replaces the component whose weight has the smallest magnitude.

algorithm for Support Vector Machines [18], a decision table majority classifier [15], a logistic regression classifier [8] and a multilayer perceptron classifier [21].

Since the available data is heavily imbalanced (for every possible molecular function, most gene products will not be associated with it), we decided to use Matthews Correlation as our performance measure [6,11,16], which describes the statistical correlation between the predicted label and the true one and is 0 if these are uncorrelated and 1 if there is perfect positive correlation. As discussed, e.g., in [11], other standard metrics for classification such as accuracy or the F_1 score can lead to overoptimistic results on greatly imbalanced datasets. The Matthews Correlation Coefficient makes use of all four cells of the confusion matrix (true/false, positives/negatives), and it assigns the same importance to "positive" and "negative" examples. It has a natural statistical interpretation: it can be seen as the special case of the Pearson Correlation Coefficient in which variables may only take one of two values.

Data Preparation. We prepared the data as follows: first, we removed all gene product annotations listed as "dubious" in the Saccharomyces Genome Database, as well as the annotations to the three uninformative top-level terms of the three sub-ontologies. Then we picked from the mapping file of the Saccharomyces Genome Database gene products with at least three annotations of type "Cellular Component" or "Biological Process". Then we chose as the labels to predict the "Molecular Function" type annotations that occur in at least one hundred of the above gene products, and selected as features the "Cellular Component" or "Biological Process" terms that apply to at least one of these gene products. This resulted in a dataset of 4,595 gene products, each one of which has 120 features and 17 possible labels. For each of these labels, we split the gene products in five folds, maintaining the same proportions of true labels.

We reserved five of these labels for final testing, using the others for developing our approach to learning threshold expressions and for tuning our baselines. This highlighted in particular that, in the cases of Decision Majority Tables, Logistic Classifiers and Support Vector Machines, it was necessary to correct the unbalancedness of the data by oversampling the positive examples during training.

Evaluation. Finally, we tested our approach on the reserved labels and the corresponding datasets, training our method and our baselines—for each of the five labels in the reserved dataset—on four folds and testing it on the remaining one. The results are summarized in Table 1 . The performance varies between labels and for some of them it is not very high, which was only to be expected since in general the biological processes to which a gene product participates and the cellular components in which it is found are not adequate information to infer their molecular function; but what is of interest for our purposes is that the performance of threshold expressions (despite the very basic approach that we took to their learning) follows roughly that of our baselines and is overall as good as them. This supports our hypothesis that threshold expressions, and very simple ones at that, can adequately capture complex concepts in real world scenarios

Table 1. Matthews Correlations of predictions on five Molecular Function terms. We report averages between five folds and standard deviation. (Leading zeros are omitted.) RF = Random Forest, SVM = Support Vector Machine, DT = Decision Table, LR = Logistic Regression, MLP = Multilayer Perceptron, $\mathbb{W}$ = our Threshold Expressions. The five rows correspond to the Molecular Function Gene Ontology terms GO:0016787 (hydrolase activity), GO:0016301 (kinase activity), GO:0030234 (enzyme regulator activity), GO:0022857 (transmembrane transporter activity) and GO:0016740 (transferase activity).

	RF	SVM	DT	LR	MLP	$\mathbb{W}$
GO:0016787	.34 (.02)	.30 (.03)	.22 (.03)	.30 (.03)	.26 (.07)	.22 (.06)
GO:0016301	.67 (.07)	.53 (.06)	.51 (.09)	.66 (.06)	.79 (.03)	.75 (.04)
GO:0030234	.25 (.06)	.18 (.01)	.12 (.03)	.20 (.04)	.22 (.07)	.27 (.06)
GO:0022857	.80 (.02)	.71 (.04)	.55 (.02)	.79 (.02)	.75 (.03)	.72 (.05)
GO:0016740	.50 (.01)	.48 (.03)	.47 (.04)	.45 (.04)	.48 (.02)	.47 (.03)

as well as more sophisticated models despite being of simpler understanding and (as we saw) easier to integrate with logical reasoning.

4   Conclusions

The results of this work lend support to the feasibility of adding threshold connectives to knowledge representation languages. As showed in Sect. 2, such connectives can be added to the language of any DL that has all Boolean connectives without increasing the complexity of the corresponding inference problem, and thus reasoning services for any such DL $\mathcal{L}$ can be also used (after translation) also for the corresponding extension $\mathcal{L}(\mathbb{W})$.

Furthermore, as we showed in Sect. 3 with a practical example over the Gene Ontology, even simple instances of perceptron connectives are expressive enough to represent complex notions in real use cases.

Much more can be done. A particularly intriguing aspect is the experimental evaluation of the degree up to which threshold expressions are more human-interpretable than equivalent logical formulations, along the lines of [5]. Also, with the prospect of sharing ontologies with perceptron connectives, their addition to semantic web languages will need to be carefully pursued.

References

1. Baader, F., Brewka, G., Gil, O.F.: Adding threshold concepts to the description logic $\mathcal{EL}$. In: Lutz, C., Ranise, S. (eds.) FroCoS 2015. LNCS (LNAI), vol. 9322, pp. 33–48. Springer, Cham (2015). https://doi.org/10.1007/978-3-319-24246-0_3
2. Baader, F., Ecke, A.: Reasoning with prototypes in the description logic $\mathcal{ALC}$ using weighted tree automata. In: Dediu, A.-H., Janoušek, J., Martín-Vide, C., Truthe, B. (eds.) LATA 2016. LNCS, vol. 9618, pp. 63–75. Springer, Cham (2016). https://doi.org/10.1007/978-3-319-30000-9_5

3. Baader, F., Horrocks, I., Lutz, C., Sattler, U.: Introduction to Description Logic. Cambridge University Press, Cambridge (2017)
4. Bishop, C.M.: Pattern Recognition and Machine Learning. Springer, New York (2006)
5. Booth, S., Muise, C., Shah, J.: Evaluating the interpretability of the knowledge compilation map: communicating logical statements effectively. In: Proceedings of 28th IJCAI, pp. 5801–5807 (2019)
6. Boughorbel, S., Jarray, F., El-Anbari, M.: Optimal classifier for imbalanced data using Matthews correlation coefficient metric. PLoS ONE **12**(6), e0177678 (2017)
7. Breiman, L.: Random forests. Mach. Learn. **45**(1), 5–32 (2001). https://doi.org/10.1023/A:1010933404324
8. le Cessie, S., van Houwelingen, J.: Ridge estimators in logistic regression. Appl. Stat. **41**(1), 191–201 (1992)
9. Cherry, J.M., et al.: SGD: saccharomyces genome database. Nucleic Acids Res. **26**(1), 73–79 (1998)
10. Cherry, J.M., et al.: Saccharomyces genome database: the genomics resource of budding yeast. Nucleic Acids Res. **40**(D1), D700–D705 (2012)
11. Chicco, D., Jurman, G.: The advantages of the Matthews correlation coefficient (MCC) over F1 score and accuracy in binary classification evaluation. BMC Genom. **21**(1), 6 (2020)
12. Consortium, G.O.: The Gene Ontology (GO) database and informatics resource. Nucleic Acids Res. **32**(suppl_1), D258–D261 (2004)
13. Galliani, P., Kutz, O., Porello, D., Righetti, G., Troquard, N.: On knowledge dependence in weighted description logic. In: Proceedings of the 5th Global Conference on Artificial Intelligence (GCAI 2019), pp. 17–19 (2019)
14. Holmes, G., Donkin, A., Witten, I.H.: Weka: a machine learning workbench. In: Proceedings of ANZIIS'94-Australian New Zealand Intelligent Information Systems Conference, pp. 357–361. IEEE (1994)
15. Kohavi, R.: The power of decision tables. In: Lavrac, N., Wrobel, S. (eds.) ECML 1995. LNCS, vol. 912, pp. 174–189. Springer, Heidelberg (1995). https://doi.org/10.1007/3-540-59286-5_57
16. Matthews, B.W.: Comparison of the predicted and observed secondary structure of t4 phage lysozyme. Biochimica et Biophysica Acta (BBA)-Protein Struct. **405**(2), 442–451 (1975)
17. Murphy, G.: The Big Book of Concepts. The MIT Press, Cambridge (2002)
18. Platt, J.: Fast training of support vector machines using sequential minimal optimization. In: Advances in Kernel Methods-Support Vector Learning, AJ, pp. 185–208. MIT Press, Cambridge (1999)
19. Porello, D., Kutz, O., Righetti, G., Troquard, N., Galliani, P., Masolo, C.: A toothful of concepts: Towards a theory of weighted concept combination. In: Proceedings of the 32nd International Workshop on Description Logics, vol. 2373. CEUR-WS (2019). http://ceur-ws.org/Vol-2373/paper-24.pdf
20. Righetti, G., Porello, D., Kutz, O., Troquard, N., Masolo, C.: Pink panthers and toothless tigers: three problems in classification. In: Proceedings of the 5th International Workshop on Artificial Intelligence and Cognition. Manchester, 10–11 September (2019)
21. Rosenblatt, F.: Principles of neurodynamics. Perceptrons and the theory of brain mechanisms. Technical report, Cornell Aeronautical Lab Inc., Buffalo (1961)
22. Vollmer, H.: Introduction to Circuit Complexity: A Uniform Approach. Springer, Heidelberg (2013)

On the Formal Representation and Annotation of Cellular Genealogies

Patryk Burek[1], Nico Scherf[2,3($\boxtimes$)], and Heinrich Herre[4]

[1] Institute of Computer Science, Faculty of Mathematics, Physics and Computer Science,
Marii Curie-Sklodowskiej University, Lublin, Poland
`patryk.burek@poczta.umcs.lublin.pl`
[2] Institute for Medical Informatics and Biometry, Carl Gustav Carus Faculty of Medicine,
School of Medicine, TU Dresden, Dresden, Germany
`nico.scherf@tu-dresden.de`
[3] Max Planck Institute for Human Cognitive and Brain Sciences, Leipzig, Germany
[4] Institute for Medical Informatics, Statistics and Epidemiology,
University of Leipzig, Leipzig, Germany
`heinrich.herre@imise.uni-leipzig.de`

Abstract. Time-lapse microscopy is a primary experimental tool for biologists
to study development: the dynamic process by which an entire organism forms
from an individual cell. The domain of these cellular dynamics is quite complex,
and thus, demands a conceptual and computational architecture to support the
integration of knowledge obtained across experiments and theories. In previous
work, we have addressed the conceptual level and developed an axiomatic theory
of cellular genealogies. In this work, we will address the other fundamental part of
theory formation: the experimental level, where we have to deal with actual observations and discoveries. In the case of experiments from time-lapse microscopy,
we need to go from the individual images taken at discrete time points to a full
conceptual description of the underlying continuous cellular processes. In this
work, we take a first step to bridge the general theory T(CO) and the experimental level by investigating individual cases. Any time-lapse experiment is linked
to a real spatiotemporal genealogy, and we assume that these entities are particular instances of the general theory. We will investigate how this individual
experimental information can be organised and represented.

Keywords: Knowledge management · Ontology of biological reality · Theories
of developmental biology · Microscopy · Time-lapse imaging · Cell tracking

1 Introduction

Cellular dynamics and interactions shape multicellular life as it develops from a single
fertilised egg into a complex organism. These (inter-)cellular processes also maintain
the structure and function of the organism during its lifetime. To fully understand the
principles underlying this self-organising process, we have to be able to observe and
analyse the cellular dynamics and cellular states from experiments [1]. One milestone

© Springer Nature Switzerland AG 2020
C. M. Keet and M. Dumontier (Eds.): EKAW 2020, LNAI 12387, pp. 194–203, 2020.
https://doi.org/10.1007/978-3-030-61244-3_14

of time-lapse experiments has undoubtedly been the reconstruction of the embryonic lineage tree of the nematode *Caenorhabditis elegans* [2]. From these roots, modern fluorescence microscopy has turned into a powerful tool to resolve the dynamics of thousands of cells together with readouts of cellular states by fluorescent labels [1, 3] across a wide range of biological questions from developmental biology to stem cell biology and oncology. But imaging and visualizing cellular dynamics is only one part of the problem, we also have to extract and quantify the resulting cellular dynamics. Beyond simple experiments with only a few cells, manual analysis of cell tracking experiments is mostly infeasible. Consequently, a variety of methods have been developed to computationally track individual cells in time-lapse movies [4, 5]. Beyond computational tracking of cells there waits another challenge, however: How can we formalise and extract knowledge from the automated (or manual) tracking results? Here, we need to develop and refine concepts and theories to make sense of the patterns we observe [6]. The first step is to establish standard data formats that serve as the core to annotate and share the tracking results [7]. We should base these annotations on a solid theoretical foundation and carefully develop the underlying terminology and formal concepts themselves as theories about the biological world [8]. We have recently [9] made a first step into this direction and developed the essential parts of a conceptual architecture that supports integration and interoperability of cell tracking experiments. This framework is based on the *Cellular Genealogy* as a fundamental notion for the development of a *Cell Tracking Ontology*. Some core components and patterns of which have already been presented in [10, 11]. In this work, we will now explore the experimental level of theory formation, where we have to deal with actual observations. Both aspects need to be addressed when developing an empirical theory about an area of reality. In the case of time-lapse experiments, we need to go from individual images taken at discrete time points by a microscope to a full, conceptual description of the underlying continuous cellular processes. Here, we take a step to bridge the general theory T(CO) and the experimental level by investigating individual cases. We will examine how different experimental information can be organised and represented.

2 Towards a Formal Theory of Cellular Genealogies

Developmental biology is the science that investigates how a variety of interacting processes (at the molecular, cellular and tissue level) generate the various shapes, size, and structural features that arise throughout the life cycles of multicellular organisms. This field also encompasses the biology of regeneration, metamorphosis, and the growth and the differentiation of stem cells in the adult organism and is thus intimately linked with stem cell biology and basic research in regenerative medicine and oncology.

We would like to note one fundamental problem here: there is no clear consensus on how to define the boundary between the animate and inanimate. Typical defining properties of life are, among others, metabolism, adaptivity and interaction with the environment, self-organisation, reproduction, heredity, and growth. These conditions define a system which must satisfy at least the following basic properties. It should have a boundary, demarcating the system from the environment, and it should have inner parts.

It should further be able to sense and interact with the environment[1]. In biology, the cell is the simplest system satisfying these assumptions. Thus, in our view, the self-organised development of a cellular genealogy, starting from a zygote, seems to be an essential feature of the animate.

Hence, the ontology of biology should consider the existence of cellular genealogies as one of the essential features demarcating biology from other fields of natural science, as physics or chemistry. The cellular genealogy of an animal is determined by the whole developmental process of this animal from the initial zygote to the multicellular organism that is focused on the cell level. At any time-point of an animal's life, a collection of cells are present. During development, these cell collectives permanently change, by e.g. cell division, cell differentiation and cell death. Hence, a cellular genealogy is a process which is determined by the development of an animal's cell collectives. Cellular genealogies possess a certain structure which can be specified by using the notion of a cell collective and cell situation, and the process connecting them. There are various important structural parameters of a cellular genealogy. How many cells exist in a complete genealogy of an animal? What can be said about the sequence of the maximal time-intervals during which there is no change of the corresponding cell-collectives? As a next step, these cell collectives can be extended by adding relations, such as the morphology of the single cells, or cell groups, or their localisation in space. Cell collectives extended by additional relations are called cell situations. Since cells may divide and eventually die the number of cells within a region under consideration (e.g. a developing organism) changes through time. Let us consider a time-segment (time-interval) I, such that during I no cell-division and no cell death occurs. Then, the cells existing during I form a collective Cells(I) that can be considered as a continuant through I.

In [9], we introduced the notion of Cell-Collective-Genealogy (denoted by CollGen), and Cell-Situation-Genealogy (SitGen). The lifetime of an organism is assumed to be a closed time interval. We assume that the time is presented by time-points and time-intervals, whereas the time-points have the order-type of the real numbers. Let us consider a time-segment (time-interval) I such that during I no cell-division and no cell death occurs; then we call the set of cells associated with this interval a cell collective. During times when the number of cells changes, new cells may occur, and cells may disappear (i.e. die). We consider the life of an organism Org from fertilisation to death. Org starts as a single cell, the zygote, develops into a multicellular structure through time collectives of cells, lives in a dynamic equilibrium and finally dies, i.e. the dynamic, functional structures dissolve. We divide the lifetime T of Org into a sequence of non-overlapping time-intervals I(1), ..., I(n) such that the following conditions are satisfied:

(1) The intervals I(m) have a first point (they are left-closed), but no last point (right open). More precisely, they have the form [a(m), a(m + 1)) specifying the set {c : a(m) $\leq$ c < a(m + 1)}, where 0 $\leq$ m $\leq$ n. Further, LifeT(Org) = $\cup$\{I(m) : 0 $\leq$ m $\leq$ n\}.

---

[1] Cf. *Autopoiesis* as an attempt to define living matter using concepts from general systems theory such as self-organisation.

(2) Let Cells(I(k)) be the set of cells existing during I(k), then no cell death or division occurs during the interval I(k), k ≺ n. Further, we assume that Cells(I(k)) ≠ Cells (I(k + 1)).

These conditions imply further properties: From Cells(I(k)) to Cells(I(k + 1)) the number of existing cells changes. We consider two types: cell division and cell death. If a division of a cell c ∈ I(k) occurs then this process ends up with two daughter cells starting their existence at the left boundary of the interval I(k + 1). Analogously, if a cell undergoes cell death during I(k) then this ends at the left-boundary of I(k + 1). The final definition of CollGen(start) then must specify which cells from Cells(k) are related to which cells in Cells(k + 1). To this end, we introduce two relations: div(x, y, z): a cell x of Cells(k) undergoes a cell division during I(k) resulting in two daughter cells y and z starting their existence at the left-boundary of I(k + 1). We also introduce the relation id(x, y) stating that x belongs to Cells(k) and y belongs to Cells(k + 1) and both cells are identical. We further say that a cell x in Cells(k) has a successor cell y in Cells(k + 1), if y is either a daughter cell of z or if y is identical with x, denoted by succ(x, y). The cell collective genealogy CellGen(c(0)), is then specified by the following system CollGen(c(0)) = ({Cells(k) | 0 ≤ k ≤ n}, div(x, y, z), id(x, y)). We call the intervals I(k) invariance intervals because during these intervals no cell-change occurs. The structure of such a cell-collective genealogy is an important, uniquely determined feature of the organism. The following theorem we postulate without proof.[2]

Theorem. For any organism Org there exists a uniquely determined cell-collective genealogy associated with Org.

As outlined, for every cell collective x there is a uniquely determined time-interval I such that no changes occur during I. This time-interval is called the *invariance interval* of the cell-collective; it has a left-boundary and no right-boundary.

A cell situation genealogy is an extension of the cell collection genealogy: We start with the system CollGen(c(0)) and extend any collective of cells(k) into an object-situation Sit(k). Sit(k) contains exactly the cells of Cells(k) as objects, and it is embedded into an object-situation with the timeframe I(k) and a specified spaceframe. The collective Cells(k) then spans a certain space, which contains at least the spatial convex closure of the objects in Cells(k). We must specify the situation type determined by a signature Σ. A situation-genealogy is based on signature-extension of a cell collective genealogy, i.e., to the signature Σ(0) further symbols from a signature Σ(1) are added; we assume that Σ(0) ∩ Σ(1) = ∅. For every signature Σ(1) we may introduce a model-structure that models the corresponding cell-situation genealogy, called SitGen = (CollGen, int(Σ(1))).

Based on the signature Σ(0) we created an initial theory about cell-collective genealogies, denoted by T(0)(CG), and presented in [9]. The further development and refinement of this theory is a future research field of its own. Here, we would like to concentrate on the experimental level of theory formation.

---

[2] Because of limitation of space for the current paper, the proof is presented [9].

3   The Experimental Framework

Humans access the independent reality by various components and levels of their cognitive systems. The immediate interaction between the subject and reality, subject and object, is realised through the senses by the process of perception. These sense-data are organised, clustered, and then concepts and relations between the data are formed. We call this basic information, acquired by the subject, phenomena, and data. A theory about a domain should formulate certain conditions that explain the domain's phenomena. The higher levels of cognition use principles of causation to establish a theory about a part of reality.

A theory T consists of propositions which are postulated to be true in D. An experiment is a mediator between a theory and the real domain under consideration. We want to get data about the CG which are not captured by the given theory T(CG). What can be said about the types of the involved cells, and about the structure of the cellular genealogies of concrete species? The Gene Ontology (GO) provides many features about the cells which are not yet considered in the current theory TG. However, all this information is needed to extend the initial theory T(CG)(0) so we can get a complete picture of the behavioural dynamics of cells. Time-lapse experiments are one important source of such information.

These real-world genealogies are analysed by cell tracking experiments. Such experiments yield snapshots by a microscope M of a continuously developing cell situation genealogy SitGen. Related to SitGen the microscope M generates a finite sequence of images that correspond to presentic situations, determined by SitGen. These images are called frames, and the resulting finite ordered set of frames is called the frame sequence of the experiment. An experiment of this type establishes a relation between SitGen, the microscope M, and the frame sequence FSeq, denoted by Exp(SitGen, M, FSeq), whereas M serves as a mediator[3] between the original entity SitGen and the output FSeq in the form of a finite sequence of images. The frame-sequence provides important information about the evolving cell situation genealogy. The snapshot of a situation is an independent ontological entity, which is classified in the framework of GFO as a material presentic object, or simply as a material presential. With this assumed preconditions, a formal description of the relation Exp(SitGen, FSeq) is useful, because it provides a deeper understanding of the relation between the reality of SitGen and the data, generated by M, and provides a frame sequence FSeq, briefly denoted by FSeq(SitGen). The interaction between cellular genealogies and frame sequences are described by axioms. Here, we only sketch the basic ideas; further details are presented in [9].

FSeq(x) := x is a frame-sequence, and its components are called frames. Every frame is a snapshot of a situation, denoted by PSit. We introduce a linear ordering between the components of a frame-sequence, hence such a sequence can be presented by the structure $FSeq = (\{F(1), ..., F(n)\}, <)$, where $F(1) < ... < F(n)$. Let FSeq be a frame sequence, we say that a component G is a successor of the component F, if $F < G$ and there is no frame between F and G; we say that G is subsequent to F.

---

[3] The development of such mediators (imaging techniques) play an important role in the advancement of science and its applications in general. A significant example is magnetic resonance imaging (MRI)

We assume that in any frame there occur cells, that these cells are presentials, and any such presentic cell is a snapshot of a uniquely determined cell (with lifetime > 0). We introduce relations such as assoc(F, t): "the frame F is associated with the time point t" (F is a snapshot at time-point t) and component(x, y): x is a component of the frame y, distance(a, b, r): the presentic cell a and the presentic cell b have distance r.

For every frame sequence FSeq there exists a cell collective genealogy CollGen such that any component of FSeq is a snapshot of a cell collective in CollGen.

4 From Frames to the Representation of Cellular Genealogies

The data acquired by the experiment are taken from snapshots which are presented in the frame sequences. Hence, we use the frame-sequence and some basic knowledge about the sequences' structure. For the tracking of single cells (as individual instances) we must introduce constants $c(1), \ldots, c(n)$, denoting these (presentic) cells. These constants are associated with the different frames, $F(1), \ldots, F(n)$ being snapshots at certain time-points, say $t(1), \ldots, t(n)$. Since we are not sure, whether a cell **a** in frame $F(i)$ is the same as the cell **b** in $F(i + 1)$ (the same for daughter cells and divisions etc.), we are forced - in the first step – to consider the presentic cells for any frame separately. For this purpose, we may associate to any constant c a timestamp, say expressed by c@t (the presentic cell occurs in the frame F(t)). For the construction of a representation of the genealogy, we need to know whether some of the following conditions hold: $id(a@i, b@(i + 1))$, or $div(a@i, b@(i + 1), c@(i + 1))$, $Death(c@i)$ (and other relations according to the situation). To answer these questions background knowledge using existing ontologies, the concepts of which can be applied to annotate the frames and their parts. Another important method could be machine learning, and – of course – other methods of artificial intelligence. Symbolic artificial intelligence can be used to abstract temporal patterns from temporalised data (i.e. data of the form c@t).

We further distinguish atomic from complex data. Atomic data have the form of atomic sentences, for example, $id(a@i, b@(i + 1))$ (with the meaning: a@i and b@(i + 1) are snapshots of a cell c). Complex data are particular combinations of atomic data, for example we may consider $id(a@i, b@(i + 1))$/and $id(b@(i + 1), c@(i + 2))$ which says that the cells a@i, b@(i + 1), c@(i + 2) are equivalent, hence present the same cell.

Individual data can be annotated by additional information, taken from existing bio-ontologies. For example, the complex datum [$id(a@i, b@(i + 1))$ and $id(b@(i + 1), c@(i + 2))$)] can be annotated by a cell-type T.

Let us consider a frame $F(i) = (PSit, c(1), \ldots, c(m), r(1), \ldots, r(n))$, and $F(i + 1)$ a successor frame of the sequence. $F(i), F(i + 1)$ reflect snapshots of certain situations S, S' of the genealogy. Are $F(i)$ and $F(i + 1)$ snapshots of the same situations, or from different situations? One may either assume that both are from the same situation, or that $F(i)$ and $F(i + 1)$ are taken from succeeding situations:

(1) $F(i)$ and $F(i + 1)$ are from the same situation $Si(k)$, i.e. no cell division or cell death occurs, and the cells in $F(i)$ and $F(i + 1)$ are snapshots of the same cell. We then need to know for which c' in $F(i)$ and c'' in $F(i + 1)$ there is a cell c in Sit (being an object),

such that c′ and c″ are snapshots of the same cell c. Furthermore, a cell division might occur during Sit. We need to know whether a certain cell in F(i) and F(i + 1), identified as the same cell, is in the process of cell division, as might be deduced from the shape of the cell (e.g. its nuclear structures) or by some additional signal such as fluorescent markers of specific proteins [12]. The process of identifying cells across snapshots is called *cell tracking* and typically uses either engineered features or Machine Learning to establish a set of rules when the identified c′ and c″ are "similar enough" to be considered snapshots of the same cell [4, 13, 14].

(2) F(i) is from situation Sit(j) and F(i + 1) is from situation Sit(j), hence S(j + 1) is the successor situation of S(j). In this case, there is a change of cells from S(j) to S(j + 1). Then, we need to know how the cells in F(i) relate to the cells in F(i + 1): Which cells in F(i) have no successor in F(i + 1)? Which cells c in F(i) give rise to daughter cells c′, c″ in F(i + 1)? Which cells c′ in F(i) and c″ in F(i + 1) are snapshots of the same cell?

As mentioned above, we assume those assignments between observed cells in F(i) and F(i + 1) have been estimated either using computational or manual cell tracking. The information from (1) and (2) can then be used to construct a formal representation out of the experiment. In constructing a representation of an individual genealogy, we must introduce constants in the language; every cell that we detect in a frame is denoted by a constant. The number of constants may change as new cells may occur (after cell division). When using FOL as a representation language, we thus add atomic sentences to the specification. For example, if c′ and c″ are constants and we know that c′ and c″ are daughter cells of c, we add to following sentences to the representation: daughter(c, c′), daughter(c, c″), div(a, b, c) etc. Analogously, we may add id(c, d), or (not exists x such that successor(c, x)), or Dead(c). We can also represent this information about the constants as a knowledge graph using a graph-theoretical representation. We summarise some of the representational formalisms using an example. FOL is the most expressive formalism. We distinguish (in a generalisation of similar notions of DL (description logic)), the FO-TBox, FO-Abox, and FO-extABox. An FO-Tbox (first-order TBox) contains those formulas with variables and quantifiers. FO-Abox (first-order ABox) contains only atomic sentences (i.e. no variables, no quantifiers), FO-extABox (extended first-order ABox) contains variable-free propositions composed of atomic sentences/propositions and propositional connectives. Let us consider a specific example to demonstrate FO-TBox, FO-Abox, and FO-extABox: $T = \{\forall x \forall y \forall z \ (div(x, y, z) \rightarrow daughter(y, x) \wedge daughter(z, x) \wedge y \neq z)\}$ belongs to FO-TBox.

The atomic sentences {div(a, b, c), daughter(b, a), daughter(c, a)} belong to FO-ABox. The FO-ABox must be consistent with the FO-TBox. Hence, the FO-ABox must not contain the atomic sentence b = c. The FO-extABox could also contain sentences like c ≠ b. These propositions can then be formalised within DL, OWL using FOL/CL. As a result of the analysis of the frame-sequences, we get a set of atomic sentences. Our strategy is to develop a system FO-TBox and FO-ABox and transform this representation into DL and OWL.

We ultimately want to provide a solution that enables interoperability among cell tracking experiments. There is not yet a widely-accepted standard for storing, annotating and exchanging cell tracking results and the tools used in the domain usually come with their own ad hoc formats. However important first attempts have been made to define a standard data format [7]. Furthermore, there are already several ontologies available and organised within the Open Biological and Biomedical Ontology (OBO) Foundry [15]. Among those there are many ontologies that are relevant to cell tracking experiments. We are particularly interested in ontologies that describe (1) experiments, such as the Ontology for Biomedical Investigations (OBI) [16], (2) cells, e.g. the Cell Ontology [17] or (3) cell characteristics and behaviours, such as the Phenotype and Trait Ontology [18] or the Cell Behavior Ontology (CBO) [19]. Therefore, a straightforward approach (illustrated in Fig. 1) is the annotation of raw data using one or several of these relevant ontologies. Raw data usually contains only presentic information obtained from FSeq(x) such as frames, presential cells and presential situations and therefore the proposed solution serves well for querying raw data on presentic entities, e.g. return all frames containing cells of a given type or shape. However, the existing frameworks would not support more advanced queries which go beyond presentic entities, e.g. one cannot query for cellular genealogies in which all cells of a certain sub-lineage died, or for a subpopulation of stem cells which gave rise to a certain pattern of differentiated cells. This is the consequence of the missing formalisation in the basic data structures that are typically used. Our work aims to close this gap. Therefore, on top of the solution presented so far, we also need to facilitate cross-experiment and cross-systems queries as well as data exploration that is not limited to presentic entities. In Fig. 1, we propose an architecture built on the core formalism of cellular genealogies. It consists of n cell tracking systems, each supporting their own format for representing the results of the experiments. The raw data from each system is then translated into the OWL-Abox by means of the Cell Tracking Annotation (CTA) Tool, e.g. [20]. The CTA will provide interfaces for specific raw data formats and will support the automatic translation of raw data into an interoperable format based on OWL-TBox of the Cell Tracking Ontology (CTO). That way, the information about the presentic entities detected in the images, such as presentic cells, their characteristics or presentic cell collections can be correctly represented in the ontology. Next, the CTA automatically augments the presentic information by means of frame-sequences axioms. Basing on an OWL-ABox containing information on presentic entities and their sequences, CTA allows reconstruction of (1) time extended entities such as cells (objects) together with their characteristics, as well as (2) intercellular processes, such as cell divisions and finally, (3) complex structures such as cellular genealogies. Similarly, these reconstructed entities can themselves be further annotated with the help of the biomedical ontologies integrated into CTO. The whole knowledge graph extracted from the reconstructed entities is then added to the original OWL-ABox, which then can be used as a source for cross-system services such as, e.g. cross-system querying.

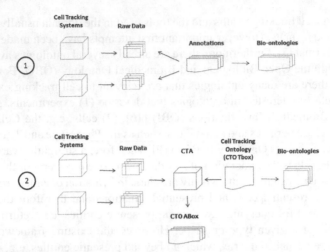

Fig. 1. (1) presents a straightforward architecture for introducing interoperability in cell tracking domain by annotation with existing bio-ontologies. (2) depicts the architecture based on the Cell Tracking Ontology and the Cell Tracking Annotation Tool which supports the transformation of raw data into CTO ABox which increases the possibilities of information retrieval on cellular genealogies.

5 Conclusions

As a continuation of the work presented in [9], we present here a generic framework for specifying a basic relation between empirical theories and the corresponding experiments as mediators between the theory and the world of individual entities. An essential component is the symbolic presentation of the data, acquired by experiments from real-world entities. We applied this framework to the domain D(CG) of cellular genealogies. The symbolic reconstruction and representation of cellular genealogies from data, acquired by experiments, uses techniques of information technology, including various forms of data representation as formal logics, description logics, and implemented languages like OWL. We argue that such a broad framework is needed as it provides the components and modules to achieve the overall aim that can be summarised by the following conditions:

1. Extraction and interpretation of biological data from systems-level experiments, and support of the interoperability between and across different types of observations at the single-cell level (e.g. time-lapse microscopy and single-cell sequencing).
2. Integration of data and knowledge that should lead to new forms of organisation of biological knowledge.
3. Supporting and augmenting the scientific progress by the use of techniques of machine learning and symbolic artificial intelligence.

We hope that our approach and framework paves the way for further research topics in these directions.

References

1. Wallingford, J.B.: The 200-year effort to see the embryo. Science **365**, 758–759 (2019)
2. Schnabel, R., Hutter, H., Moerman, D., Schnabel, H.: Assessing normal embryogenesis in caenorhabditis elegans using a 4D microscope: variability of development and regional specification. Dev. Biol. **184**, 234–265 (1997)
3. Megason, S.G., Fraser, S.E.: Imaging in systems biology. Cell **130**, 784–795 (2007)
4. Ulman, V., et al.: An objective comparison of cell-tracking algorithms. Nat. Methods **14**, 1141–1152 (2017)
5. Moen, E., Bannon, D., Kudo, T., Graf, W., Covert, M., Van Valen, D.: Deep learning for cellular image analysis. Nat. Methods (2019). https://doi.org/10.1038/s41592-019-0403-1
6. Wellmann, J.: Model and movement: studying cell movement in early morphogenesis, 1900 to the present. Hist. Philos. Life Sci. **40**(3), 1–25 (2018). https://doi.org/10.1007/s40656-018-0223-0
7. Gonzalez-Beltran, A.N., et al.: Community Standards for Open Cell Migration Data (2019). https://www.biorxiv.org/content/10.1101/803064v1. https://doi.org/10.1101/803064
8. Leonelli, S.: The challenges of big data biology. Elife **8** (2019). https://doi.org/10.7554/eLife.47381
9. Burek, P., Scherf, N., Herre, H.: On the Ontological Foundations of Cellular Development (2020). https://www.biorxiv.org/content/10.1101/2020.05.30.124875v1. https://doi.org/10.1101/2020.05.30.124875
10. Burek, P., Scherf, N., Herre, H.: A pattern-based approach to a cell tracking ontology. Procedia Comput. Sci. **159**, 784–793 (2019)
11. Burek, P., Scherf, N., Herre, H.: Ontology patterns for the representation of quality changes of cells in time. J. Biomed. Semant. **10**, 16 (2019)
12. Zerjatke, T., et al.: Quantitative cell cycle analysis based on an endogenous all-in-one reporter for cell tracking and classification. Cell Rep. **19**, 1953–1966 (2017)
13. Moen, E., et al.: Accurate cell tracking and lineage construction in live-cell imaging experiments with deep learning (2019). https://www.biorxiv.org/content/10.1101/803205v2. https://doi.org/10.1101/803205
14. Kwok, R.: Deep learning powers a motion-tracking revolution. Nature **574**, 137–138 (2019)
15. Smith, B., et al.: The OBO Foundry: coordinated evolution of ontologies to support biomedical data integration. Nat. Biotechnol. **25**, 1251–1255 (2007)
16. Bandrowski, A., et al.: The ontology for biomedical investigations. PLoS ONE **11**, e0154556 (2016)
17. Diehl, A.D., et al.: The Cell Ontology 2016: enhanced content, modularization, and ontology interoperability. J. Biomed. Semantics. **7**, 44 (2016)
18. Gkoutos, G.V., Schofield, P.N., Hoehndorf, R.: The anatomy of phenotype ontologies: principles, properties and applications. Brief. Bioinform. **19**, 1008–1021 (2018)
19. Sluka, J.P., Shirinifard, A., Swat, M., Cosmanescu, A., Heiland, R.W., Glazier, J.A.: The cell behavior ontology: describing the intrinsic biological behaviors of real and model cells seen as active agents. Bioinformatics **30**, 2367–2374 (2014)
20. Wagner, S., Thierbach, K., Zerjatke, T., Glauche, I., Roeder, I., Scherf, N.: TraCurate: efficiently curating cell tracks (2020). https://www.biorxiv.org/content/10.1101/2020.02.14.936740v1. https://doi.org/10.1101/2020.02.14.936740

Task-Oriented Uncertainty Evaluation for Linked Data Based on Graph Interlinks

Ahmed El Amine Djebri(✉) ⓘ, Andrea G.B. Tettamanziⓘ,
and Fabien Gandonⓘ

Université Côte d'Azur, Inria, CNRS, I3S, Biot, France
djebri.emp@gmail.com

Abstract. For data sources to ensure providing reliable linked data, they need to indicate information about the (un)certainty of their data based on the views of their consumers. In Addition, uncertainty information in terms of Semantic Web has also to be encoded into a readable, publishable, and exchangeable format to increase the interoperability of systems. This paper introduces a novel approach to evaluate the uncertainty of data in an RDF dataset based on its links with other datasets. We propose to evaluate uncertainty for sets of statements related to user-selected resources by exploiting their similarity interlinks with external resources. Our data-driven approach translates each interlink into a set of links referring to the position of a target dataset from a reference dataset, based on both object and predicate similarities. We show how our approach can be implemented and present an evaluation with real-world datasets. Finally, we discuss updating the publishable uncertainty values.

Keywords: Uncertainty · Semantic Web · Graph interlinks

1 Introduction

We are witnessing an era fulfilling the vision to create a Web of linked intelligent systems [1], thriving through sharing data they own or have processed. In this context, many challenges present themselves to developers of such platforms to retain reliable data that allows enriching their existing knowledge bases using robust reasoning or with the help of more external relevant content. The latter is using links with extra pieces of information revealing new dimensions for users to explore with their requests. Uncertainty is a major issue when related to content brought out on the Web, or Semantic Web by extension. Nevertheless, most data providers do not present explicit information about the uncertainty of their data. On the other hand, completely mistrusting a data source is unfair: while some data providers may not be reliable on one subject or provide false information about it, they are experts on other subjects and the pieces of information they

© Springer Nature Switzerland AG 2020
C. M. Keet and M. Dumontier (Eds.): EKAW 2020, LNAI 12387, pp. 204–215, 2020.
https://doi.org/10.1007/978-3-030-61244-3_15

provide should not be ignored. In some cases, references about data provenance and/or related data are given, from which a data consumer may hope to get further validation from other data sources.

In this paper, we address the need to evaluate uncertainty in linked data sources. In our approach, a data source may auto-evaluate the level of uncertainty of its data according to what is being presented by other data sources and for a specific use-case. We leverage the fact that different knowledge graphs may provide complementary and/or extra information enabling the assessment of the conformity of a target source. We also think that a user's preferences should be taken into consideration while evaluating uncertainty. Our work is built on top of the $mUnc$ model [2] to represent and publish uncertainty on the Semantic Web. The main question we aim to answer is: *How to evaluate uncertainty in a data source, based on its data, other linked data sources, and with respect to a specific use-case?*

To answer this question, we propose an approach to evaluate the uncertainty of a target data source, based on graph interlinks with other reference data sources. We propose to annotate statements with uncertainty values in a publishable format and provide a method to manipulate and update such values if existed. The intuition behind this work is that often users who need to confirm a piece of information will look for different sources that confirm or contradict it. For instance, the traditional verification techniques in journalism include the "two-sources rule" asking to verify that at least two independent trustworthy sources confirm a piece of information.

The rest of the paper is organized as follows. Section 2 surveys related work and positions our contribution accordingly. In Sect. 3 we discuss similarity assessment between two focus graphs of one resource and our choices of indicators. In Sect. 4 we present our main contribution, with a method to evaluate uncertainty based on existing links and transform it into reusable information that annotates statements in the data source of interest. In Sect. 5 we discuss the experimental workflow and present our tool for uncertainty evaluation and annotation. We conclude with a snapshot of our work and our future goals.

2   Related Works

According to Paulheim [3], external error-detection approaches in knowledge graphs are based on interconnections between data sources: they take advantage of the links (identity links or simply IRI reuse) to check for errors in the data source of interest. Paulheim [4] proposes in another work an external approach to detect outlier interlinks between datasets by creating a feature vector representation of each interlink based on types and incoming/outgoing links to all instances of a class. That work is meant to evaluate links, whilst here we check the reliability of data based on presumed correct interlinks. Other works are based on a statistical analysis of feature vectors associated with predicates that are linked to interlinked resources [5,6]. Another interesting idea is identity quantification between two linked data sets. It explores the idea of isomorphism quantification between two sets presumably representative of the same real-world entity. Similar works inspiring data-driven ontology alignment were discussed by Shvaiko *et al.* [7].

Christodoulou *et al.* [8] discusses the use of similarity measurements and Bayesian updating to help to align ontologies from different data sources and using precomputed values provided by ontology matchers. The authors depend on the Linked Open Vocabularies[1] to calculate the likelihood of equivalence vs. non-equivalence of two distinct classes and use that measure to update the local probability of similarity between two classes using Bayesian update. Authors of [6] propose a statistical data-driven approach to detect incorrect property mappings among the different language chapters of DBpedia. The work focuses on detecting the wrong mappings and the analysis is run through the whole datasets.

The aforementioned works mostly treated the reliability of the similarity links between data sources or detecting wrong schema-mappings. Different from our problem that requires analyzing data based on a use-case. The previous works present a promising set of measures to analyze data uncertainty based on links. Nevertheless, we notice the absence of specific sets of interest encapsulating the linked resources. Moreover, the said works are more in the spirit of ontology-matching techniques relying on linking all instances of two classes.

The problem relates in general to ontology alignment approaches and is also inspired by quasi-key detection problems. Most of the literature is assessing the link quality and not depending on the links themselves to assess data quality. We believe that it is original to discuss uncertainty evaluation with a task-centered perspective based on graph interlinks.

3   Uncertainty Assessment in Linked Data

3.1   Terminology and Definitions for Uncertainty

We introduce the terminology and the formalism used in the paper to propose an evaluation of uncertainty based on existing links between graphs.

Definition 1. *RDF-dataset—a set of statements (triples) in the form $\langle subject, predicate, object \rangle \in (I \cup B) \times I \times (I \cup B \cup L)$ where I is a set of IRIs, B a set of blank nodes, L a set of literals, I, B and L are pairwise disjoint and for every two RDF-datasets D_1, D_2 the sets of blank nodes are disjoint. we also denote I_D the set of IRIs used in statements of the RDF-dataset D.*

Definition 2. *Target dataset—an RDF-dataset noted as D_t that is the target of the uncertainty evaluation.*

Definition 3. *Reference dataset—an RDF-dataset noted as D_r that represents a reference for the evaluation of the uncertainty of a target dataset.*

---

[1] https://lov.linkeddata.es/.

Definition 4. *RDF-graph—a graph $G = (V, E)$, where $V \subset (I \cup B \cup L)$ is a set of vertices, and $E \subset I$ is a set of directed edges.*

Definition 5. *Focus graph—an RDF-graph noted as $G_D(e) \subset D$, where D is the dataset including the graph (target or reference) and $e \in I$ is a focused resource for which $G_D(e)$ is considered representative according to the use-case.*

Definition 6. *Set of Linking predicates—a non-empty set of predicates explicitly chosen to link between the target dataset and the reference dataset. We note it as $P_l \subset I$. Example: $P_l = \{\texttt{owl:sameAs, skos:exactMatch}\}$.*

Definition 7. *Contextual Linkset—as defined in the VOID² vocabulary, a linkset is a set of RDF triples where all subjects are in one dataset and all objects are in another dataset. We call a contextual linkset the one containing links between focused resources of D_t and those of D_r. A contextual linkset defines the set of focused resources of each dataset as well as the links between them. A link between a target focused resource e_t and a reference focused resource e_r is also a link between the focus graphs $G_{D_t}(e_t)$ and $G_{D_r}(e_r)$: $LS(D_t, D_r) = \{\langle e_t, p, e_r \rangle \mid p \in P_l, e_t \in I_{D_t}, e_r \in I_{D_r}\};$*

Definition 8. *Evidence link—a relationship between two statements $t_t \in G_{D_t}(e_t)$, $t_r \in G_{D_t}(e_r)$ discovered using similarity analysis, that supports the link between two linked focus graphs $G_{D_t}(e_t)$ and $G_{D_t}(e_r)$. The evidence link refers to a considered relationship between the predicates and/or the objects of two statements t_t and t_r. We note $E(G_{D_t}(e_t), G_{D_t}(e_r))$ the set of evidence links discovered between the two focus graphs $G_{D_t}(e_t)$ and $G_{D_t}(e_r)$.*

Our purpose is to find a method to assess the reliability of the information in each target focus graph $G_{D_t}(e_t)$ centered around a target focused resource e_t. To this end, we translated the existing link between the resource e_t of a target dataset and the resource e_r of a reference dataset ($\langle e_t, p, e_r \rangle \in LS(G_{D_t}(e_t), G_{D_t}(e_r)), p \in P_l$) to a set of evidence links between the target focus graph $G_{D_t}(e_t)$ and the reference focus graph $G_{D_t}(e_r)$. We statistically analyze the extracted evidence links to obtain a set of indicators enabling the evaluation of the overall semantic similarity between the predicates of linked focus graphs. Finally, we use the extracted evidence links to calculate the uncertainty of each focus graph based on its local ones.

3.2   Choosing Target Focused Resources

The problem of matching, whether it is data-driven or schema-driven, is context-related and may not be evident to users or useful for their request if done without involving them in the process [9]. We consider the concept of uncertainty to be also context-specific and that it is possible to choose a different evaluation method for each use case.

---

² https://www.w3.org/TR/void/#linkset.

A focus graph $G_D(e)$ is meant to be the image that represents e in the context of the application. Hence, the choice of the set of focused resources is necessary to ensure that uncertainty assessment is built on a user-centered view. The set of targeted focused resources $e \in I_{D_t}$ (I_{D_t} being the set of IRIs in the dataset D_t) depends on the type of validation a user intends to have within the data-source and depending on the use-case.

We also need to present a sufficient focus graph—in the context of the use-case—reflective of information about the resource. As an example with music artists, a focus graph may contain simple information like their names and birth-places and deeper-level information like songs from their albums. To limit the issue in our current use-case, we rely on the proposal[3] made by Strikler, aiming to create a focused subgraph centered around and describing a resource, called a *Concise-Bounded Description* and noted as *CBD*. Some Linked Data stores like *Virtuoso*[4] propose their proper definition of *CBD* and use it as the mapping of DESCRIBE SPARQL queries. For our current use-case, we find the definition of *CBD* an intuitive, simple yet interesting one to define our $G_D(e)$.

3.3   Linking Predicates and Contextual Linkset

Unlike the approaches to ontology matching or alignment, we take existing links in the contextual linkset as ground truth. The first links one may find between two data sources can be established by reusing IRIs of resources from one in the other. Moreover, the *RDFS* and *OWL* standards provide predicates such as `owl:sameAs`, `rdfs:seeAlso` with debatable semantics to link between resources [10,11]. Other commonly used ontologies propose more predicates to indicate the matching between two resources (example: `skos:exactMatch` [12]).

4   Approach and Uncertainty Assessment Pipeline

We propose a level-based architecture where each level depends on the previous one, from isolating candidate evidence links to exporting update-ready uncertainty values. A link between a target focused resource e_t and a reference focused resource e_r can be seen as a link between the focus graph of each. The evidence links supporting that link are discovered and selected based on defined similarity indicators.

Considering two statements $t_1 : \langle s_1, p_1, o_1 \rangle, t_2 : \langle s_2, p_2, o_2 \rangle$ where $t_1 \in G_{D_t}(e_t)$ and $t_2 \in G_{D_r}(e_r)$ and a prior knowledge indicating the existence of a link between the two resources e_t and e_r: $\langle e_t, l, e_r \rangle \in LS(D_t, D_r)$. We define here a set of similarity indicators to be used for uncertainty assessment.

---

[3] https://www.w3.org/Submission/CBD/.
[4] http://docs.openlinksw.com/virtuoso/rdfsqlfromsparqldescribe/.

4.1 Precomputing: Augmentation and Clustering

During this step, we apply the chosen definition of focus graphs on D_t based on $LS(D_t, D_r)$. Beforehand, we use OWL [11] semantics for properties to augment the data source by calculating the transitive closure of our target dataset D_t. This helps to unveil more potential evidence links between the linked focus graphs.

4.2 Level 1: Identifying Possible Evidence Links Based on Syntactic Similarity Between Objects of Statements in Linked Focus Graphs

In the first level, we produce a set of evidence links for each pair of linked focus graphs using an *object similarity* measure defined as follows.

Definition 9. *Object similarity—We denote $sym_o(t_1, t_2)$ (Eq. 1) as the weighted similarity between objects of statements t_1 and t_2 (between o_1 and o_2). This measure refers to what extent the two objects share the same nature (literal, URI), the same datatype(xsd:short, xsd:integer, etc.[5]) and/or the same value:*

$$sym_o(t_1, t_2) = (1 - w_{val}) \times typeMatch(o_1, o_2) + w_{val} \times valMatch(o_1, o_2). \quad (1)$$

The binary function *typeMatch* returns 1 if both nature (IRI, Literal) and datatypes are similar and 0 otherwise. The *valMatch* function can be any syntactic similarity measure (Jaccard, Levenshtein, Jaro-Winkler distance, n-grams, etc.). Once the first level measures are established, a positive threshold $\tau_{obj} \leq 1$ restricts the discovered evidence links to ones of higher object similarity.

4.3 Level 2: Identifying Evidence Link Patterns Using Semantic Similarity of Predicates in the Overall Linked Focus Graphs

The second level introduces semantic similarity between evidence links while taking into account: the fact that the same predicates are used in schemas of the different data sources, and specific semantics related to the current use case by the mean of predicate similarity indicators. This view is inspired by the example in [8] but adapted to fit predicates due to the generalized, class-independent definition of $LS(D_t, D_r)$.

Definition 10. *Predicate similarity—We denote $sym_p(t_1, t_2)$ (Eq. 3) the statistical similarity between predicates of statements t_1 and t_2 (between p_1 and p_2). This measure is built on all the linked focus graphs and represents the use-case related semantic similarity of the two predicates p_1 and p_2.*

---

[5] https://www.w3.org/2011/rdf-wg/wiki/XSD_Datatypes.

Table 1. Semantic similarity indicators for each pair of linked focus graphs.

Indicator	Definition
$I_1(G_{D_t}(e_t), G_{D_r}(e_r))$	The number of evidence links between the two focus graphs $G_{D_t}(e_t)$ and $G_{D_r}(e_r)$. i.e. the number of links supporting the similarity hypothesis between the two resources e_t and e_r
$I_2(G_{D_t}(e_t), G_{D_r}(e_r))$	The set of predicate pairs in evidence links between statements of the two focus graphs $G_{D_t}(e_t)$ and $G_{D_r}(e_r)$. i.e: the set of pairs (p_1, p_2) where an evidence link exists between t_1 and t_2
$I_3(G_{D_t}(e_t), G_{D_r}(e_r), p_1, p_2)$	The count of evidence links relying on two predicates p_1, p_2 between the two focus graphs $G_{D_t}(e_t)$ and $G_{D_r}(e_r)$
$I_4(G_{D_t}(e_t), G_{D_r}(e_r), p_1, p_2)$	The total number of possible combinations between statements using each p_1 or p_2 in the two linked focus graphs $G_{D_t}(e_t), G_{D_r}(e_r)$ (For instance, if three statements in $G_{D_t}(e_t)$ use p_1 and two statements in $G_{D_r}(e_r)$ use p_2 then the total number of links would be six. So this represents the maximum possible number of evidence links that can be found linking p_1 and p_2)
$I_5(G_{D_t}(e_t), G_{D_r}(e_r), p_1, p_2)$	The sum of the quality of evidence links relying on two predicates p_1, p_2 between the two focus graphs $G_{D_t}(e_t)$ and $G_{D_r}(e_r)$. i.e. the sum of object similarities of discovered evidence links between $G_{D_t}(e_t)$ and $G_{D_r}(e_r)$ linking statements using respectively p_1 and p_2

Table 2. Normalised local ratios for each pair of linked focus graphs.

Ratio	Definition
$R_1(G_{D_t}(e_t), G_{D_r}(e_r), p_1, p_2)$	I_3 is normalised using I_1 to reflect the participation of evidence links between two statements having p_1 and p_2 as predicates, in the overall evidence links between the two linked focus graphs
$R_2(G_{D_t}(e_t), G_{D_r}(e_r), p_1, p_2)$	I_3 is normalised using I_4 to reflect the portion of existing statement that actually participate with a link. If all existing statements between two focus graphs, with p_1 and p_2 as predicates are linked with evidence links, it indicates that the predicates may be functional, or that this information is a common knowledge that usually have a lower cardinal (like homepages for artists)
$R_3(G_{D_t}(e_t), G_{D_r}(e_r), p_1, p_2)$	I_5 is normalised using I_3 to get the average quality of each evidence link between statements having p_1 and p_2 as predicates

To evaluate semantic similarity, we first define four indicators (Table 1) to be statistically extracted for each pair of linked focus graphs $G_{D_t}(e_t)$ and $G_{D_r}(e_r)$. From the previous indicators and for each pair of linked focus graphs $G_{D_t}(e_t)$ and $G_{D_r}(e_r)$, we also calculate three local ratios (Table 2).

To evaluate the semantic similarity between p_1 and p_2 on the overall contextual linkset, we average for each pair of predicates p_1 and p_2 with an evidence link between t_1 and t_2 in all linked focus graphs, and add another indicator $\hat{R}_0$ for the equality $p_1 = p_2$ (as it will stay the same if averaged). We get a vector of averaged ratios $\hat{R}(p_1, p_2) = [\hat{R}_0(p_1, p_2), \hat{R}_1(p_1, p_2), \hat{R}_2(p_1, p_2), \hat{R}_3(p_1, p_2)]$, with

$$\hat{R}_i(p_1, p_2) = \frac{1}{|LS(D_t, D_r)|} \sum_{\langle e_t, p_l, e_r \rangle \in LS(D_t, D_r)} R_i(G_{D_t}(e_t), G_{D_r}(e_r), p_1, p_2) \quad (2)$$

and for which we define a vector of semantic weights $\omega_{sem} = [\omega_0, \omega_1, \omega_2, \omega_3]$ with $\sum \omega_i = 1, \omega_i \geq 0$. We select only the predicate pairs having an average of link quality equal or greater than a positive defined threshold τ_{sem} where $\tau_{sem} \leq \hat{R}_3(p_1, p_2) \leq 1$. Hence, we can define $sym_p(t_1, t_2)$ of statements t_1 and t_2 as the dot product of the two vectors $\hat{R}(p_1, p_2)$ and ω_{sem}:

$$sym_p(t_1, t_2) = \omega_{sem} \cdot \hat{R}(p_1, p_2) \quad (3)$$

Similarly to the previous level, the overall quality of considered evidence links should also respect the average quality threshold τ_{sem}.

4.4 Level 3: Evaluating Contextual Uncertainty of Target Focus Graphs

At this level, the previous similarity measures are combined into one value reflecting the degree of uncertainty of a target focus graph $G_{D_t}(e_t)$ regarding its linked reference focus graph $G_{D_r}(e_r)$. For this, we define the notion of contextual uncertainty to be the measure of one of a target focus graph based on its evidence links.

Definition 11. *Contextual Uncertainty—We define contextual uncertainty of a target focus graph $G_{D_t}(e_t)$ compared to a reference focus graph $G_{D_r}(e_r)$, with a link existing between e_t and e_r in the contextual linkset $LS(D_t, D_r)$, as the sum of products of object(syntactic) and predicate(semantic) similarity scores of the statements linked by each $l \in E(G_{D_t}(e_t), G_{D_r}(e_r))$, on the number of evidence links in $E(G_{D_t}(e_t), G_{D_r}(e_r))$.*

$$U(G_{D_t}(e_t) \mid \langle e_t, p_l, e_r \rangle) = \frac{\sum_{<t_1, l, t_2> \in E(G_{D_t}(e_t), G_{D_r}(e_r))} sym_o(t_1, t_2) \times sym_p(t_1, t_2)}{|E(G_{D_t}(e_t), G_{D_r}(e_r))|}$$

$$(4)$$

5   Experiment and Evaluation

We evaluate a dataset with 714 artists from *MusicBrainz* against their linked information from the English chapter of *dbpedia*. The used dataset including focus graphs and contextual linkset is available online.

To validate our approach, we developed *Archer*[6], a tool for analyzing and annotating link data with uncertainty values. *Archer* uses the proposed approach to extract the object and predicate similarity with respect to the links between focus graphs. The tool allows the user to query for identity links, extract focus graphs from both the target and the reference datasets, and evaluate the uncertainty of each focus graph in the target dataset. It further allows analyzing and visualizing pairs of linked focus graphs individually as well as the different indicators for the overall analysis.

For the experiment, we chose both a Jaccard distance and a string equality measures as a *valMatch()* function. Plots in Fig. 1 show the effect of the size of the contextual linkset $|LS(D_t, D_r)|$ on the overall count of evidence links $\sum I_1(G_{D_t}(e_t), G_{D_r}(e_r))$ and the number of distinct predicate-pair $|\bigcup I_2(G_{D_t}(e_t), G_{D_r}(e_r))|$. We fixed $\tau_{sem} = 0$ to see the effect of τ_{obj} on the evidence link count specifically. We then changed the value to $\tau_{sem} = 0.5$ to visualise the effect specifically on the distinct count of predicate-pairs that are considered as similar in the context of the application. For both experiments, we chose $\omega_{val} = 1$ to see the effect of each object similarity function as well. We notice that:

- in all of (a_1, a_2, a_3, a_4), the number of evidence links is proportional to the number of analyzed focus graphs. This points to the fact that focus graphs in both sides share a certain structure allowing to maintain a relatively fixed ratio of evidence links per pair of focus graphs. Moreover, in (a_1) compared to the absence of a threshold, more than half the evidence links were ignored in $(\tau_{obj} = 0.25)$ indicating that those evidence links were of bad quality. As for the string equality, the local threshold is not needed as the indicators R_1 and R_3 will be the same (for each discovered evidence link, the quality is 1 at $\omega_{val} = 1$), so no evidence links will be dropped.
- as seen in (b_1, b_3), the effect of τ_{obj} on the number of evidence links is also predictable. The threshold will only allow links with better quality to be part of the overall evaluation.
- the number of predicate-pairs increases with the number of linked focus graphs. This is due to discovering predicate-pairs that did not have any evidence links in the first analyzed focus graphs. It is notable that for both object similarity methods, the number converges after analyzing more than 400 pairs of focus graphs. Furthermore, the effect of τ_{obj} can be observed confirming that some predicate-pairs were dropped as they presented only bad quality links.
- when increasing τ_{sem}, the plots in (a_2) move closer to each other and converging towards (a_4) as it represents strict equality, resulting as well in similar

---

[6] http://github.com/djebr/archer.

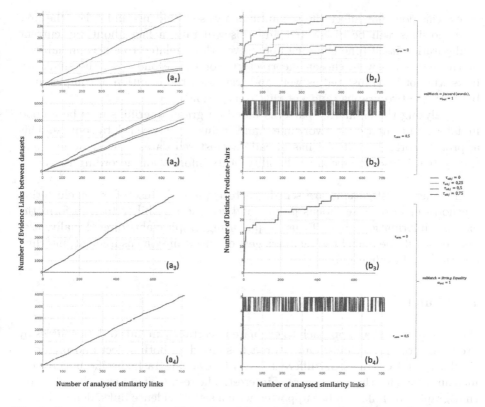

Fig. 1. Results for analysing 714 pairs of linked focus graphs: (a_i) total number of discovered evidence links (b_i) Number of distinct discovered predicate-pairs.

shapes for (b_2) and (b_4). The fluctuation is due to the fact that the overall quality of some predicate-pairs evidence links might drops when considering new pairs of focus graphs that do not support the hypothesis. However, the plot remains constant proving that on the overall analysis, five predicate-pairs can be considered as best candidates to support the graph interlink.

- the difference between the number of predicate-pairs in (b_3) and (b_4) is remarkable. Comparing to 28 predicate-pairs in the first with 6600 evidence links, the second has only 5 predicate-pairs with almost 6000 evidence links. This further provides proof that most of the discovered links were not of general use (not common information between focus graph pairs).

6   Discussion

An argument about statistical extraction of semantics would be the fact that a target dataset can be completely wrong, or somehow unrelated to the reference dataset like having the same information but in a different language. In both cases, this does not affect the semantic analysis of evidence links. For the first case, no links will be discovered and this will raise a flag about the current configuration itself (one is wrong about everything related to a certain subject, or the references were chosen incorrectly). For the second case, the similarity links will not be translated as well, and triggering the intuition of completeness between the two graphs (and not that of negation).

Analyzing the similarity patterns based on graph interlinks may be a good first base to evaluate trustworthiness and inclusion between data sources. This approach works best if one has already a clustered dataset by structure, and the system is used to see the reliability of its information according to known sources.

Further investigations are scheduled to explore the use of other clustering methods, or customized focus graphs and see the possibility to transform the existing information about focus graphs using graph embedding. Finally, user queries should be one of the main triggers of uncertainty measurement, interlink creation, and evaluation.

7   Conclusion

We have proposed an approach to evaluate uncertainty in linked data sources by providing graph interlinks. Our approach is based on both object and predicate similarity and operates on different levels to evaluate task-specific uncertainty measurements for the data source of interest. The results of our experiments show that graph interlinks can be supported with a set of evidence links, depending on the use-case and the user's choice of quality parameters. Using our tool enables us to assess the quality of a dataset regarding a certain task, and annotate its data accordingly while producing reusable and publishable uncertainty measurements. Future work will focus on learning the most suitable structure for a focus graph, generalizing our approach to consider a set of reference resources, and including more parameters such as scores from ontology matchers.

References

1. Gandon, F.: Web Science, Artificial Intelligence and Intelligence Augmentation (in Dagstuhl Perspectives Workshop 18262–10 Years of Web Science: Closing The Loop). Other, Dagstuhl (2019). https://hal.inria.fr/hal-01976768
2. Djebri, A.E.A., Tettamanzi, A.G.B., Gandon, F.: Publishing uncertainty on the semantic web: blurring the LOD bubbles. In: Endres, D., Alam, M., Şotropa, D. (eds.) ICCS 2019. LNCS (LNAI), vol. 11530, pp. 42–56. Springer, Cham (2019). https://doi.org/10.1007/978-3-030-23182-8_4
3. Paulheim, H.: Knowledge graph refinement: a survey of approaches and evaluation methods. Semant. Web **8**(3), 489–508 (2017)
4. Paulheim, H.: Identifying wrong links between datasets by multi-dimensional outlier detection. In: WoDOOM, pp. 27–38 (2014)

5. Hogan, A., Polleres, A., Umbrich, J., Zimmermann, A.: Some entities are more equal than others: statistical methods to consolidate linked data. In: 4th International Workshop on New Forms of Reasoning for the Semantic Web: Scalable and Dynamic (NeFoRS2010) (2010)
6. Rico, M., Mihindukulasooriya, N., Kontokostas, D., Paulheim, H., Hellmann, S., Gómez-Pérez, A.: Predicting incorrect mappings: a data-driven approach applied to DBpedia. In: Proceedings of the 33rd Annual ACMsymposium on Applied Computing, pp. 323–330 (2018)
7. Shvaiko, P., Euzenat, J.: A survey of schema-based matching approaches. In: Spaccapietra, S. (ed.) Journal on Data Semantics IV. LNCS, vol. 3730, pp. 146–171. Springer, Heidelberg (2005). https://doi.org/10.1007/11603412_5
8. Christodoulou, K., Serrano, F.R.S., Fernandes, A.A.A., Paton, N.W.: Quantifying and propagating uncertainty in automated linked data integration. In: Hameurlain, A., Wagner, R. (eds.) Transactions on Large-Scale Data- and Knowledge-Centered Systems XXXVII. LNCS, vol. 10940, pp. 81–112. Springer, Heidelberg (2018). https://doi.org/10.1007/978-3-662-57932-9_3
9. Cheatham, M., Cruz, I.F., Euzenat, J., Pesquita, C.: Special issue on ontologyand linked data matching. Semant. Web 8(2), 183–184 (2017). https://doi.org/10.3233/SW-160251
10. Brickley, D., Guha, R.V., McBride, B.: RDF Schema 1.1. W3C Recommendation 25, 2004–2014 (2014)
11. McGuinness, D.L., Van Harmelen, F., et al.: OWL web ontology language overview. W3C Recommendation 10(10), 2004 (2004)
12. Miles, A., Bechhofer, S.: SKOS simple knowledge organization system reference. W3C Recommendation 18, W3C (2009)

In Use Papers

ResearchFlow: Understanding the Knowledge Flow Between Academia and Industry

Angelo Salatino(✉) ⓘD, Francesco Osborne ⓘD, and Enrico Motta ⓘD

Knowledge Media Institute, The Open University, Milton Keynes MK7 6AA, UK
{angelo.salatino,francesco.osborne,enrico.motta}@open.ac.uk

Abstract. Understanding, monitoring, and predicting the flow of knowledge between academia and industry is of critical importance for a variety of stakeholders, including governments, funding bodies, researchers, investors, and companies. To this purpose, we introduce ResearchFlow, an approach that integrates semantic technologies and machine learning to quantifying the diachronic behaviour of research topics across academia and industry. ResearchFlow exploits the novel Academia/Industry DynAmics (AIDA) Knowledge Graph in order to characterize each topic according to the frequency in time of the related i) publications from academia, ii) publications from industry, iii) patents from academia, and iv) patents from industry. This representation is then used to produce several analytics regarding the academia/industry knowledge flow and to forecast the impact of research topics on industry. We applied ResearchFlow to a dataset of 3.5M papers and 2M patents in Computer Science and highlighted several interesting patterns. We found that 89.8% of the topics first emerge in academic publications, which typically precede industrial publications by about 5.6 years and industrial patents by about 6.6 years. However this does not mean that academia always dictates the research agenda. In fact, our analysis also shows that industrial trends tend to influence academia more than academic trends affect industry. We evaluated ResearchFlow on the task of forecasting the impact of research topics on the industrial sector and found that its granular characterization of topics improves significantly the performance with respect to alternative solutions.

Keywords: Scholarly data · Digital libraries · Knowledge graph · Topic ontology · Bibliographic data · Topic detection · Science of science

1 Introduction

Understanding, monitoring, and predicting the flow of knowledge between academia and industry is of primary importance for a variety of stakeholders, such as governments, funding bodies, researchers, investors, and companies. In particular, government and funding bodies need accurate tools to measure research impact, while companies may wish to monitor the flow of knowledge from academia to industry to ensure they stay on top of the latest scientific and innovation trends.

The complex relationship between academia and industry has been analysed from several perspectives in the literature, e.g., focusing on the characteristics of direct collaborations [1], on the influence of industrial trends on curricula [2], and the quality of

© Springer Nature Switzerland AG 2020
C. M. Keet and M. Dumontier (Eds.): EKAW 2020, LNAI 12387, pp. 219–236, 2020.
https://doi.org/10.1007/978-3-030-61244-3_16

the knowledge transfer [3]. However, approaches to monitoring and/or predicting the evolution of research topics typically focus either on academia [4–7] or industry [8, 9]. The few solutions that have tried to take advantage of features from both contexts have been limited to small-scale datasets, or they have focused on very specific research questions [10, 11]. Therefore, we still lack large-scale quantitative approaches to monitoring and predicting the evolution of research topics, which can integrate information from papers and patents, while also considering their provenance: academia or industry.

In this paper, we introduce ResearchFlow, a new approach for quantifying the diachronic behaviour of research topics in academia and industry. ResearchFlow builds on the Academia/Industry DynAmics (AIDA) Knowledge Graph[1] [12], a resource that we recently developed for supporting large scale analyses of academia and industry. The current version of AIDA describes 14M publications and 8M patents according to the research topics drawn from the Computer Science Ontology (CSO) [13]. Moreover, 4M publications and 5M patents are characterized according to the type of the author's affiliations (e.g., academia, industry, collaborative) and the industrial sectors (e.g., automotive, financial, energy, electronics).

ResearchFlow represents the evolution of each topic in terms of the relevant i) papers from academia, ii) papers from industry, iii) patents from academia, and iv) patents from industry. This semantic characterization takes in account the structure of the topic taxonomy described in CSO and it is used for a) producing several analytics regarding the topic evolution and the research flow between academy and industry and b) predicting the impact of research topics on the industrial sector. The resulting knowledge base, which is available at http://doi.org/10.21954/ou.rd.12805307, describes the trends of 5K topics in *Computer Science* over 2.9M papers from academia, 676K papers from industry, 2M patents from industry, and 46K patents from academia in the period 1990–2018.

The data shows that about 89.8% of the topics first appear in academic publications, 3.0% in industrial publications, and only 7.2% in patents, confirming the leading position of universities in investigating new research areas. On the average, academic publications precede industrial publications by about 5.6 years and industrial patents by about 6.6 years. However, this does not mean that academia always dictates the research agenda. In fact, if we consider only the topics for which the publication trends by academia and industry sync, after compensating for a delay, the trends from industry appear to influence academia more than academic trends influence industry. This may be due to the fact that academia tends to be quite reactive to the rise of a topic in industry (e.g., social media), which typically causes a surge of relevant academic publications in the following years. Conversely, industry appears less receptive to the emergence of topics in academia, which can be neglected for a variety of reasons – e.g., because the relevant technologies are not mature enough to support commercial products.

We evaluated ResearchFlow on the task of forecasting the impact of research topics in the industrial sector by applying several machine learning classifiers on different combinations of features. We found that the characterization of the topics produced by ResearchFlow outperforms significantly alternative solutions.

In summary, the main contributions of this paper are: i) a new approach to quantifying and forecasting the evolution of topics in academia and industry; ii) a new dataset derived

---

[1] Academia/Industry DynAmics Knowledge Graph - http://w3id.org/aida.

from AIDA which describes the diachronic behaviour of 5K topics across 29 years (1990–2018); iii) an analysis of the patterns of knowledge flow in the field of Computer Science; and iv) a gold standard of about 39 K time series that can be used for training and evaluating approaches to predicting the impact of emerging research topics on the industrial sector.

The rest of the paper is organised as follows. In Sect. 2, we review the literature on current approaches to studying the relationship between academia and industry, pointing out the existing gaps. In Sect. 3, we describe ResearchFlow and in Sect. 4 we provide a brief overview of the evolution of research topics in Computer Science. Section 5 reports the evaluation. Finally, in Sect. 6 we summarise the main conclusions and outline future directions of research.

2 Literature Review

Analysing the relationship between academia and industry allows us to understand their role within the whole knowledge economy [14]: from production, towards adoption, enrichment, and ultimately deployment as a new commercial product or service. Academia and industry typically influence each other by exchanging ideas, resources, and researchers [11]. In some cases, academia and industry engage in collaborations as an opportunity for a more productive division of tasks: academia focusing on scientific insights, and industry on commercialisation [10]. A recent book by Stilgoe [15] discusses the main drivers of scientific innovation and focuses on the central role of the industry sector in pushing innovation by constantly deploying new technologies. However, it can be argued that innovation is not simply the result of the development of new technologies, but it also emerges through a more complex journey, which involves the birth of a new scientific area, the development of its theoretical framework, and the creation of innovative products that capitalise on the new knowledge [16].

So far, there has been limited investigation of this relationship. Typically, the two sectors are either analysed separately [15, 17–20] or together on a small scale [10, 11], using a limited sample of papers and patents. Most of these analyses rely on knowledge graphs describing research publications, such as Microsoft Academic Graph [21], Scopus[2], Semantic Scholar[3], Aminer [22], Core [23], OpenCitations [24], and others. Other resources, such as Dimensions[4], the United States Patent and Trademark Office corpus[5], the PatentScope corpus[6] and the European Patent Office dataset[7], offer a similar description of patents. The Semantic Web community has produces several ontologies for representing these data and the relevant research entities such as SWRC[8], BIBO[9],

---

[2] Scopus - https://www.scopus.com/.

[3] Semantic Scholar - https://www.semanticscholar.org/.

[4] Dimensions.ai - https://www.dimensions.ai/.

[5] United States Patent and Trademark Office (USPTO) - https://www.uspto.gov/.

[6] PatentScope corpus - https://patentscope.wipo.int/.

[7] European Patent Office - https://data.epo.org/linked-data/.

[8] SWRC - http://ontoware.org/swrc.

[9] BIBO - http://bibliontology.com.

SPAR[10] [25], ModSci [26], and AI-KG[11] [27]. However, current knowledge graphs cannot be directly used to analyse the research dynamics of academia and industry since they lack a high quality characterization of research topics and industrial sectors. For this reason, we recently introduced the AIDA knowledge graph, which characterizes publications from MAG and patents from Dimensions according to the topics of CSO[12], the affiliation types of Global Research Identifier Database (GRID)[13], and the industrial sectors of the Industrial Sector Ontology (INDUSO)[14].

The relationship between academia and industry has been studied according to both qualitative and quantitative methods. A good example of the former is the work by Michaudel et al. [28] in which the authors share their personal experience on how the collaboration between industry and academia impacted their research program. Similarly, Grimpe et al. [29] performed a survey-based analysis to understand the innovation performance associated with collaborations between German manufacturers and universities. We can also find more quantitative approaches, such as Larivière et al. [30], who employed both research papers and patents to understand the primary interests of both sides in this symbiosis. Huang et al. [31] analysed 20K research papers and 8K patents in the area of *fuel cells*, in order to gain an understanding of the benefits for the two parties, which derive from industry-academic collaborations. However, all of these approaches either focus on relatively narrow areas of science or are restricted to a limited number of research questions. Other approaches focus instead on trend detection [4–6]. Typically, these methods use statistical techniques to identify, and possibly predict, the evolution of new significant areas of research. A common limitation of these techniques is that they do not take into account the types of the publications as we do. In this paper, we aim to widen the scope of this line of enquiry by developing a novel and comprehensive approach for monitoring and predicting the diffusion of research topics across academia and industry.

3   The ResearchFlow Approach

The ResearchFlow approach consists of three main steps: i) generation of AIDA knowledge graph, ii) data analysis, iii) impact forecasting.

In the first phase, we generate Academia/Industry DynAmics (AIDA) Knowledge Graph, by integrating the data sources containing information about scientific articles and patents and then we enrich them by classifying documents according to i) their research topics and ii) the type of author's affiliation (academia or industry). This allows us to represent each topic according to four time series reporting the time frequency of i) papers from academia, ii) papers from industry, iii) patents from academia, and iv) patents from industry. In the second phase, we analyse the resulting time series to assess the topic trends and to identify patterns of knowledge flow. In the third phase, we use a deep learning forecaster to predict the impact of research topics.

---

[10] SPAR - http://www.sparontologies.net/.

[11] AI-KG - http://w3id.org/aikg/.

[12] CSO - https://cso.kmi.open.ac.uk/.

[13] Global Research Identifier Database - https://www.grid.ac/.

[14] INDUSO - http://aida.kmi.open.ac.uk/downloads/induso.ttl.

3.1 Generation of AIDA Knowledge Graph

In order to perform a large-scale analysis of academia and industry, we need four key elements: papers, patents, research topics, and information about organizations. For this reason, we developed the AIDA knowledge graph that currently integrates 14M publications from MAG and 8M patents from Dimensions. These are described according to the topics drawn from the Computer Science Ontology (CSO) [13] and information from Global Research Identifier Database (GRID), DBpedia, and INDUSO. AIDA is generated automatically by a pipeline that is run periodically on new corpora of publications and patents. This process consists of four main steps: i) selection and integration of the relevant documents, ii) topic detection, iii) extraction of affiliation types, and iv) classification of industrial sectors.

First, we download all publications from MAG and all patents from Dimensions. MAG is a scientific knowledge base containing publication records, citations, authors, institutions, journals, conferences, and fields of study. It is one of the largest datasets of scholarly data publicly available, and, as of May 2020, it contains more than 233 million publications. Dimensions is a heterogeneous dataset containing grants, research publications, citations, clinical trials and patents. The current version includes more than 39 million patents. We then filter the resulting documents to retain only those in the field of *Computer Science*. To achieve this, we select all papers in MAG classified under "Computer Science" according to their *field of science* (FoS) [32], which is an in-house taxonomy of research areas developed by Microsoft. The patents in Dimensions are instead classified both according to the International Patent Classification (IPC) and the *fields of research* (FoR) taxonomy, which is part of the Australian and New Zealand Standard Research Classification (ANZSRC). To filter the patents in the field of Computer Science, we retain only the relevant IPC identifiers.

Since both fields of study in MAG and fields of research in Dimensions are too high level to allow a granular analysis of the knowledge flow, as a second step we annotate each paper and patent with the research topics from the Computer Science Ontology (CSO). CSO [13] is a large-scale automatically generated taxonomy of research topics in Computer Science. The current version (3.2) includes 14K research topics and 159K semantic relationships. The CSO data model is an extension of SKOS[15] and the main semantic relationships are *superTopicOf*, which is used to define the hierarchical structure of the Computer Science domain (e.g., *<artificial intelligence, superTopicOf, machine learning>*) and *relatedEquivalent*, which is used to define alternative labels for the same topic (e.g., *<ontology matching, relatedEquivalent, ontology alignment>*). We annotated publications and patents using the CSO Classifier[16] [33], an open-source Python tool for annotating documents with research topics from CSO. This is the same classifier that powers the Smart Topic Miner [34], which is the application used by Springer Nature for annotating Proceedings Book in Computer Science. The resulting set of topics was enriched by including all their super-topics in CSO. For instance, a paper tagged as *neural network* was also tagged with *machine learning* and *artificial intelligence*. This solution aims to obtain a better characterization of high-level topics that are not often directly referred in the documents.

---

[15] SKOS Simple Knowledge Organization System - http://www.w3.org/2004/02/skos.

[16] CSO Classifier - https://pypi.org/project/cso-classifier/.

As a third step, we classify papers and patents according to the nature of their authors' affiliations in the GRID database. GRID is a publicly available knowledge graph describing 97K organizations involved in the research. MAG and Dimensions associate the affiliations of the authors to their ID on GRID and in turn GRID associates each ID with information such as geographical location, date of establishment, alternative labels, external links, and *type of institution*, which consists of values such as Education, Healthcare, Company, Archive, Nonprofit, Government, Facility, Other. We classify a document as *academia*, if all the authors have an affiliation of kind 'education' on GRID; and *industry*, if all the authors have an affiliation of kind 'company'. For the purpose of this work, we focus on these two types and ignore the collaborative efforts which constitute about 1.4% of the documents. We also do not consider the other types, which are associated with an even smaller number of documents. We plan to address both in future work.

Finally, we characterise the industrial papers and patents according to their industrial sectors. Specifically, for each industrial affiliation, we use their Wikipedia URL in GRID to query DBpedia, which is a project aiming at extracting information from Wikipedia and publish them as linked data. We exploit the predicates "About:Purpose" and "About:Industry" to retrieve the industrial sectors of each affiliation. These are then mapped to 66 main sectors described in INDUSO. Industrial sectors are not used in the current version of ResearchFlow, but they will be incorporated in the future.

AIDA is available at http://w3id.ord/aida and can be downloaded as a dump or queried via SPARQL. More details on AIDA are available in Angioni et al. [12].

3.2 Analysis

In order to focus on the main research topics, we select from AIDA only the documents associated with the most frequent n topics. In this paper we used $n = 5,000$, resulting in 3.5M papers and 2M patents. We then associate each topic K with four time series, or signals: i) research publications from academia ($RA^K = \{RA_t^K; t \in T\}$), ii) research publications from industry ($RI^K = \{RI_t^K; t \in T\}$), iii) patents from academia ($PA^K = \{PA_t^K; t \in T\}$) and iv) patents from industry ($PI^K = \{PI_t^K; t \in T\}$), where T is the set of years considered $\{1990 \ldots 2018\}$.

We perform three analyses on the resulting signals. First, we study the diachronic behaviour of topics in order to characterize their trajectory across academia and industry (Sect. 3.2.1). Second, we compare each pair of signals to understand which one typically precedes the other and in which order they usually tackle a research topic (Sect. 3.2.2). Finally, we assess how signals influence each other by identifying pairs of signals that are highly correlated, after compensating for a time delay (Sect. 3.2.3).

3.2.1 Diachronic Analysis of Topics

This phase aims to quantify the evolution of a topic in previous years according to the type of documents associated with it (publications or patents) and the authors of these documents (academia or industry). For instance, we may want to detect which topics are shifting from a more academic fingerprint to a more industrial one.

As a first step we need to combine the different time series of a given topic to obtain the number of research publications (R), patents (P), documents from academia (A) and documents from industry (I) using the following formula:

$$R_t^K = RA_t^K + RI_t^K; \quad P_t^K = PA_t^K + PI_t^K;$$
$$A_t^K = RA_t^K + PA_t^K; \quad I_t^K = RI_t^K + PI_t^K; \qquad t \in T$$

For example, given a topic K, its research papers time series ($R^K = \{R_t^K; t \in T\}$) is obtained by summing the number of papers from academia (RA) and industry (RI).

As second step, each point in time of each time series of each topic is normalised according to its global value for the whole Computer Science.

Therefore, given $R^{CS} = \{R_t^{CS}; t \in T\}$ the time series of research papers in Computer Science, the normalised time series of research papers R of topic K becomes:

$$R_{norm}^K = \left\{ \frac{R_t^K}{R_t^{CS}}; t \in T \right\}$$

The other time series, i.e. patents (P), documents from academia (A) and documents from industry (I), are similarly obtained by combining the appropriate signals.

As a third step, we chunk our time-range in a number of time windows. For instance, if we want to observe how a particular topic changed over a period of 12 years, we may want to split it in 4 windows of 3 years. Then, for each time window w and for each topic K, we sum the contributions of each time series within that time window. For instance, the contribution of research papers (R_w^K) is given by:

$$R_w^K = \sum_{t=w_{init}}^{w_{end}} R_t^K$$

where w_{init} and w_{end} are the years in which the time windows respectively start and end. Similarly, we can compute the contributions of patents (P), academia (A), and industry (I).

At this stage, for a given time window, each research topic is represented by four points: total number of research publications (R_w^K), total number of patents (P_w^K), and total number of documents from academia (A_w^K) and industry (I_w^K). Then, for each topic K and for each window w, we define two indexes:

$$RP_w^K = \frac{R_w^K - P_w^K}{R_w^K + P_w^K}; \qquad AI_w^K = \frac{A_w^K - I_w^K}{A_w^K + I_w^K}$$

The index RP allows us to observe whether in a particular time window, w, in proportion, a topic tends to be associated with a higher number of publications, if $RP_w^K > 0$, or patents, if $RP_w^K < 0$. The index AI instead indicates whether, in the same time window, w, in proportion, the topic is mostly populated by academia ($AI_w^K > 0$) or industry ($AI_w^K < 0$). In brief, for a given topic K, we now have a reduced set of time series $RP^K = \{RP_w^K; w \in W\}$ and $AI^K = \{AI_w^K; w \in W\}$, where W is the set of windows in which our initial time-frame has been divided.

In order to monitor the evolution of a topic, we can now analyse the trends of RP and AI over time. In particular, we use the least-squares approximation to determine the linear regression of both time series $f(x) = \alpha \cdot x + \beta$. Then, as trends of time series we take the slopes α^{RP} and α^{AI} of their approximated lines. If α^{RP} is positive, it means that the values in RP are growing positively over time and thus there are more papers published. On the other hand, if α^{RP} is negative it means that the number of patents is increasing in proportion. If α^{AI} is positive, it means that the topic is becoming more academic over time, whereas, if it is negative, it is becoming more industrial.

3.2.2 Analysis of Topic Emergence

In this phase, we want to asses which signal precedes another in addressing a certain topic. For instance, the topic *gamification* emerged in RA in 2008 and only five years later in RI. In the context of this analysis, we consider a topic as emergent for a certain signal when it becomes associated with at least n documents ($n = 10$ in the current implementation). Therefore, we iterate over the topics and calculate the time elapsed between the emergence of a topic for each pair of signals. Section 4.2 reports the results of this analysis on the field of Computer Science.

3.2.3 Trend Analysis

In this phase, we detect the signals that seem to influence each other by checking if they synchronize after making allowance for their mutual delay. For instance, if we consider the topic *bluetooth*, the trends of RI regularly anticipate RA, suggesting that industry is leading the research efforts for this topic. Indeed, if we align the two signals by shifting ahead RI by one year, the two signals yield a correlation coefficient $\rho = 0.975$.

In order to detect this phenomenon, we perform pairwise sliding of the time series and determine when two signals have the maximum correlation. We first normalise the time series RA^K, RI^K, PI^K and PA^K using the time series associated to the topic *Computer Science*, RA^{CS}, RI^{CS}, PI^{CS} and PA^{CS}. As a second step, for each pair of time series, we compute the sliding Pearson's correlation coefficient on the overlapping part between the time series. For each couple of signals, such as RA-RI where RA is the first signal (S1) and RI the second (S2), we can define the sliding Pearson's correlation coefficient as:

$$\rho_\tau^{S1-S2} = \frac{cov(S1, S2(-\tau))}{\sigma^{S1} \cdot \sigma^{S2}}; \qquad -len(S2) + 1 \leq \tau \leq len(S1) - 1$$

where $S2(-\tau)$ is the time series of the second signal that has been shifted of $-\tau$ positions. Since $len(S2) = len(S1)$, this process produces a list of $2 \cdot len(S1) - 1$ Pearson's correlation coefficients. Having done this, we can then determine for which τ we have the highest correlation. If the maximum correlation appears for a negative value of τ, e.g. $\tau = -5$, it means that the second signal (S2:RI in the example) anticipates the first signal (S1:RA). Conversely, if τ is positive, S1 anticipates S2. However, we have observed that, within the array of correlation coefficients, there can be a number of local maxima with similar magnitude and selecting the absolute maximum may not be the appropriate solution. Therefore, to identify the value of τ that synchronises the signals we observe for which local maxima of the Pearson's correlation coefficients the two signals have also the lowest Euclidean distance.

3.3 Impact Forecasting

In this section, given the limited amount of space in this paper, we will focus specifically on predicting the impact of a research topic on the industrial landscape. Having said so, it should be emphasised that the forecaster that we have developed could indeed be used for predicting the behaviour of any of the four time series.

A good measure of the impact of a topic on industry is the number of relevant patents granted to companies. For instance, according to our data, the topic *wearable sensors* was granted only 2 patents during 2009, after which it experienced a strong acceleration, ultimately producing 135 patents in 2018. The literature proposes a wide range of approaches to patent and technology prediction through patents data, using for instance weighted association rules [9], Bayesian clustering [35], and various statistical models [36] (e.g., Bass, Gompertz, Logistic, Richards). In the last few years, we saw also the emergence of several approaches based on Neural Networks [8, 37], which often yield the most competitive results. However, most of these tools focus only on patents, and do not integrate research publication data, nor can they distinguish patents and publications produced by academia or industry.

The ResearchFlow approach can naturally support all these solutions since it produces a large quantity of granular data that can be used to train and test machine learning classifiers. Furthermore, we hypothesize that an input which integrates all the information about publications and patents should offer a richer set of features and would be more robust in situations in which patents data are scarce, ultimately yielding a better performance in comparison to approaches which rely solely on patent data.

In order to train a forecaster, we created a gold standard, in which for each topic in CSO, we selected all the time-frames of five years in which the topic had not yet emerged (less than 10 patents). We then labelled each of these samples as *True* if the topic produced more than 50 industrial patents (PI) in the following 10 years and *False* otherwise. The resulting dataset includes 9,776 labelled samples, each composed of four time series (RA, RI, PA, PI). We then implemented a neural network forecaster which uses one Long short-term memory (LSTM) hidden layer of 128 units and one output layer computing the softmax function. We use binary cross-entropy as loss function and train the model over 50 epochs. Section 5 reports the evaluation of this architecture versus alternative approaches.

4   Results from the Analysis of Computer Science

We used ResearchFlow to quantify the trends of 5K topics in *Computer Science* over 2.9M research papers from academia (RA), 676K research papers from industry (RI), 2M patents from industry (PI), and 46K patents from academia (PA) in the period 1990–2018. Because of space restrictions, we will focus the discussion only on the main insights that emerged from our experiments.

4.1 Diachronic Analysis

Figure 1 shows the distribution of all topics in a 2-dimensional diagram with AI on the horizontal axis and RP on the vertical axis (computed as described in Sect. 3.2.1). Interestingly, most topics are tightly distributed around the bisector.

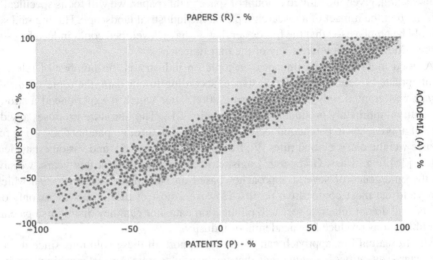

Fig. 1. Top 5,000 topics in computer science according to their RP and AI indexes.

The topics which attract most interest from academia mainly produce research papers (top-right quadrant). Conversely, the topics which are more interesting for industry tend to generate prevalently patents (bottom left quadrant). This distribution follows a classic pattern, consistent with the analysis of Larivière et al. [30], which suggest that academia is mostly interested on the dissemination of knowledge through scientific articles, while companies focus more on preserving their intellectual property by producing patents.

In the top-right quadrant we find research topics, such as *e-learning systems, scholarly communication, smart environment, community detection, decision tree algorithms*, which are mostly populated by academics. In the bottom-left quadrant we tend to find more applied areas, such as *optoelectronic devices, high power lasers, network interface, flip-flop, optical signals, magnetic disk storage*.

We applied the diachronic topic analysis described in Sect. 3.2.1 to highlight the topics that experienced the most dramatic shift in this space. We focused on the last 12 years (2007–18), using 4 windows of 3 years each. Table 1, Table 2, Table 3, and Table 4 report the top 5 topics that have respectively the strongest trends towards publications ($\alpha^{RP} > 0$), patents ($\alpha^{RP} < 0$), academia ($\alpha^{AI} > 0$), and industry ($\alpha^{AI} < 0$). We also report the values of the two indexes (RP and AI) in the first (2007–2009, RP_1 and AI_1) and the last (2016–2018, RP_4 and AI_4) time windows. Although it is not possible without additional analysis to come to definitive conclusions, these tables provide valuable information by highlighting areas of relative high/low activity.

Table 1. Topics with strongest trends towards publications.

Topic	α^{RP}	RP_1	RP_4
Smart grid	27.2	−21.1	65.1
Internet of things	26.6	−8.5	76.8
Energy harvesting	23.3	−58.1	13.8
Matrix factorization	22.2	6.8	72.1
Slot antennas	22.1	−52.5	18.7

Table 2. Topics with strongest trends towards patents.

Topic	α^{RP}	RP_1	RP_4
Long term evolution (lte)	−31.0	89.0	−0.9
Mode decision (coding)	−27.7	46	−36.2
3d video	−26.9	72.5	−4.1
Overlay networks	−25.2	81.5	6.8
Hand gesture	−23.1	59.1	−6.5

Table 3. Topics with strongest trends towards academia.

Topic	α^{AI}	AI_1	AI_4
Smart grid	26.9	−14.2	68.5
Internet of things	25.2	−6.0	68.9
Encrypted data	24.9	−62.4	9.88
Distribution systems	23.4	−17.9	52.9
Energy harvesting	22.1	−44.9	22.7

Table 4. Topics with strongest trends towards industry.

Topic	α^{AI}	AI_1	AI_4
overlay networks	−21.8	72.8	7.5
mode decision (coding)	−21.5	30.4	−34.5
long term evolution (lte)	−19.2	52.4	−3.2
wearable computing	−18.6	72.8	16.08
video encoder	17.1	−14.1	−66.2

Overall, the top five entries which had a strong increment in the direction of academia and publications (Table 1 and 3) can be categorized in three macro areas: energy production (e.g., *smart grid, energy harvesting*), technologies for telecommunication (e.g., *internet of things, slot antennas*), and data security (e.g., *encrypted data*). Conversely, the main entries for industry and patents (Table 2 and 4) focus prevalently on technologies for telecommunication (e.g., *overlay networks, long term evolution, coding mode*), user interfaces (e.g., *hand gesture, wearable computing*), and image processing (e.g., *video encoder, 3d video*).

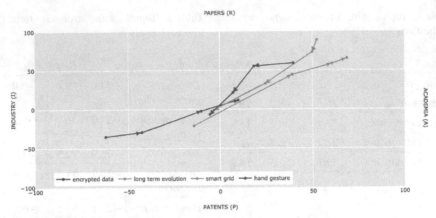

Fig. 2. Trajectories of *encrypted data, long term evolution, smart grid* and *hand gesture*. (Color figure online)

Figure 2 shows as example the trajectories of four topics that exhibited a dramatic shift in the period 2007–2018: *encrypted data, long term evolution* (a standard for broadband wireless technology), *smart grid*, and *hand gesture*. *Encrypted data* (red line) was in the left-bottom area, which characterizes prominently industrial topics, counting 178 documents from academia (A) and 560 from industry (I) in the first windows (2007–09), before being increasingly adopted by academia and moving up to the top-right area, counting A = 894 and I = 453 in the last window (2016–18). *Smart grid* (light blue line) followed a similar trajectory. On the other hand, *long term evolution* (orange line) and *hand gesture* (dark blue line) followed the opposite trajectory. Specifically, in the first window *hand gesture* was primarily an academic topic, counting A = 1,107 and I = 348; it then became more and more industrial over the years, increasing the number of documents from academia to 2,218, and from industry to 2,133. Similarly, *long term evolution* was initially in the top-right quadrant finding more industrial application over time as it became a well adopted standard.

4.2 Analysis of Topic Emergence

In this section we report the results of the analysis described in Sect. 3.2.2 on the 3,484 topics that according to their four associated signals emerged after 1990, which is the first year of our dataset.

We found that 89.8% of the topics first emerge in academic publications, 3.0% in industrial publications, 7.2% in industrial patents, and none in academic patents. On average, publications from academia (RA) precede publications from industry (RI, see Fig. 3) by 5.6 ± 5.6 years, and in turn RI precedes patents from industry (PI, see Fig. 4) by 1.0 ± 5.8 years. RA also precedes by 6.7 ± 7.4 years patents from industry (PI, see Fig. 5). However, just considering the average would be misleading in this case. Indeed, as depicted by Fig. 3, in 15.7% of cases the topics emerged in RI only one year later than RA, and in the 11.7% two years later.

For the sake of space we do not show the distributions involving PA, that counts only 1,897 emerging topics. An analysis of this set showed that topics in PA appear on average 20.4 ± 7.0 years after they emerge in RA, 14.8 ± 7.2 after RI, and 13.7 ± 7.3 after PI. In conclusion, these results confirm that the academia is usually the first to investigate a topic and suggest that industrial publications are conducive to patents.

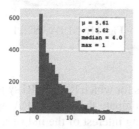 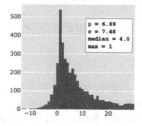

Fig. 3. S1:RA - S2:RI   **Fig. 4.** S1:RI - S2:PI   **Fig. 5.** S1:RA - S2:PI.

4.3 Trend Analysis

We performed the analysis described in Sect. 3.2.3 on all the topics and determined the time delay (τ) between each pair of time series S1 and S2. The following figures show the distributions of the delay for the six pairwise comparisons between the four time series. The x-axis represents the time lag τ, while the y-axis represents the number of topics in which the maximum Pearson's correlation coefficient was found in τ. We included only maxima in which $\rho \geq 0.7$, which is traditionally considered a strong direct correlation. We remind the reader that, as per our convention, the signal S2 is sliding over S1, and a maximum correlation in a negative τ means that S2 anticipates S1. Conversely, a positive τ means that S1 anticipates S2.

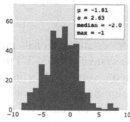 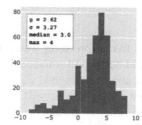 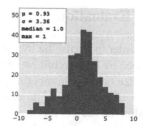

Fig. 6. S1:RA - S2:RI   **Fig. 7.** S1:RI - S2:PI   **Fig. 8.** S1:RA -S2:PI

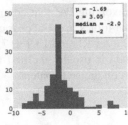
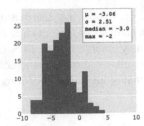
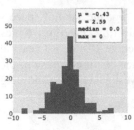

Fig. 9. S1:PA - S2:RA   **Fig. 10.** S1:PA - S2:RI   **Fig. 11.** S1:PA - S2:PI

Figure 6 shows that when we consider only the 327 topics for which RA and RI sync after compensating for a delay, the trends of RI tend to anticipate the ones of RA by almost 1.8 years on the average. In other words, an increasing interest of the industrial sector appears to often trigger a reaction in academia, while the opposite case is less frequent. A more in depth analysis on the involved topics seems to suggest that this is due to the fact that academia often reacts to the emergence of a topic in industry (e.g., social media, mobile devices, internet of things) by further investigating it. Conversely, industry tends to be less receptive and in some cases to ignore or react slowly to the emergence of topics in academia. This asymmetry is an intriguing phenomenon that we intend to further investigate in future works.

Another interesting dynamics is that the trends of industrial patents (PI) are anticipated by the trends of publications from industry (RI) with a delay of about 2.6 years (Fig. 7) and by academic publications (RA) by 1 year (Fig. 8). This suggests that both could be good predictors for patents. Finally, on average patents from academia (PA) tend to sync with publications from academia with a delay of almost 1.7 years (Fig. 9), industrial publications by 3.0 years (Fig. 10), and industrial patents by 0.4 year (Fig. 11).

5   Evaluation

In order to verify the hypothesis that a forecaster which integrates all the signals produced by ResearchFlow will yield better performance than the systems [8, 35–37] that utilize only the number of publications or patents, we evaluated several models on the task of predicting if an emergent research topic will have a significant impact on the industrial sector, producing more than 50 patents in the following 10 years. We thus trained five machine learning classifiers on the gold standard introduced in Sect. 3.3: Logistic Regression (LR), Random Forest (RF), AdaBoost (AB), Convoluted Neural Network (CNN), and Long Short-term Memory Neural Network (LSTM). We ran each of them on research papers (R), patents (P), and the 15 possible combinations of the four time series in order to assess which set of features would yield the best results. We performed a 10-fold cross-validation of the data and measured the performance of the classifiers by computing the average precision (P), recall (R), and F1 (F). The dataset, the results of experiments, the parameter and implementation details, and the best models are available at http://doi.org/10.21954/ou.rd.12805307.

Table 5 shows the results of the evaluation. We report all combinations in order to assess the contributions of the different time series. LSTM outperforms all the other solutions, yielding the highest F1 for 12 of the 17 feature combinations and the highest average F1 (73.7%). CNN (72.8%) and AB (72.3%) also produce competitive results. For the sake of space, here we will focus on the performance of the LSTM models.

As hypothesized, using the full set of features produced by ResearchFlow (RA-RI-PA-PI) significantly ($p < 0.0001$) outperforms (F1: 84.6%) the solution which uses only the number of patents by companies (74.8%). Splitting each of the two main time series (publications and patents) in its components (academia and industry) also increases performance: RA-RI (80.7%) significantly ($p < 0.0001$) outperforms R (68.2%) while PA-PI (75.2%) is marginally better than P (74.8%). This confirms that the more granular representation of the document origin can increase the forecaster performance.

When considering the models produced with only one of the time series, we find that the number of publications from industry (RI) is a significant ($p = 0.004$) better indicator than PI, yielding a F1 of 76.9%, followed by RA, and PA. If we zoom on the models trained on two time series, the best results are obtained by the combinations RI-PI (81.4%), when considering three, RA-RI-PI yields the best performance (84.7%).

In conclusion, this evaluation substantiates the hypothesis that considering the four time series separately is conducive to higher quality predictions and suggests that RI and RA are good indicators for PI.

Table 5. Performance of the five classifiers on 17 combinations of time series. In bold the best F1 (F) for each combination.

	LR			RF			AB			CNN			LSTM		
	P%	R%	F%	P%	R%	F%	P%	R%	F%	P%	R%	F%	P%	R%	F%
RA	70.8	45.2	55.2	63.3	55.8	59.2	66.0	58.4	61.9	64.1	66.3	**65.0**	65.2	64.2	64.6
RI	83.5	67.1	74.4	78.9	69.8	74.0	80.0	73.1	76.4	79.2	75.1	**77.0**	79.1	74.8	76.9
PA	58.3	15.3	24.2	60.4	15.4	24.5	59.3	16.0	**25.2**	60.5	15.7	24.9	60.8	15.6	24.8
PI	76.5	69.0	72.5	73.9	68.4	71.0	75.6	71.8	73.6	73.7	76.6	75.0	74.1	76.6	**75.2**
R	73.7	48.8	58.7	65.5	59.7	62.5	68.6	63.1	65.6	67.6	69.2	**68.3**	67.2	69.4	68.2
P	76.5	68.6	72.3	72.8	67.6	70.0	74.4	71.6	73.0	73.2	76.1	74.6	73.1	76.6	**74.8**
RA-RI	85.7	70.9	77.6	80.5	76.0	78.2	82.6	76.6	79.5	78.9	75.1	76.8	82.2	79.3	**80.7**
RA-PA	70.3	47.0	56.3	63.1	55.5	59.0	66.5	59.3	62.6	64.5	65.1	64.5	65.4	64.2	**64.6**
RA-PI	79.6	73.7	76.5	77.2	74.3	75.7	79.1	76.5	77.7	75.2	76.3	75.7	77.4	81.9	**79.5**
RI-PA	83.3	67.0	74.3	77.9	70.8	74.1	79.6	73.0	76.1	78.6	75.6	77.0	79.1	75.2	**77.1**
RI-PI	83.4	77.3	80.2	81.0	77.3	79.1	82.7	78.6	80.6	82.0	78.6	80.2	81.7	81.2	**81.4**
PA-PI	76.7	68.6	72.4	74.2	69.0	71.5	75.9	71.5	73.6	71.1	70.8	70.9	73.8	76.7	**75.2**
RA-RI-PA	85.2	71.4	77.7	80.8	75.4	78.0	82.5	77.0	79.6	82.6	78.1	**80.3**	82.6	78.2	80.3
RA-RI-PI	85.4	79.8	82.5	84.5	80.5	82.4	84.6	81.2	82.9	83.8	84.7	84.2	84.1	85.4	**84.7**
RA-PA-PI	79.6	73.9	76.6	77.5	74.4	75.9	79.2	76.5	77.8	78.9	78.6	78.6	77.4	81.4	**79.2**
RI-PA-PI	83.6	77.5	80.4	81.1	78.0	79.5	82.7	78.6	80.6	82.2	80.9	**81.5**	81.1	81.0	81.1
RA-RI-PA-PI	85.4	79.8	82.5	83.8	80.0	81.8	84.6	81.2	82.9	84.7	81.3	82.9	83.2	86.1	**84.6**
Average	78.7	64.8	70.2	75.1	67.5	70.4	76.7	69.6	72.3	75.4	72.0	72.8	75.7	73.4	**73.7**

6 Conclusions and Future Work

In this paper, we introduced ResearchFlow, an approach to analysing and forecasting the knowledge flows between academia and industry. We applied ResearchFlow on a dataset of publications and patents in Computer Science, and produced a knowledge base that described the behaviour of topics across academia and industry. Our analysis indicates that academia is the first to investigate most of these topics; on the average, academic publications precede industrial publications by about 5.6 years and industrial patents by about 6.6 years. However, industrial trends actually appears to influence academia more often than academic trends affect industry, suggesting that in several cases it is industry that dictates the research direction. Finally, we showed that quantifying research topics according to the four time series described in this work can significantly increase the performance of a forecaster.

We are now working on a more comprehensive analysis of Computer Science which will include the full range of analytics that we can produce with ResearchFlow and a more detailed discussion. In particular, we intend to investigate further the specific mechanisms that allow industry to influence academia and the other way round. We also intend to analyse documents with mixed affiliations and extend this analysis to other kinds of organisations, such as healthcare, government, and non-profit.

References

1. Ankrah, S., AL-Tabbaa, O.: Universities-industry collaboration: a systematic review. Scand. J. Manag. **31**, 387–408 (2015). https://doi.org/10.1016/j.scaman.2015.02.003
2. Weinstein, L., Kellar, G., Hall, D.: Comparing topic importance perceptions of industry and business school faculty: is the tail wagging the dog? Acad. Educ. Leadersh. J. **20**, 62 (2016)
3. Ankrah, S.N., Burgess, T.F., Grimshaw, P., Shaw, N.E.: Asking both university and industry actors about their engagement in knowledge transfer: what single-group studies of motives omit. Technovation **33**, 50–65 (2013)
4. Ohniwa, R.L., Hibino, A., Takeyasu, K.: Trends in research foci in life science fields over the last 30 years monitored by emerging topics. Scientometrics **85**, 111–127 (2010)
5. Salatino, A.A., Osborne, F., Motta, E.: AUGUR: forecasting the emergence of new research topics. In: Joint Conference on Digital Libraries 2018, Fort Worth, Texas, pp. 1–10 (2018)
6. Bolelli, L., Ertekin, Ş., Giles, C.L.: Topic and trend detection in text collections using latent dirichlet allocation. In: Boughanem, M., Berrut, C., Mothe, J., Soule-Dupuy, C. (eds.) ECIR 2009. LNCS, vol. 5478, pp. 776–780. Springer, Heidelberg (2009). https://doi.org/10.1007/978-3-642-00958-7_84
7. Salatino, A.A., Osborne, F., Motta, E.: How are topics born? Understanding the research dynamics preceding the emergence of new areas. PeerJ Comput. Sci. **3**, e119 (2017). https://doi.org/10.7717/peerj-cs.119
8. Zang, X., Niu, Y.: The forecast model of patents granted in colleges based on genetic neural network. In: 2011 Proceedings of the International Conference on Electrical and Control Engineering, ICECE 2011, pp. 5090–5093 (2011)
9. Altuntas, S., Dereli, T., Kusiak, A.: Analysis of patent documents with weighted association rules. Technol. Forecast. Soc. Change **92**, 249–262 (2015)
10. Bikard, M., Vakili, K., Teodoridis, F.: When collaboration bridges institutions: the impact of university-industry collaboration on academic productivity. Organ. Sci. **30**, 426–445 (2019). https://doi.org/10.1287/orsc.2018.1235

11. Anderson, M.S.: The complex relations between the academy and industry: views from the literature. J. High. Educ. **72**, 226–246 (2001). https://doi.org/10.2307/2649323
12. Angioni, S., Salatino, A.A., Osborne, F., Recupero, D.R., Motta, E.: Integrating knowledge graphs for analysing academia and industry dynamics. In: Bellatreche, L., et al. (eds.) TPDL/ADBIS -2020. CCIS, vol. 1260, pp. 219–225. Springer, Cham (2020). https://doi.org/10.1007/978-3-030-55814-7_18
13. Salatino, A.A., Thanapalasingam, T., Mannocci, A., Osborne, F., Motta, E.: The computer science ontology: a large-scale taxonomy of research areas. In: Vrandečić, D., et al. (eds.) ISWC 2018. LNCS, vol. 11137, pp. 187–205. Springer, Cham (2018). https://doi.org/10.1007/978-3-030-00668-6_12
14. Powell, W.W., Snellman, K.: The knowledge economy. Ann. Rev. Sociol. **30**, 199–220 (2004). https://doi.org/10.1146/annurev.soc.29.010202.100037
15. Stilgoe, J.: Who's Driving Innovation? New Technologies and the Collaborative State. Palgrave Macmillan, Cham (2020)
16. Kuhn, T.S.: The Structure of Scientific Revolutions. University of Chicago Press, Chicago (2012)
17. Becher, T., Trowler, P.: Academic Tribes and Territories: Intellectual Enquiry and the Culture of Disciplines. Open University Press (2001)
18. Krumov, L., Fretter, C., Müller-Hannemann, M., Weihe, K., Hütt, M.-T.: Motifs in co-authorship networks and their relation to the impact of scientific publications. Eur. Phys. J. B **84**(4), 535–540 (2011). https://doi.org/10.1140/EPJB/E2011-10746-5
19. Varlamis, I., Tsatsaronis, G.: Visualizing bibliographic databases as graphs and mining potential research synergies. In: Proceedings of the 2011 International Conference on Advances in Social Networks Analysis and Mining, ASONAM 2011, pp. 53–60 (2011). https://doi.org/10.1109/ASONAM.2011.52
20. Frank, M.R., Wang, D., Cebrian, M., Rahwan, I.: The evolution of citation graphs in artificial intelligence research (2019). https://www.nature.com/articles/s42256-019-0024-5. https://doi.org/10.1038/s42256-019-0024-5
21. Wang, K., Shen, Z., Huang, C., Wu, C.-H., Dong, Y., Kanakia, A.: Microsoft academic graph: when experts are not enough. Quant. Sci. Stud. **1**, 396–413 (2020)
22. Zhang, Y., Zhang, F., Yao, P., Tang, J.: Name disambiguation in AMiner: clustering, maintenance, and human in the loop. In: KDD 2018, p. 10 (2018)
23. Knoth, P., Zdrahal, Z.: CORE: three access levels to underpin open access. D-Lib Mag. **18** (2012). https://doi.org/10.1045/november2012-knoth
24. Peroni, S., Shotton, D.: OpenCitations, an infrastructure organization for open scholarship. Quant. Sci. Stud. **1**, 428–444 (2020). https://doi.org/10.1162/qss_a_00023
25. Peroni, S., Dutton, A., Gray, T., Shotton, D.: Setting our bibliographic references free: towards open citation data. J. Doc. **71**, 253–277 (2015)
26. Fathalla, S., Auer, S., Lange, C.: Towards the semantic formalization of science (2020). https://doi.org/10.1145/3341105.3374132
27. Dessì, D., Osborne, F., Recupero, D.R., Buscaldi, D., Motta, E., Sack, H.: AI-KG: an automatically generated knowledge graph of artificial intelligence. In: The Semantic Web – ISWC 2020. Springer (2020)
28. Michaudel, Q., Ishihara, Y., Baran, P.S.: Academia-industry symbiosis in organic chemistry. Acc. Chem. Res. **48**, 712–721 (2015). https://doi.org/10.1021/ar500424a
29. Grimpe, C., Hussinger, K.: Formal and informal knowledge and technology transfer from academia to industry: complementarity effects and innovation performance. Ind. Innov. **20**, 683–700 (2013). https://doi.org/10.1080/13662716.2013.856620
30. Larivière, V., Macaluso, B., Mongeon, P., Siler, K., Sugimoto, C.R.: Vanishing industries and the rising monopoly of universities in published research (2018)

31. Huang, M.-H., Yang, H.-W., Chen, D.-Z.: Industry–academia collaboration in fuel cells: a perspective from paper and patent analysis. Scientometrics **105**(2), 1301–1318 (2015). https://doi.org/10.1007/s11192-015-1748-6
32. Sinha, A., et al.: An overview of microsoft academic service (MAS) and applications. In: Proceedings of the 24th International Conference on World Wide Web - WWW 2015 Companion, pp. 243–246. ACM Press, New York (2015)
33. Salatino, Angelo A., Osborne, F., Thanapalasingam, T., Motta, E.: The CSO classifier: ontology-driven detection of research topics in scholarly articles. In: Doucet, A., Isaac, A., Golub, K., Aalberg, T., Jatowt, A. (eds.) TPDL 2019. LNCS, vol. 11799, pp. 296–311. Springer, Cham (2019). https://doi.org/10.1007/978-3-030-30760-8_26
34. Salatino, A.A., Osborne, F., Birukou, A., Motta, E.: Improving editorial workflow and metadata quality at springer nature. In: Ghidini, C., et al. (eds.) ISWC 2019. LNCS, vol. 11779, pp. 507–525. Springer, Cham (2019). https://doi.org/10.1007/978-3-030-30796-7_31
35. Choi, S., Jun, S.: Vacant technology forecasting using new Bayesian patent clustering. Technol. Anal. Strateg. Manag. **26**, 241–251 (2014)
36. Marinakis, Y.D.: Forecasting technology diffusion with the Richards model. Technol. Forecast. Soc. Change **79**, 172–179 (2012)
37. Ramadhan, M.H., Malik, V.I., Sjafrizal, T.: Artificial neural network approach for technology life cycle construction on patent data. In: 2018 5th International Conference on Industrial Engineering and Applications, ICIEA 2018, pp. 499–503 (2018)

A Knowledge Graph Enhanced Learner Model to Predict Outcomes to Questions in the Medical Field

Antonia Ettorre[1]($\boxtimes$), Oscar Rocha Rodríguez[1,2] , Catherine Faron[1] ,
Franck Michel[1] , and Fabien Gandon[1]

[1] University Côte d'Azur, CNRS, Inria, I3S, Biot, France
`aettorre@i3s.unice.fr`
[2] Teach on Mars, Mougins, France

Abstract. The training curriculum for medical doctors requires the intensive and rapid assimilation of a lot of knowledge. To help medical students optimize their learning path, the *SIDES 3.0* national French project aims to extend an existing platform with intelligent learning services. This platform contains a large number of annotated learning resources, from training and evaluation questions to students' learning traces, available as an RDF knowledge graph. In order for the platform to provide personalized learning services, the knowledge and skills progressively acquired by students on each subject should be taken into account when choosing the training and evaluation questions to be presented to them, in the form of customized quizzes. To achieve such recommendation, a first step lies in the ability to predict the outcome of students when answering questions (success or failure). With this objective in mind, in this paper we propose a model of the students' learning on the *SIDES* platform, able to make such predictions. The model extends a state-of-the-art approach to fit the specificity of medical data, and to take into account additional knowledge extracted from the *OntoSIDES* knowledge graph in the form of graph embeddings. Through an evaluation based on learning traces for pediatrics and cardiovascular specialties, we show that considering the vector representations of answers, questions and students nodes substantially improves the prediction results compared to baseline models.

Keywords: Semantic web · Graph embedding · Prediction · Learner model · Medical field

1 Introduction

Since 2013, teachers of French medical schools have been using a common national platform to create and give local evaluation tests on different devices. The Web-based platform, named *SIDES* (*Intelligent Health Education System*[1]),

---

[1] Système Intelligent d'Enseignement en Santé. http://side-sante.org.

C. M. Keet and M. Dumontier (Eds.): EKAW 2020, LNAI 12387, pp. 237–251, 2020.
https://doi.org/10.1007/978-3-030-61244-3_17

allows to share these tests among medical schools to form a national database for training, and supports the preparation of medical students for the ECNi (National Computerized Ranking Tests).

The French national project *SIDES 3.0* started at the end of 2017 and aims to develop a new version of the platform meant to offer user-centered intelligent services such as individual monitoring, enriched dashboards, personalized recommendations, augmented corrections for self-assessment, and a standardized digital environment for knowledge sharing. To achieve these goals, the approach taken leverages semantic Web models and technologies to enrich and integrate these resources in RDF with OWL ontologies. As part of the *SIDES 3.0* project, existing data from the platform, such as annotated questions and students' learning traces, were converted into structured data expressed in RDF using the *OntoSIDES OWL ontology* [13], and stored in the *OntoSIDES* knowledge graph.

Recommending questions to the students (i.e. the *learners*) in an intelligent way is a key element to achieve personalized and efficient individual learning. This requires the ability to take into account their profile, learning objectives and current level of knowledge in order to guide them in progressively improving their knowledge about a medical specialty. An important criterion for this tailored recommendation is the prediction of the outcomes of students to questions, since such predictions should allow to more effectively detect and adjust students' gaps.

Throughout the years, several research works have addressed this prediction relying on diverse machine learning techniques. Our goal is to propose a hybrid approach that combines Machine Learning and Knowledge Representation to take advantage of the most advanced learning architectures while exploiting the information provided by the knowledge graph. In this context, this paper addresses the following research questions:

- How to model students' learning on the *SIDES* platform to predict their outcomes to medical questions?
- Which set of features should be extracted from the *OntoSIDES* knowledge graph and considered for learning the student model?
- Can taking into account the knowledge graph structure of *OntoSIDES* improve the performance of the prediction of students answers to questions?

To answer these questions, in this paper we present (1) our model to predict the outcome of students' answers to questions, and (2) an evaluation of our model focused on the pediatrics and cardiovascular specialties. Our model was created on the basis of two state-of-the-art works on this domain: Knowledge Tracing Machines [20] and Deep Knowledge Tracing Machines (DeepFM) [7]. We adapted the learning models proposed in these works to the *OntoSIDES* knowledge graph, and extended them with calculated features and embeddings of graph nodes to exploit the knowledge captured in the *OntoSIDES* graph. Through experimentation and evaluation, we validated a new model that makes the most accurate predictions by considering these features in the DeepFM machine learning algorithm.

The remainder of this paper is organized as follows: In Sect. 2, we review existing related works. We describe the *OntoSIDES* knowledge graph in Sect. 3. The features extracted or computed from the *OntoSIDES* knowledge graph to model students' learning are detailed in Sect. 4. In Sect. 5, we present the experiments performed in order to define our model, and we analyse the results of these experiments in Sect. 5.2. Finally, conclusions and future work are presented in Sect. 6.

2   Related Work

Several models have been proposed in the literature to measure and predict students' outcomes to questions. The Classical Test Theory (CTT) [12] is a foundational work developed in the context of psychological tests. It builds on the assumption that the measurement of a test cannot be completely error-free. Thus, student's observed score on a test is the sum of a true score (a score obtained if there were no measurement errors) and an error score. Several shortcomings of the CTT were underlined in [8], yet the major limitation with respect to our goal is that CTT is test-oriented and therefore is not suitable for modeling answers to individual items of a test.

The Item Response Theory (IRT) [8] was proposed to overcome the shortcomings of the CTT. IRT models the relationship between persons and test items in order to predict the response of any student to any item even if similar students have never answered similar items before. The probability of correctly responding to an item is a monotonically increasing function of the measured latent trait (ability) of the student and some parameters of the question item (e.g. difficulty). For dichotomous question items, there are 4 IRT models, from one (1PL) to four parameters (4PL) models. The 1PL model (also called the *Rasch model* as it was originally suggested by Rasch [16]) is the simplest IRT model. It describes the test items in terms of only one parameter: the item difficulty. The probability of responding correctly to an item given its difficulty and the ability level of the student is given by a logistic function. The 2PL model generalizes the 1PL model by adding the *discrimination parameter*. The 3PL model (which is not a logistic model unlike the previous two) generalizes the 2PL model by adding the *(pseudo)guessing parameter* which expresses the property that even very low ability persons have a positive probability of answering an item correctly, simply by randomly guessing the correct answer. Finally, the 4PL model adds a fourth parameter that models the "inattention" of high ability students failing to answer an easy item correctly.

Unlike IRT models, which are suitable for analyzing students' responses to items that measure a single latent trait, mIRT [17] models allow to analyze richer question items that measure multiple latent traits simultaneously.

Additive Factors Model (AFM) [3] is a predictive learning model based on the Logistic Regression algorithm, that takes into account student skill parameters, skill parameters and learning rates. In [14], the authors propose the Performance

Factors Analysis (PFA) model. This model is also based on the Logistic Regression, however, unlike AFM, it takes into account the prior students' failures and successes on each skill to make predictions.

Bayesian Knowledge Tracing (BKT) [4] is one of the most popular methods for modeling students' knowledge. It models the student's prior incorrect and correct responses to items of a particular skill in a Hidden Markov Model to estimate the probability that a student has mastered or not that skill. Its major limitation is that it cannot model the fact that question items may involve multiple skills.

Taking advantage of the advances of Deep Learning [10], in 2015, the Deep Knowledge Tracing (DKT) [15] model was proposed to overcome the limitations of BKT. This model is based on the use of Recurrent Neural Networks (RNNs) to model student's learning and predict the outcomes to questions based upon students' prior activity. More specifically, two different types of RNNs are applied: a vanilla RNN model with sigmoid units and a Long Short Term Memory (LSTM) mode. However, in 2016, authors of [22] have shown how IRT-based methods matched or even outperformed DKT. In particular, a hierarchical extension of IRT that captured item grouping structure performed the best. Additionally, a temporal extension of IRT improved performance over standard IRT while the RNN-based method did not.

More recently, Vie and Kashima proposed the Knowledge Tracing Machines (KTM) [21] approach based on factorization machines (FM) [18] to model and estimate students' learning. KTM encompasses several existing models in the educational literature as special cases, such as AFM, PFA, and mIRT. In addition, this approach provides a test bed to try new combinations of features in order to improve existing models. Finally, in [20], an approach similar to the previous one is presented, but based on Deep Factorization Machines (DeepFM) [7] as a classification algorithm. DeepFM combines the power of FM for recommendation and Deep Learning for feature learning. The article compares the results obtained with DeepFM with the ones obtained using logistic regression and Vanilla FM, showing that it outperforms the other algorithms. This is why, for the research work presented in this paper, we have taken this framework as the basis for testing new features and combinations of features to improve predictions.

When compared to the above-mentioned research works, the novelty of our model is that it exploits the knowledge captured in the *OntoSIDES* knowledge graph by means of text and graph embeddings of nodes.

3   OntoSIDES

OntoSIDES [13] is a knowledge graph that comprises a domain ontology represented in OWL and a set of factual statements about the entities on the SIDES platform, linking them to the ontology classes and properties. Being an RDF graph, it is possible to query *OntoSIDES* with the standard query language SPARQL. The *OntoSIDES* knowledge graph was automatically generated from the relational database of the *SIDES* platform, and by enriching these data with the developed ontology.

The current version of the *OntoSIDES OWL ontology* contains 52 classes and 50 properties, mainly describing universities, faculties, users (students, professors, and administrative staff), tests, questions and answers. Here are the top classes of interest for our work:

Action (`sides:action`): the root class of actions that students can perform when they interact with the pedagogical resources of the *SIDES* platform. For example, it is possible to characterize the action of selecting the proposal of an answer to a question with subclass `sides:action_to_answer`.

Content (`sides:content`): the root class of the hierarchy of resource types available in the *SIDES* platform. The class of questions (`sides:question`), the class of proposed answers to a question (`sides:proposal_of_answer`) and the class of answers (`sides:answer`) of a student to a question, are subclasses of `sides:content`.

Person (`sides:person`): class of persons involved in medical studies. Its subclasses correspond to the specific roles of *SIDES* users: for example, the class `sides:student` is a subclass of `sides:person`.

Figure 1 depicts the RDF graph representing an answer given by a student to a question with multiple possible answers. For each attempt of a student to a question, an instance of the class `sides:answer` is created. This answer is directly linked to the student through property `sides:done_by` and to the question through `sides:correspond_to_question`. An answer is linked to multiple instances of `sides:action_to_answer`, each one representing the action of selecting a single `sides:proposal_of_answer` for the question. For example, question q666472 in Fig. 1 is a multiple choice question (QMA) associated to two possible answers, prop3017738 and prop3017739, and student stu27880, while answering, has selected (`sides:has_wrongly_ticked`) the wrong option `sides:prop3017739`. The instances of `sides:action_to_answer` are used to compute the number of misticked and non-ticked answers and then the level of correctness of the given answer, value of property `sides:has_for_result`. Other useful nodes further describe questions: `sides:has_for_textual_content` gives the text of a question, and `sides:is_linked_to_the_medical_speciality` relates a question to the medical specialties it belongs to. It is also worth pointing out that questions are normally organized in evaluations that group sets of questions related to similar topics or concerning the same clinical case.

The *OntoSIDES* graph currently includes the description of 569,762,878 answers to 1,797,180 questions related to 31 medical specialties and given by 173,533 students. In total the knowledge graph contains more than 9.2 billion triples.

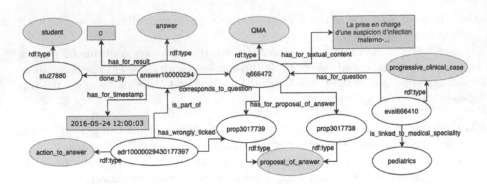

Fig. 1. RDF graph describing an answer of a student to a question. Blue bubbles are owl:Classes, white bubbles are instances and grey rectangles are literal values. (Color figure online)

4 Features Selected or Computed from OntoSIDES to Learn a Student Model

Based on the *OntoSIDES* knowledge graph, our aim is to predict the outcome of a student to a question, that is, the value related to an instance of sides:answer by property sides:has_for_result, which is equal to 1 if the student answered the question correctly, and 0 otherwise. Therefore this amounts to a binary classification.

In this section, we describe the candidate features that we selected or computed from the *OntoSIDES* knowledge graph to build a student model. We hypothesize that these features may improve the quality of the binary classification carried out by the algorithm to predict a student's outcome to a question. In Sect. 5.2, we draw some conclusions with respect to this hypothesis based on the results of our experiments.

4.1 Basic Features

A first set of basic (or raw) features concerns the entities that can be extracted by simply querying the *OntoSIDES* knowledge graph, without further processing. These features are as follows:

student: the identifier of a student who answers a question, specifically, the URI of an instance of class sides:student related to an instance of sides:answer by property sides:done_by.

answer: the identifier of an answer given by a student, that is, the URI of an instance of the class sides:answer.

question: the identifier of a question answered by a student, that is, the URI of an instance of the class sides:question.

timestamp: the date and time when a student answered a question, that is, the value related to an instance of sides:answer by property sides:has_for_timestamp.

4.2   Calculated Features Conveying a Temporal Dimension

A set of additional features is computed from the above described raw features. They are meant to provide insight into students' level of knowledge over time, difficulty level of questions and number of prior attempts that a student carried out to answer a question. Together, they convey a temporal dimension to the model that is richer than the raw timestamp. These features are as follows:

wins: given a question and a student, it represents the number of times that this student has previously answered that question correctly.

fails: given a question and a student, it represents the number of times that this student has previously answered that question incorrectly.

attempts: wins + fails.

question_difficulty: for a given question, it is an estimation of its difficulty and assumes values between 0 and 1, 1 being the highest difficulty. It is computed by dividing the number of incorrect answers by the number of answers given to that question.

static_student_ability: a static estimate of the student's overall ability, valued between 0 and 1, 1 being the highest ability. It is computed as the student's total number of correct answers divided by the student's total number of answers.

progressive_student_ability: this feature follows the evolution of the student's ability over time. It draws her learning curve. For each attempt, it is computed as the ratio between the number of correct answers and the number of all the answers given by the student up to that moment. At the beginning of the training, the student's ratio of correct answers is likely to be low to medium. Then, in time, this ratio increases, reflecting the growth of her level of knowledge and expertise.

4.3   Text Embeddings of Questions

We hypothesize that questions' text may provide valuable information to predict the answer of a student to a question. To test this hypothesis, we queried the OntoSIDES knowledge graph to extract the text of the questions, i.e. the value of the property sides:has_for_textual_content, and we computed their vector representation by using the state-of-the-art word embedding algorithm *fastText* [2]. We used the *flair framework* [1] implementation which provides embeddings pre-trained with the French Wikipedia. Applying this approach to the text of each question yields vectors of 300 dimensions. Later on, we refer to this set of vectors as **questions_temb**.

4.4   Knowledge Graph Embeddings of Questions, Answers, and Users

Lastly, we hypothesize that the *OntoSIDES* graph topology may convey valuable knowledge to predict the answer of a student to a question. To test this hypothesis, we used the state-of-the-art *node2vec* algorithm [6] to construct vector representations of the knowledge graph nodes. *node2vec* learns continuous feature representations for the nodes in a graph by mapping each node to a low-dimensional space of features that maximizes the likelihood of preserving network neighborhoods of nodes. To do this, we used the SNAP project implementation [11][2] of *node2vec* to extract vector representations of dimension 100 for each of the nodes in our training dataset (described in Sect. 5). In the following, we refer to these vectors as **answers_gemb**, **questions_gemb** and **students_gemb** respectively.

5   Empirical Determination of a Learner Model

This section describes a comparative evaluation of several student models, that we carried out to determine which of them produces the best prediction of the students' answers to questions. Each model relies on a specific set of features selected among those described in Sect. 4.

5.1   Experimental Settings

Training Data. We trained the different models on a sub-graph of the SIDES knowledge graph containing the answers given by the sixth-year medical students during the 2018–2019 academic year. The sixth year corresponds to the last year of the second cycle of medical studies. Thus, predicting the outcomes of these students is a particularly relevant task because their activities are the most reliable indicator of their performance during the National Computerized Ranking Tests (ECNi).

The extracted sub-graph contains 96,511,040 answers to 831,057 different questions, given by 8,776 students. Given the large size of this sub-graph, to be able to train the models within reasonable time we decided to limit our experiments to the answers to questions related to pediatrics and cardiovascular, the two specialties with the largest number of answers. For each specialty, we randomly extracted 100,000 answers, obtaining the following sub-graphs:

- pediatrics: 100,000 answers to 22,551 questions, given by 8,535 students;
- cardiovascular: 100,000 answers to 22,505 questions, given by 8,655 students.

Candidate Models. Relying on the benchmarking approach presented in [20], we defined 15 different models by combining the features described in Sect. 4, in order to comparatively evaluate them and determine which one allows the classification algorithms to obtain the best prediction scores.

Each model is identified by a label whose letters each denotes a feature: **s**: students identifiers; **q**: questions identifiers; **a**: number of attempts; **w**: number of wins; **f**: number of fails; **d**: question_difficulty; **b**: static_student_ability;

---

b': progressive_student_ability; **T**: questions_temb; **Q**: questions_gemb; **S**: students_gemb; **R**: answers_gemb. With this notation, the candidate models are as follows.

The first three models correspond to state-of-the-art models and will serve as a baseline for richer models:

sq is equivalent to the *1PL IRT* model when used with the Logistic Regression algorithm. Used with the FM algorithm configured with a "number of factors used for pairwise interactions" greater than 0 $(d > 20)$, this model is equivalent to the *mIRT* model [20].

sqa is inspired by the *AFM* model as it takes into account the number of previous attempts but not the skills which is not among our features.

sqawf is inspired by the *AFM* and *PFA* models as it takes into account the number of previous attempts and the distinction between correct and incorrect attempts.

Additionally, we consider the following models that test other possible features combinations, notably involving text and graph embeddings: **sqawfd, sqawfb, sqawfb', sqawfdbb', sqawfdbb'T, sqawfdbb'R, sqawfdbb'Q, sqawfdbb'S, sqawfdbb'RQ, sqawfdbb'TRQ, sqawfdbb'RQS** and **sqawfdbb'TRQS**.

Classification Algorithm. As a result of our survey of related works (Sect. 2), we chose to rely on the **DeepFM** classification algorithm for our experiments. We used the DeepCTR[3] Python implementation. The results reported in this paper were obtained with 256 layers of 256 units each, parameter *initialize std of embedding vector* was set to 0.001, and an L2 regularizer strength applied to embedding vector was set to 1e−06.

Hardware Setup. We used a *Dell T640* GPU node equipped with 4 *GTX 1080 Ti* GPU cards, 2 *Xeon Silver 4110* CPUs, 96 GB of RAM and 4 RAID-0 SSDs of 600 GB.

Temporality-Aware Cross-Validation. The performance of each model was evaluated by means of the *student-based* 5-fold cross-validation technique, in order to take into account the temporal dimension of the knowledge in the graph. Specifically, the list of students included in our dataset is split into five folds; four of them are directly used as training data while the remaining one is split again in two parts following the chronological order of answers: the first half is included into the training data while the last half is used as test set. The rationale behind this splitting method is as follows: for each fold, we train the model using the complete learning path of four fifths of the students, thus learning the entire trend of the students' knowledge acquisition, and learning information about all

---

[3] https://github.com/shenweichen/DeepCTR.

the questions. Then, using as training data the partial learning traces of the remaining students ensures that the training involves all the students. But by testing on their latest answers, we approach the real use case, in which we want to forecast future answers based on the training history of the student.

Evaluation Metrics. We evaluate the average of the results obtained on each fold in terms of Accuracy (ACC) which measures the percentage of correct predictions out of the total number of predictions, Area Under the ROC Curve (AUC) which measures the probability of correctness of each answer, F1-score and execution time.

5.2 Results and Discussion

Table 1 shows the results of the evaluation of each model on the pediatrics subgraph, using the DeepFM algorithm. Columns "F1-score (pos.)" and "F1-score (ne.g.)" report the F1-score for the prediction of positive answers and negative answers respectively. The best results were obtained with the *sqawfdbb'TRQS* model (*students, questions, attempts, wins, fails, question difficulty, student abilities (static and progressive), questions_temb, answers_gemb, questions_gemb, students_gemb*), that is all of the features presented in Sect. 4 (AUC = 0.797, ACC = 0.796).

Table 1. Results for the pediatrics sub-graph. Models with the highest AUC are in bold.

Model	ACC	AUC	F1-score (neg.)	F1-score (pos.)	Execution time
sq	0.712	0.711	0.729	0.693	0:01:38
sqa	0.715	0.710	0.739	0.692	0:01:48
sqawf	0.710	0.708	0.729	0.686	0:02:05
sqawfd	0.736	0.734	0.752	0.716	0:02:12
sqawfb	0.709	0.708	0.727	0.687	0:02:15
sqawfb'	0.722	0.723	0.734	0.707	0:02:14
sqawfdbb'	0.745	0.742	0.767	0.718	0:02:38
sqawfdbb'T	0.696	0.696	0.713	0.675	0:06:52
sqawfdbb'R	0.764	0.763	0.780	0.745	0:03:49
sqawfdbb'Q	0.708	0.706	0.725	0.687	0:03:55
sqawfdbb'S	0.706	0.704	0.730	0.677	0:03:56
sqawfdbb'RQ	0.776	0.775	0.789	0.759	0:06:26
sqawfdbb'TRQ	0.781	0.780	0.794	0.765	0:12:09
sqawfdbb'RQS	0.790	0.788	0.803	0.773	0:08:22
sqawfdbb'TRQS	**0.797**	**0.796**	**0.811**	**0.779**	0:14:10

Beyond this overall result, comparing the scores obtained with each of the models can help us point out the contribution (positive, neutral or negative) of some of the features to the predictions:

question difficulty, student abilities: When comparing the results obtained with models *sqawf* and *sqawfdbb'*, we notice that adding the features *question_difficulty, static_student_ability* and *progressive_student_ability*, increases both the ACC and AUC by approximately 3%. In particular, by comparing the models *sqawfd, sqawfb* and *sqawfb'* we see that the largest improvement (2.6%) in terms of AUC and ACC is due to introduction of the feature *question_difficulty*, whereas *static_student_ability* has almost no effect on the quality of the prediction.

questions_temb: By comparing models *sqawfdbb'* and *sqawfdbb'T*, we notice that the results are significantly worse when including feature *questions_temb*: ACC and AUC both decrease by about 5%. This result is somehow counter-intuitive and may be related to the specificity and variety of medical vocabulary. To investigate further, additional experiments shall test the impact on word embeddings of techniques such as negative sampling, sub-sampling of common words or pre-processing to rewrite common medical expressions into single tokens.

Let us also underline that including this feature substantially increases the execution time of the classification algorithm.

questions_gemb: When comparing the results obtained with models *sqawfdbb'* and *sqawfdbb'Q*, we observe that this feature has a negative impact on the prediction results in terms of ACC, AUC and F1-score. Again, this negative impact can seem counter-intuitive, in particular when considering that the embeddings of the answers have a significant positive impact (as described afterwards).

students_gemb: Similarly, feature *students_gemb* seems to worsen the quality of the prediction. The values of ACC, AUC and F1-score are very close to those obtained when using *questions_gemb*, presenting a decrease of 4% w.r.t. the same model without graph embeddings (*sqawfdbb'*).

answers_gemb: Comparing the results obtained with models *sqawfdbb'* and *sqawfdbb'R* shows that this feature yields an improvement of 2% in terms of AUC and ACC. Also, a higher F1-score of 0.780 and 0.745 was obtained for the negative and positive responses respectively. Execution time remained low at 3 min approximately.

Although the contribution of the single features may seem negligible when they are considered separately, and, in some cases, even negative, the best performance in terms of ACC, AUC and F1-score is obtained when all the features are included in the model. Indeed, the best model *sqawfdbb'TRQS* presents an ACC and AUC around 80%, with a substantial increment (about 9%) when compared with the basic model (*sq*). It is also worth pointing out that even partial combinations of these newly added features bring significant improvements with respect to the models in which the single features are used alone.

For example, even though *students_gemb* and *questions_gemb* do not improve the quality of the prediction when used separately, they yield a 3.5% increase of ACC and AUC when used in conjunction with *answers_gemb*, as can be seen by comparing *sqawfdbb'R* and *sqawfdbb'RQS*. This could be explained by the fact that our model captures high-degree interactions between some features, interactions that, in some cases, turn out to be much more meaningful than the single features themselves.

Comparing the results of *sqawfdbb'RQS* and *sqawfdbb'TRQS* suggests that the improvement which *questions_temb* is accountable for is ancillary, while it entails a significant execution time increase (14 min for *sqawfdbb'TRQS* vs. 8 min for *sqawfdbb'RQS*). At a first sight, this may appear as a hindrance considering that we are only using a small fraction of the original data at our disposal. Nevertheless, we observe that, even with this small dataset, the quality of the prediction is fairly good. This suggests that, in the production environment of the SIDES platform, there shall be no need for training the algorithm on a much larger dataset in order to achieve good performance in the prediction task. We shall investigate further to determine a reasonable trade-off between the size of the dataset subset, the learning time and the quality of the prediction.

In order to validate our model and assess its flexibility with respect to the considered medical specialty, we trained and tested the DeepFM learning algorithm on the sub-graph related to the cardiovascular answers, extracted as described in Sect. 5.1.

Table 2. Results for the cardiovascular sub-graph. Models with the highest AUC are in bold.

Model	ACC	AUC	F1-score (neg.)	F1-score (pos.)	Execution time
sq	0.727	0.726	0.737	0.713	0:01:39
sqa	0.715	0.713	0.728	0.697	0:01:47
sqawf	0.719	0.718	0.730	0.705	0:02:05
sqawfd	0.741	0.741	0.750	0.730	0:02:54
sqawfb	0.720	0.719	0.733	0.705	0:02:55
sqawfb'	0.721	0.720	0.732	0.707	0:02:52
sqawfdbb'	0.746	0.745	0.757	0.733	0:02:12
sqawfdbb'T	0.701	0.701	0.714	0.687	0:07:04
sqawfdbb'R	0.770	0.769	0.778	0.759	0:03:49
sqawfdbb'Q	0.708	0.706	0.719	0.693	0:03:49
sqawfdbb'S	0.702	0.701	0.711	0.690	0:03:48
sqawfdbb'RQ	0.788	0.787	0.798	0.776	0:05:24
sqawfdbb'TRQ	0.791	0.789	0.798	0.781	0:10:18
sqawfdbb'RQS	0.796	0.795	0.806	0.784	0:07:00
sqawfdbb'TRQS	**0.799**	**0.798**	**0.808**	**0.789**	0:11:52

As it can be seen in Table 2, the results for this new specialty are consistent and confirm what we observed earlier for the pediatrics sub-graph. As for the previous experiments, the best model appears to be *sqawfdbb'TRQS*, including all the possible features, i.e. basic and computed features and both text and graph embeddings. It produces the highest values of ACC (0.799), AUC (0.798) and F1-score (0.808 and 0.789 for positive and negative classes respectively). The new results confirm the modest impact of the *questions_temb* feature, as can be seen by comparing the models *sqawfdbb'TRQS* and *sqawfdbb'RQS*. They also confirm the importance of the interactions between answers, questions and students graph embeddings. Indeed, in line with the previous case, we observe that, when used alone, features *questions_gemb* and *students_gemb* have a negative impact on the accuracy and AUC of the model, while when used together with *answers_gemb*, the quality of the prediction is improved.

To sum up, our experiments show that the best student model combines a set of basic features obtained by directly querying the *OntoSIDES* knowledge graph – questions, attempts, wins, fails –, a set of additional features computed based on the basic ones – question difficulty, student ability (static and progressive) –, and the vector representations of the answers, questions and students nodes in the *OntoSIDES* knowledge graph, as well as the vector representation of questions' text despite a modest impact.

6 Conclusions and Future Work

In this article, we have presented, evaluated and compared several models to predict the outcome of medical students' answers to questions in pediatrics and cardiovascular specialties, on the *SIDES* platform, with the final goal of answering the three research questions presented in Sect. 1. We have identified as the best model for our task the one based on Deep Knowledge Tracing Machines and relying on a rich set of features including state-of-the-art features such as wins, fails, questions' difficulties and students' abilities; textual information processed through NLP techniques (questions' text embeddings) and the structural knowledge provided by the OntoSIDES knowledge graph. In particular, we have shown that considering the vector representations of answers, questions and students nodes had a positive impact on the prediction results: when these three features are used in conjunction, the accuracy and AUC measures of the predictions made by the DeepFM algorithm improved significantly.

As future work, we intend to consider several leads of improvement. First, we plan to evaluate our approach with other state-of-the-art graph representation algorithms, such as Complex [19], ConvE [5] and LiteralE [9]. Second, we wish to further exploit the knowledge contained into the graph by taking into account not only the assertional knowledge but also the ontology. Furthermore, we wish to investigate the reason why some features, such as the graph embeddings of question nodes, have a limited impact when used alone, while the impact is more important when they are used jointly with embeddings of other nodes. We also plan to extend our evaluation to questions and answers from other medical specialties present in the *OntoSIDES* graph.

In the mid-term, we plan to identify other existing knowledge graphs containing medical training data to apply, evaluate and improve our approach. With respect to the *SIDES 3.0* project, our final goal, beyond predicting answers, is to use the resulting trained model to design an algorithm that, by considering additional criteria, will be able to recommend to medical students a customized learning path that automatically adapts to their learning objectives and their current progress.

Acknowledgement. This work is supported by the ANR DUNE project SIDES 3.0 (ANR-16-DUNE-0002-02).

References

1. Akbik, A., Blythe, D., Vollgraf, R.: Contextual string embeddings for sequence labeling. In: Proceedings of the 27th International Conference on Computational Linguistics (COLING 2018), pp. 1638–1649 (2018)
2. Bojanowski, P., Grave, E., Joulin, A., Mikolov, T.: Enriching word vectors with subword information. Trans. Assoc. Comput. Linguist. **5**, 135–146 (2017)
3. Cen, H., Koedinger, K., Junker, B.: Learning factors analysis – a general method for cognitive model evaluation and improvement. In: Ikeda, M., Ashley, K.D., Chan, T.-W. (eds.) ITS 2006. LNCS, vol. 4053, pp. 164–175. Springer, Heidelberg (2006). https://doi.org/10.1007/11774303_17
4. Corbett, A.T., Anderson, J.R.: Knowledge tracing: modeling the acquisition of procedural knowledge. User Model. User-Adap. Inter. **4**(4), 253–278 (1994). https://doi.org/10.1007/BF01099821
5. Dettmers, T., Minervini, P., Stenetorp, P., Riedel, S.: Convolutional 2D knowledge graph embeddings. In: Proceedings of the 32nd AAAI Conference on Artificial Intelligence (AAAI 2018) (2018)
6. Grover, A., Leskovec, J.: node2vec: Scalable Feature Learning for Networks. CoRR (2016). http://arxiv.org/abs/1607.00653
7. Guo, H., Tang, R., Ye, Y., Li, Z., He, X.: DeepFM: a factorization-machine based neural network for CTR prediction. In: Proceedings of the 26th International Joint Conference on Artificial Intelligence, pp. 1725–1731. Melbourne, Australia, August 2017. https://doi.org/10.24963/ijcai.2017/239
8. Hambleton, R., Swaminathan, H., Rogers, H.: Fundamentals of Item Response Theory. Measurement Methods for the Social Science. SAGE Publications (1991)
9. Kristiadi, A., Khan, M.A., Lukovnikov, D., Lehmann, J., Fischer, A.: Incorporating literals into knowledge graph embeddings. In: Ghidini, C., Hartig, O., Maleshkova, M., Svátek, V., Cruz, I., Hogan, A., Song, J., Lefrançois, M., Gandon, F. (eds.) ISWC 2019. LNCS, vol. 11778, pp. 347–363. Springer, Cham (2019). https://doi.org/10.1007/978-3-030-30793-6_20
10. LeCun, Y., Bengio, Y., Hinton, G.E.: Deep learning. Nature **521**(7553), 436–444 (2015). https://doi.org/10.1038/nature14539
11. Leskovec, J., Sosič, R.: SNAP: a general-purpose network analysis and graph-mining library. ACM Trans. Intell. Syst. Technol. (TIST) **8**(1), 1 (2016)
12. Novick, M.R.: The axioms and principal results of classical test theory. J. Math. Psychol. **3**(1), 1–18 (1966). https://doi.org/10.1016/0022-2496(66)90002-2

13. Palombi, O., Jouanot, F., Nziengam, N., Omidvar-Tehrani, B., Rousset, M.C., Sanchez, A.: OntoSIDES: ontology-based student progress monitoring on the national evaluation system of French Medical Schools. Artif. Intell. Med. **96**, 59–67 (2019)
14. Pavlik, P.I., Cen, H., Koedinger, K.R.: Performance factors analysis -a new alternative to knowledge tracing. In: Proceedings of the 2009 Conference on Artificial Intelligence in Education: Building Learning Systems That Care: From Knowledge Representation to Affective Modelling, pp. 531–538. IOS Press, Amsterdam (2009)
15. Piech, C., et al.: Deep knowledge tracing. In: Cortes, C., Lawrence, N.D., Lee, D.D., Sugiyama, M., Garnett, R. (eds.) Advances in Neural Information Processing Systems 28, pp. 505–513. Curran Associates, Inc. (2015)
16. Rasch, G.: Probabilistic Models for Some Intelligence and Attainment Tests. Studies in mathematical psychology, Danmarks Paedagogiske Institut (1960)
17. Reckase, M.D.: The past and future of multidimensional item response theory. Appl. Psychol. Meas. **21**(1), 25–36 (1997). https://doi.org/10.1177/0146621697211002
18. Rendle, S.: Factorization machines. In: Proceedings of the 2010 IEEE International Conference on Data Mining, pp. 995–1000. ICDM 2010. IEEE Computer Society, Washington, DC (2010). https://doi.org/10.1109/ICDM.2010.127
19. Trouillon, T., Dance, C.R., Welbl, J., Riedel, S., Gaussier, É., Bouchard, G.: Knowledge graph completion via complex tensor factorization. J. Mach. Learn. Res. abs/1702.06879 (2017)
20. Vie, J.J.: Deep factorization machines for knowledge tracing. In: Proceedings of the 13th Workshop on Innovative Use of NLP for Building Educational Applications. New Orleans, Louisiana (USA) (2018)
21. Vie, J.J., Kashima, H.: Knowledge tracing machines: factorization machines for knowledge tracing. In: Proceedings of the 33th AAAI Conference on Artificial Intelligence (AAAI 2019). Honolulu, Hawai (USA) (2019)
22. Wilson, K.H., Karklin, Y., Han, B., Ekanadham, C.: Back to the basics: Bayesian extensions of IRT outperform neural networks for proficiency estimation. In: Proceedings of the 9th International Conference on Educational Data Mining (EDM 2016). Association for Computational Linguistics, Raleigh (2016)

Position Papers

Coming to Terms with FAIR Ontologies
A Position Paper

María Poveda-Villalón[1]([✉]) [iD], Paola Espinoza-Arias[1]([✉]) [iD], Daniel Garijo[2] [iD],
and Oscar Corcho[1] [iD]

[1] Ontology Engineering Group, Universidad Politécnica de Madrid, Madrid, Spain
{mpoveda,pespinoza,ocorcho}@fi.upm.es
[2] Information Sciences Institute, University of Southern California, Los Angeles, USA
dgarijo@isi.edu

Abstract. Ontologies are widely used nowadays for many different purposes and in many different contexts, like industry and research, and in domains ranging from geosciences, biology, chemistry or medicine. When used for research, ontologies should be treated as other research artefacts, such as data, software, methods, etc.; following the same principles used to make them findable, accessible, interoperable and reusable (FAIR) to others. However, in comparison to the number of guides, indicators and recommendations available for making research data FAIR, not much attention has been paid so far on how to publish ontologies following the FAIR principles. This position paper reviews the technical and social needs required to define a roadmap for generating and publishing FAIR ontologies on the Web. We analyze four initiatives for ontology publication, aligning them in a common framework for comparison. The paper concludes by opening a discussion about existing, ongoing and required initiatives and instruments to facilitate FAIR ontology sharing on the Web.

Keywords: FAIR principles · Ontologies · Semantics

1 Introduction

Since its inception in 2016, the FAIR (Findable, Accessible, Interoperable, Reusable) data principles [35] have gained an increasing importance in the context of research data management, and are being adopted by a large number of private and public organisations worldwide, including initiatives such as the European Open Science Cloud[1] (EOSC) or the Research Data alliance[2] (RDA).

Ontologies play a relevant role in some of the FAIR data principles, especially in relation to providing support for data "interoperability" and "reusability". The need for ontologies (also called vocabularies) is pointed out in the

---

[1] https://www.eosc-portal.eu/.
[2] https://www.rd-alliance.org/.

© Springer Nature Switzerland AG 2020
C. M. Keet and M. Dumontier (Eds.): EKAW 2020, LNAI 12387, pp. 255–270, 2020.
https://doi.org/10.1007/978-3-030-61244-3_18

following principles: data and metadata should (I2)[3] use vocabularies that follow FAIR principles, (I1) use a formal, accessible, shared, and broadly applicable language for knowledge representation; (I3) include qualified references to other (meta)data, and (R1.3) meet domain-relevant community standards. Ontologies are also relevant in terms of "findability", (F2) requiring to describe data with rich metadata.

The research community has already acknowledged the need for ontologies to follow the FAIR principles [7]. First, there is a clear movement towards expanding the application of the FAIR principles beyond research data, as described in the ongoing EOSC Interoperability Framework [8]. Since ontologies are often the result of research activities or fundamental components in many areas of research, the FAIR principles should be applied to them, independently of whether they are used to describe data or metadata. Second, ontologies are already identified as a relevant artefact in the principles (even though the term *vocabulary* is used more generally and there is a general preference to talk about semantic artefacts, including thesauri, glossaries, shared UML models, etc.). Therefore, we consider that it is critical for the community to discuss and analyse how the FAIR principles should be applied to these artefacts.

However, we do not start from scratch when it comes to making ontologies available to others. Before the appearance and general acceptance of FAIR principles in research, many approaches had already focused on how to publish ontologies on the Web following Linked Data principles, ensuring the existence of permanent identifiers and making them available through standardised protocols like HTTP [4,18,21]. Other approaches focused on making ontologies findable by creating metadata schemas and ontologies to describe them and register them in ontology catalogues and repositories [9,16,22,28,32,34,37].

Some initial studies and reports on how to make ontologies FAIR have recently appeared [24,26]. For the time being they can be considered as initial proposals coming from working or interest groups under the umbrella of Open Science projects or initiatives (e.g., the FAIRsFAIR EU project,[4] the GO-FAIR implementation network GO-INTER,[5] the RDA Vocabulary Services Interest Group[6]). Other proposals like [11] focus mostly on the technical implementation of some of the FAIR principles. These initiatives are developing proposals and recommendations that may not necessarily fit the view of the Ontology Engineering community at large.

In this position paper we 1) argue that there is a need to open a broader and more open discussion of the technical and social consequences of adopting the FAIR principles for the publication and sharing of ontologies, and that such discussion should incorporate the views of the Ontology Engineering community;

---

[3] We point in parentheses to the principles numeration used in the original FAIR paper [35].

[4] https://fairsfair.eu/.

[5] https://www.go-fair.org/implementation-networks/overview/go-inter/.

[6] https://www.rd-alliance.org/groups/vocabulary-services-interest-group.html.

2) analyze and compare existing approaches for making ontologies FAIR; and 3) describe the challenges ahead.

We start the paper with a general review of the FAIR and LOD principles (Sect. 2), moving then into how they have been already considered in seminal approaches that focus on the FAIRification of ontologies, providing both the description of such approaches (Sect. 3) and a comparative analysis of them (Sect. 4). We discuss previous work that may be reused in this context; provide concrete recommendations needed in order to make ontologies FAIR; and expose what we consider to be the next steps towards developing a community recommendation on how to make ontologies FAIR (Sect. 5).

2   Background

The Linked Data principles[7] were proposed in 2006 as a set of guidelines for publishing and linking data on the Web [4]. The Linked Data principles may be summarized as: 1) use URIs for naming things, 2) use HTTP URIs to search things, 3) use standards (e.g., RDF) to provide useful information about URIs and 4) include links to other URIs. These principles were extended further in 2010, with the 5-star rating system for publishing Linked **Open** Data, which can be summarized as: make the data available in the Web with 1) an open licence, 2) in a machine readable manner, 3) in a non-proprietary format, 4) using RDF to identify and describe things and 5) linking to other data.

In 2016, the FAIR principles [35] were defined as a technology-agnostic and domain-independent guide to enhancing scientific data management and stewardship. Such principles are considered guidelines for those wishing to enhance the reusability of their data. In short, the four high-level FAIR principles stand that data must be easy to find, be accessible by standardized protocols, be machine-readable to enhance interoperability, and be well-described in order to be reusable for both humans and machines. The complete list of FAIR principles is provided in Annex A.

Despite both sets of principles having similar goals and definitions they also exhibit slight differences among them. Both approaches share the goal of using permanent identifiers to identify data (Uniform Resource Identifiers - URIs - for Linked Data, Persistent Identifiers - PIDs - for FAIR), and both promote using standards to provide further information about data, including references to other data. They also share the idea of using a standardized communication protocol to retrieve data (HTTP for Linked Data, and not specified for FAIR). Even though both approaches make explicit the need for licensing data, Linked Data principles are more restrictive in the sense than an open license is imposed while FAIR does not restrict any license permissions. However, unlike Linked Data, FAIR makes an explicit and strong focus on metadata management in order to enable resource findability and reusability. Finally, FAIR includes a set of principles to ease data and metadata findability, which are not covered by Linked Data principles. For further discussion about distinctions an overlaps

---

[7] https://www.w3.org/DesignIssues/LinkedData.html.

among LOD and FAIR principles we refer readers to the analysis provided by Hasnain and Rebholz-Schuhmann in 2018 [17].

3   Applying Linked Data and FAIR Principles for Publishing Semantic Artefacts

Throughout this document, we use the term *semantic artefact* to refer to a specification of a conceptualization that may be represented by different levels of formalization [27] (including controlled lists, thesauri and ontologies - either lightweight or heavyweight). This section describes the most relevant proposals to address the FAIRness of semantic artefacts as a complement to the FAIR data principles. This includes the ongoing effort from the FAIRsFAIR EU project [24] and the recent guidelines for publishing FAIR ontologies [11], released by co-authors of the present position paper. We also describe existing recommendations for improving the publication of ontologies on the Web. Even though there is a large number of methodologies, guidelines and techniques that may be reused and considered to publish FAIR ontologies, we only consider in this work those initiatives adapting the LOD 5-star schema for ontologies.

A full analysis of the existing methods, guidelines, techniques and tools available for FAIR ontologies may be subject of a dedicated systematic review, beyond the scope of this position paper.

3.1   FAIRsFAIR Recommendations for Ontology Publication

The FAIRsFAIR project, started in 2019, is a European effort aiming to provide practical solutions for the use of the FAIR data principles throughout the research data lifecycle. This project is in close cooperation with other ongoing European projects and several stakeholders to work in an overall knowledge infrastructure on academic quality data management, procedures, standards, metrics, and related matters based on the FAIR principles for the research data providers and repositories. FAIRsFAIR's activities include a specific task dedicated to semantic interoperability, with the aim to support the creation of a federated semantic space. In 2020, this task released a deliverable [24] that provides a list of 17 preliminary recommendations related to the application of FAIR principles to improve the global FAIRness of semantic artefacts. Each recommendation and best practice is related to one or more FAIR principles and links to existing recommendations and related stakeholders (e.g: practitioners, repositories or the Semantic Web community). The list of recommendations [24] includes:

P-Rec1: Use Globally Unique, Persistent and Resolvable Identifier for Semantic Artefacts, their content and their versions.
P-Rec2: Use Globally Unique, Persistent and Resolvable Identifier for Semantic Artefact Metadata Record.
P-Rec3: Use a common minimum metadata schema to describe semantic artefacts and their content.

P-Rec4: Publish the Semantic Artefact and its content in a semantic repository.

P-Rec5: Semantic repositories should offer a common API to access semantic artefacts and their content in various serializations for both use/reuse and indexation by any search engines.

P-Rec6: Build semantic artefacts' search engines that operate across different semantic repositories.

P-Rec7: Repositories should offer a secure protocol and user access control functionalities.

P-Rec8: Define human and machine-readable persistency policies for semantic artefacts metadata.

P-Rec9: Semantic artefacts should be represented using common serialization formats, e.g., Semantic Web and Linked Data standards.

P-Rec10: Use a Foundational Ontology to align semantic artefacts.

P-Rec11: Use a standardized language for describing semantic artefacts.

P-Rec12: Semantic mappings between the different elements of semantic artefacts should use machine-readable formats based on W3C standards.

P-Rec13: Crosswalks, mappings and bridging between semantic artefacts should be documented, published and curated.

P-Rec14: Use standard vocabularies to describe semantic artefacts.

P-Rec15: Make the references to the reused third-party semantic artefacts explicit.

P-Rec16: The semantic artefact should be clearly licensed for machines and humans.

P-Rec17: Provenance should be clear for both humans and machines.

The work proposed in [24] also identifies a list of 10 best practices (e.g use of naming conventions, use of ontology design patterns, workflows definition between formats, etc.) that go beyond the FAIR scope. Such practices are mostly inspired by the OBO foundry[8] and Industry Ontology Foundry principles[9] and are not necessarily related to any of the FAIR principles. Hence they fall out of scope of our analysis.

3.2 Best Practices for Implementing FAIR Vocabularies and Ontologies on the Web

A coetaneous effort with the FAIRsFAIR recommendation are the best practices for implementing vocabularies and ontologies on the Web [11]. In this work, specific practical guidelines are provided to help users in the following activities:

- Design of Accessible Ontology URIs
  1. Design ontology name and prefix
  2. Decide between hash or slash URIs
  3. Decide whether to use opaque URIs

---

[8] http://www.obofoundry.org/principles/fp-000-summary.html.
[9] https://www.industrialontologies.org/?page_id=87.

4. Define an ontology versioning strategy
5. Use of permanent URIs
- Generate reusable ontology documentation
  6. Generate ontology metadata
  7. Generate HTML documentation
  8. Generate diagrams
- Publish an ontology on the Web
  9. Provide the ontology online in multiple formats (HTML and ontology serializations)
  10. Make the ontology findable on the Web

3.3 Initiatives for 5-Star Vocabularies

The 5-star schema for publishing Linked Open Data has been adapted to vocabularies by two different approaches. More precisely, the first approach of 5-star vocabularies was published by Bernard Vatant as a blog post[10] in 2012. The proposed 5-stars for vocabularies are defined as follows:

1. ☆ Publish your vocabulary on the Web at a stable URI with a open license.[11]
2. ☆☆ Provide human-readable documentation and basic metadata such as creator, publisher, date of creation, last modification, version number.
3. ☆☆☆ Provide labels and descriptions, if possible in several languages, to make your vocabulary usable in multiple linguistic scopes.
4. ☆☆☆☆ Make your vocabulary available via its namespace URI, both as a formal file and human-readable documentation, using content negotiation.
5. ☆☆☆☆☆ Link to other vocabularies by re-using elements rather than re-inventing.

Later, in 2014, an editorial paper from the Semantic Web Journal [21] adapted the idea of 5-stars for vocabularies to the following schema:

1. ☆ There is dereferenceable human-readable information about the used vocabulary.
2. ☆☆ The information is available as machine-readable explicit axiomatization of the vocabulary.
3. ☆☆☆ The vocabulary is linked to other vocabularies.
4. ☆☆☆☆ Metadata about the vocabulary is available (in a dereferencable and machine-readable form).
5. ☆☆☆☆☆ The vocabulary is linked to by other vocabularies.

---

[10] https://bvatant.blogspot.com/2012/02/is-your-linked-data-vocabulary-5-star_9588.html.

[11] Note that the "open license" is added to the first star as a comment by the author as a reaction to the feedback, but not shown in the original list.

While these vocabulary-oriented 5-star schemes have not been widely adopted by the community so far, they are often referred to by reviewers when assessing ontology papers for journals and conferences, and ontology repositories are promoting their use. For example, in the Linked Open Vocabularies [32] registry, a vocabulary should 1) be written in RDF and be dereferenceable; 2) be parsed without errors; 3) provide `rdfs:label` for all of its terms; 4) refer to and reuse relevant existing vocabularies; and 5) provide some metadata. These constraints force authors to follow the stars 1, 2, 3 and 5 from 2012; although it does not force authors to provide human readable documentation with content negotiation nor an open license. Another case is the Smart Cities ontology catalogue [29], where quality indicators are established for ontologies taking into account: a) whether an ontology is available on the Web, in RDF and/or HTML: b) whether an ontology follows the W3C standards (e.g., RDF-S or OWL); and c) whether an ontology is available under an open license.

4   An Analysis Framework for FAIR Ontologies

In this section we discuss and compare the initiatives described in Sect. 3, with the aim of providing insight and food for thought for the next wave of recommendations to be made for the FAIRification of semantic artefacts. We review each of the initiatives and align them with the FAIR principles. The results of our analysis are shown in Table 1, where FAIR principles are listed in columns and guidelines are listed in rows, grouped by initiatives. The numbering of the guidelines corresponds to the numbering provided in Sect. 3 and all FAIR principles are listed in Annex A.[12] The values provided for each cell are: "x" when a guideline (row) and a FAIR principle (column) have similar scope; "<" to indicate that the guideline is less strict than the principle; and ">" to indicate that the guideline is more strict than the principle.

Since the FAIR principles focus on data (and its related metadata) and the analyzed initiatives target semantic artefacts (including ontologies), we have considered that a semantic artefact corresponds to the term 'data' in the principles.

Note that the table values for the FAIRsFAIR guidelines have been taken from the original draft publication [24]. The table includes question marks (highlighted in bold blue letters in Table 1) for matches that are not clear to the authors and that will be subject to further discussion below. For the rest of the initiatives, the cell values presented in this table reflect the agreement by the authors and incorporate external feedback and comments from other colleagues at the Ontology Engineering Group at UPM.

The following mismatches have been found between [24] and our understanding of the guidelines and the FAIR principles. It is worth noting that these mismatches, among others, haven been also reported and discussed with FAIRsFAIR representatives and will be reported publicly in the corresponding GitHub repositories when made available, as agreed with them. Indeed, we have included this

---

[12] To ease the reading of the rest of the paper we recommend to have the FAIR principles list (Annex A) and Sect. 3 at hand.

discussion on mismatches in this paper since it shows the need for an extensive discussion on this topic. In our opinion:

- P-REC12, P-REC13 and P-REC14 relations with the FAIR principles may be revised. Our proposals are: **A)** P-REC12 may be related to I3 and I1 instead of R1.3. The reason is that P-REC12 describes the need for machine-readable descriptions of the mappings, what is more related to interoperability than to community standards. **B)** P-REC13 may be related to I3 instead of R1.3. The rationale behind this is that P-REC13 describes the need for documenting mappings and also mentions sharing such resources. This seems to be more related to interoperability than to community standards, as discussed for the case of P-REC12. **C)** P-REC14 may also be linked to R1.3, since the recommendation explicitly refers to relevant community standards to be used to describe semantic artefacts.
- P-REC10 is related to interoperability principles, emphasizing the need to align semantic artefacts to foundational ontologies, such as DOLCE [5] or UFO [15]. While we acknowledge the benefits that foundational ontologies may bring into ontology development, first, we consider this as a very strong requirement at this stage, considering that many domain ontology developers may have difficulties to understand how to align their semantic artefacts to these ontologies, as shown by the small amount of published ontologies that are currently aligned to them. Second, we think that the definition of foundational ontology could be broaden so that it includes reference ontologies that are well-adopted within some communities, such as the case of schema.org [13], Wikidata, etc. Taking this into account, the description of P-REC10 may be relaxed to emphasize the benefits of linking to foundational ontologies rather than the need to do it, that is stating it as a possibility rather than an obligation.
- P-REC9 and P-REC11 present some inaccuracies when analysed from a Semantic Web perspective. First, P-REC11 is entitled "use a standardised language for describing semantic artefacts" pointing to SHACL [23], SWRL[13] and OntoUML [14]. SHACL is the only official recommendation from a standardisation body, while RDF(S) [6] and OWL [3,19] are mentioned in P-REC9. Second, P-REC9 mentions that semantic artefacts should be represented using common serializations formats, however from the Semantic Web perspective the different serializations of an ontology or dataset are just different ways of implementing them in a particular format and syntax, but the semantics are equivalent and are defined by the ontology language, not the serialization. The rationale behind P-REC9 seems to promote the use of standardised ontology implementation languages for defining semantic artefacts and for P-REC11 to extend them with more complex languages when the former are not enough. Hence our proposal would be to merge both recommendations into one proposing the use of standardized languages like RDF(S) and OWL for implementing ontologies, extending them with SHACL for constraint definitions if applicable, and using SKOS [2] for the implementation

---

[13] https://www.w3.org/Submission/SWRL/.

of thesauri. Some mentions may then be included to other initiatives, not yet standardized, like SWRL, or SheX.[14]

Table 1. Relationship between initiatives for FAIR semantic artefacts and FAIR principles. In the guidelines the row numbering corresponds to the numbering provided in Sect. 3 and the FAIR principles column numbering corresponds to the list provided in Annex A.

	Guidelines ↓	FAIR Principles														
		F1	F2	F3	F4	A1	A1.1	A1.2	A2	I1	I2	I3	R1	R1.1	R1.2	R1.3
FAIRsFAIR	P-Rec1	x														
	P-Rec2	x		x												
	P-Rec3		x										x	x	x	x
	P-Rec4				x											
	P-Rec5				x	x	x									
	P-Rec6				x											
	P-Rec7					x										
	P-Rec8							x								
	P-Rec9								x							
	P-Rec10								x	x	x					
	P-Rec11								x							
	P-Rec12								x		x					x?
	P-Rec13										?				x	x?
	P-Rec14									x						?
	P-Rec15										x			x		
	P-Rec16											x				
	P-Rec17													x		
FAIR ontologies	1	x														
	2	x														
	3	x														
	4										x					
	5	x														
	6		x						x		x		x	x	x	x
	7				x					x	x					
	8										x					
	9				x				x							
	10				x											x
5-stars 2012	1	<				>								>		
	2											x				
	3		x									x				
	4	<				x	x		x							
	5													x		
5-stars 2014	1					x										
	2					x			x							
	3										x					
	4					x					x					
	5															

Furthermore, we have additional comments related to some other principles.

– F3 encourages making clear and explicit references from the metadata to the data. This is poorly addressed by the guidelines, being absent from the Semantic Web oriented guidelines (FAIR ontology, and the 5-stars schemas). This may be a consequence of the fact that in the Semantic Web, ontology metadata is commonly embedded in the ontology itself and not as a first-class citizen, and would be retrieved by looking up the ontology URIs, therefore there is no clear need for this link.

---

[14] http://shex.io/shex-primer/.

- A1.2 and A2 are also lacking guidelines. On the one hand, A1.2 is not described in the 5-stars2012 because it is assumed that the vocabulary will be open (star 1). In addition, all the Semantic Web oriented guidelines assume HTTP and HTTPS as protocols to share the semantic artefacts. On the other hand, the absence of A2 is related to the fact that usually ontologies themselves contain their metadata together in a unique artefact, as discussed above.

Finally, it should be mentioned that the fifth star from the schema proposed by [21] is not related to any of the principles. The reason is that the star states that the vocabulary should be linked to by other vocabularies and this is a measure of the success of the vocabulary after being published rather than recommendation or an action to be taken by the developers or publishers. That is, even though it is related to interoperability, it is not related to any principle in particular as there is no equivalent principle stating that the data should be linked back from other data.

5   Towards FAIR Ontology Engineering Practices

This Section aims at providing a summary of the items that we consider that should be further discussed by the Ontology Engineering (OE) and Open Science (OS) communities, so as to propose our contributions towards a unified recommendation on how to make ontologies FAIR.

To be Findable

The F1 principle refers to using globally unique and persistent identifiers. In the OE community URIs are already used to refer to one ontology or SKOS schema, and sometimes for their elements as well. This practice complies with the "unique" definition of FAIR, which means that an identifier refers to only one entity. It is worth noting that the use of "unique" in the FAIR principles is different from (and compatible with) the meaning of "unique" in the non-unique naming assumption used in OWL, which means that one entity may be identified by more than one name. Regarding persistence, even though there are good practices and services (w3id or purl) for generating permanent URIs, no strict rules are defined to ensure persistence and no mechanisms as the use of DOIs are established to persist URIs. The Semantic Web community background on the Web of documents has modelled the practitioners to understand and work with the Web as a living ecosystem, where resources may disappear, in contrast to other communities that are more oriented to archiving and preservation practices. In order to align this principle to the publication of semantic artefacts, the following questions should be subject to discussion: Should the Semantic Web community establish mechanisms and authorities to coin persistent identifiers (PIDs) for semantic artefacts? Should these PIDs refer only to semantic artefacts as a whole or also to each of their components (e.g., specific concepts or properties, specific SKOS concepts)?

The F2 principle refers to describing data with rich metadata. As documented in [20] F2 refers to metadata to allow for data findability in contrast to metadata to improve its reusability, which is mentioned in principle R1. In this sense the OE community should agree on a minimum set of metadata that semantic artefacts should have. This does not imply imposing a specific vocabulary, but defining which attributes (e.g., license, title, creators, etc.) the community considers as crucial for ensuring findability of a semantic artefact. For example, the WIDOCO Best Practices[15] recommend stating the creator(s) of an ontology, which can be identified by using `dcterms:creator`, `dc:creator`, `schema:creator`, `prov:wasAttributedTo` or `pav:createdBy`. In this sense, DCAT or Dublin Core should be considered as reference vocabularies for providing metadata, however some communities might use their own common vocabularies. Finally, it is also needed to provide more practical guidelines for declaring metadata, for example generating templates, of how these annotations are implemented in each case and defining clearly what is embedded in semantic artefacts, for example in OWL ontologies.

Nowadays, the F3 principle is not applicable to ontologies because in practice they contain the metadata that describes them, both as a resource and for each ontology element defined. Therefore, the question here is in which cases metadata should be provided as a separate object? This principle might not be applicable from the Semantic Web perspective unless we refer to metadata assets managed by third-party applications like ontology indexes and registries rather than the metadata provided by ontology publishers.

F4 suggests that data and metadata are indexed in searchable resources. While there are general ontology registries and community or domain oriented ones, a federation model for ontologies should be defined. Regarding repositories and search engines that would be needed to find semantic artefacts, P-REC6 proposes to build search engines to operate across distributed and heterogeneous repositories. However no existing recommendations are listed for this. For doing this some federation models existing for data as for example the European Data Portal,[16] based on DCAT, or the JoinUp initiative, based on ADMS, may be considered as examples. For the semantic artefacts case the DCAT2 vocabulary[17] may be used for the federation system. This federation mechanism would be closely related to the F2 principle regarding the agreement on metadata for findability. Other practice to be taken into account is the inclusion of metadata in the form of JSON-LD [30] snippets within the HTML describing ontologies in order to be indexed by web search engines, as it is currently done by WIDOCO [10] and Agroportal [22]. Finally, any of these federation approaches may be combined with the idea of de-centralized web exposed in [33] in which each semantic artefact owner will store and manage the data about the published artefact to be integrated by third party registries or applications. Standard definitions of

---

[15] https://w3id.org/widoco/bestPractices.
[16] European Data Portal https://www.europeandataportal.eu/en.
[17] https://www.w3.org/TR/vocab-dcat-2.

SAODs (Semantic Artefact Online Data[18]) should be created as well as SAODs discovery approaches.

To be Accessible

Ontologies published following the Semantic Web technologies and best practices use HTTP URIs as identifiers and are shared under HTTP or HTTPS protocols; complying with A1, A1.1, A1.2 principles. These already existing technologies and protocols are suggested to be adopted by FAIR implementations.

The A2 principle requires keeping metadata accessible even when the data is no longer available. This principle clashes with the (Semantic) Web aspect where resources as ontologies may become unavailable at any moment, as it happens for websites. Complying to this principle would involve developing registries or infrastructures to act as ontology libraries, to preserve the metadata. From the Semantic Web perspective, having preservation policies (for example how long a semantic artefact will be preserved, what version will be retained, what serialization formats will be stored, etc.) for publishing resources may be a good practice to adopt [1].

To be Interoperable

To be compliant with the I1 principle, semantic artefacts should use knowledge representation languages proposed by a standardization body, such as W3C. To this end, as commented in Sect. 3 in regards with P-REC9 and P-REC11, well-known W3C recommendations like RDF(S) and OWL are used for implementing ontologies, and SKOS [2] for thesauri. In addition, SHACL may be used to extend ontologies with additional data constraints definitions.

The I2 principle states that (meta)data should use vocabularies that follow FAIR principles. An attempt to translate this principle to ontologies would be recommending the reuse of FAIR semantic artefacts to the extent possible, in addition to the common practice about reusing ontologies that follow best practices and Linked Data principles. This also applies to the reuse of other ontologies for annotating ontology metadata. This leads us to the need of indicators that describe compliance with FAIR principles in order to decide whether an ontology is FAIR, such as the ones proposed by the RDA maturity model [12]. Therefore, validators should be developed to automatically compute these indicators, such as proposed in [36]. However, this principle should not force to reuse only (and at least one) FAIR vocabulary, as circular references would appear, that is, if a vocabulary should (re)use other FAIR vocabularies, how would be the first FAIR vocabulary be considered as such?

In order to comply with I3, ontologies should include qualified references to other ontologies. The Semantic Web technologies already provide a number of mechanisms to refer to other ontologies. When referring to another ontology element URI the reference is explicit and in addition the relations could be

---

[18] Acronym adapted from the PODs defined in [33] as Personal Online Data.

explicit by using `owl:equivalentClass`, `owl:equivalentProperty` or the different relations for SKOS concepts. Finally, the `owl:import` construct also allows for referring to (and importing) other ontologies explicitly and in a machine readable way.

To be Reusable

The minimum set of metadata mentioned in F2 should also contain the minimum attributes to assess whether a semantic artefact is appropriate for reuse as required by R1. For example, provenance, term detailed descriptions (usually included in the ontologies by using `rdfs:comment` annotations), rationales behind the inclusion of terms, examples of use, etc. In addition, the community should suggest vocabularies that could be used to represent such fields and the mappings between such vocabularies. Ontologies should rely on the human oriented complementary documentation such as examples of use and diagrams of the conceptualizations to ease the task of understanding the model represented in the code to potential users. Therefore, there is a need for research towards best practices to document and communicate ontologies.

Taking into account that FAIR advocates for the reuse of data as much as possible, it is advisable to provide minimum information about the permissions and conditions included in the licenses of semantic artefacts to be considered FAIR compliant with R1.1. Also, such license descriptions should be linked from the resources and provided in RDF. This could be done in two ways. The simplest way would be providing a link to the applicable license URI, which in the best case scenario would be described in RDF. A more complete way would be providing the RDF description of the license (what it is allowed, or not, and under which conditions) using vocabularies as the Creative Commons vocabulary[19] or ODRL [31].

To comply with principle R1.2 the W3C already provides the PROV-O ontology and standard specification [25] that should be adopted.

Meeting domain-relevant standards, as defined in R1.3, might refer to technological ones like the use of RDF(S) and OWL to describe ontologies as already proposed in I1. However, standards may involve another aspects which will depend on the communities. For example, in the OBO community there is a standard way of naming ontology elements while in the Semantic Web community the rule is to keep the naming convention, whichever is chosen, consistent. This principle is also related to the minimum set of metadata already defined in several communities [20]. Therefore, there is a need here for each community to agree on common standards and best practices to follow in regard to ontology engineering.

Summarizing, to pave the path for FAIR semantics publishing, understanding and exploitation, the OE community needs to:

- Agree on a minimum set of metadata suggesting vocabularies to represent it and provide more technical guidelines for its declaration.

---

[19] https://creativecommons.org/ns.

- Define a federation model for ontologies that may be combined with standard definitions of SAODs as well as SAODs discovery approaches.
- Define and adopt preservation policies for publishing resources together with mechanisms to determine whether this preservation is fulfilled.
- Use knowledge representation languages from standardization bodies.
- Define FAIR indicators for semantic artefacts.
- Define best practices to document and communicate ontologies.

Finally, the following questions remain open for discussion: 1) should the Semantic Web community establish mechanisms and authorities to coin persistent identifiers (PIDs) for semantic artefacts? and 2) in which cases metadata should be provided as a separate object and whether to define third party certification agencies is needed?

Acknowledgments. This work has been supported by a Predoctoral grant from the I+D+i program of the Universidad Politécnica de Madrid and the Spanish project DATOS 4.0: RETOS Y SOLUCIONES (TIN2016-78011-C4-4-R). Authors would like to thank Yann Le Franc for his clarifications and explanations about the FAIRsFAIR recommendations content and their development process and OEG, especially Victor Rodríguez Doncel, for all the valuable comments.

A   Annex: FAIR Principles

The list of FAIR guiding principles defined in [35] is:

- To be Findable
  - F1. (meta)data are assigned a globally unique and persistent identifier
  - F2. data are described with rich metadata (defined by R1 below)
  - F3. metadata clearly and explicitly include the identifier of the data it describes
  - F4. (meta)data are registered or indexed in a searchable resource
- To be Accesible
  - A1. (meta)data are retrievable by their identifier using a standardized communications protocol
  - A1.1 the protocol is open, free, and universally implementable
  - A1.2 the protocol allows for an authentication and authorization procedure, where necessary
  - A2. metadata are accessible, even when the data are no longer available
- To be Interoperable
  - I1. (meta)data use a formal, accessible, shared, and broadly applicable language for knowledge representation.
  - I2. (meta)data use vocabularies that follow FAIR principles
  - I3. (meta)data include qualified references to other (meta)data
- To be Reusable
  - R1. meta(data) are richly described with a plurality of accurate and relevant attributes
  - R1.1. (meta)data are released with a clear and accessible data usage license
  - R1.2. (meta)data are associated with detailed provenance
  - R1.3. (meta)data meet domain-relevant community standards

References

1. Baker, T., Vandenbussche, P.Y., Vatant, B.: Requirements for vocabulary preservation and governance. Library Hi Tech **31**(4), 657–668 (2013)
2. Bechhofer, S., Miles, A.: SKOS simple knowledge organization system reference. W3C recommendation, W3C (2009)
3. Bechhofer, S., et al.: OWL web ontology language reference. W3C recommendation **10**(02) (2004)
4. Bizer, C., Heath, T., Berners-Lee, T.: Linked data: the story so far. In: Semantic Services, Interoperability and Web Applications: Emerging Concepts, pp. 205–227. IGI Global (2011)
5. Borgo, S., Masolo, C.: Foundational choices in DOLCE. In: Staab, S., Studer, R. (eds.) Handbook on Ontologies. IHIS, pp. 361–381. Springer, Heidelberg (2009). https://doi.org/10.1007/978-3-540-92673-3_16
6. Brickley, D., Guha, R.V., McBride, B.: RDF Schema 1.1. W3C recommendation 25 (2014)
7. Collins, S., et al.: Turning FAIR into reality: final report and action plan from the European Commission expert group on FAIR data (2018). https://doi.org/10.2777/54599
8. Corcho, O., et al.: EOSC interoperability framework, May 2020. https://www.eoscsecretariat.eu/sites/default/files/eosc-interoperability-framework-v1.0.pdf
9. Côté, R.G., Jones, P., Apweiler, R., Hermjakob, H.: The Ontology Lookup Service, a lightweight cross-platform tool for controlled vocabulary queries. BMC Bioinform. **7**(1), 97 (2006)
10. Garijo, D.: WIDOCO: a wizard for documenting ontologies. In: d'Amato, C., et al. (eds.) ISWC 2017. LNCS, vol. 10588, pp. 94–102. Springer, Cham (2017). https://doi.org/10.1007/978-3-319-68204-4_9
11. Garijo, D., Poveda-Villalón, M.: Best practices for implementing FAIR vocabularies and ontologies on the Web, March 2020. https://arxiv.org/abs/2003.13084
12. Group, F.D.M.M.W.: FAIR Data Maturity Model: specification and guidelines, April 2020. https://doi.org/10.15497/RDA00045
13. Guha, R.V., Brickley, D., Macbeth, S.: Schema.org: evolution of structured data on the web. Commun. ACM **59**(2), 44–51 (2016)
14. Guizzardi, G.: Ontological foundations for structural conceptual models (2005)
15. Guizzardi, G., Wagner, G.: Towards ontological foundations for agent modelling concepts using the unified fundational ontology (UFO). In: Bresciani, P., Giorgini, P., Henderson-Sellers, B., Low, G., Winikoff, M. (eds.) AOIS -2004. LNCS (LNAI), vol. 3508, pp. 110–124. Springer, Heidelberg (2005). https://doi.org/10.1007/11426714_8
16. Hartmann, J., Sure, Y., Haase, P., Palma, R., Suarez-Figueroa, M.: OMV-ontology metadata vocabulary. In: ISWC, vol. 3729 (2005)
17. Hasnain, A., Rebholz-Schuhmann, D.: Assessing FAIR data principles against the 5-star open data principles. In: Gangemi, A., et al. (eds.) ESWC 2018. LNCS, vol. 11155, pp. 469–477. Springer, Cham (2018). https://doi.org/10.1007/978-3-319-98192-5_60
18. Heath, T., Bizer, C.: Linked data: evolving the web into a global data space. Synth. Lect. Semantic Web: Theory Technol. **1**(1), 1–136 (2011)
19. Hitzler, P., et al.: OWL 2 web ontology language primer. W3C Recommendation **27**(1), 123 (2009)

20. Jacobsen, A., et al.: FAIR principles: interpretations and implementation considerations. Data Intell. **2**(1–2), 10–29 (2020). https://doi.org/10.1162/dint_r_00024
21. Janowicz, K., et al.: Five stars of linked data vocabulary use. Semantic Web **5**(3), 173–176 (2014)
22. Jonquet, C., et al.: Agroportal: a vocabulary and ontology repository for agronomy. Comput. Electron. Agric. **144**, 126–143 (2018)
23. Knublauch, H., Kontokostas, D.: Shapes constraint language (SHACL). World Wide Web Consortium recommendation (2017)
24. Le Franc, Y., Parland-von Essen, J., Bonino, L., Lehväslaiho, H., Coen, G., Staiger, C.: D2.2 FAIR semantics: first recommendations, March 2020. https://doi.org/10.5281/zenodo.3707985
25. Lebo, T., et al.: Prov-o: The prov ontology. W3C recommendation (2013)
26. Lehväslaiho, et al.: D2.1 Report on FAIR requirements for persistence and interoperability 2019, November 2019. https://doi.org/10.5281/zenodo.3557381
27. McGuinness, D.L.: Ontologies come of age. In: Spinning the Semantic Web: Bringing the World Wide Web to Its Full Potential, pp. 171–194. MIT Press, Cambridge (2002)
28. Palma, R., Haase, P.: Oyster – sharing and re-using ontologies in a peer-to-peer community. In: Gil, Y., Motta, E., Benjamins, V.R., Musen, M.A. (eds.) ISWC 2005. LNCS, vol. 3729, pp. 1059–1062. Springer, Heidelberg (2005). https://doi.org/10.1007/11574620_77
29. Poveda-Villalón, M., García-Castro, R., Gómez-Pérez, A.: Building an ontology catalogue for smart cities. In: Proceedings of the 10th European Conference on Product and Process Modelling, ECPPM 2014, pp. 1–8 (2014)
30. Sporny, M., Longley, D., Kellogg, G., Lanthaler, M., Lindström, N.: JSON-LD 1.0: a JSON-based serialization for linked data. World Wide Web Consortium recommendation (2014)
31. Steidl, M., Iannella, R., Myles, S., Rodríguez-Doncel, V.: ODRL vocabulary & expression 2.2. W3C recommendation, W3C, February 2018
32. Vandenbussche, P.Y., Atemezing, G.A., Poveda-Villalón, M., Vatant, B.: Linked open vocabularies (LOV): a gateway to reusable semantic vocabularies on the Web. Semantic Web **8**(3), 437–452 (2017)
33. Verborgh, R.: Re-decentralizing the Web, for good this time. In: Seneviratne, O., Hendler, J. (eds.) Linking the World's Information: Tim Berners-Lee's Invention of the World Wide Web. ACM (2020). https://ruben.verborgh.org/articles/redecentralizing-the-web/
34. Whetzel, P.L., et al.: Bioportal: enhanced functionality via new web services from the National Center for Biomedical Ontology to access and use ontologies in software applications. Nucleic Acids Res. **39**(Suppl_2), W541–W545 (2011)
35. Wilkinson, M.D., et al.: The FAIR Guiding Principles for scientific data management and stewardship. Sci. Data **3** (2016)
36. Wilkinson, M.D., et al.: Evaluating FAIR maturity through a scalable, automated, community-governed framework. Sci. Data **6**(1), 1–12 (2019)
37. Xiang, Z., Mungall, C., Ruttenberg, A., He, Y.: Ontobee: a linked data server and browser for ontology terms. In: ICBO (2011)

Challenges of Linking Organizational Information in Open Government Data to Knowledge Graphs

Jan Portisch[1]([✉])(iD), Omaima Fallatah[2](iD), Sebastian Neumaier[3](iD),
Mohamad Yaser Jaradeh[5](iD), and Axel Polleres[3,4](iD)

[1] Data and Web Science Group, University of Mannheim, Mannheim, Germany
jan@informatik.uni-mannheim.de
[2] Information School, The University of Sheffield, Sheffield, UK
oafallatah1@sheffield.ac.uk
[3] Vienna University of Economics and Business, Vienna, Austria
{sebastian.neumaier,axel.polleres}@wu.ac.at
[4] Complexity Science Hub Vienna, Vienna, Austria
[5] L3S Research Center, Leibniz University Hannover, Hanover, Germany
jaradeh@l3s.de

Abstract. Open Government Data (OGD) is being published by various public administration organizations around the globe. Within the metadata of OGD data catalogs, the publishing organizations (1) are not uniquely and unambiguously identifiable and, even worse, (2) change over time, by public administration units being merged or restructured. In order to enable fine-grained analyzes or searches on Open Government Data on the level of publishing organizations, linking those from OGD portals to publicly available knowledge graphs (KGs) such as *Wikidata* and *DBpedia* seems like an obvious solution. Still, as we show in this position paper, organization linking faces significant challenges, both in terms of available (portal) metadata and KGs in terms of data quality and completeness. We herein specifically highlight five main challenges, namely regarding (1) temporal changes in organizations and in the portal metadata, (2) lack of a base ontology for describing organizational structures and changes in public knowledge graphs, (3) metadata and KG data quality, (4) multilinguality, and (5) disambiguating public sector organizations. Based on available OGD portal metadata from the *Open Data Portal Watch*, we provide an in-depth analysis of these issues, make suggestions for concrete starting points on how to tackle them along with a call to the community to jointly work on these open challenges.

Keywords: Open data · Dataset evolution · Entity linking · Knowledge graphs · Knowledge graph evolution

1 Introduction

Open Data from public administrations, also called *Open Government Data* (OGD), provides a rich source of structured data that has become a key com-

© Springer Nature Switzerland AG 2020
C. M. Keet and M. Dumontier (Eds.): EKAW 2020, LNAI 12387, pp. 271–286, 2020.
https://doi.org/10.1007/978-3-030-61244-3_19

ponent of an evolving Web of Data. The key factors for the success of OGD initiatives are on the one hand the incentives for publishing organizations to demonstrate transparency or compliance to regulations, but on the other hand also the availability of agreed standards and best practices for publishing OGD: de facto publishing standards for metadata on OGD portals such as *DCAT* or, more recently, Schema.org's dataset vocabulary [3], as well as widely used open publishing software frameworks such as *CKAN* or *Socrata*, provide technical means to publish structured data along with descriptive metadata. There are over 250 (governmental) portals worldwide relying on these software frameworks for describing and publishing datasets [16]. Yet, as more and more data is becoming available, findability, as well as quality and trust are of utmost importance in order to utilize the data. While in terms of findability, metadata about the temporal and geo-spatial scope of datasets are most relevant [10,15], *provenance* information has to be known to assess the trustworthiness of OGD. This is usually done in the form of giving a speaking label of the publishing body in the metadata. For instance, "European Commission" is mentioned as a publisher of 12,448 datasets on https://data.europa.eu/; an organization that can be uniquely referenced also in existing knowledge graphs (KGs) such as DBpedia (`dbr:/European_Commission`)[1] or Wikidata (`Q8880`), however, such links are not (yet) explicit. Moreover, in other cases, different publishing organizations within the metadata have non-descriptive names such as "Parlament"[2] (on https://data.gv.at/), which only in the context of the portal itself make sense.[3] Apparently, the publisher here actually refers to the *Austrian Parliament*. Alternatively, in other cases in addition, the contact information (e.g. an e-mail address or URL) found in the metadata can provide additional context on the publishing organization.

Summarizing, organizational information is usually not yet standardized in OGD portals by means of unique identifiers. Notably, this problem is aggravated by the fact that public bodies – just as any institution – are affected by *organizational changes*, that is, for instance ministries are being merged or restructured, and, therefore, the publishers may change over time and across different versions of datasets. Overall, this means that, while several qualitative comparisons of Open Data initiatives exist on a country level[4], tracking the success of Open Data policies on the level of publishing organizations, or, respectively, tracking the development of these organizations in terms of mergers and re-structuring is hardly possible at the moment.

We argue that unambiguously linking Open Data publishers to URIs in public KGs would both increase findability of datasets (e.g. queries for datasets by statistical offices located in the European Union would be possible) as well as

---

[1] URL prefixes such as `dbo:`, `dbp:`, `wdt:`, or `schema:` can be referenced in `prefix.cc`.
[2] German writing of the English word "parliament".
[3] As https://data.gv.at/ is the Austrian national data portal, the label "Parlament" refers to the Austrian parliament.
[4] cf. for instance http://opendatamonitor.eu or
http://europeandataportal.eu/dashboard.

make it easier for data consumers to trust in the data, given reliable provenance information. Additionally, advanced queries for dataset monitoring and analyses would become possible. Lastly, even changes in organizations (such as mergers and renamings) would be less confusing for dataset users as long as the organizations still remain correctly linked. We therefore believe that linking Open Government Data and metadata with entities found in open KGs could be a solution to the stated ambiguity problems. Yet, to the best of our knowledge, neither the coverage of OGD publishing organizations, nor the specific challenges of this organizational linking problem have been investigated so far. The focus of of the present position paper is therefore to study the feasibility and main open research problems for providing working solutions in this area. More concretely, we identify five challenges that are yet to be solved when linking organizations of public datasets to knowledge graphs, for each of which, we discuss potential solutions to be applied by Open Data publishers, the knowledge graph community, or – where possible – through automated linking approaches.

The rest of the paper is structured as follows: Sect. 2 provides an overview of the most important related work to our target contributions. In Sect. 3 we analyze and briefly show the (non-)performance of state-of-the-art entity linking systems. This analysis is based on a gold standard that we created to further analyze and motivate underlying issues; subsequently, the identified main challenges in our opinion primarily responsible for this poor performance are discussed one by one in Sect. 4, whereupon Sect. 5 discusses possible directions and starting points to tackle them. We conclude in Sect. 6 with an outlook and call for future work.

2 Background and Related Work

Our analysis and observations are mainly based on the data gathered by the *Open Data Portal Watch* (ODPW) project[5]. ODPW provides a large collection of Open Data metadata which has been compiled in order to monitor the quality of OGD portals: the ODPW project is regularly collecting metadata from over 250 portals world-wide, providing access to metadata dumps as weekly snapshots as well as various quality metrics [14,16] per portal, i.e., typically at country-level. However, a more fine-grained analysis of Open Data quality, as well as analysis of Open Data *on the level of single publishing organizations* is not yet supported, for the reasons we will outline in the following sections.

As for other related work on connecting Open Data to KGs, in [7] the authors propose a system to integrate user-generated mappings of attributes into an existing Open Data ecosystem; however, this system did not yet allow links to public KGs. Moreover, the temporal aspects of changes, that we will focus upon herein, were not covered there. The system was part of the former EU Open Data Portal[6] but is currently not available there anymore.

---

[5] https://data.wu.ac.at/portalwatch.
[6] https://data.europa.eu/euodp/de/data.

Tygel et al. [19] present a system to link datasets from different Open Data portals by extracting the tags and keywords from metadata descriptions: the tags get reconciled using automated translations and similarity measures, and re-published using unique URIs and meta-information for the reconciled tags. Again, specifically, links to organizations and temporal changes were not taken into account in this approach. However, the approach tries to solve multilinguality-issues using automated machine translation, which as we will discuss below, are also relevant in our context.

Overall, we observe that so far not much work has been carried out in terms of matching organizational information from OGD datasets to KGs. The most prominent recent contribution is the Google Dataset Search [4] service which offers a dedicated search engine for public datasets. To do so, Google links the identified datasets to their internal knowledge graph, in particular by partially mapping the publishing organizations. While no details about the actual matching approach and its coverage are provided, as a main challenge (besides data quality) they identify the ambiguity of organization names which are tackled by considering the website context for the mappings.

Related to our addressed challenge of linking organisations in the context of OGD is the heterogeneity of academic/research organisations; this is addressed by the EU-funded project RISIS.[7] The goal of this project is to provide a comprehensive register of public-sector research and higher education organizations in European countries. Each entry in the register provides a stable identifier and a set of characteristics of the entities, such as the website, country, and the entity type. While the register is a valuable source in the domain of research organisations, there is no coverage in the domain of OGD.

Notably, there are already existing standards and vocabularies which aim to solve the problem of heterogeneous metadata and missing links to publishing organizations. For instance, the *Semantic Government Vocabulary* (SGoV) [11], the *Data Catalog Vocabulary* (DCAT) [12], etc. – for publishing OGD. Yet, in practice, where these vocabularies are used (or mapped to, as in [14]) the respective attributes to link to publishing organizations are rather linking to (ambiguous) string labels than to URIs.

3   On the Performance of Current Entity Linking Systems

In order to analyze the challenges of linking organizational information to knowledge graphs' entities in depth, three methods have been applied which are presented in the following.

3.1   Analysis of the ODPW Database

To assess the linking problem quantitatively, we focus on metadata from the Open Data Portal Watch data base [16], accessible via a public API. The data

---

[7] http://risis.eu/orgreg/.

base consists of weekly metadata crawls from 252 data portals starting in early 2016. As of November 2019, when we conducted this analysis, the data covered 2,552,114 individual datasets. Under scrutiny for this work are the organizational metadata details and changes of those over the observed time frame. All statistical figures concerning organizational metadata in public datasets given in this paper refer to this metadata corpus unless stated otherwise.

3.2   Gold Standard for Change Analysis and Linker Evaluation

From the corpus, we created links from randomly chosen ODPW datasets by manually assigning the publishing organizations in terms of their existing Wikidata and DBpedia entities. We linked 200 distinct organizations of 174 distinct datasets. A match was only added to the gold standard when at least a link to Wikidata could be found. Each link was checked by at least two authors of this paper and only added if there was agreement concerning the link. The annotated instances in the final gold standard are from 57 different data portals and cover publishing organizations in different parts of the world. Notably, out of these 200, only 72.5% of the organizations could be manually matched to DBpedia which suggests a lower organization coverage for public administration institutions compared to Wikidata.

The gold standard also covers organizational changes in the datasets in terms of updates on the `dcat:publisher` property:[8] for 26 datasets direct changes can be observed in terms of updated label for the `dcat:publisher`; that is, 26 out of the 200 linked instances potentially reflect an organizational change, some of which could indeed be mapped to different organizations (whereas others only indicate a refinement or correction). The gold standard is publicly available on GitHub[9] under the CC-BY license. It can also be used to evaluate linking systems on their ability to match organizational entities.

3.3   Evaluation of Current Matching Systems

To make the point of limited usability of currently available entity linkers "off-the-shelf", we evaluated multiple state-of-the-art linkers (on the `dcat:publisher` label information only) and also implemented a naïve baseline entity linker based on *term frequency - inverse document frequency (TF/iDF)* by comparing whole metadata descriptions with DBpedia and Wikidata abstracts. For each target entity, i.e. an entity of a public KG, a document is built consisting of its labels, alternative forms, as well as its `dbo:abstract` in the case of DBpedia, and `schema:description` in case of Wikidata. The linker produces a one-to-many mapping by ranking TF/iDF matches in decreasing order according to their similarity scores. To obtain a one-to-one mapping, only the top-1

---

[8] The ODPW metadata already maps different schemata uniformly to DCAT, cf. [17].
[9] https://github.com/YaserJaradeh/LinkingODPublishers/blob/master/GoldStandard.csv.

match is considered for the evaluation. The linker is implemented in Python and is available on GitHub[10].

In order to give a quick overview on the performance of current entity linking systems, seven state-of-the-art systems as well as our introduced baseline linker have been run on the datesets of our manually created gold standard. While linking to Wikidata achieves generally better results due to a higher concept coverage, the performance scores even for the best linking systems are clearly too low for a fully automated approach.

Table 1. Performance of different linking systems for the two target KGs Wikidata and DBpedia. The best F1 scores of each KG are represented in bold print. Most systems evaluated here are tailored to one specific target graph. The symbol (-) indicates that the system does not work on the stated knowledge graph.

	DBpedia			Wikidata		
	P	R	F1	P	R	F1
Exact Matching	0.071	0.059	0.063	0.099	0.102	0.1
DBpedia Spotlight [13]	0.214	0.223	0.217	–	–	–
Text Razor [1]	–	–	–	0.214	0.206	0.207
EARL [6]	0.204	0.2	0.201	–	–	–
TagMe [9]	0.055	0.067	0.06	–	–	–
Meaning Cloud [2]	0.105	0.104	0.103	–	–	–
FALCON [18]	0.266	0.254	0.258	–	–	–
Open Tapioca [5]	–	–	–	0.432	0.42	0.423
Simple TF-IDF Linker	0.39	0.373	**0.378**	0.621	0.587	**0.596**

This small experiment clearly demonstrates that relying solely on exact string matching techniques, or comparing abstracts with metadata descriptions achieves poor results as shown in Table 1. We argue that the problem is indeed not purely based in the non-suitability of matching techniques themselves but fundamentally related to open challenges brought by the nature of organizational data and their representation in KGs.

Though a simple TF/iDF approach is used for the naïve linker, it is still outperforming other baselines. One reason is that this simple linker only searches a part of the entire search space, namely the collection of organizations found in the knowledge graph. Other general purpose tools (e.g. DBpedia Spotlight) try first to find out what the entity type is and perform the actual linking afterwards. Therefore, in the case of the simple linker, the search space is more restricted and the disambiguation process is more accurate.

---

[10] https://github.com/YaserJaradeh/LinkingODPublishers/tree/master/Scripts.

4   Challenges

In the following section we identify fundamental and in our opinion open challenges that complicate automated linking of organizations to KGs; each identified challenge will be illustrated and where possible quantitatively analyzed on our corpus or, respectively the KGs under consideration (DBpedia and Wikidata).

4.1   Challenge 1: Temporal Changes in Organizations

Challenge Statement. Organizations change over time due to mergers, splits, or renamings. On the other hand, the metadata of open datasets also changes over time. Both types of changes complicate the automated linking process.

Challenge Analysis. While the actual change in organizational structures is not in itself problematic, there are many consequences which affect the linking process. For instance, information about a change might not be reflected in the dataset's metadata and/or in public KGs, or respectively be reflected asynchronously: there is latency in terms of both when/whether the change is updated in the metadata and the KGs. Furthermore, it is not clear how such temporal changes shall be reflected in public KGs (see Subsect. 4.2).

In terms of temporal changes on the metadata level, we analyzed changes of individual dataset publishers per dataset and data portal over time. In order to take into account the sheer size of our metadata corpus and to increase the performance of our analysis, a heuristic was applied: only datasets where the organization label of the first occurrence is different from the organization label in the last occurrence were considered in this statistical evaluation. In total, 109,280 organizational changes could be identified in this way.

In a second step, the distribution of the number of organizational changes on a per dataset basis was analyzed. The maximum number of organizational changes is 11, meaning the organization of a single dataset on a data portal was changed 11 times. Figure 1 shows the distribution of changes. It can be seen that the distribution follows a power law: while 4 and more changes are relatively unlikely, datasets with one change clearly dominate the distribution with 78,378 occurrences.

It was further analyzed how many organizational changes cause the changes on dataset level, i.e. whether there are bulk changes that propagate across different datasets and portals (e.g. through "harvesting portals" that import metadata from other portals), and how these changes are distributed. The fact that there are only 33,879 distinct organization labels in the dataset but that there are more than 90,000 changes on a per-dataset level, indicates that bulk changes occur. We found that these roughly 90,000 changes on dataset level are caused by 12,489 individual changes of organization labels. It is important to note that the number of changes here does not necessarily reflect changes on distinct organizations — multiple renamings of the same organization are also counted (which can likewise be seen in Table 2). Figure 2 shows the distribution of individual organization label changes. Although there are few changes that are heavily picked up in the datasets, the distribution is more linear compared to the one in Fig. 1. Table 2 displays the ten most frequent label changes on ODPW.

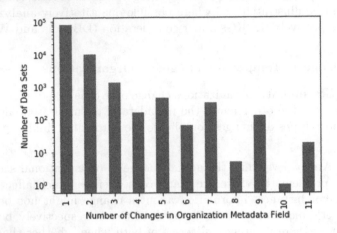

Fig. 1. The distribution of organizational changes for individual datasets. On the X-axis, the number of times an organization has been changed for a dataset on a particular data portal is shown while the overall frequency of such a change is reflected on the Y-axis. Note that the Y-axis is log-scale.

Overall, in our analysis of the Open Data Portal Watch data base, we qualitatively identify six reasons for organizational metadata changes – only two of them (I and II) being an actual change of the organization:

I **Renaming:** Organizational changes due to actual renamings of the publishing institution such as from *Department for Communities and Local Government* to *Ministry of Housing, Communities and Local Government*.

II **Structural Changes:** Changes due to structural transitions of the publishing organization such as mergers, divisions, or other restructurings. An example here would be the *Department of Energy and Climate Change* that was merged with the *Department for Business, Innovation and Skills* to form the *Department for Business, Energy and Industrial Strategy*.

III **Specialization:** Changes to further specify which organization is meant such as changing the label *Department of Education* to *Department Of Education (Northern Ireland)*. In this category also fall changes that further define which part of the organization was involved in the dataset creation or provision such as from *Bristol City Council* to *Bristol City Council - Sustainability Team*.

IV **Generalization:** Changes that generalize the authorship – most likely in order to make the publisher easier to find and to identify. An example here would be a change from *Martin Farrell* to *West Sussex County Council*.

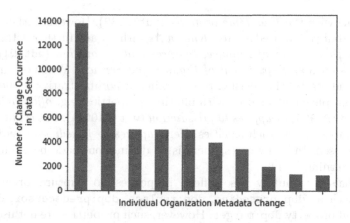

Fig. 2. The number of datasets in which an individual change, such as an organizational renaming, occurs. Each bar represents an individual change (cf. Table 2), e.g., the first one refers to the change from "NSGIC GIS Inventory (aka Ramona)" to "NSGIC GIS Inventory" and was propagated to almost 14000 individual datasets.

V **Editorial/Error Correction:** Changes due to corrections e.g. from *Ordance Survey* to *Ordnance Survey*.

VI **Other:** Changes that we could not further classify, such as from *Frederick Manby, Noah Linden* to *Science* or from *Daryl Beggs, Ruth Oulton, Benjamin Lang* to *Benjamin Lang, Daryl Beggs, Ruth Oulton*, neither of which are mappable to an actual organization.

4.2 Challenge 2: Lack of Consistently Used Base Ontology for Modeling Organizations in Knowledge Graphs

Challenge Statement. Organizations change over time — however, this change cannot be sufficiently expressed in current knowledge graphs' ontologies or, respectively, existing capabilities of the vocabulary are not broadly used. Additionally, the vocabulary is insufficient in terms of expressing the relation between a geographic area and its governing body.

Challenge Analysis. Wikidata offers specific properties for capturing different types of organizational changes. For example, *Also Known As* (skos:altLabel), *Official Names* (wdt:P1448), *Replaces* (wdt:P1365), *Replaced By* (wdt:P1366), and *Follows* (wdt:P155). *Wikidata*'s model also offers a property named *The Point In Time* (wdt:P585) which indicates the date from when a fact considered true. However, in the majority of the studied instances, these properties were not used to reflect organizational changes. In only 50% of all cases, an organizational change was reflected in Wikidata – mainly by using *Also Known As* and *Official Names* properties. For instance, the *Department for Environment and Water* (wdt:Q5260295) formally known as *Department of Environment, Water and Natural Resources*, is correctly listed in Wikidata using the property *official* *names* along with the *End Time* property (wdt:P582). However, other captured changes are only annotated as *Also Known As* without any further details. A case in point is *Department of Finance, Services and Innovation* (wdt:Q17004340) previously known as *Department of Finance and Services*. While on the level of countries and states, the relation to governing or administrative bodies is clear through multiple concepts used with multiple properties (e.g. *office held by head of state* (wdt:P1906) or *applies to jurisdiction* (wdt:P1001)), this is not true anymore for smaller areas such as cities. Here, *applies to jurisdiction* (wdt:P1001) is typically used. In many cases, there is no distinction made between the area and the governing body.

DBpedia's vocabulary also offers properties to capture organizational changes, such as dbp:preceding, dbp:replace, dbp:predecessor, dbp:successor, and property dbp:merger. However, such properties are not used widely to reflect actual changes. Furthermore, DBpedia lacks the temporal dimension that can be easily expressed in Wikidata. For instance, there is a property dbo:mergerDate – however, this property's rdfs:domain is dbo:Place which is, in fact, disjoint with dbo:Organisation's parent class dbo:Agent and consequently cannot be used to express the temporal details of an organizational merger. To quantify these statements, in the sampled organizational changes, only 34% of the conducted organizational changes were reflected in DBpedia entities. Moreover, similar to Wikidata, changes are rarely supported with details that describe the change. For instance, *London Fire and Emergency Planning Authority*[11] which replaces *London Fire and Civil Defence Authority*[12], is captured by dbp:predecessor and dbp:successor properties in both instances – however, without any timeline information. In terms of the relation between geospatial areas and governing bodies on DBpedia, it is available to some extent in the vocabulary through multiple properties such as dbp:governingBody, but the vocabulary is rarely used.[13] Similar to Wikidata, in many cases no distinction is made between areas and the governing body. We note even that the DBpedia entities themselves are inconsistent in this regard, such as European_Union both being typed as dbo:Country and dbo:Organisation, two classes labelled as owl:disjointWith.

4.3 Challenge 3: Metadata Quality

Challenge Statement. Varying metadata quality among data portals complicates the automated linking process.

Challenge Analysis. Poor metadata quality in provenance information is a major issue when linking organizations to unique KG entities. This issue has also been addressed by Google [4] and could be confirmed by our analysis of the

---

[11] dbr:London_Fire_and_Emergency_Planning_Authority.

[12] dbr:London_Fire_and_Civil_Defence_Authority.

[13] A SPARQL query for dbp:governingBody resulted in ~ 6,000 usages with only 930 distinct objects over all of DBpedia.

ODPW data base: as an example, Table 2 displays the most frequent organization metadata changes on ODPW. It can be noted that from the 10 most frequent changes, at least 4 are not meaningful, and in fact loosing semantics (marked in *italic*, i.e. not indicating any derferenceable publishing organization, but rather generic departments names or individual authors (potentially raising additional privacy problems).

Table 2. Top 10 organization changes by label together with the number of occurrences of the change within datasets listed in ODPW.

Old Organization Label	New Organization Label	Frequency
NSGIC GIS Inventory (aka Ramona)	NSGIC GIS Inventory	13,793
Geoscience Australia	*Corp*	7,111
Daryl Beggs, Ruth Oulton, Benjamin Lang,	*Benjamin Lang, Daryl Beggs, Ruth Oulton,*	5,007
Daryl Beggs, Ruth Oulton, Benjamin Lang,	*Engineering*	5,007
Benjamin Lang, Daryl Beggs, Ruth Oulton,	*Engineering*	5,007
Ivan Begtin	Федеральная служба статистики	3,359
Archive bot	Национальный цифровой архив России	1,925
Senatsverwaltung für Gesundheit und Soziales	Senatsverwaltung für Gesundheit und Soziales Berlin	1,298
Senatsverwaltung für Gesundheit und Soziales Berlin	Senatsverwaltung für Gesundheit und Soziales	1,273
PAT S. Statistica	ISPAT	1,121

4.4 Challenge 4: Multilinguality

Challenge Statement. As public dataset providers are spread around the world, different language identifiers further complicate the linking process. For example, the Chinese Central Bank is called *People's Bank of China* in English, *Chinesische Volksbank* in German, and 中国人民银行 in Chinese.

Challenge Analysis. The analysis of the ODPW data base showed that organizational labels are typically stated in the language where the publishing institution resides and that translations are often not given. An exception here is the European Data Portal (europeandataportal.eu): this portal harvests datasets from all member states, and the labels are automatically translated to English. However, automated translations do not necessarily correspond to the correct labels in other languages. DBpedia is not entirely multilingual in a sense that multiple labels are given in various languages for organizations in all cases: instead, there are dedicated DBpedia versions for multiple languages. Wikidata is more aligned in this regard: it is possible to define multiple labels in any given language. The People's Bank of China, for instance, can also be found using its Chinese label. Even though multilingual labels can be defined on Wikidata, this is often not sufficient for our case.

For example, the concept *Russian Federal State Statistics Service* (Федеральная служба статистики) *does* exist on Wikidata[14] – but there is no

---

[14] https://web.archive.org/web/20190403150124/https://www.wikidata.org/wiki/Q2624680.

Russian label defined for it as of April 2020. Yet, this label appears more than 3,000 times in the ODPW data base as publisher.

Figure 3 shows the distribution of languages in which a label is given for Wikidata entities typed as organization on a logarithmic scale. As it can be seen, the distribution follows a power-law: For most organizations labels are defined only in a single language.

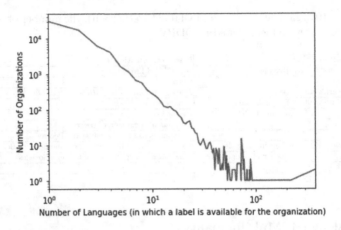

Fig. 3. Distribution of the number of languages in which labels exist for Wikidata concepts of type *Organization*. The axes are logarithmically scaled. The distribution follows a power-law.

4.5   Challenge 5: Disambiguating Public Sector Organizations

Challenge Statement. While companies can mostly be linked to one named entity without too much effort, this task is harder for public bodies.

Challenge Analysis. The disambiguation problem is two-sided: (i) When only states and cities are quoted as originator of a dataset, there is ambiguity in terms of the actual concept that is referred to in the KG which may hold multiple entities for a particular label. For example: Does *New York* refer to the city of New York, the state of New York, or some particular administrative body of New York City? Wikidata contains entities for all three cases but the disambiguation is complicated without further context. (ii) Similarly, given a concept in a KG, it can be hard to link it to dataset publishers due to the ambiguities – in particular when acronyms are uses; this has also been pointed out by Google [4]. Also institution names common in several countries (e.g. *"Statistics Office"* could be hard to disambiguate, though the portal context of nationally operated OGD portals may help here.

5   Towards Solutions for Linking Organizations

In order to tackle the aforementioned challenges we outline possible solutions paths and starting points below.

5.1   Challenge 1: Temporal Changes in Organizations

The fact that organizations change over time is a given. It is, therefore, important to acknowledge this and improve current technologies, including publicly available KGs and data portals, to better and more consistently represent such changes. For example, on data portals, the metadata should be timestamped so that it is clear as of which date the information is valid. It may, in addition, help not to only store the most recent version but to keep a history of organizational labels and metadata since a change may not yet be reflected in the target to which the organization is mapped.

5.2   Challenge 2: The Lack of a Base Ontology for Public Knowledge Graphs

At least as important as the design of a capable base ontology is the application. Our analysis showed, for instance, that the existing capabilities of the Wikidata and DBpedia vocabulary to reflect organizational changes are rarely exploited. Therefore, in order to automate and maintain mappings of such information, efforts to semantically represent organizational changes within KGs are required. This can be done by promoting currently available properties that express changes in organizations e.g. in the form of best practices for editors. At the same time, existing ontologies can be extended to better capture organizations and administrative units.

5.3   Challenge 3: Metadata Quality

Improving the quality of metadata across different open datasets will significantly improve the linking quality. As mentioned earlier, while some of the observed changes are meaningful, such as "NSGIC GIS Inventory (aka Ramona)" to "NSGIC GIS Inventory" or "Ivan Begtin" to "*Федеральная служба статистики*" (*Russian Federal State Statistics Service*), there is a concerning number of random changes occurring across datasets such as "Corp". One way to improve the metadata that is provided is to refine information extraction methods used to create such datasets. Furthermore, dataset publishers should be urged and motivated to keep their metadata as current and as accurate as possible. Moreover, as we are aware that the data quality will not improve instantly, automated linking systems need to be able to handle a certain amount of noise. As our analysis showed, the metadata changes rather frequently (this is also observed by Google [4]) – hence, it is important to monitor meaningful changes on regular basis. Dataset harvesters, such as

ODPW, can be beneficial for this purpose by regularly retrieving metadata and detecting potential changes.[15]

5.4   Challenge 4: Multilinguality

Multilinguality can be addressed by exploiting the multilingual capabilities of the Semantic Web. The problem is less pronounced for Wikidata compared to DBpedia. An active promotion of multilingual content (in KGs as well as on knowledge portals) can help in overcoming multilingual issues. For example, if multiple organization labels in multiple languages for the same organization would be available in the dataset metadata as well as in KGs, an overlap which might lead to a match becomes more likely. In addition, the use of dictionaries, such as *WordNet* [8] or *Wiktionary*, may help in some cases. For DBpedia, interlanguage links could be exploited to allow for multilinguality to a certain extent.

5.5   Challenge 5: Disambiguating Public Sector Organizations

One of the most pronounced problems is the disambiguation of labels. Here, the context has to be very broad to also include, for instance, the local top level domain (indicator for the country), contact e-mail addresses, and data portal URLs. Specialized linking systems are required for this task as current generic solutions fail to successfully disambiguate organizations. We believe that exploring the context of the dataset during the linking process can provide more accurate predication of the linked resource. Information such as the portal ID or URL provides more indications of the organization's context such as the country. For example, utilizing the country of an organization which is often found as part of portal ID can improve linking accuracy: if two organizations have the same name but are coming from different countries (e.g. *Ministry of Education*) the broader context helps to disambiguate them.

5.6   Across Challenges 1–5: Enabling a Community-Driven Linking Process

As outlined above, a fully-automated linking process is as of now not available. Therefore, we argue that while the community is working on improving the boundary conditions, a manual lookup service is required that allows a data science community as well as dataset publishers to annotate organizational links on a dataset level together with a community effort. This can be applied by allowing humans to use a voting function to ensure a high linking quality. We believe that such a service will not only improve the linking quality but will also help in maintaining the linking results overtime. This service might look similar

---

[15] Note that to a certain extend, up-to-date metadata is available e.g. through the ODPW data base that was also used for our analysis: https://data.wu.ac.at/portalwatch/data.

to www.prefix.cc, where publishers can be quickly looked up given a dataset URL or a data portal URL together with a label. As the same unique labels are used on many portals, the service could transitively reason organizational links for datasets not yet annotated which can be up or down voted by the user community. Over time, a larger gold standard could be created to improve and fine-tune existing linking systems.

6   Conclusion and Outlook

In this paper, we discussed the need and open problems of linking organizations of public datasets to their corresponding entities in public KGs such as Wikidata and DBpedia. In order to understand the current state of this issue, we created a gold standard mapping of open dataset organizations to KGs entities. We evaluated the performance of different current entity linking approaches including our own simple approach. As the results of the automated linking approaches were disappointing, we outlined five major challenges to be addressed. This includes (1) the temporal changes that happen on a regular basis in the organizations themselves and therefore in the metadata of open datasets. Our analysis also shows (2) that KGs are not fully using their existing capabilities to express organizational changes and we also address shortfalls in the existing vocabulary. We have also addressed (3) metadata quality issues and (4) multilinguality aspects within the linking process. Lastly, we found that (5) the disambiguation of public sector organizations is a hard task. We provide directions in terms of how these challenges can be addressed in the future. For future work, we aim to explore the idea of a community-driven effort in order to improve linking quality and to maintain that linking over time.

Acknowledgements. The authors thank Vincent Emonet, Paola Espinoza-Arias, and Bilal Koteich who contributed preliminary analyses regarding the challenges addressed in this paper. We also thank the organizers of the International Semantic Web Summer school (ISWS) 2019: the idea for this paper origins in discussions at the school.

References

1. Extract meaning from your text. https://www.textrazor.com/
2. Text analytics - meaningcloud text mining solutions (2016). https://www.meaningcloud.com/
3. Assaf, A., Troncy, R., Senart, A.: HDL - towards a harmonized dataset model for open data portals. In: Workshop on Using the Web in the Age of Data (USEWOD '15) Co-located with (ESWC 2015), pp. 62–74 (2015)
4. Brickley, D., Burgess, M., Noy, N.F.: Google dataset search: building a search engine for datasets in an open web ecosystem. In: The World Wide Web Conference, WWW, pp. 1365–1375. ACM (2019)
5. Delpeuch, A.: Opentapioca: Lightweight entity linking for wikidata. CoRR abs/1904.09131 (2019). http://arxiv.org/abs/1904.09131

6. Dubey, M., Banerjee, D., Chaudhuri, D., Lehmann, J.: EARL: joint entity and relation linking for question answering over knowledge graphs. In: Vrandečić, D., et al. (eds.) ISWC 2018. LNCS, vol. 11136, pp. 108–126. Springer, Cham (2018). https://doi.org/10.1007/978-3-030-00671-6_7

7. Ermilov, I., Auer, S., Stadler, C.: User-driven semantic mapping of tabular data. In: I-SEMANTICS 2013, pp. 105–112. ACM (2013)

8. Fellbaum, C. (ed.): WordNet: An Electronic Lexical Database. Language, Speech, and Communication. MIT Press, Cambridg (1998)

9. Ferragina, P., Scaiella, U.: TAGME: on-the-fly annotation of short text fragments (by wikipedia entities). In: Proceedings of the 19th ACM Conference on Information and Knowledge Management, CIKM, pp. 1625–1628 (2010)

10. Kacprzak, E., Koesten, L., Ibáñez, L.D., Blount, T., Tennison, J., Simperl, E.: Characterising dataset search - an analysis of search logs and data requests. J. Web Semant. **55**, 37–55 (2019)

11. Kremen, P., Necaský, M.: Improving discoverability of open government data with rich metadata descriptions using semantic government vocabulary. J. Web Semant. **55**, 1–20 (2019)

12. Maali, F., Erickson, J.: Data catalog vocabulary (DCAT). W3C Recommendation (2014). http://www.w3.org/TR/vocab-dcat/

13. Mendes, P.N., Jakob, M., García-Silva, A., Bizer, C.: Dbpedia spotlight: shedding light on the web of documents. In: 7th International Conference on Semantic Systems, I-SEMANTICS 2011, Graz, Austria, 7–9 September 2011, pp. 1–8 (2011)

14. Neumaier, S.: Semantic enrichment of open data on the web. Ph.D. thesis, Vienna University of Technology (2019)

15. Neumaier, S., Thurnay, L., Lampoltshammer, T.J., Knap, T.: Search, filter, fork, and link open data: the adequate platform: data- and community-driven quality improvements. In: Companion of the The Web Conference 2018 on The Web Conference 2018, pp. 1523–1526 (2018)

16. Neumaier, S., Umbrich, J., Polleres, A.: Automated quality assessment of metadata across open data portals. J. Data Inf. Qual. **8**(1), 2:1–2:29 (2016)

17. Neumaier, S., Umbrich, J., Polleres, A.: Lifting data portals to the web of data. In: 10th Workshop on Linked Data on the Web (LDOW2017) (2017)

18. Sakor, A., et al.: Old is gold: linguistic driven approach for entity and relation linking of short text. In: Proceedings of the 2019 NAACL-HLT 2019, pp. 2336–2346 (2019)

19. Tygel, A., Auer, S., Debattista, J., Orlandi, F., Campos, M.L.M.: Towards cleaning-up open data portals: a metadata reconciliation approach. In: 10th IEEE International Conference on Semantic Computing, ICSC 2016, pp. 71–78 (2016)

Author Index

Printed in the United States
By Bookmasters